冨樫義博

Kakinotane rice cracker snacks are the best, but only with peanuts in a supporting role.

Yoshihiro Togashi

Yoshihiro Togashi's manga career began in 1986 at the age of 20, when he won the coveted Osamu Tezuka Award for new manga artists. He debuted in the Japanese **Weekly Shonen Jump** magazine in 1989 with the romantic comedy **Tende Shôwaru Cupid**. From 1990 to 1994 he wrote and drew the hit manga **YuYu Hakusho**, which was followed by the dark comedy science-fiction series **Level E**, and finally this adventure series, **Hunter x Hunter**, available from VIZ Media's SHONEN JUMP Advanced imprint. In 1999 he married the manga artist Naoko Takeuchi.

HUNTER X HUNTER Volume 32
SHONEN JUMP ADVANCED Manga Edition

STORY AND ART BY
YOSHIHIRO TOGASHI

English Adaptation & Translation/Lillian Olsen
Touch-up Art & Lettering/Mark McMurray
Design/Matt Hinrichs
Editor/Shaenon K. Garrity

HUNTERxHUNTER © POT (Yoshihiro Togashi) 2012
All rights reserved. First published in Japan in 2012 by SHUEISHA Inc.,
Tokyo. English translation rights arranged by SHUEISHA Inc.

The stories, characters and incidents mentioned in this publication are
entirely fictional.

Printed in the U.S.A.

Published by VIZ Media, LLC
P.O. Box 77010
San Francisco, CA 94107

10 9 8 7 6 5 4 3 2 1
First printing, April 2014

SHONEN JUMP ADVANCED MANGA

Volume 32

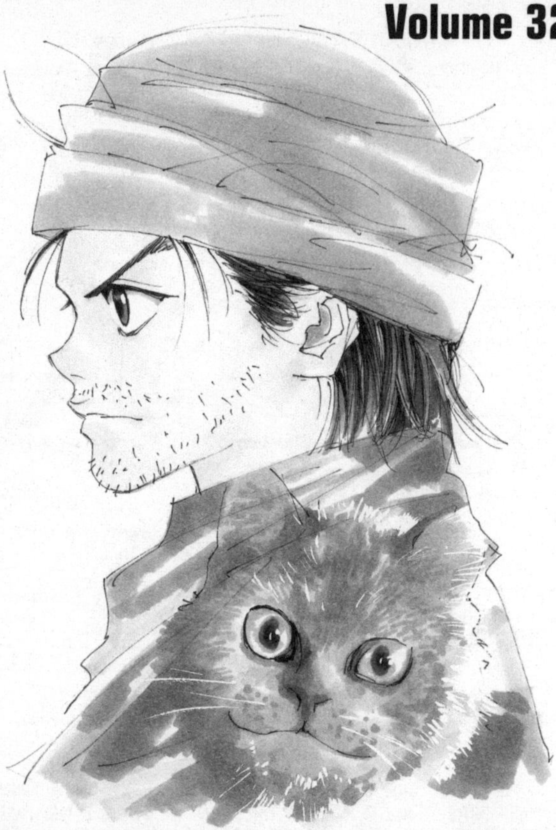

HUNTER × HUNTER

ハンター × ハンター

Story & Art by

Yoshihiro Togashi

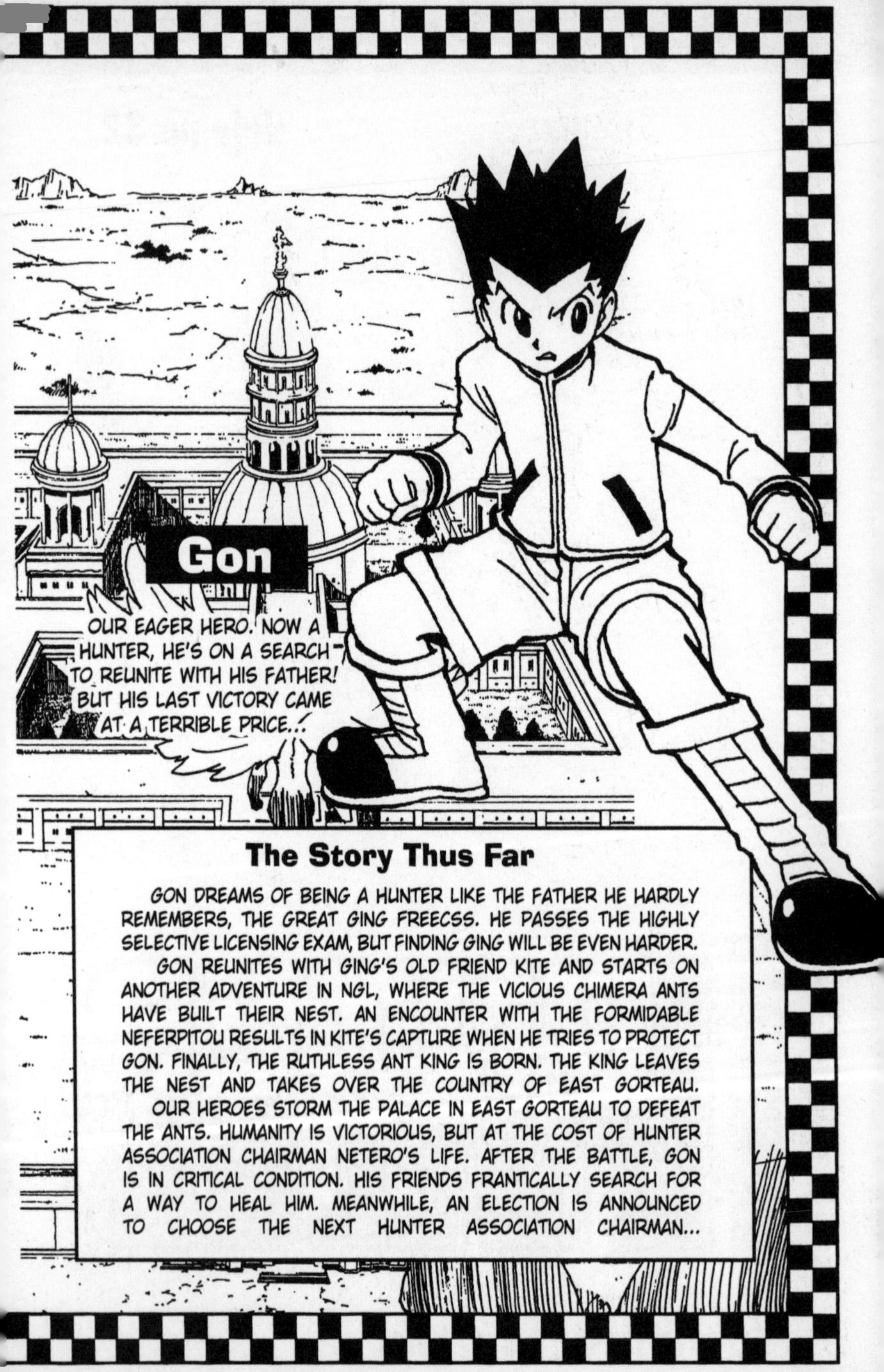
Gon
OUR EAGER HERO. NOW A HUNTER, HE'S ON A SEARCH TO REUNITE WITH HIS FATHER! BUT HIS LAST VICTORY CAME AT A TERRIBLE PRICE...

The Story Thus Far

GON DREAMS OF BEING A HUNTER LIKE THE FATHER HE HARDLY REMEMBERS, THE GREAT GING FREECSS. HE PASSES THE HIGHLY SELECTIVE LICENSING EXAM, BUT FINDING GING WILL BE EVEN HARDER.

GON REUNITES WITH GING'S OLD FRIEND KITE AND STARTS ON ANOTHER ADVENTURE IN NGL, WHERE THE VICIOUS CHIMERA ANTS HAVE BUILT THEIR NEST. AN ENCOUNTER WITH THE FORMIDABLE NEFERPITOU RESULTS IN KITE'S CAPTURE WHEN HE TRIES TO PROTECT GON. FINALLY, THE RUTHLESS ANT KING IS BORN. THE KING LEAVES THE NEST AND TAKES OVER THE COUNTRY OF EAST GORTEAU.

OUR HEROES STORM THE PALACE IN EAST GORTEAU TO DEFEAT THE ANTS. HUMANITY IS VICTORIOUS, BUT AT THE COST OF HUNTER ASSOCIATION CHAIRMAN NETERO'S LIFE. AFTER THE BATTLE, GON IS IN CRITICAL CONDITION. HIS FRIENDS FRANTICALLY SEARCH FOR A WAY TO HEAL HIM. MEANWHILE, AN ELECTION IS ANNOUNCED TO CHOOSE THE NEXT HUNTER ASSOCIATION CHAIRMAN...

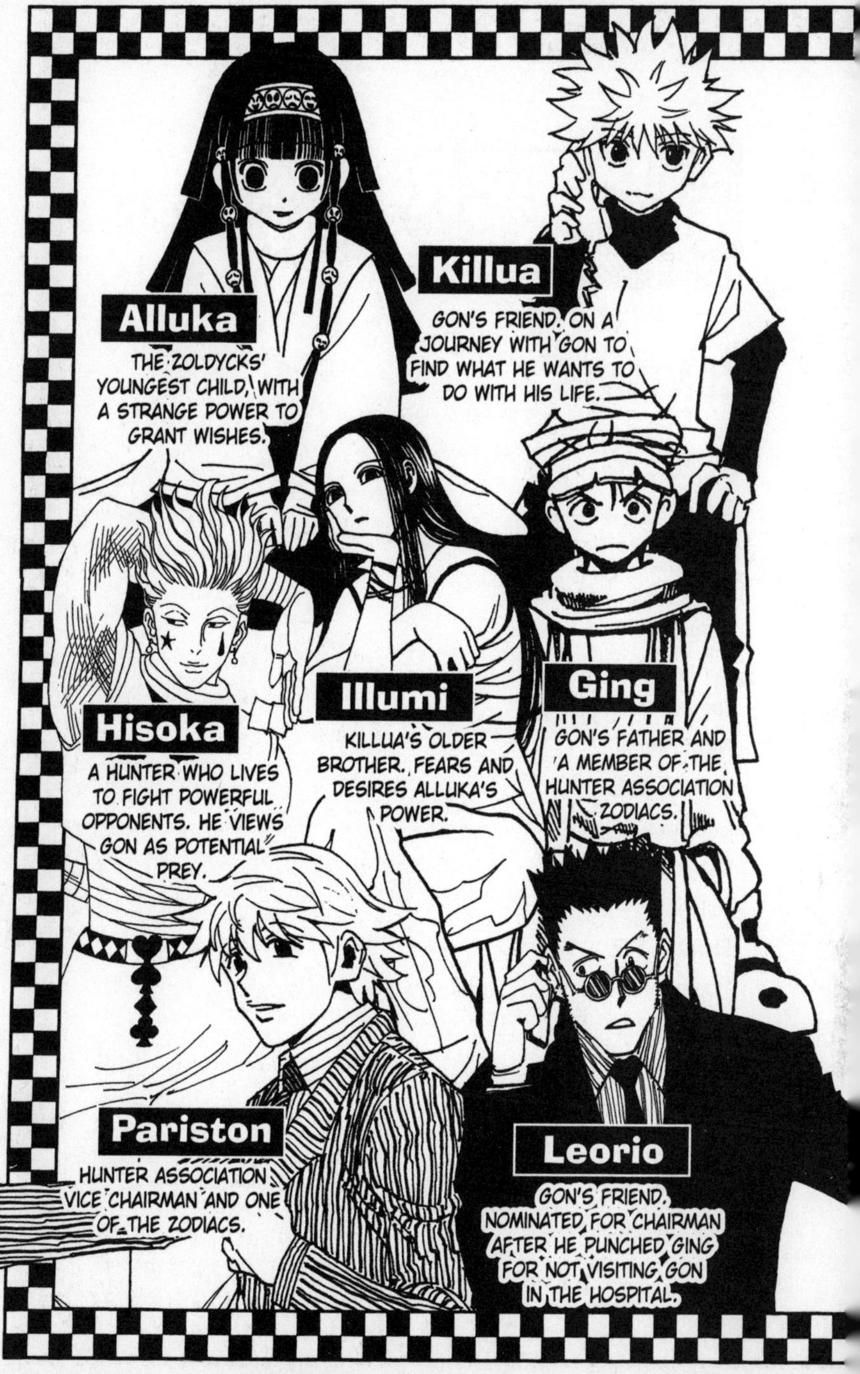

Killua
GON'S FRIEND. ON A JOURNEY WITH GON TO FIND WHAT HE WANTS TO DO WITH HIS LIFE.
Alluka
THE ZOLDYCKS' YOUNGEST CHILD, WITH A STRANGE POWER TO GRANT WISHES.
Ging
GON'S FATHER AND A MEMBER OF THE HUNTER ASSOCIATION ZODIACS.
Illumi
KILLUA'S OLDER BROTHER. FEARS AND DESIRES ALLUKA'S POWER.
Hisoka
A HUNTER WHO LIVES TO FIGHT POWERFUL OPPONENTS. HE VIEWS GON AS POTENTIAL PREY.
Leorio
GON'S FRIEND. NOMINATED FOR CHAIRMAN AFTER HE PUNCHED GING FOR NOT VISITING GON IN THE HOSPITAL.
Pariston
HUNTER ASSOCIATION VICE CHAIRMAN AND ONE OF THE ZODIACS.

Volume 32

CONTENTS

Chapter 331: Day of Reckoning

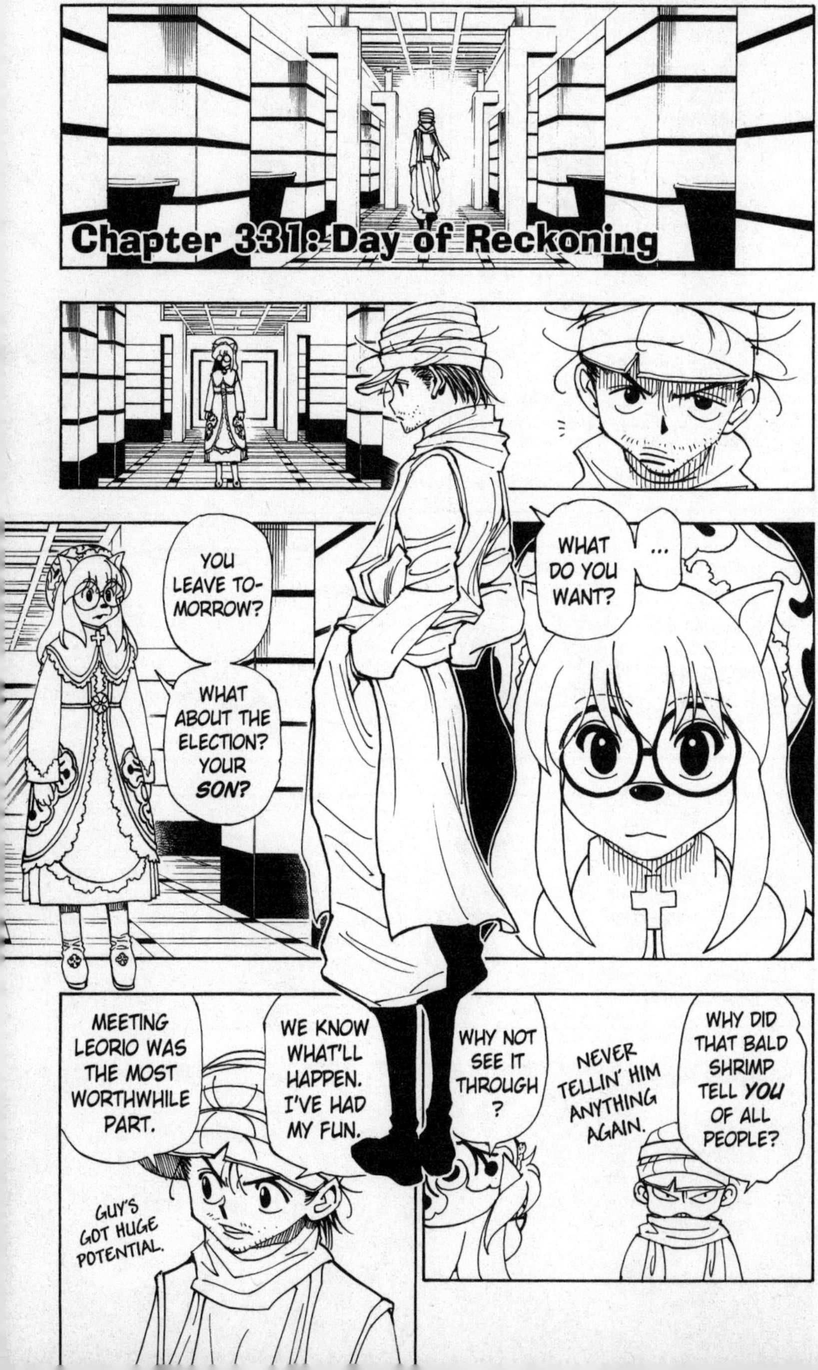
...
WHAT DO YOU WANT?
YOU LEAVE TO-MORROW?
WHAT ABOUT THE ELECTION? YOUR *SON?*
WHY DID THAT BALD SHRIMP TELL *YOU* OF ALL PEOPLE?
NEVER TELLIN' HIM ANYTHING AGAIN.
WHY NOT SEE IT THROUGH?
WE KNOW WHAT'LL HAPPEN. I'VE HAD MY FUN.
MEETING LEORIO WAS THE MOST WORTHWHILE PART.
GUY'S GOT HUGE POTENTIAL.

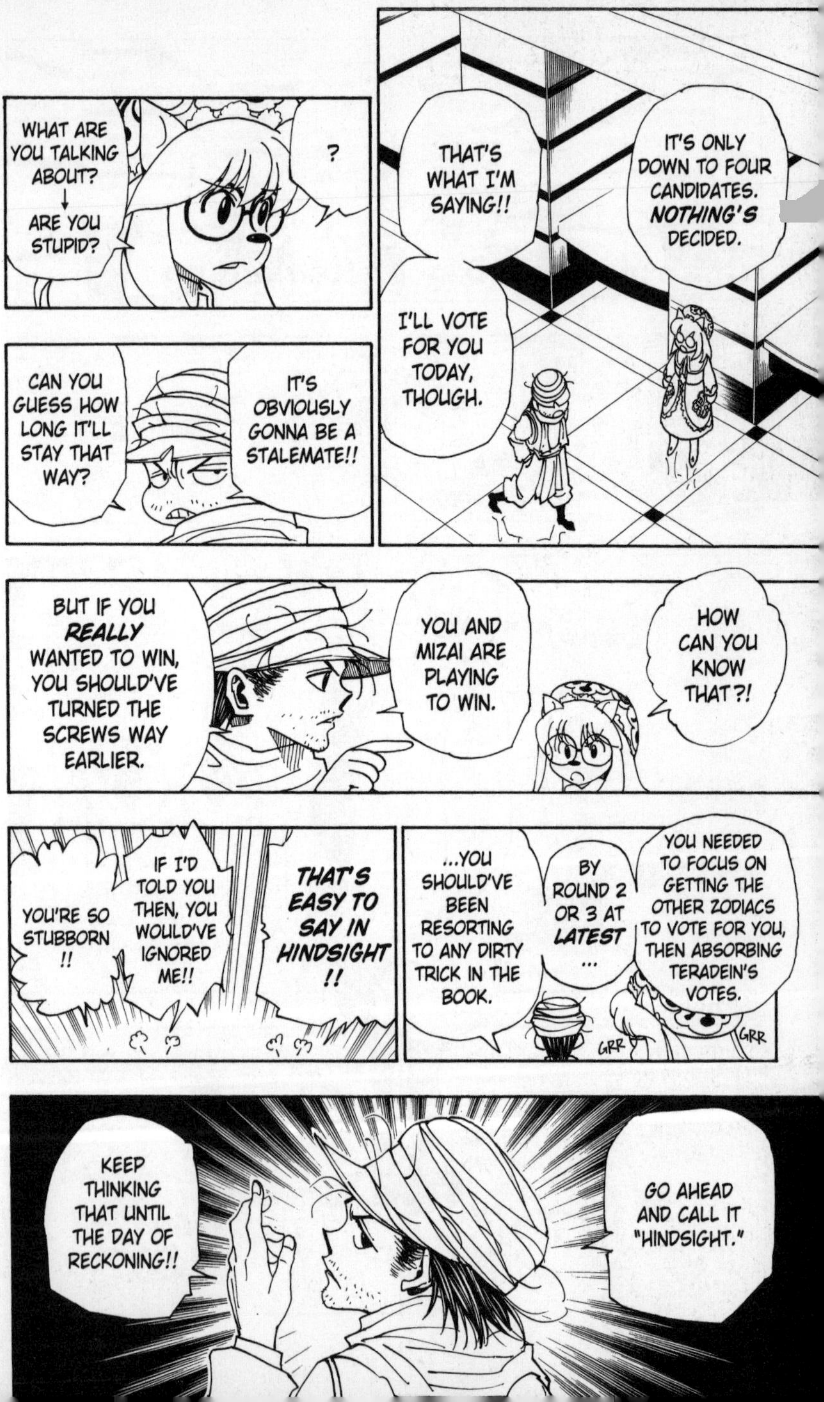
IT'S ONLY DOWN TO FOUR CANDIDATES. NOTHING'S DECIDED.
THAT'S WHAT I'M SAYING!!
I'LL VOTE FOR YOU TODAY, THOUGH.
?
WHAT ARE YOU TALKING ABOUT? ↓ ARE YOU STUPID?
IT'S OBVIOUSLY GONNA BE A STALEMATE!!
CAN YOU GUESS HOW LONG IT'LL STAY THAT WAY?
HOW CAN YOU KNOW THAT?!
YOU AND MIZAI ARE PLAYING TO WIN.
BUT IF YOU REALLY WANTED TO WIN, YOU SHOULD'VE TURNED THE SCREWS WAY EARLIER.
YOU NEEDED TO FOCUS ON GETTING THE OTHER ZODIACS TO VOTE FOR YOU, THEN ABSORBING TERADEIN'S VOTES.
GRR
BY ROUND 2 OR 3 AT LATEST ...
...YOU SHOULD'VE BEEN RESORTING TO ANY DIRTY TRICK IN THE BOOK.
GRR
THAT'S EASY TO SAY IN HINDSIGHT!!
IF I'D TOLD YOU THEN, YOU WOULD'VE IGNORED ME!!
YOU'RE SO STUBBORN!!
GO AHEAD AND CALL IT "HINDSIGHT."
KEEP THINKING THAT UNTIL THE DAY OF RECKONING!!

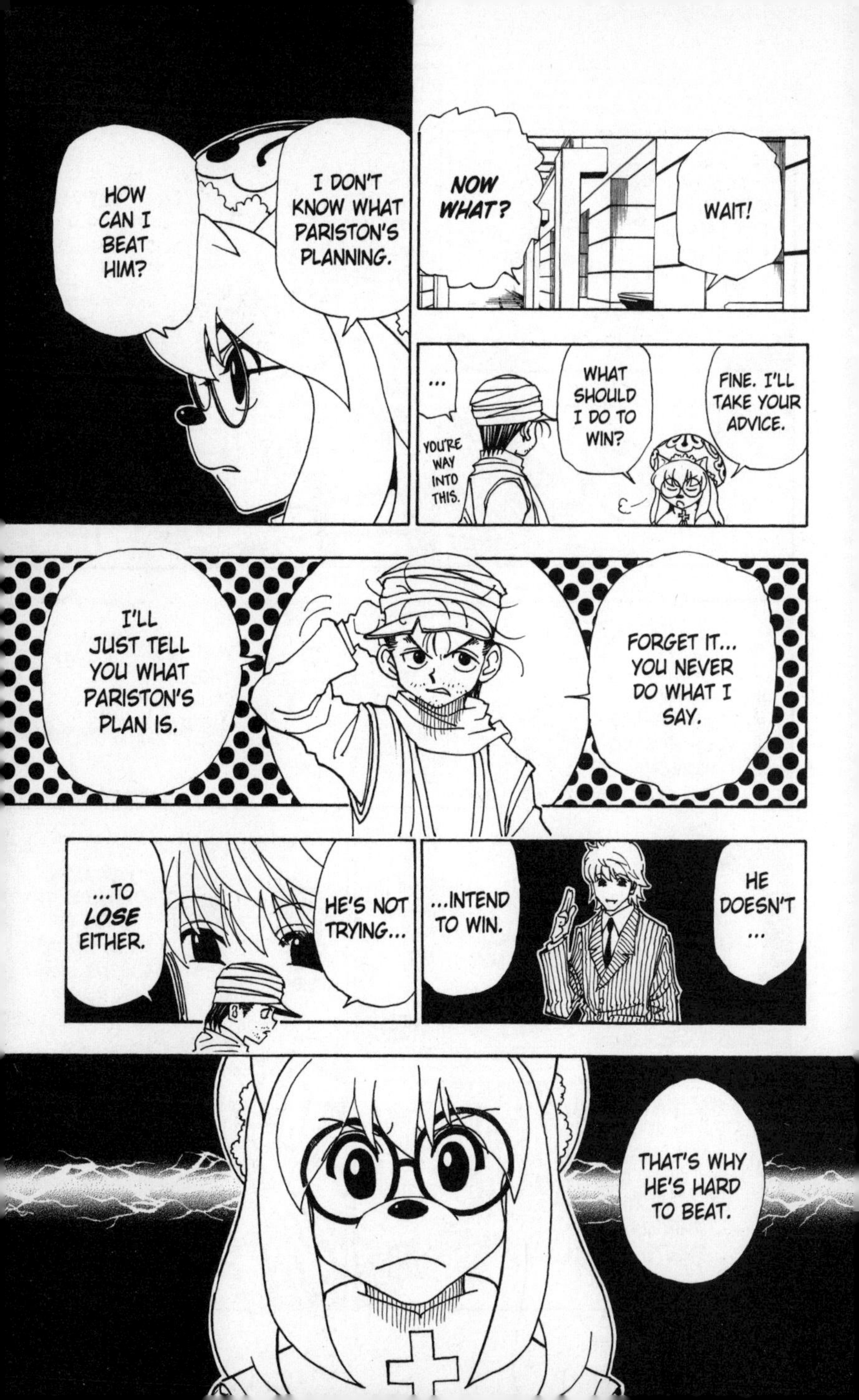
WAIT!
NOW WHAT?
FINE. I'LL TAKE YOUR ADVICE.
WHAT SHOULD I DO TO WIN?
...
YOU'RE WAY INTO THIS.
I DON'T KNOW WHAT PARISTON'S PLANNING.
HOW CAN I BEAT HIM?
FORGET IT... YOU NEVER DO WHAT I SAY.
I'LL JUST TELL YOU WHAT PARISTON'S PLAN IS.
HE DOESN'T ...
...INTEND TO WIN.
HE'S NOT TRYING...
...TO LOSE EITHER.
THAT'S WHY HE'S HARD TO BEAT.

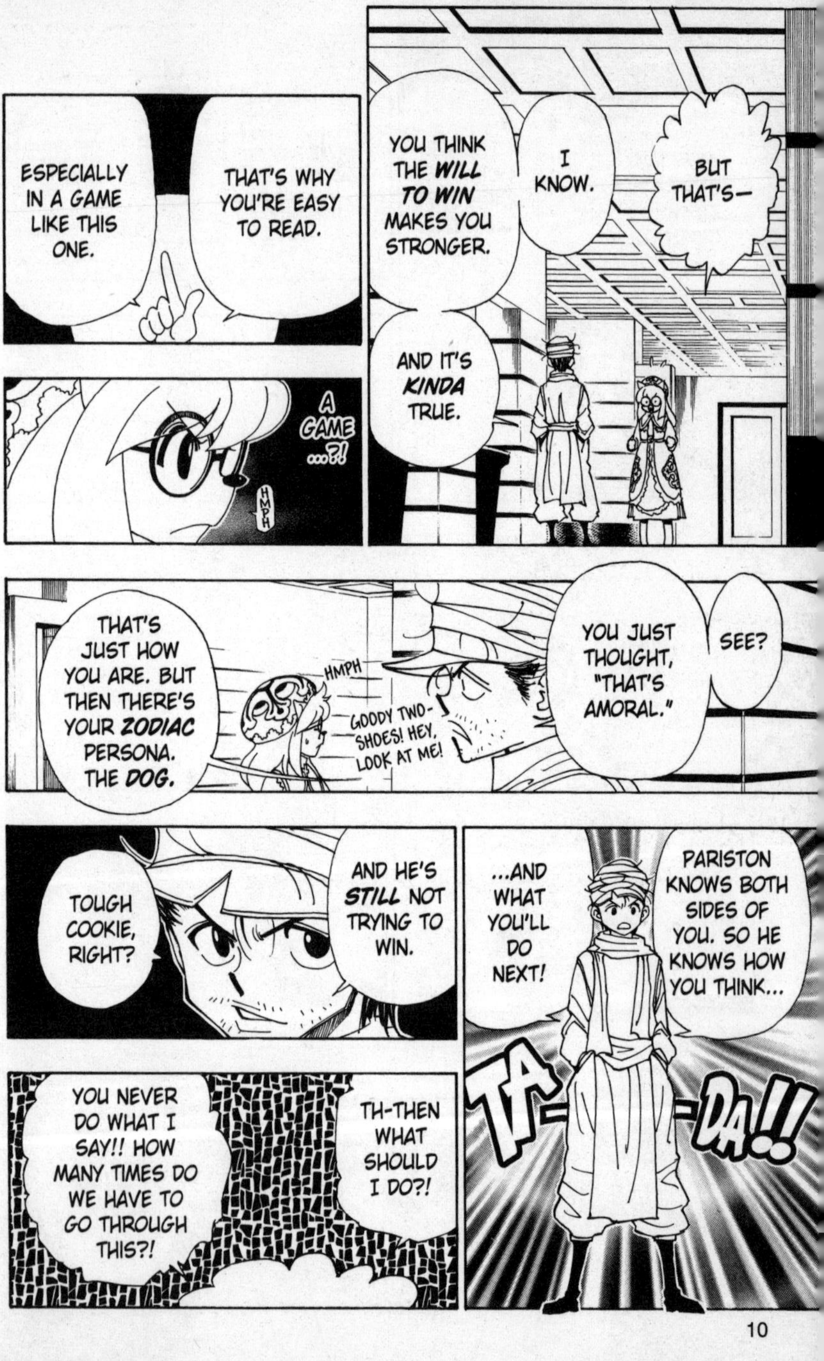
BUT THAT'S—
I KNOW.
YOU THINK THE WILL TO WIN MAKES YOU STRONGER.
AND IT'S KINDA TRUE.
THAT'S WHY YOU'RE EASY TO READ.
ESPECIALLY IN A GAME LIKE THIS ONE.
A GAME ...?!
HMPH
SEE?
YOU JUST THOUGHT, "THAT'S AMORAL."
GOODY TWO-SHOES! HEY, LOOK AT ME!
HMPH
THAT'S JUST HOW YOU ARE. BUT THEN THERE'S YOUR ZODIAC PERSONA. THE DOG.
PARISTON KNOWS BOTH SIDES OF YOU. SO HE KNOWS HOW YOU THINK...
...AND WHAT YOU'LL DO NEXT!
TA-DA!!
AND HE'S STILL NOT TRYING TO WIN.
TOUGH COOKIE, RIGHT?
TH-THEN WHAT SHOULD I DO?!
YOU NEVER DO WHAT I SAY!! HOW MANY TIMES DO WE HAVE TO GO THROUGH THIS?!

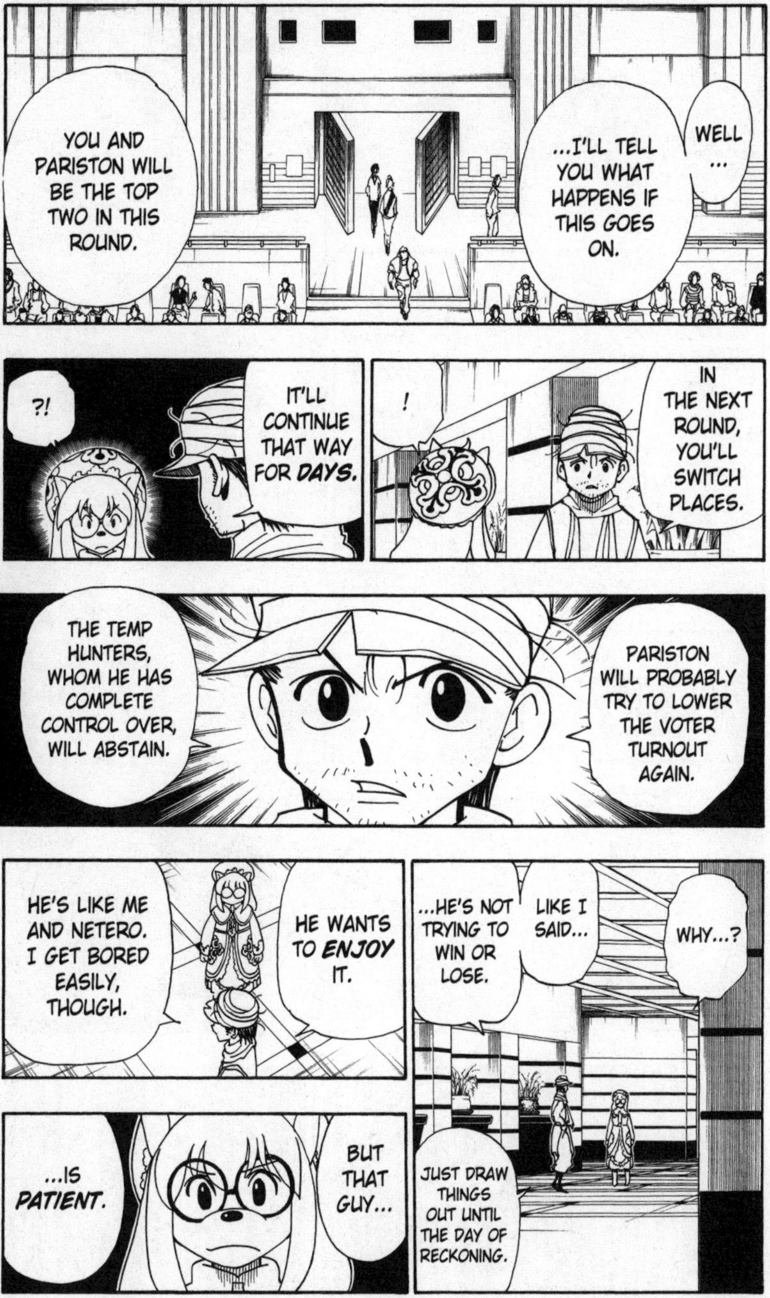
WELL ...
...I'LL TELL YOU WHAT HAPPENS IF THIS GOES ON.
YOU AND PARISTON WILL BE THE TOP TWO IN THIS ROUND.
IN THE NEXT ROUND, YOU'LL SWITCH PLACES.
!
IT'LL CONTINUE THAT WAY FOR DAYS.
?!
PARISTON WILL PROBABLY TRY TO LOWER THE VOTER TURNOUT AGAIN.
THE TEMP HUNTERS, WHOM HE HAS COMPLETE CONTROL OVER, WILL ABSTAIN.
WHY...?
LIKE I SAID...
...HE'S NOT TRYING TO WIN OR LOSE.
JUST DRAW THINGS OUT UNTIL THE DAY OF RECKONING.
HE WANTS TO ENJOY IT.
HE'S LIKE ME AND NETERO. I GET BORED EASILY, THOUGH.
BUT THAT GUY...
...IS PATIENT.

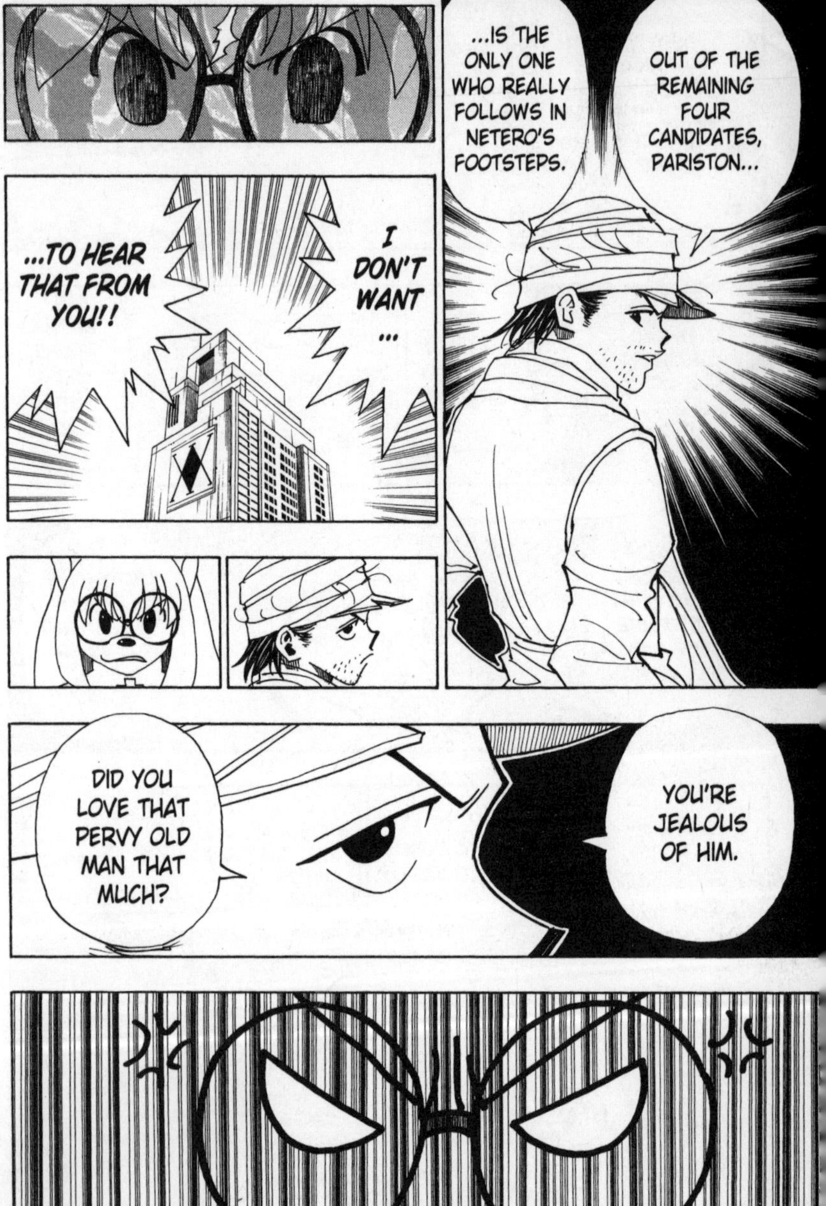
OUT OF THE REMAINING FOUR CANDIDATES, PARISTON...
...IS THE ONLY ONE WHO REALLY FOLLOWS IN NETERO'S FOOTSTEPS.
I DON'T WANT ...
...TO HEAR THAT FROM YOU!!
YOU'RE JEALOUS OF HIM.
DID YOU LOVE THAT PERVY OLD MAN THAT MUCH?

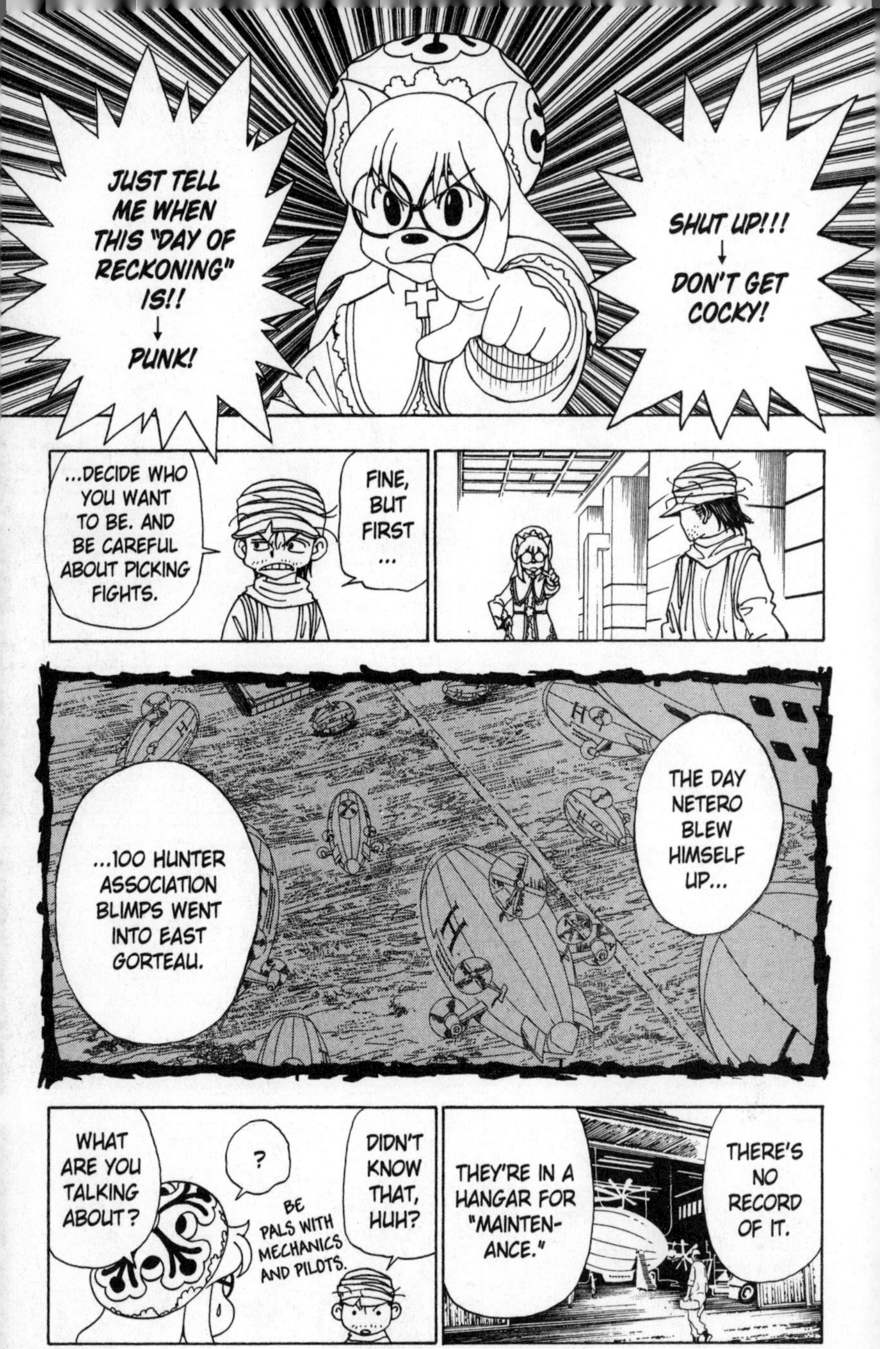
SHUT UP!!! ↓ DON'T GET COCKY!
JUST TELL ME WHEN THIS "DAY OF RECKONING" IS!! ↓ PUNK!
FINE, BUT FIRST...
...DECIDE WHO YOU WANT TO BE. AND BE CAREFUL ABOUT PICKING FIGHTS.
THE DAY NETERO BLEW HIMSELF UP...
...100 HUNTER ASSOCIATION BLIMPS WENT INTO EAST GORTEAU.
THERE'S NO RECORD OF IT.
THEY'RE IN A HANGAR FOR "MAINTENANCE."
DIDN'T KNOW THAT, HUH?
?
WHAT ARE YOU TALKING ABOUT?
BE PALS WITH MECHANICS AND PILOTS.

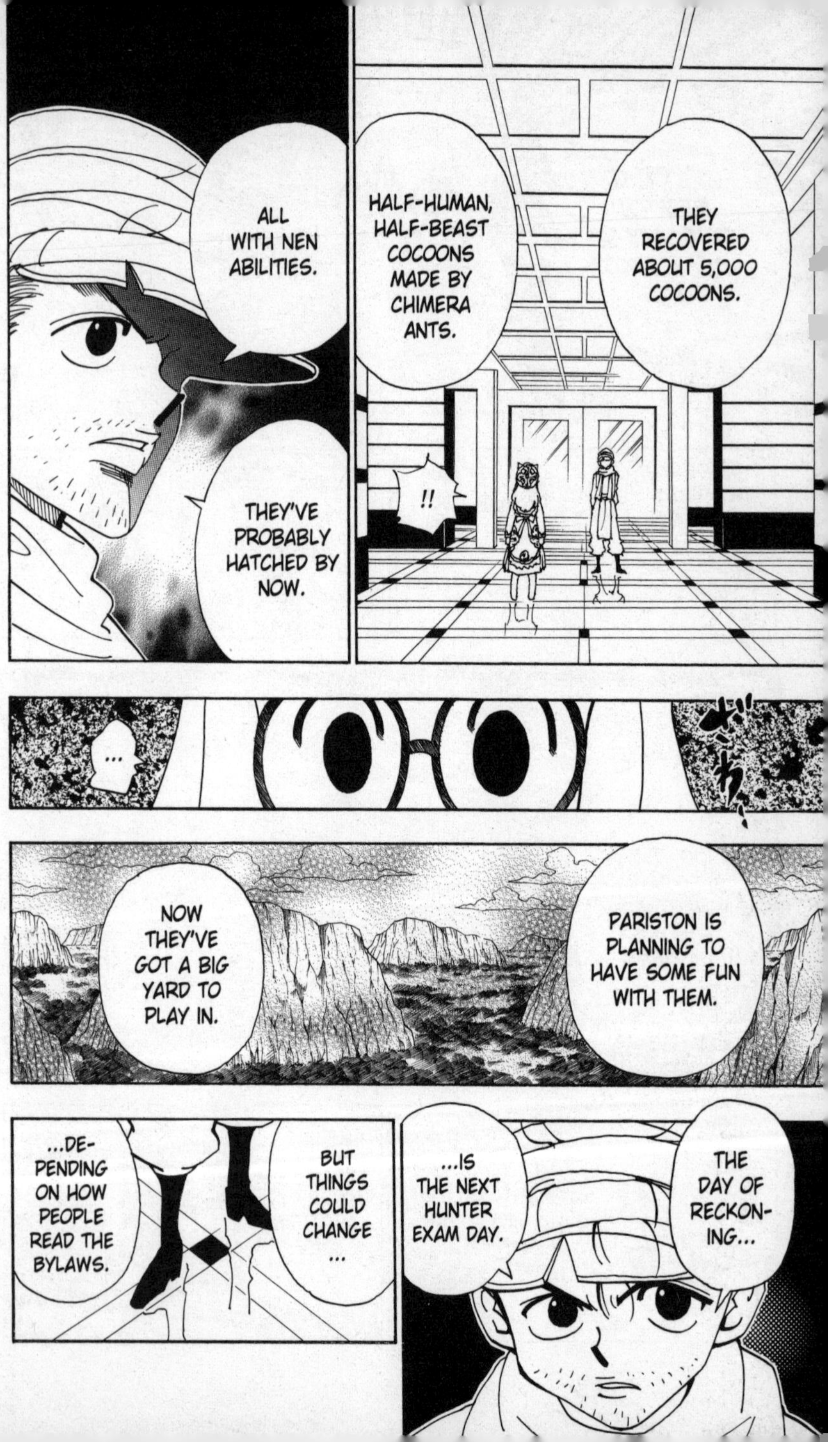
THEY RECOVERED ABOUT 5,000 COCOONS.
HALF-HUMAN, HALF-BEAST COCOONS MADE BY CHIMERA ANTS.
!!
ALL WITH NEN ABILITIES.
THEY'VE PROBABLY HATCHED BY NOW.
...
PARISTON IS PLANNING TO HAVE SOME FUN WITH THEM.
NOW THEY'VE GOT A BIG YARD TO PLAY IN.
THE DAY OF RECKON-ING...
...IS THE NEXT HUNTER EXAM DAY.
BUT THINGS COULD CHANGE ...
...DE-PENDING ON HOW PEOPLE READ THE BYLAWS.

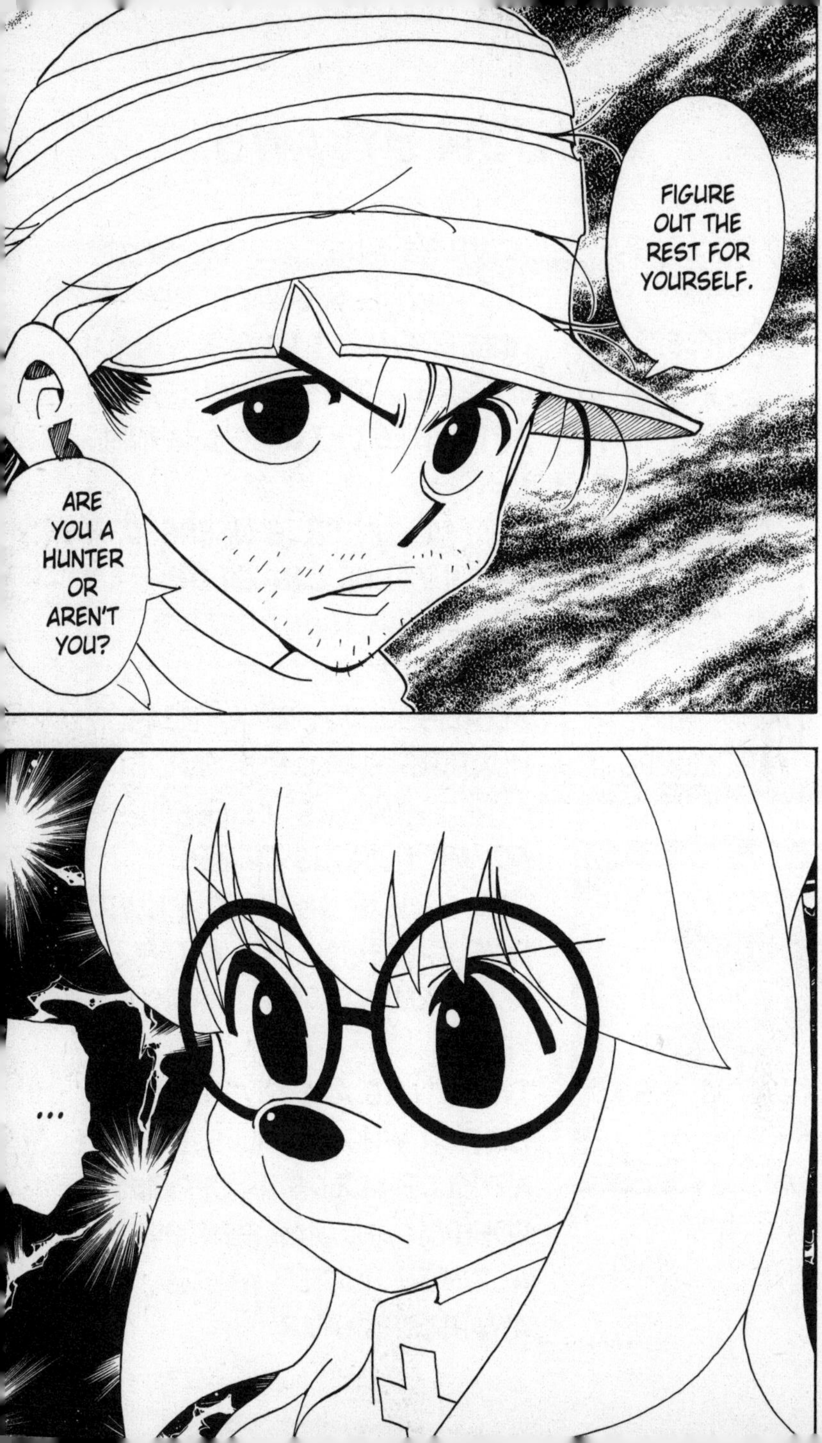
FIGURE OUT THE REST FOR YOURSELF.
ARE YOU A HUNTER OR AREN'T YOU?
...

HUNTER BYLAWS

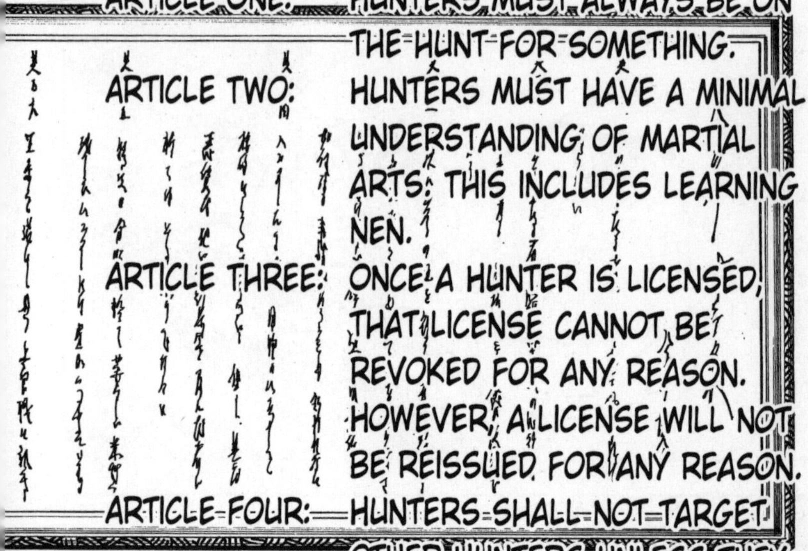

ARTICLE ONE: HUNTERS MUST ALWAYS BE ON THE HUNT FOR SOMETHING.

ARTICLE TWO: HUNTERS MUST HAVE A MINIMAL UNDERSTANDING OF MARTIAL ARTS. THIS INCLUDES LEARNING NEN.

ARTICLE THREE: ONCE A HUNTER IS LICENSED, THAT LICENSE CANNOT BE REVOKED FOR ANY REASON. HOWEVER, A LICENSE WILL NOT BE REISSUED FOR ANY REASON.

ARTICLE FOUR: HUNTERS SHALL NOT TARGET OTHER HUNTERS UNLESS THEY COMMIT HEINOUS CRIMES.

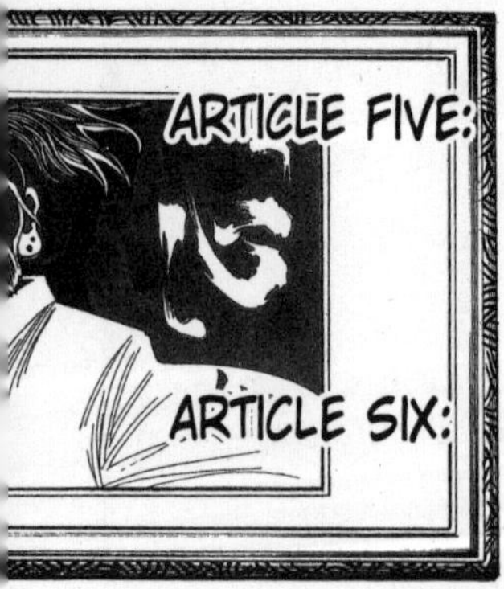

ARTICLE FIVE: ONE STAR IS GIVEN TO A HUNTER WHO PRODUCES REMARKABLE ACHIEVEMENTS IN A PARTICULAR FIELD.

ARTICLE SIX: TWO STARS ARE GIVEN TO A HUNTER WHO FULFILLS THE FIVE ARTICLES, HOLDS AN OFFICIAL POSITION AND HAS MENTORED A JUNIOR HUNTER WHO IS AWARDED A STAR.

ARTICLE SEVEN: THREE STARS ARE GIVEN TO
A HUNTER WHO FULFILLS THE
SIX ARTICLES AND PRODUCES
REMARKABLE ACHIEVEMENTS IN
MULTIPLE FIELDS.

ARTICLE EIGHT: THE CHIEF EXECUTIVE OF THE
HUNTER ASSOCIATION MUST EARN
THE CONFIDENCE OF A MAJORITY
OF HIS COLLEAGUES. WHEN THE
POSITION OF CHAIRMAN IS VACATED,
THE VOTE TO ELECT THE NEXT
CHAIRMAN MUST BE CONDUCTED
AT ONCE, AND DEPUTY POWER IS
GIVEN TO THE VICE-CHAIRMAN IN THE
MEANTIME.

ARTICLE NINE: THE AUTHORITY TO DECIDE ON A
METHOD TO SELECT NEW MEMBERS
IS GIVEN TO THE CHAIRMAN.
HOWEVER, TO SIGNIFICANTLY CHANGE
EXISTING METHODS REQUIRES THE
CONFIDENCE OF A MAJORITY OF
COLLEAGUES.

ARTICLE TEN: ANY MATTER NOT MENTIONED HERE
WILL BE DECIDED IN A CABINET
CONSISTING OF THE CHAIRMAN, VICE-
CHAIRMAN AND STAFF ADVISORS.
THE CHAIRMAN HAS THE AUTHORITY
TO SELECT THE VICE-CHAIRMAN AND
STAFF.

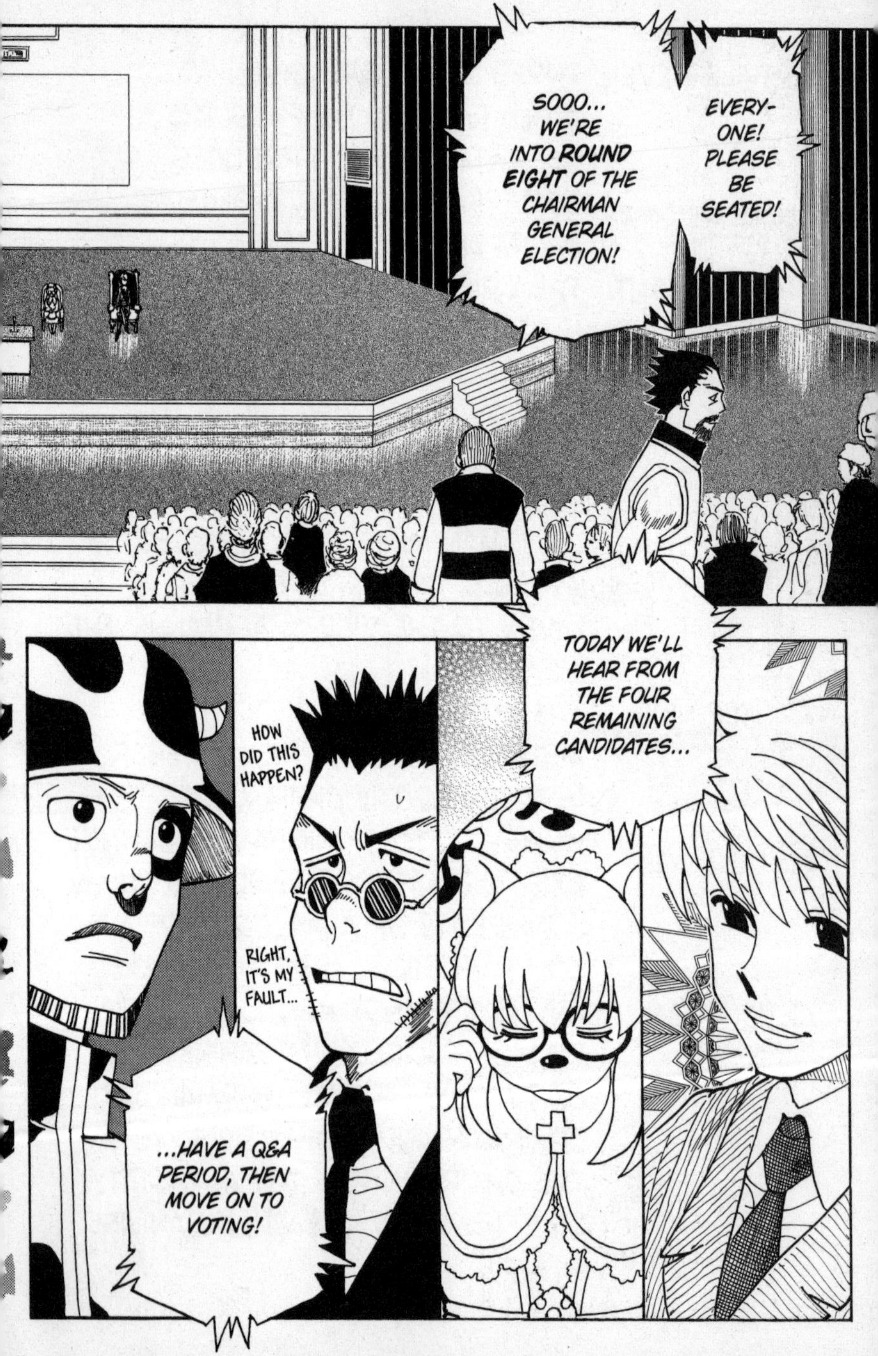
EVERY-ONE! PLEASE BE SEATED!
SOOO... WE'RE INTO ROUND EIGHT OF THE CHAIRMAN GENERAL ELECTION!
TODAY WE'LL HEAR FROM THE FOUR REMAINING CANDIDATES...
HOW DID THIS HAPPEN?
RIGHT, IT'S MY FAULT...
...HAVE A Q&A PERIOD, THEN MOVE ON TO VOTING!

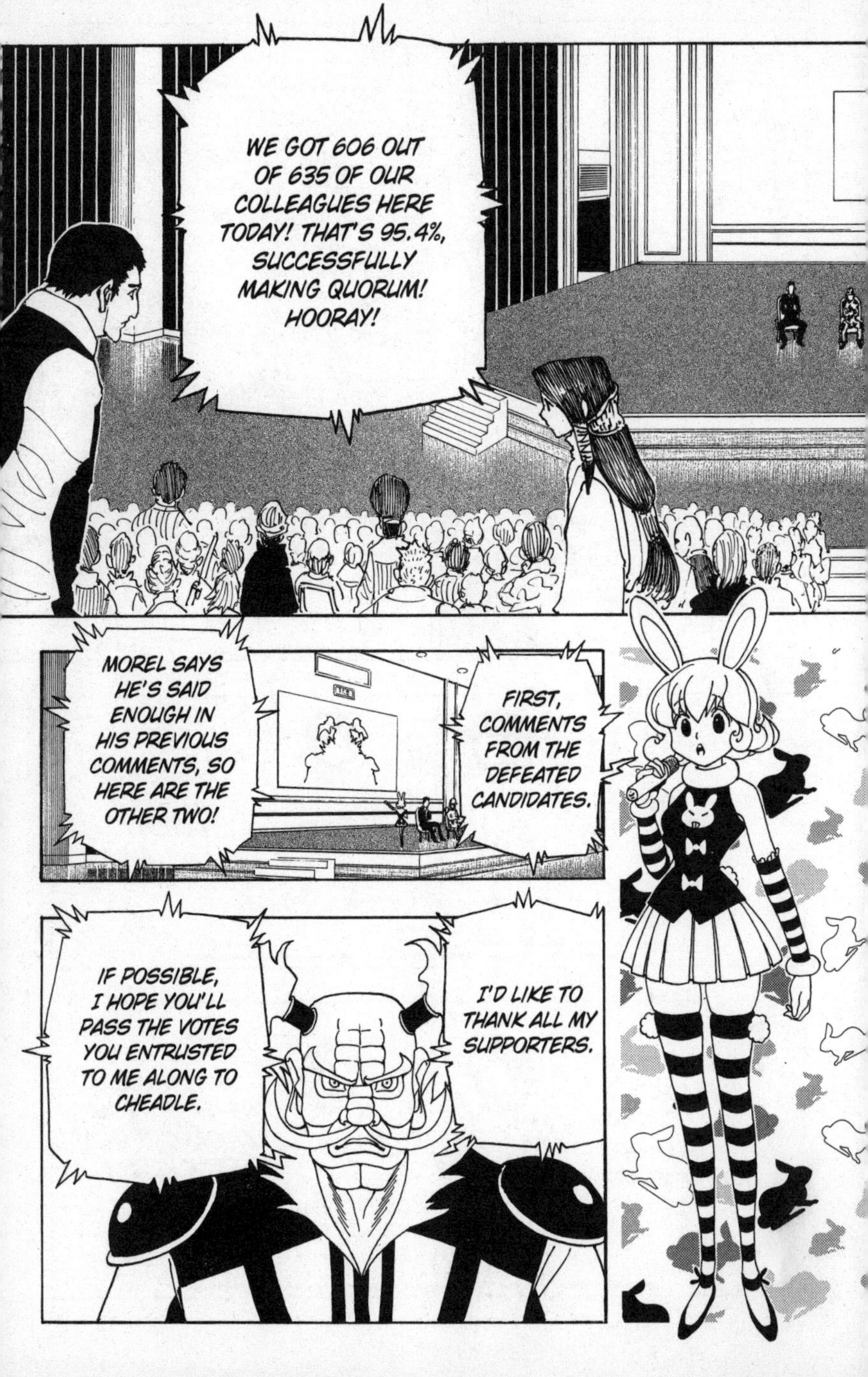
WE GOT 606 OUT OF 635 OF OUR COLLEAGUES HERE TODAY! THAT'S 95.4%, SUCCESSFULLY MAKING QUORUM! HOORAY!
FIRST, COMMENTS FROM THE DEFEATED CANDIDATES.
MOREL SAYS HE'S SAID ENOUGH IN HIS PREVIOUS COMMENTS, SO HERE ARE THE OTHER TWO!
I'D LIKE TO THANK ALL MY SUPPORTERS.
IF POSSIBLE, I HOPE YOU'LL PASS THE VOTES YOU ENTRUSTED TO ME ALONG TO CHEADLE.

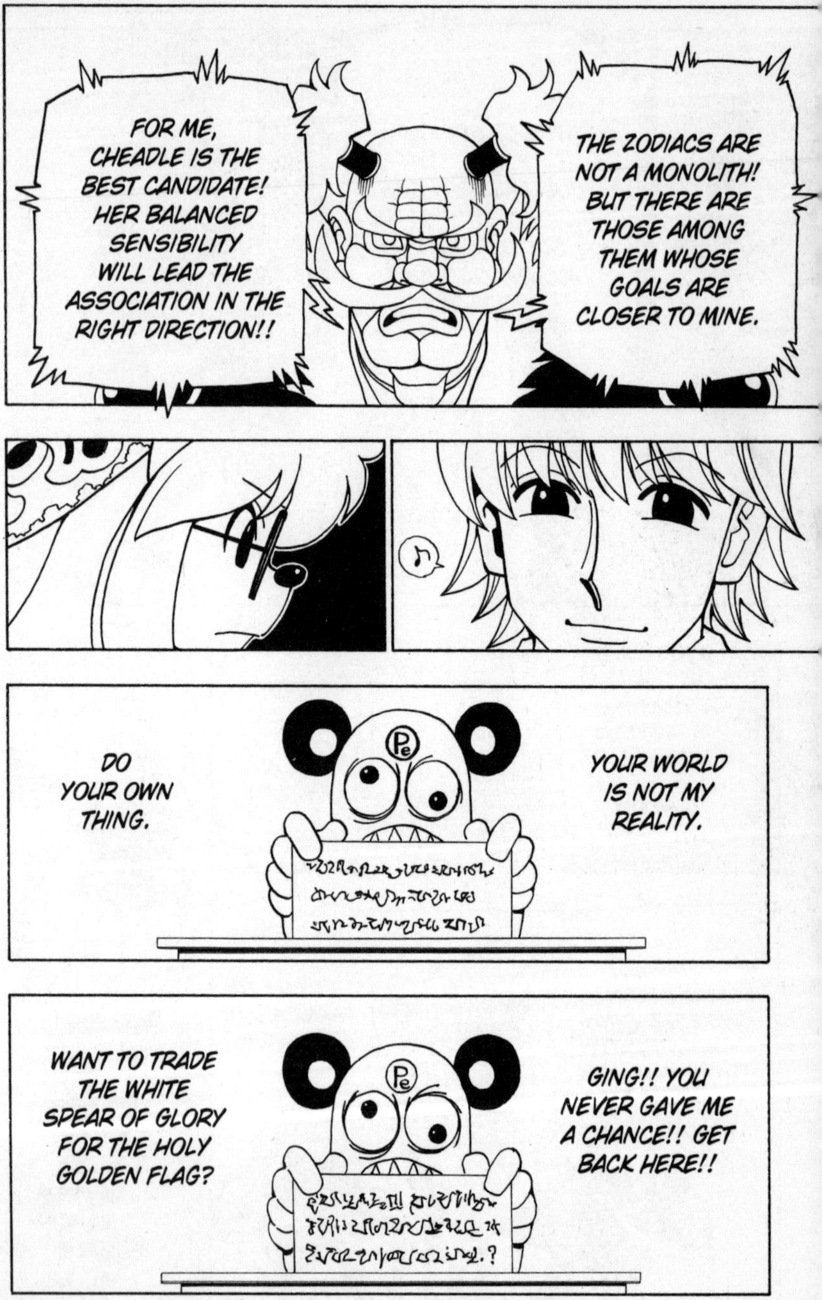
THE ZODIACS ARE NOT A MONOLITH! BUT THERE ARE THOSE AMONG THEM WHOSE GOALS ARE CLOSER TO MINE.
FOR ME, CHEADLE IS THE BEST CANDIDATE! HER BALANCED SENSIBILITY WILL LEAD THE ASSOCIATION IN THE RIGHT DIRECTION!!
♪
Pe
YOUR WORLD IS NOT MY REALITY.
DO YOUR OWN THING.
Pe
GING!! YOU NEVER GAVE ME A CHANCE!! GET BACK HERE!!
WANT TO TRADE THE WHITE SPEAR OF GLORY FOR THE HOLY GOLDEN FLAG?

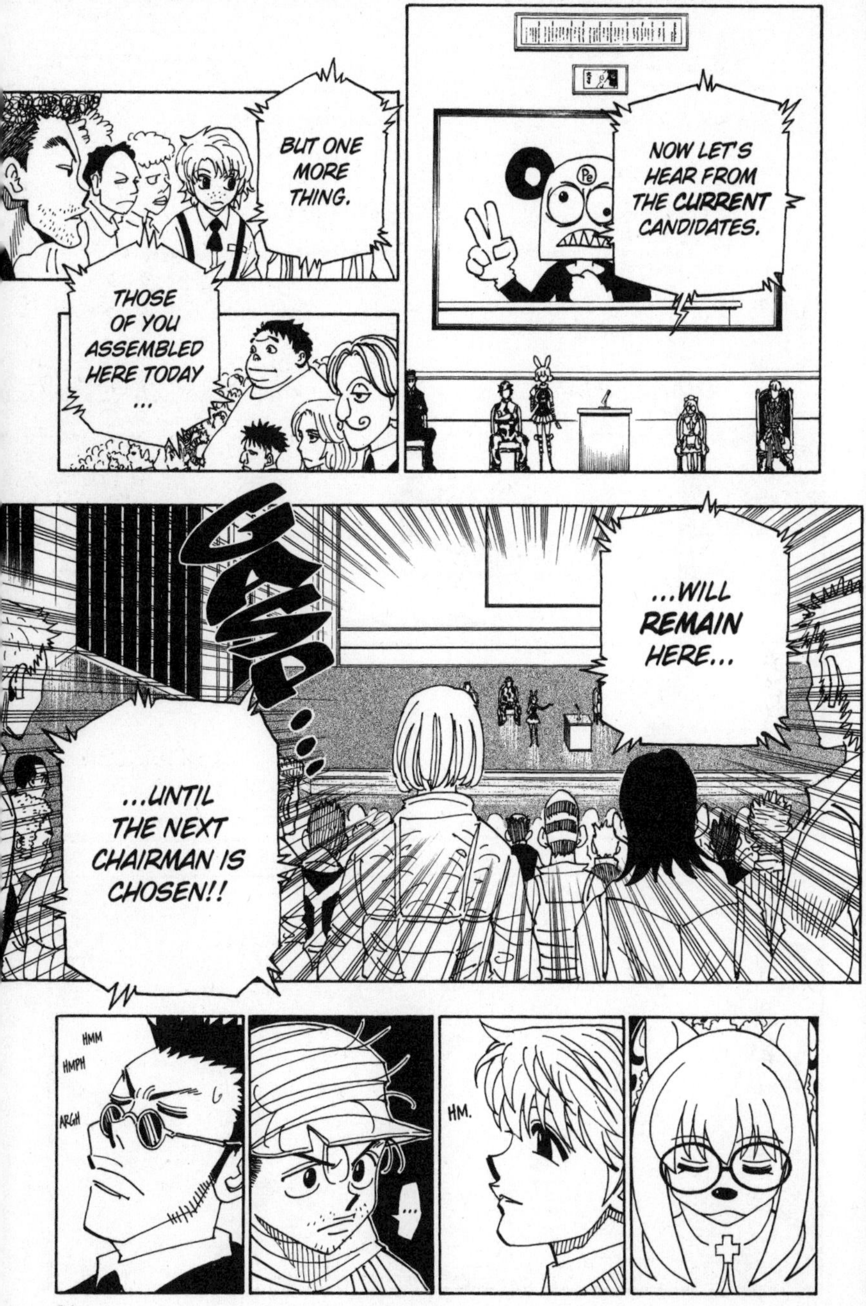
NOW LET'S HEAR FROM THE CURRENT CANDIDATES.
BUT ONE MORE THING.
THOSE OF YOU ASSEMBLED HERE TODAY ...
...WILL REMAIN HERE...
GASP...
...UNTIL THE NEXT CHAIRMAN IS CHOSEN!!
HM.
...
HMM
HMPH
ARGH

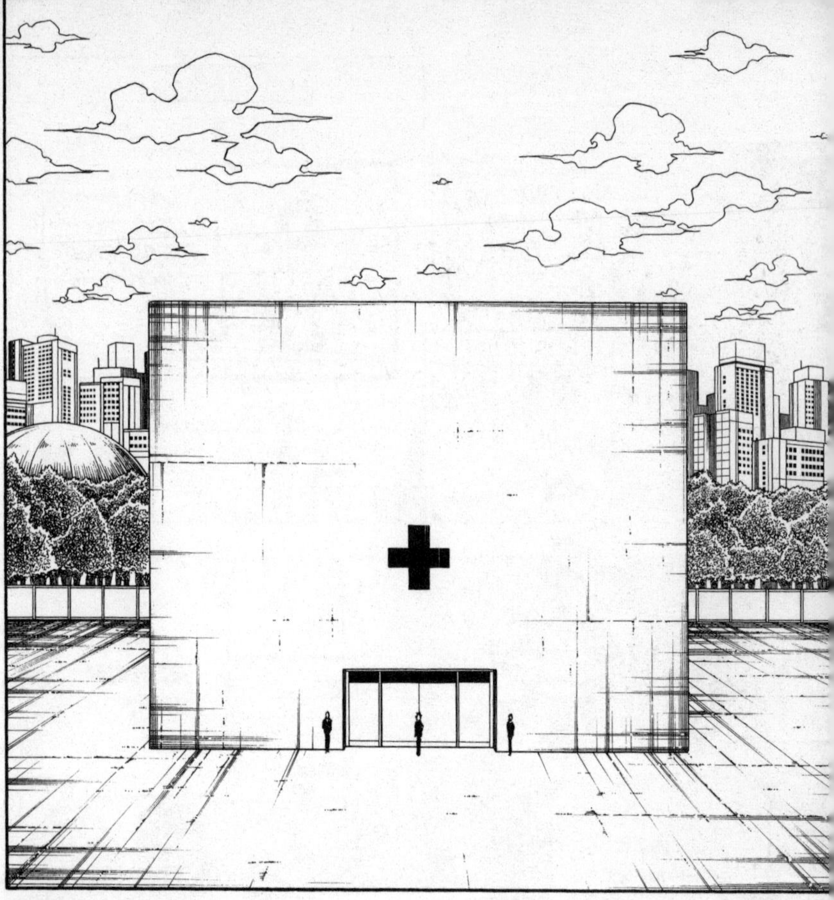

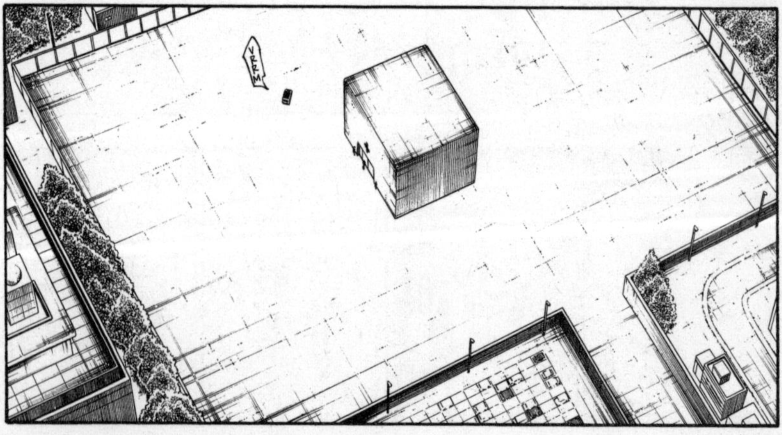
VRRM

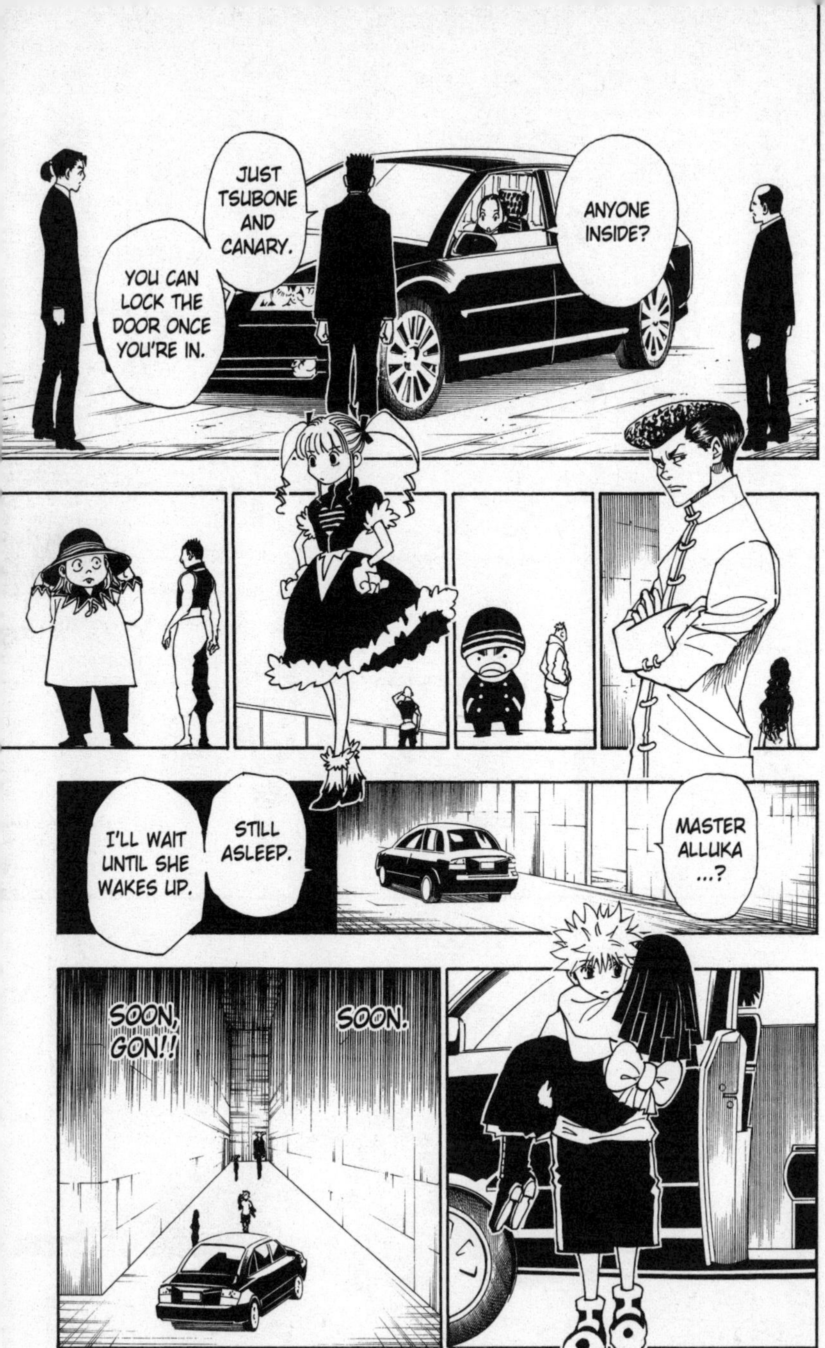
ANYONE INSIDE?
JUST TSUBONE AND CANARY.
YOU CAN LOCK THE DOOR ONCE YOU'RE IN.
MASTER ALLUKA ...?
STILL ASLEEP.
I'LL WAIT UNTIL SHE WAKES UP.
SOON.
SOON, GON!!

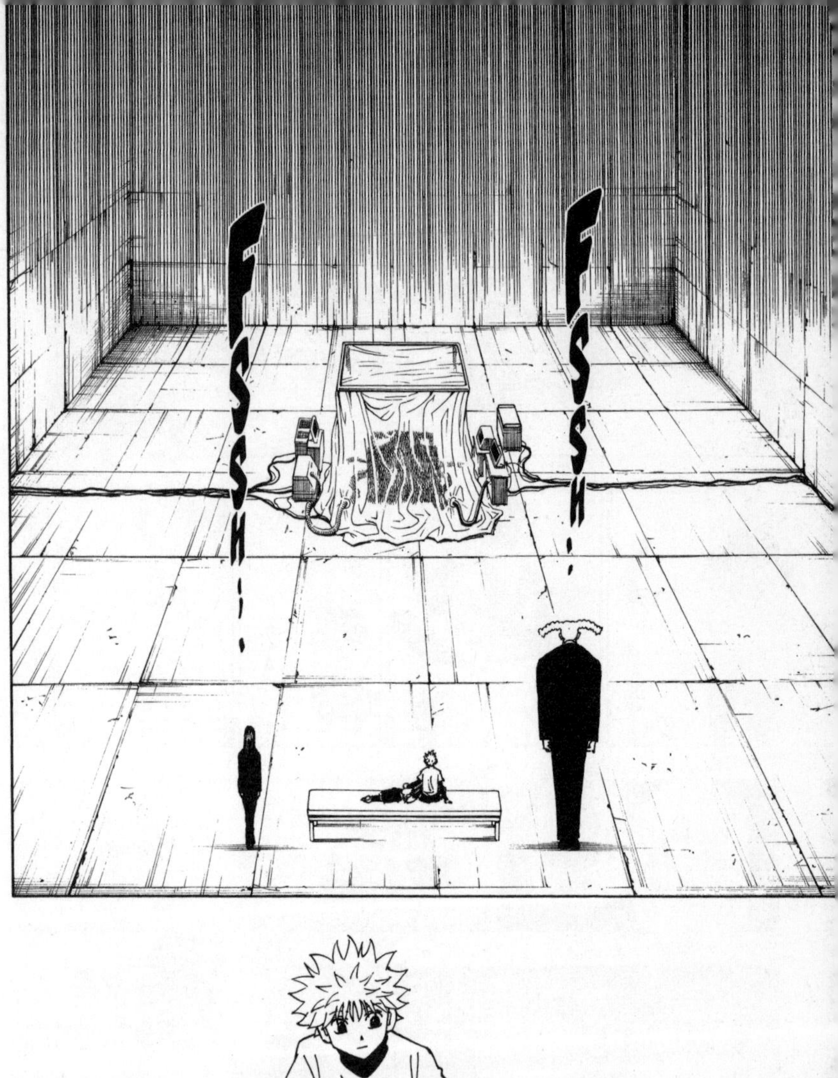
FSSH!
FSSSH!!

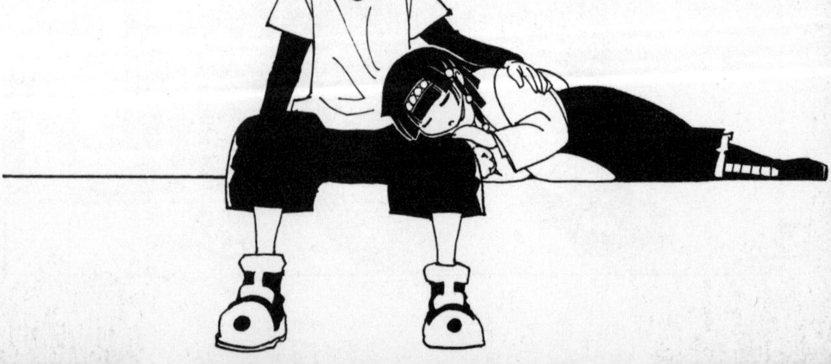

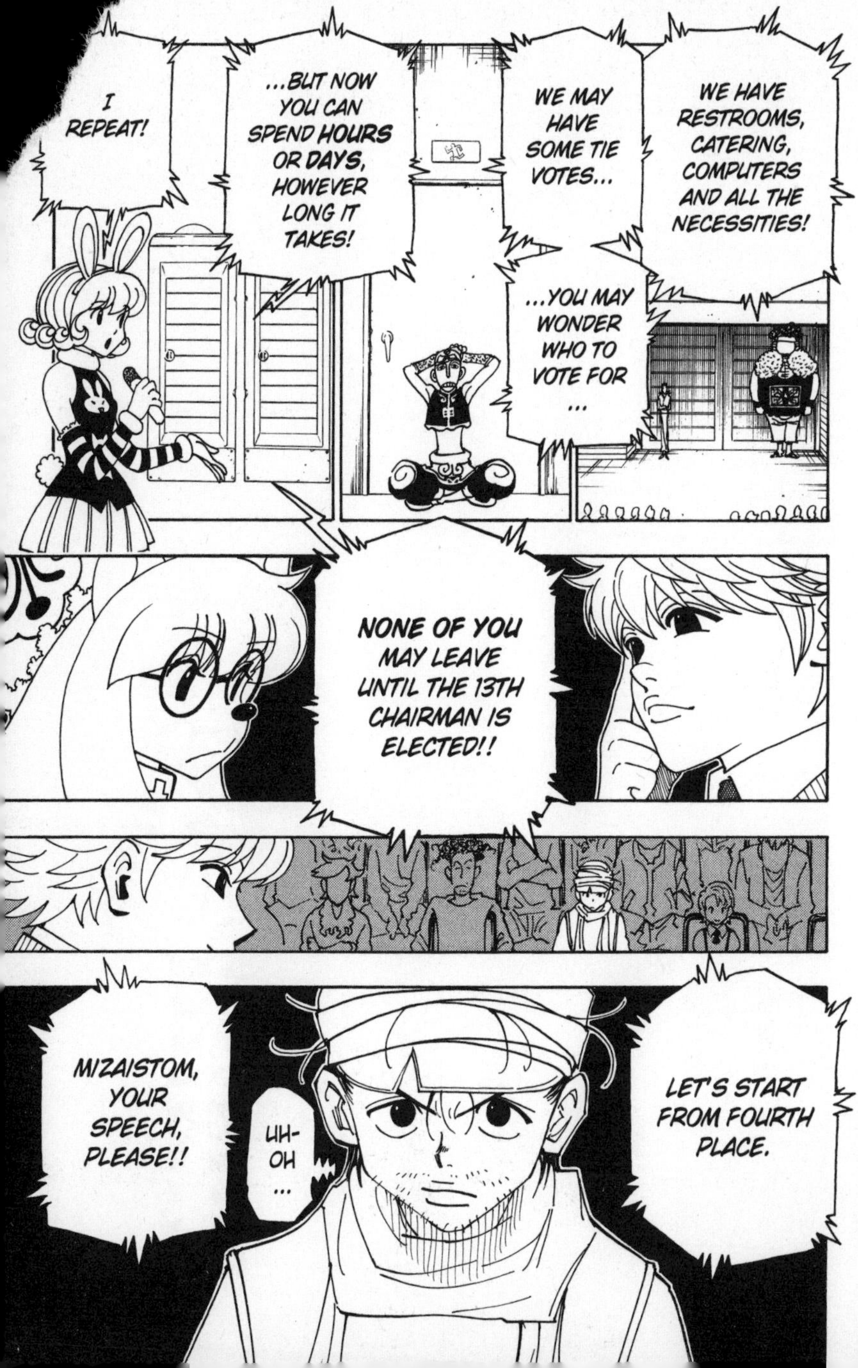
WE HAVE RESTROOMS, CATERING, COMPUTERS AND ALL THE NECESSITIES!
WE MAY HAVE SOME TIE VOTES...
...YOU MAY WONDER WHO TO VOTE FOR ...
...BUT NOW YOU CAN SPEND HOURS OR DAYS, HOWEVER LONG IT TAKES!
I REPEAT!
NONE OF YOU MAY LEAVE UNTIL THE 13TH CHAIRMAN IS ELECTED!!
LET'S START FROM FOURTH PLACE.
UH-OH ...
MIZAISTOM, YOUR SPEECH, PLEASE!!

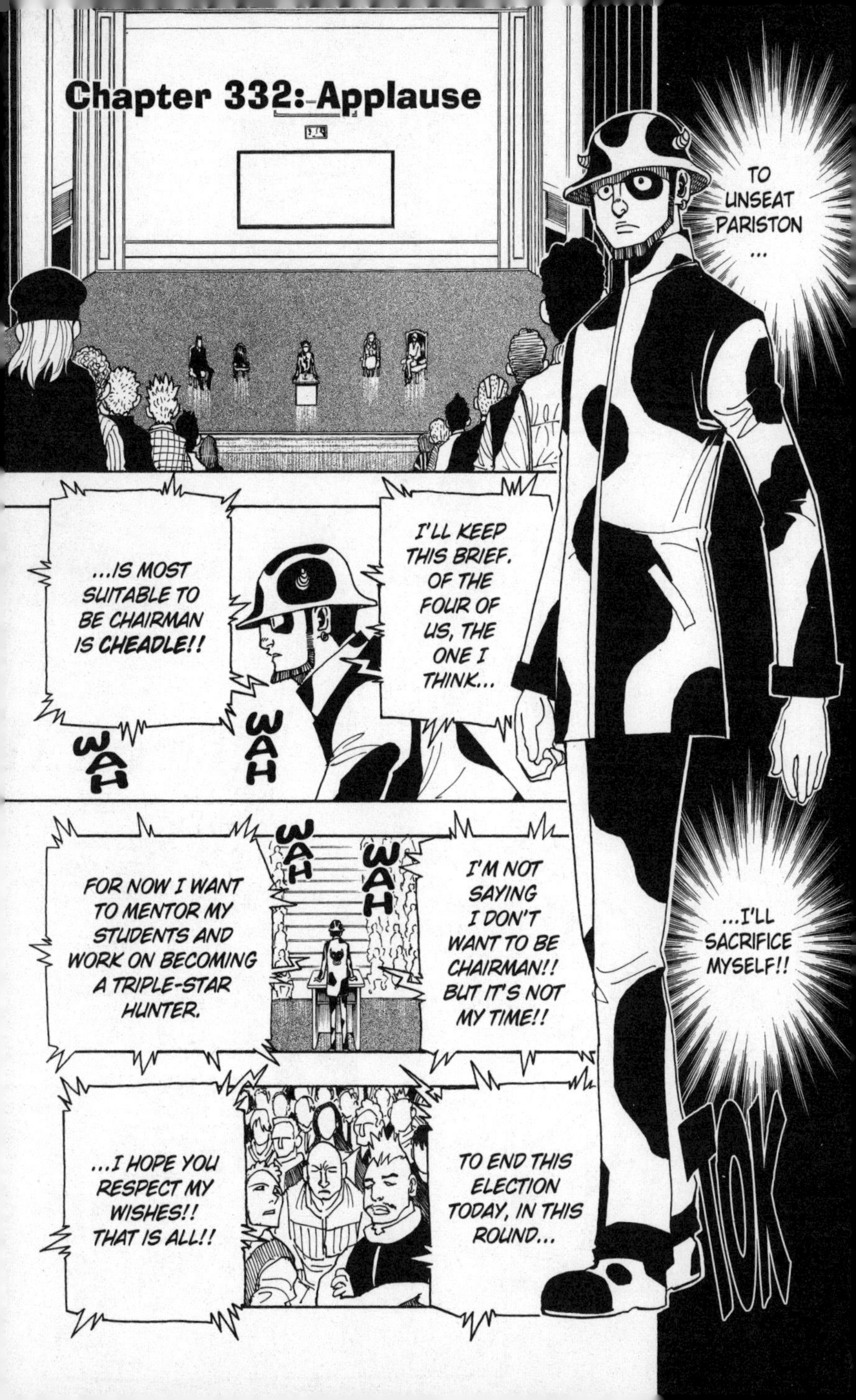
Chapter 332: Applause
I'LL KEEP THIS BRIEF. OF THE FOUR OF US, THE ONE I THINK...
...IS MOST SUITABLE TO BE CHAIRMAN IS CHEADLE!!
WAH
WAH
I'M NOT SAYING I DON'T WANT TO BE CHAIRMAN!! BUT IT'S NOT MY TIME!!
WAH
WAH
FOR NOW I WANT TO MENTOR MY STUDENTS AND WORK ON BECOMING A TRIPLE-STAR HUNTER.
TO END THIS ELECTION TODAY, IN THIS ROUND...
...I HOPE YOU RESPECT MY WISHES!! THAT IS ALL!!
TO UNSEAT PARISTON ...
...I'LL SACRIFICE MYSELF!!
TOK

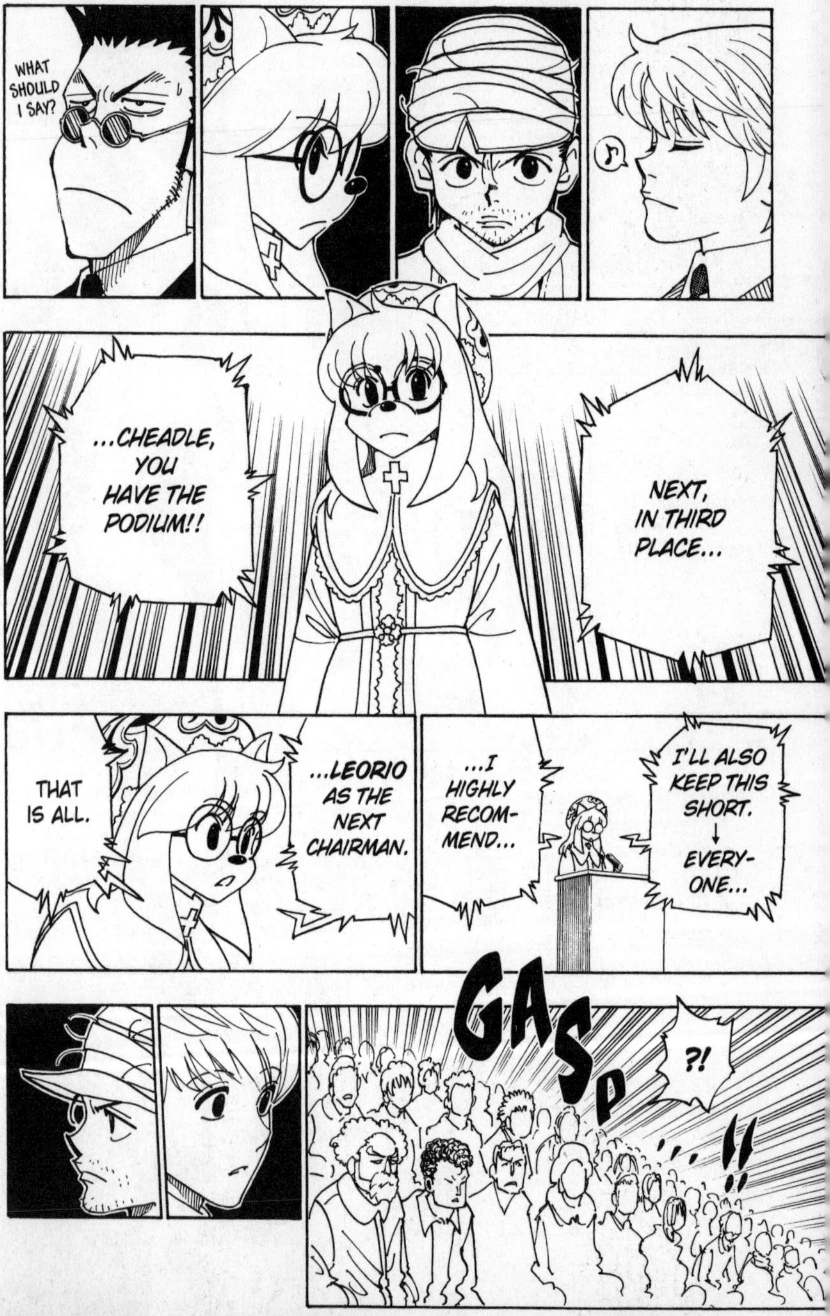
WHAT SHOULD I SAY?
NEXT, IN THIRD PLACE...
...CHEADLE, YOU HAVE THE PODIUM!!
I'LL ALSO KEEP THIS SHORT.
EVERYONE...
...I HIGHLY RECOMMEND...
...LEORIO AS THE NEXT CHAIRMAN.
THAT IS ALL.
GASP
?!

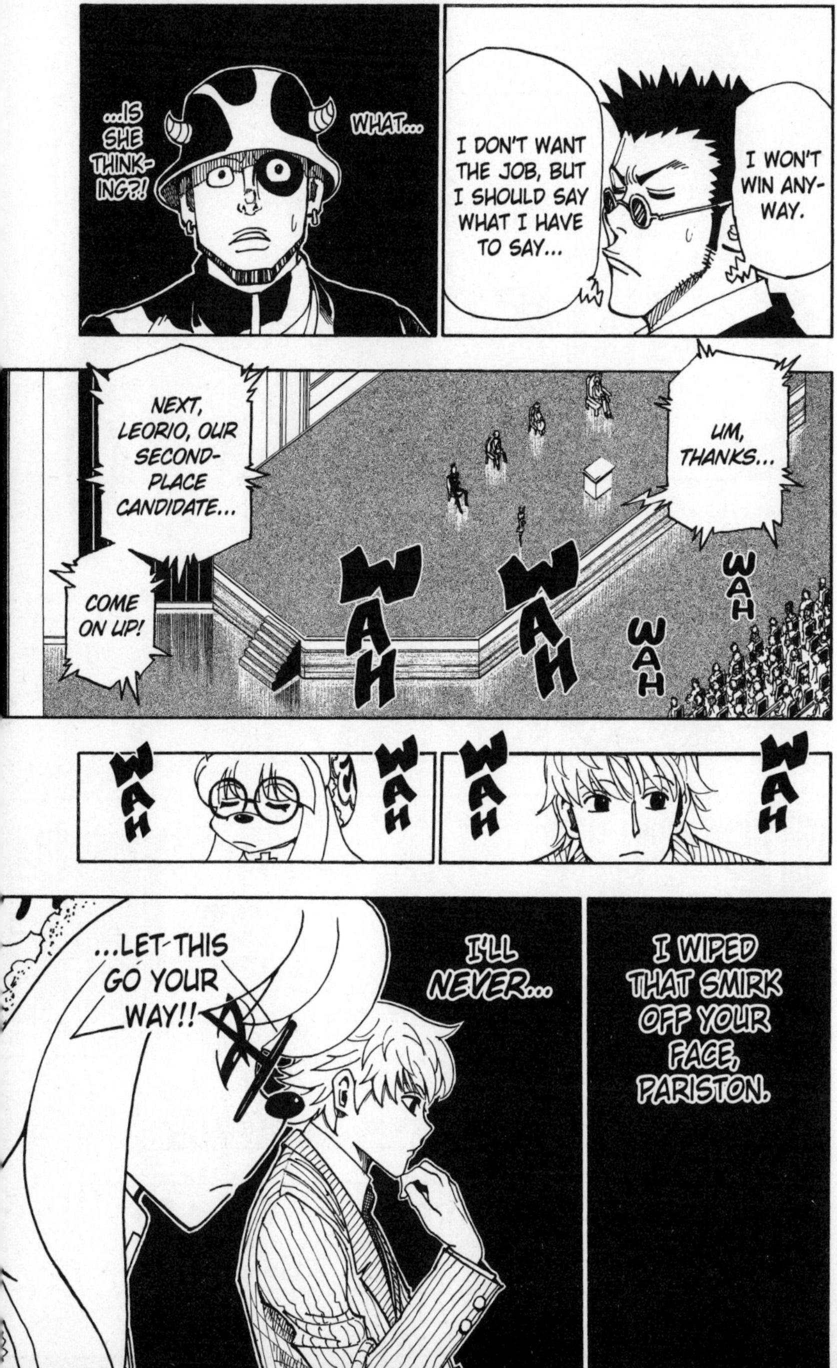
I WON'T WIN ANYWAY.
I DON'T WANT THE JOB, BUT I SHOULD SAY WHAT I HAVE TO SAY...
WHAT...
...IS SHE THINKING?!
UM, THANKS...
NEXT, LEORIO, OUR SECOND-PLACE CANDIDATE...
COME ON UP!
WAH
WAH
WAH
WAH
WAH
WAH
WAH
WAH
I WIPED THAT SMIRK OFF YOUR FACE, PARISTON.
I'LL NEVER...
...LET THIS GO YOUR WAY!!

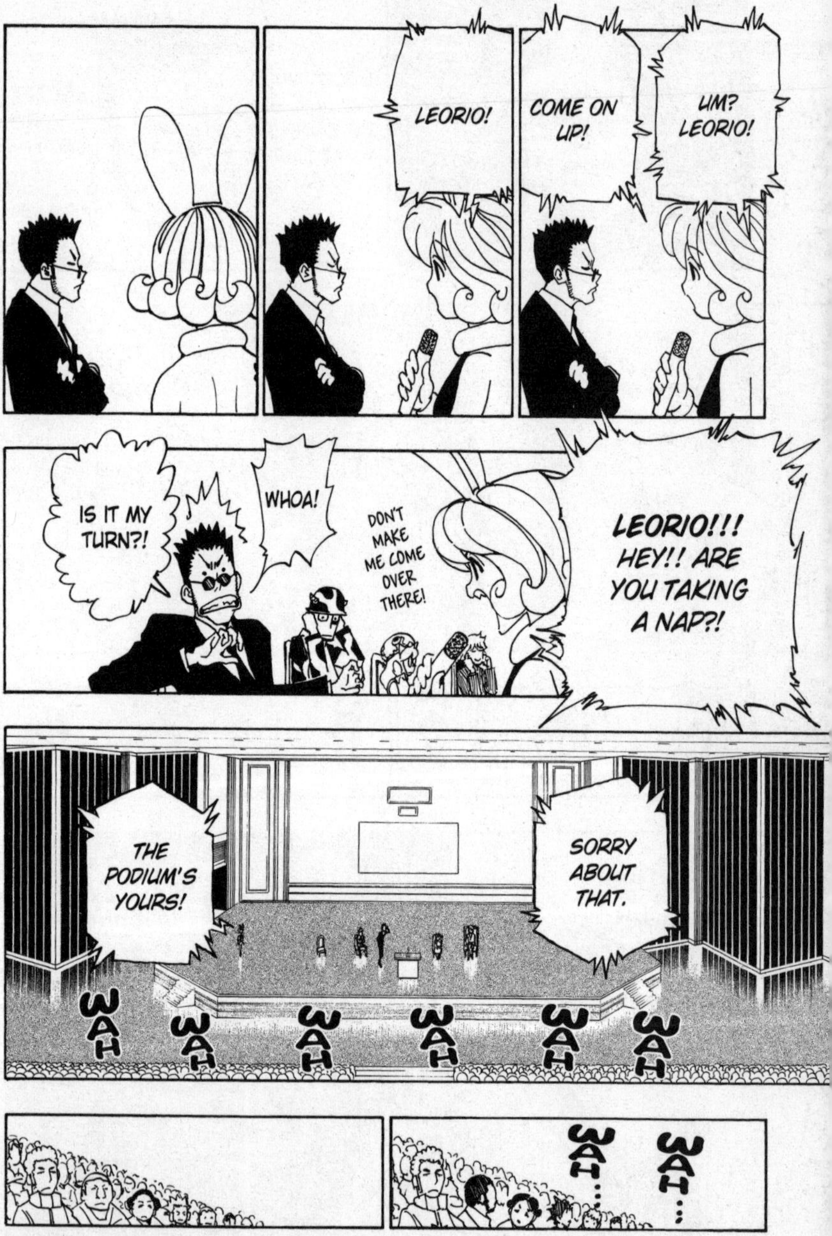
UM? LEORIO!
COME ON UP!
LEORIO!
LEORIO!!! HEY!! ARE YOU TAKING A NAP?!
DON'T MAKE ME COME OVER THERE!
WHOA!
IS IT MY TURN?!
SORRY ABOUT THAT.
THE PODIUM'S YOURS!
WAH WAH WAH WAH WAH WAH
WAH... WAH...

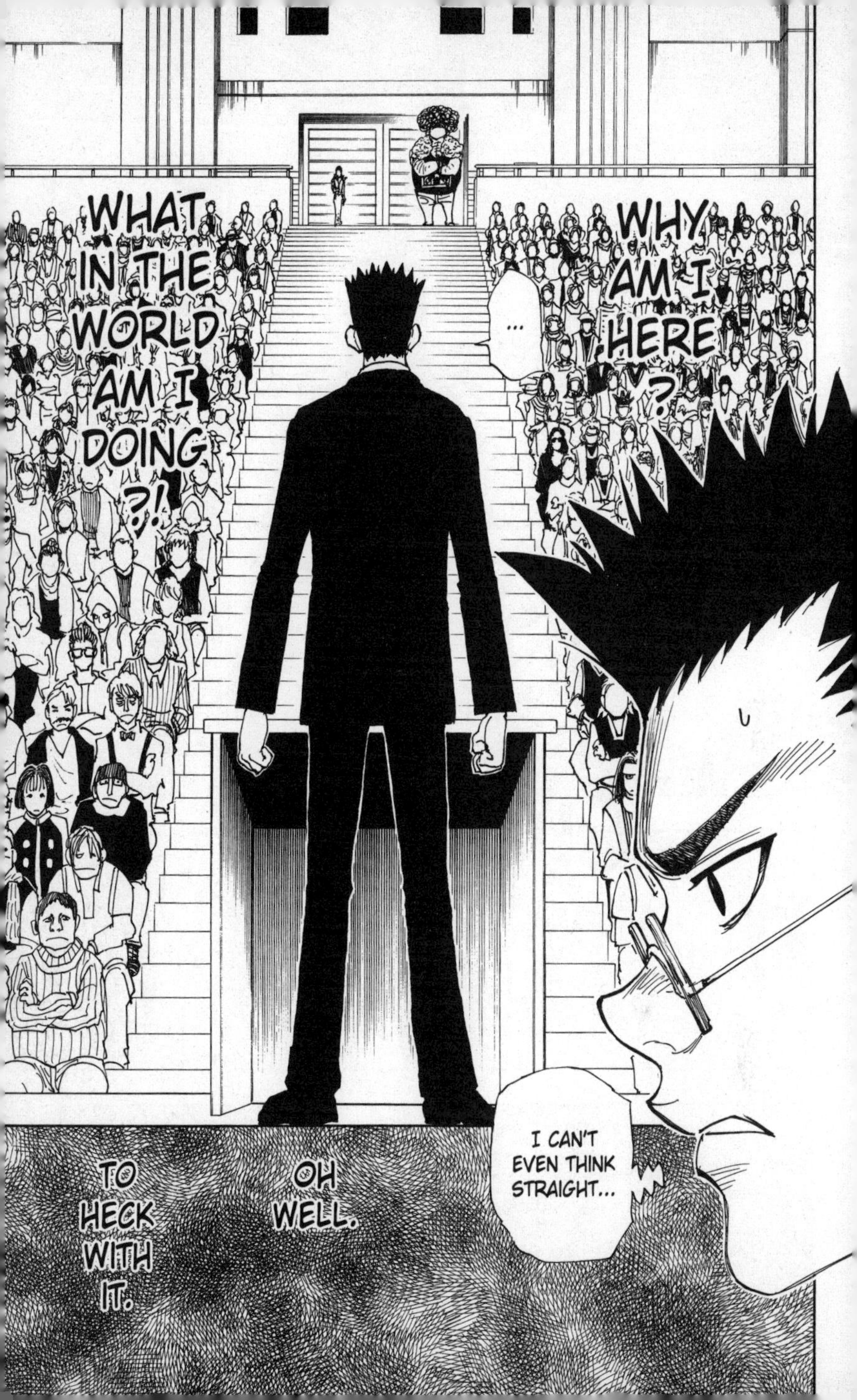
WHY AM I HERE?
...
WHAT IN THE WORLD AM I DOING?!
I CAN'T EVEN THINK STRAIGHT...
OH WELL.
TO HECK WITH IT.

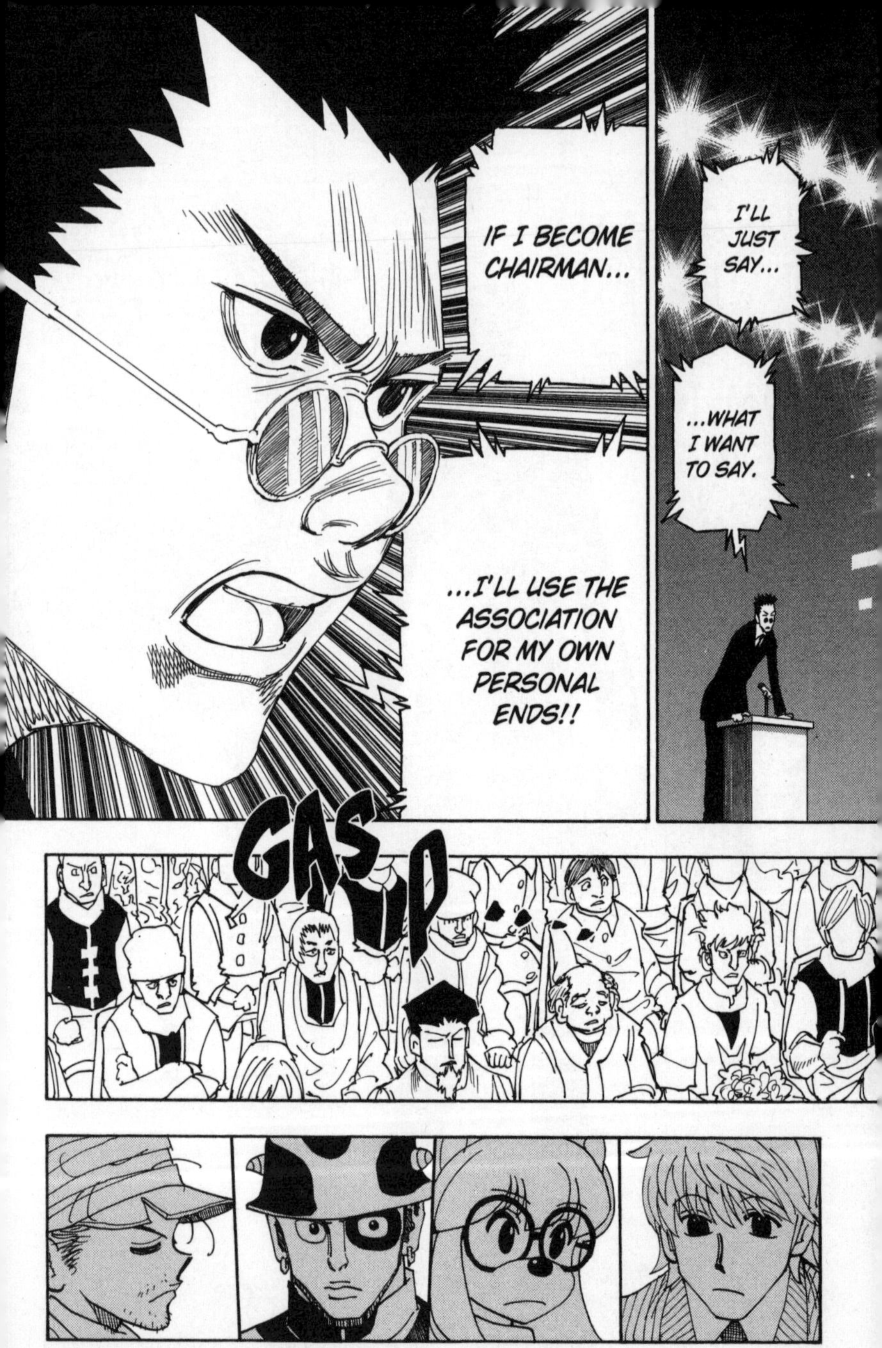
I'LL JUST SAY...
...WHAT I WANT TO SAY.
IF I BECOME CHAIRMAN...
...I'LL USE THE ASSOCIATION FOR MY OWN PERSONAL ENDS!!
GASP

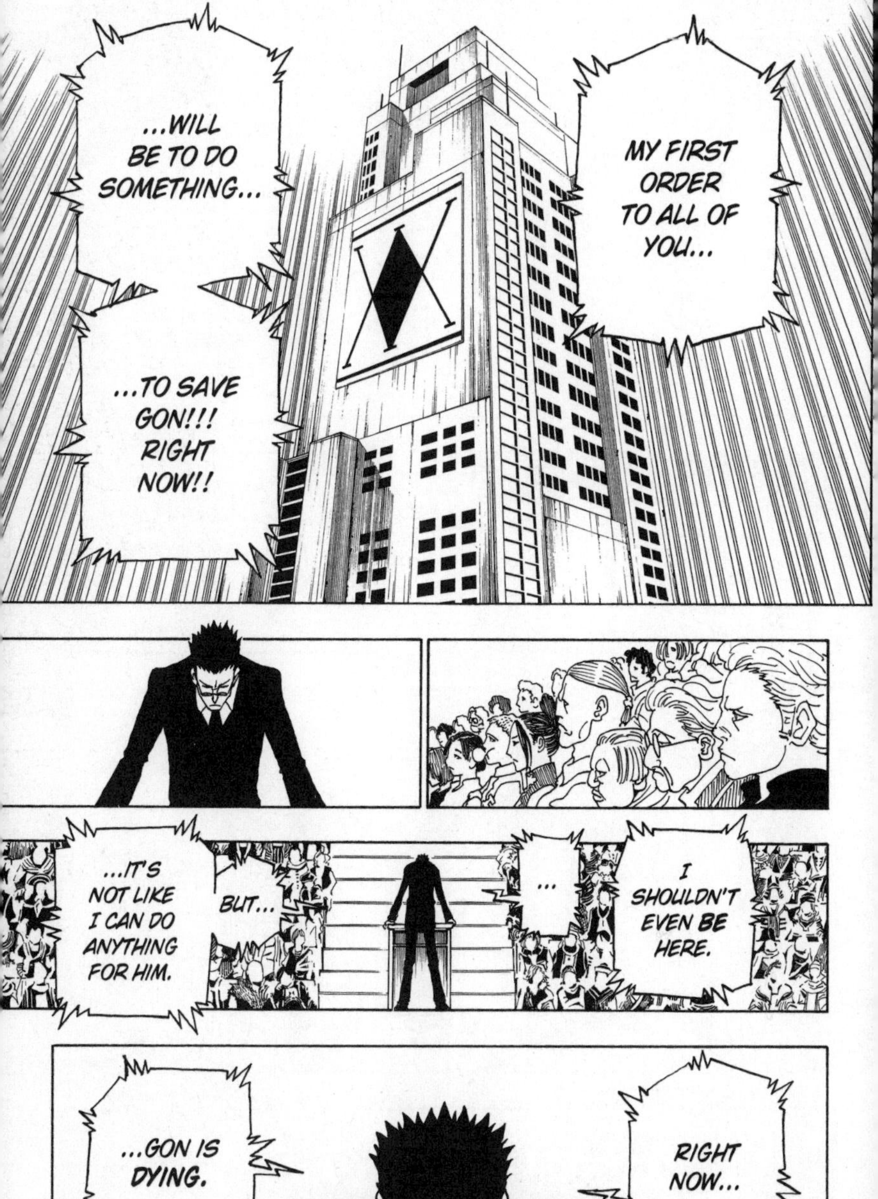
MY FIRST ORDER TO ALL OF YOU...
...WILL BE TO DO SOMETHING...
...TO SAVE GON!!! RIGHT NOW!!
I SHOULDN'T EVEN BE HERE.
...
BUT...
...IT'S NOT LIKE I CAN DO ANYTHING FOR HIM.
RIGHT NOW...
...GON IS DYING.

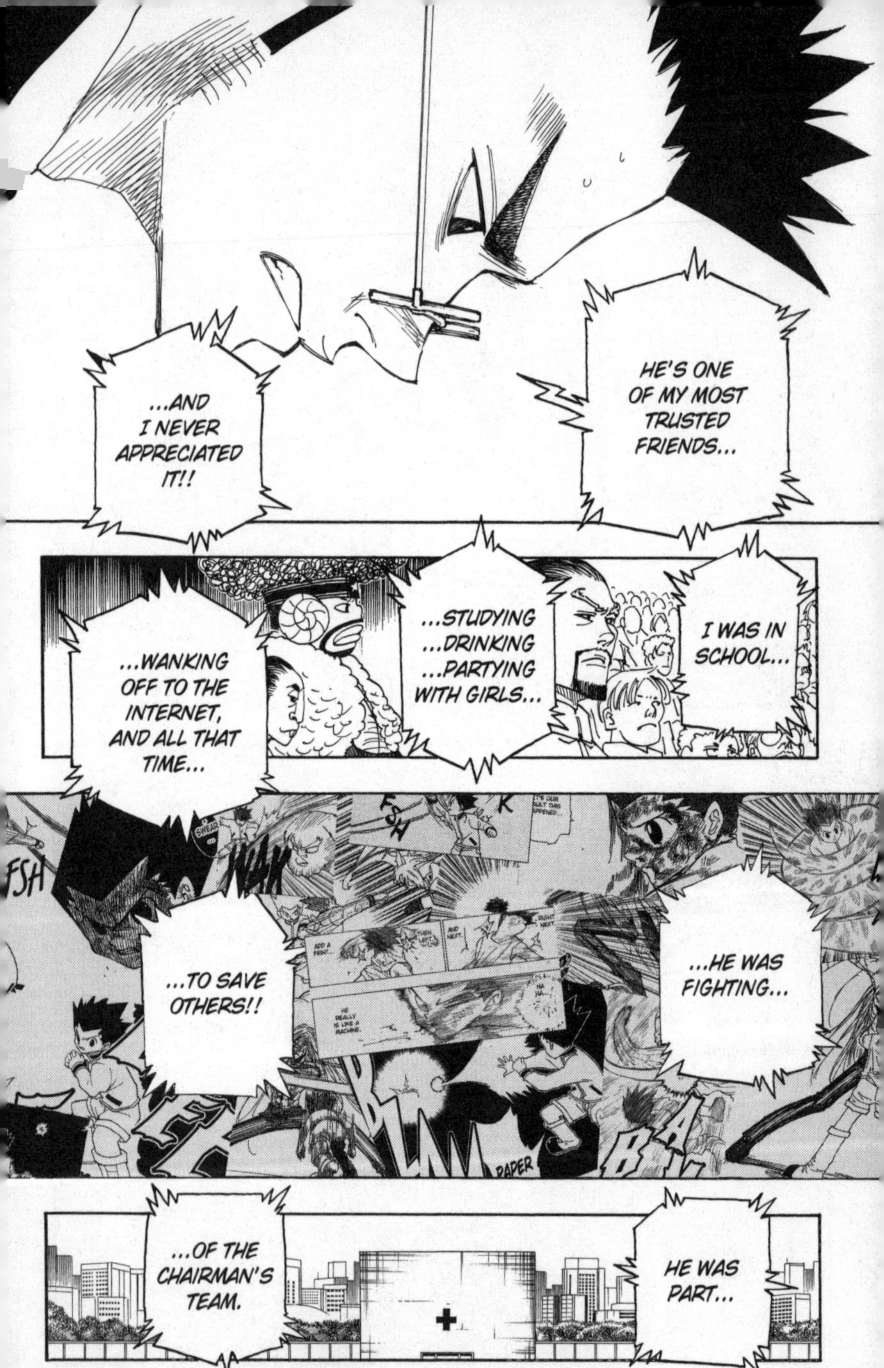
HE'S ONE OF MY MOST TRUSTED FRIENDS...
...AND I NEVER APPRECIATED IT!!
I WAS IN SCHOOL...
...STUDYING ...DRINKING ...PARTYING WITH GIRLS...
...WANKING OFF TO THE INTERNET, AND ALL THAT TIME...
...HE WAS FIGHTING...
...TO SAVE OTHERS!!
FSH
WAK
BLAM
PAPER
HE WAS PART...
...OF THE CHAIRMAN'S TEAM.

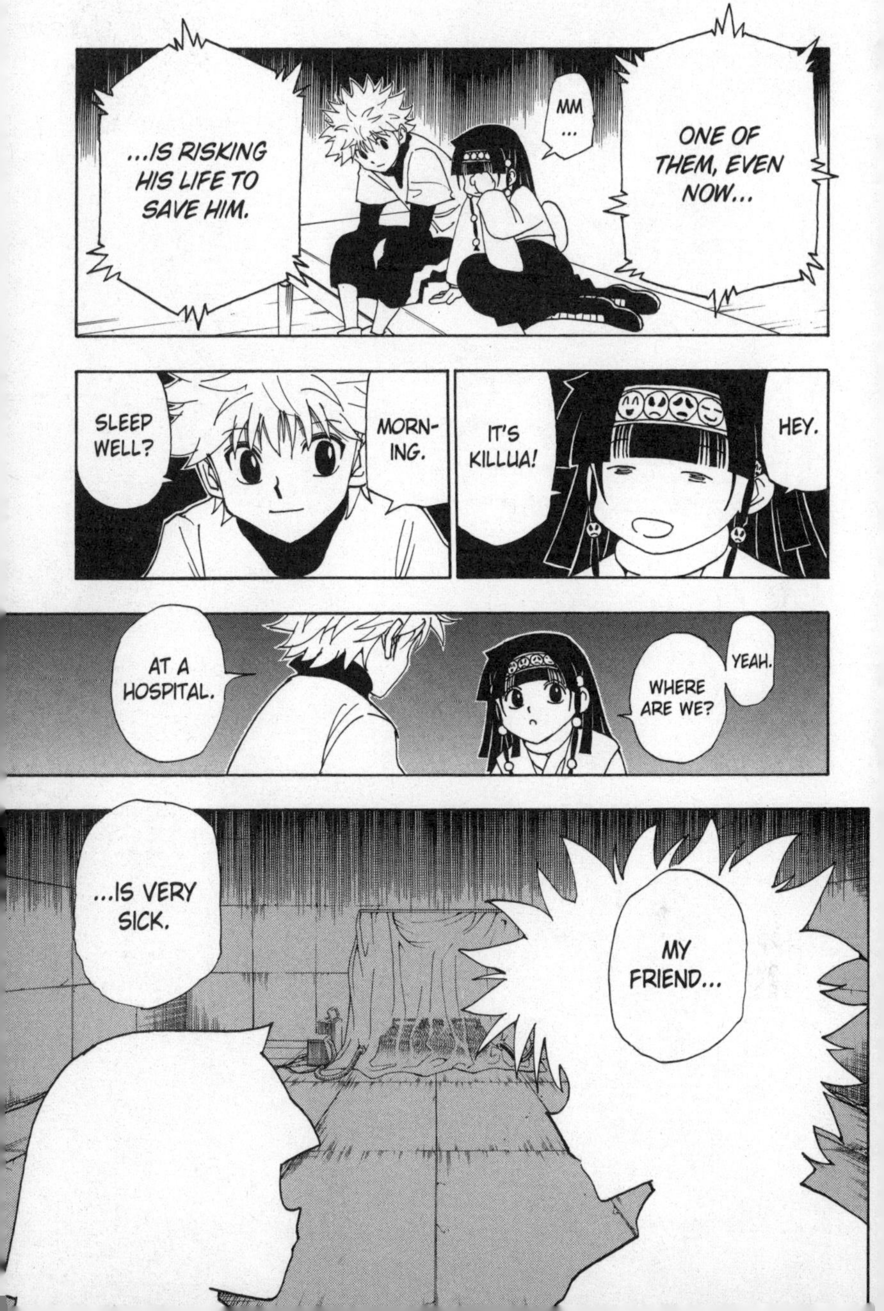
ONE OF THEM, EVEN NOW...
MM...
...IS RISKING HIS LIFE TO SAVE HIM.
HEY.
IT'S KILLUA!
MORN-ING.
SLEEP WELL?
YEAH.
WHERE ARE WE?
AT A HOSPITAL.
MY FRIEND...
...IS VERY SICK.

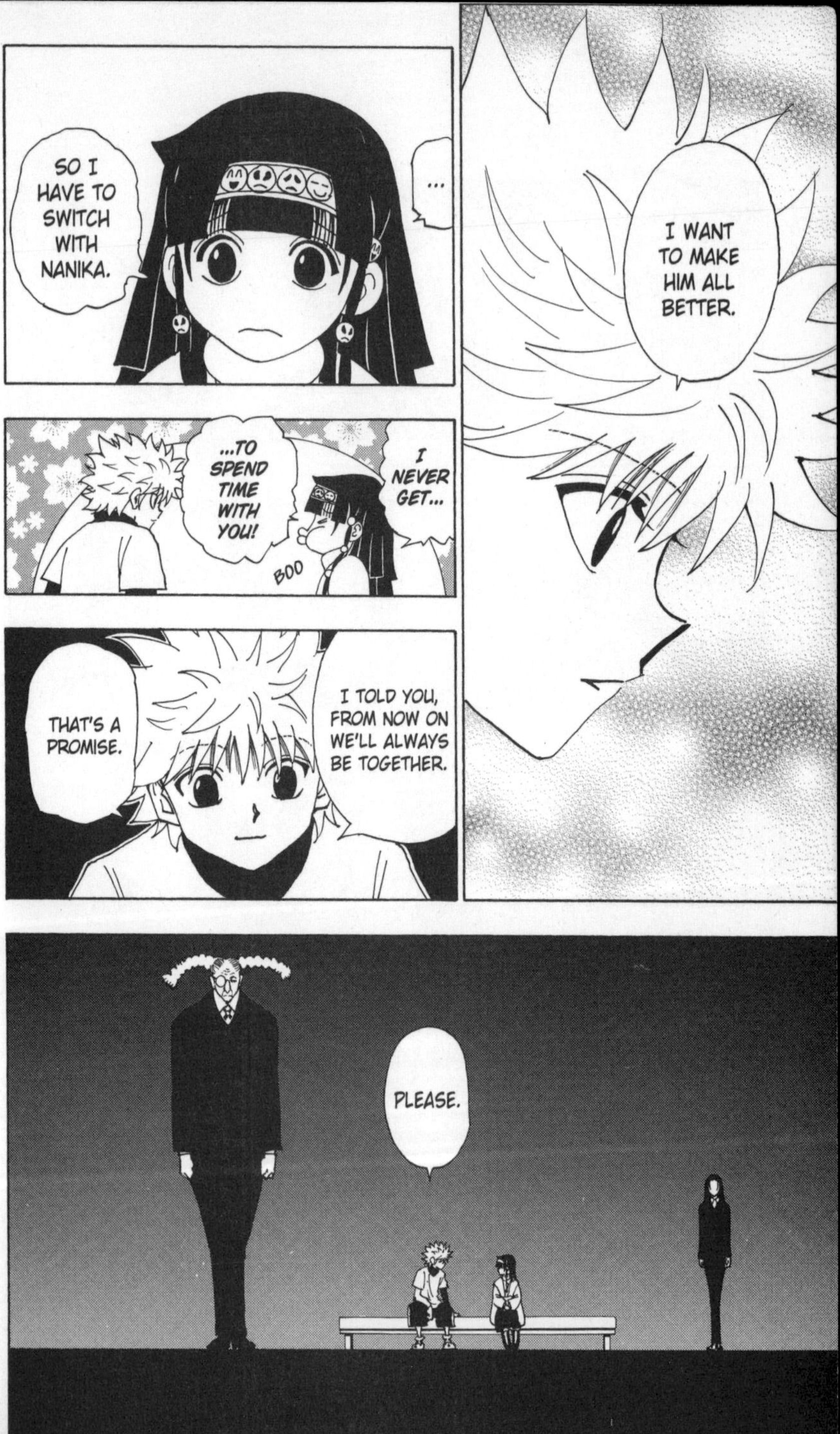
I WANT TO MAKE HIM ALL BETTER.
...
SO I HAVE TO SWITCH WITH NANIKA.
I NEVER GET...
...TO SPEND TIME WITH YOU!
BOO
I TOLD YOU, FROM NOW ON WE'LL ALWAYS BE TOGETHER.
THAT'S A PROMISE.
PLEASE.

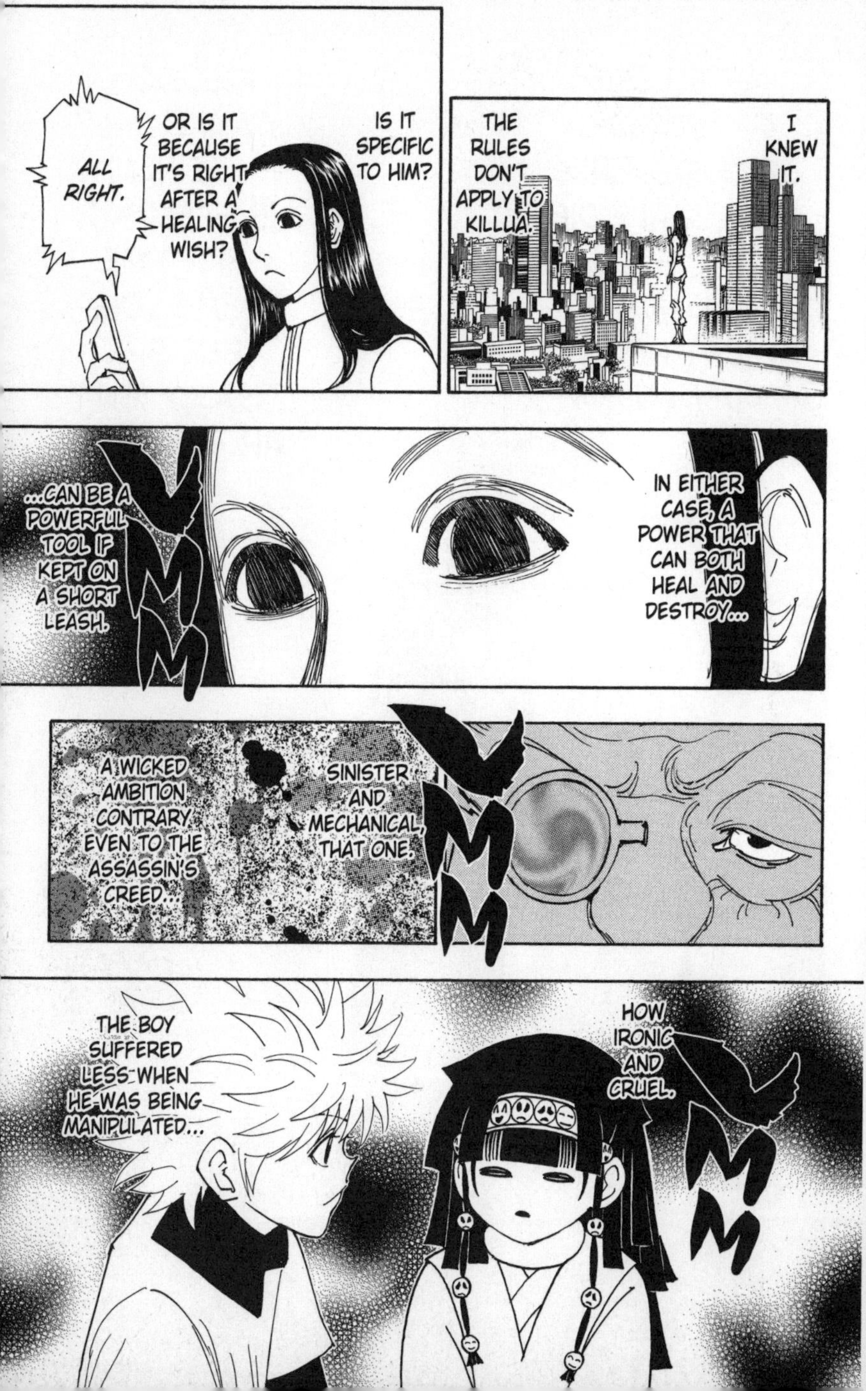
I KNEW IT.
THE RULES DON'T APPLY TO KILLUA.
IS IT SPECIFIC TO HIM?
OR IS IT BECAUSE IT'S RIGHT AFTER A HEALING WISH?
ALL RIGHT.
IN EITHER CASE, A POWER THAT CAN BOTH HEAL AND DESTROY...
...CAN BE A POWERFUL TOOL IF KEPT ON A SHORT LEASH.
SINISTER AND MECHANICAL, THAT ONE.
A WICKED AMBITION CONTRARY EVEN TO THE ASSASSIN'S CREED...
HOW IRONIC AND CRUEL.
THE BOY SUFFERED LESS WHEN HE WAS BEING MANIPULATED...

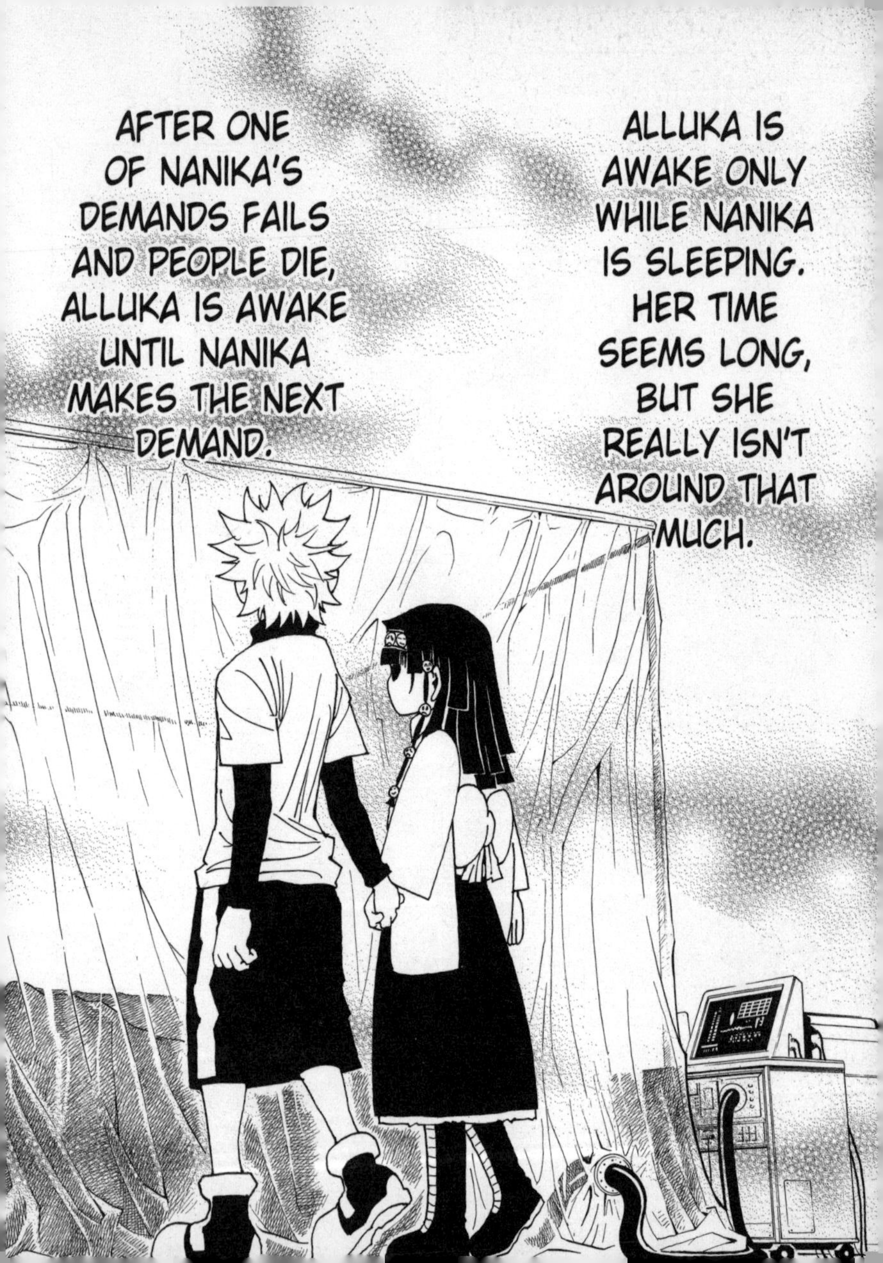
ALLUKA IS AWAKE ONLY WHILE NANIKA IS SLEEPING. HER TIME SEEMS LONG, BUT SHE REALLY ISN'T AROUND THAT MUCH.
AFTER ONE OF NANIKA'S DEMANDS FAILS AND PEOPLE DIE, ALLUKA IS AWAKE UNTIL NANIKA MAKES THE NEXT DEMAND.

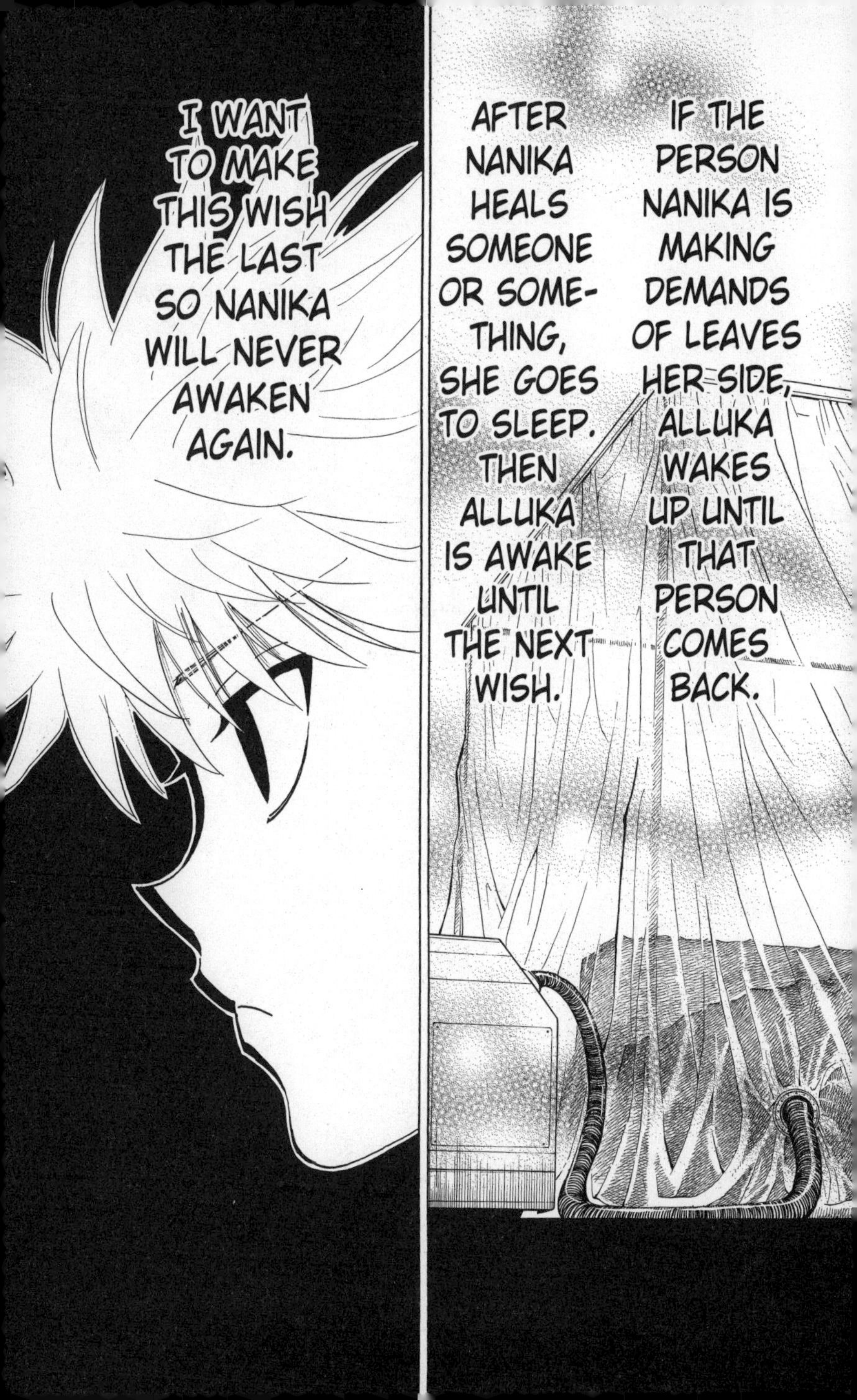
IF THE PERSON NANIKA IS MAKING DEMANDS OF LEAVES HER SIDE, ALLUKA WAKES UP UNTIL THAT PERSON COMES BACK.
AFTER NANIKA HEALS SOMEONE OR SOME-THING, SHE GOES TO SLEEP. THEN ALLUKA IS AWAKE UNTIL THE NEXT WISH.
I WANT TO MAKE THIS WISH THE LAST SO NANIKA WILL NEVER AWAKEN AGAIN.

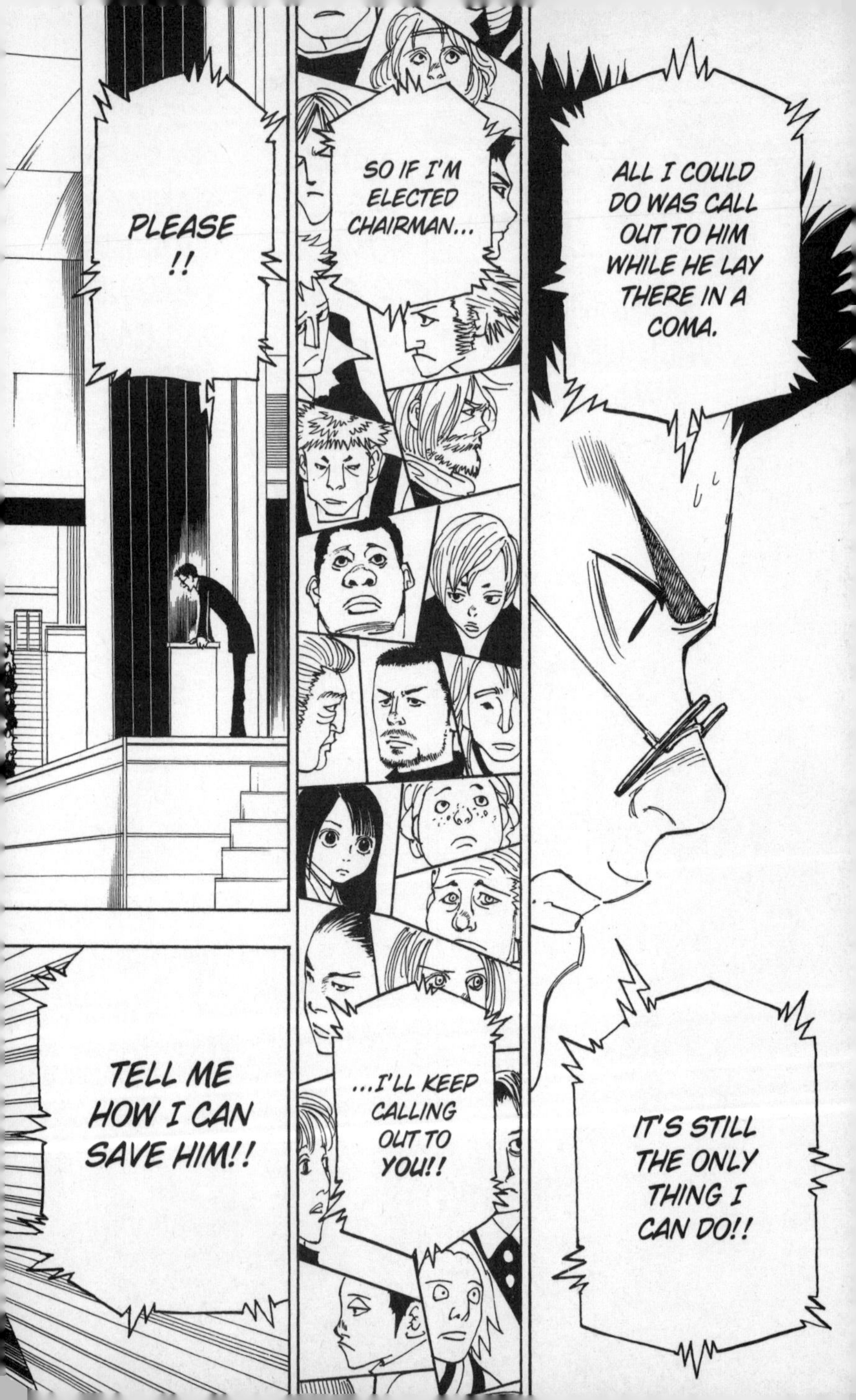
ALL I COULD DO WAS CALL OUT TO HIM WHILE HE LAY THERE IN A COMA.
IT'S STILL THE ONLY THING I CAN DO!!
SO IF I'M ELECTED CHAIRMAN...
...I'LL KEEP CALLING OUT TO YOU!!
PLEASE !!
TELL ME HOW I CAN SAVE HIM!!

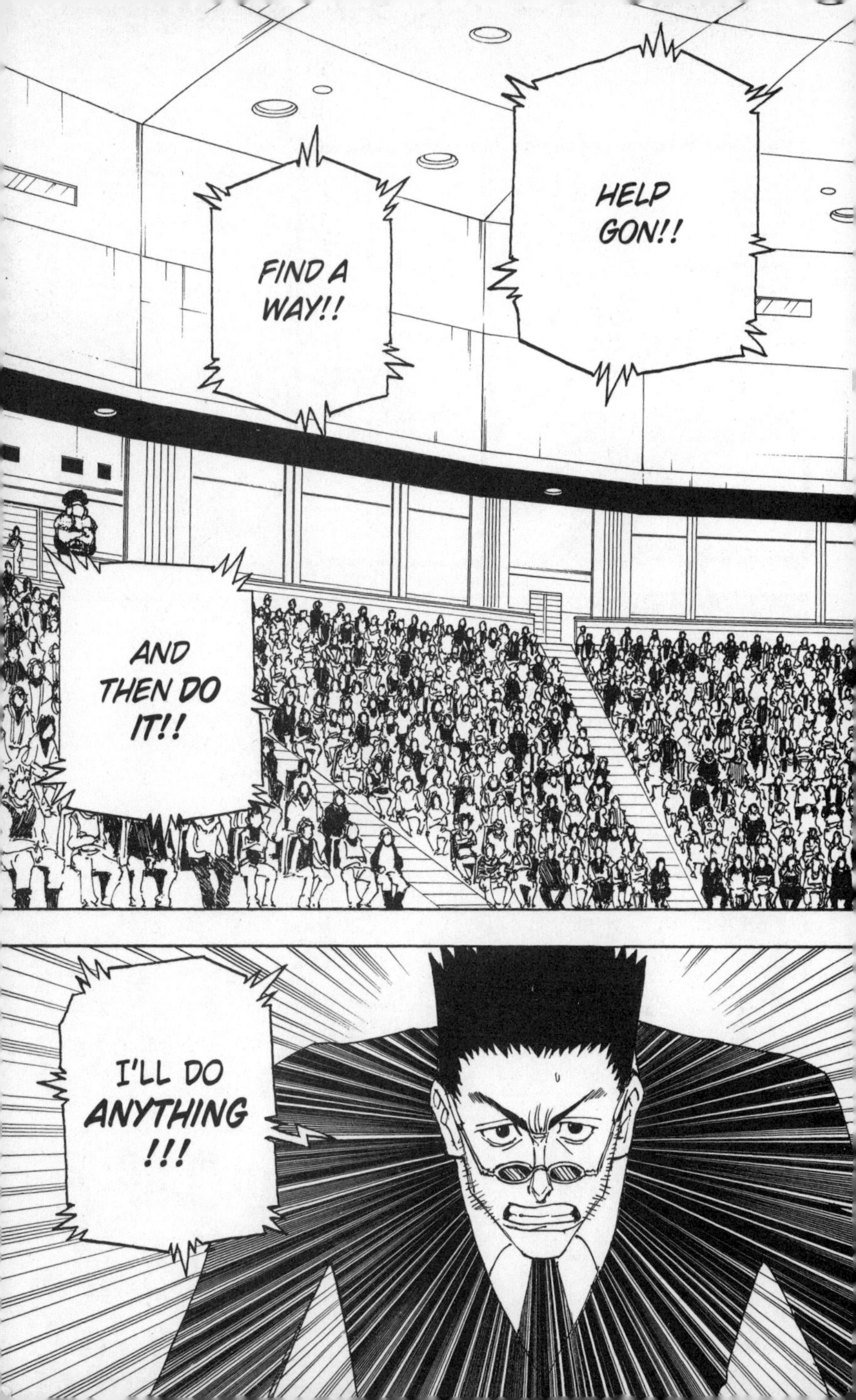
HELP GON!!
FIND A WAY!!
AND THEN DO IT!!
I'LL DO ANYTHING !!!

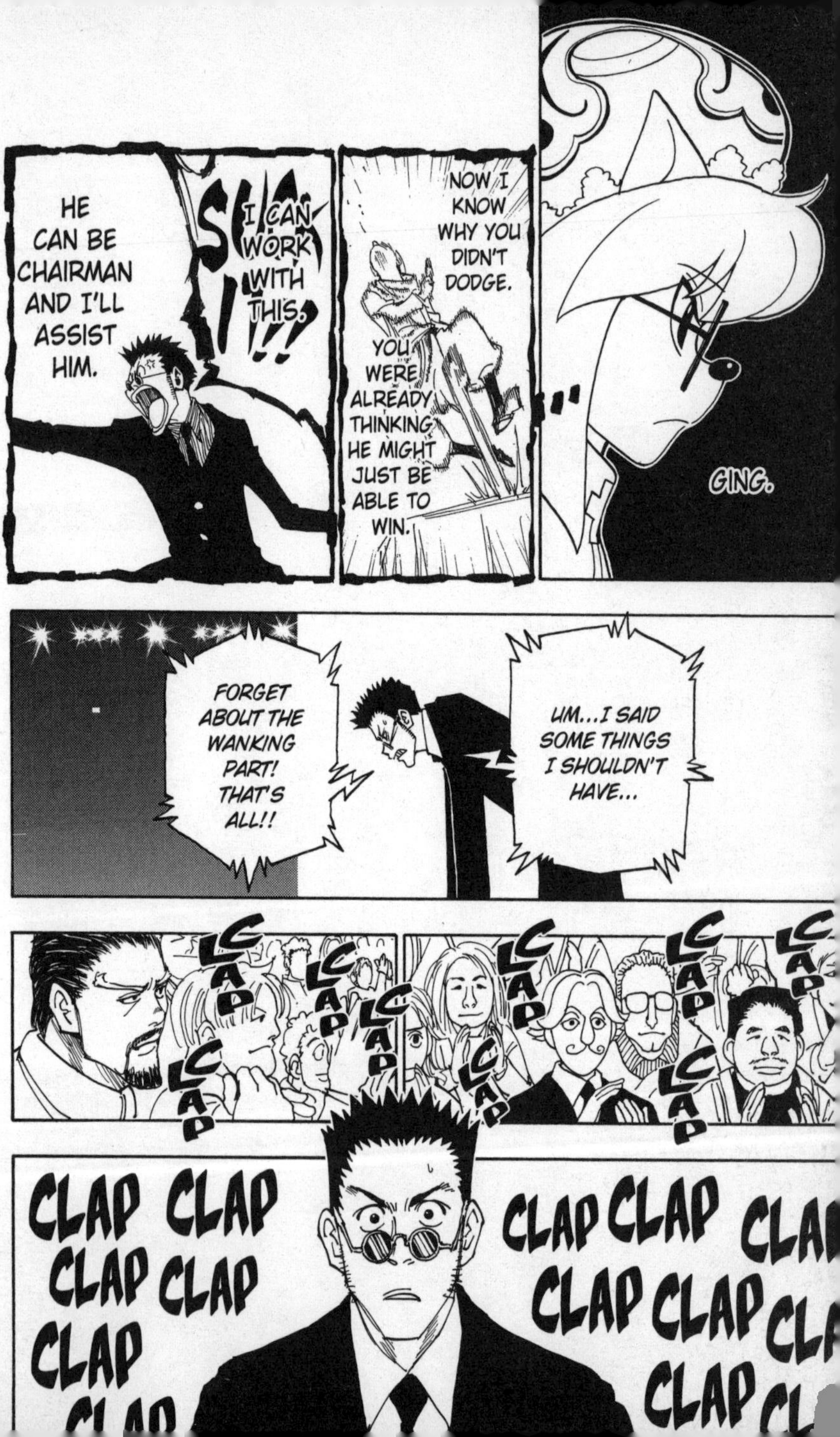
...
GING.
NOW I KNOW WHY YOU DIDN'T DODGE.
YOU WERE ALREADY THINKING HE MIGHT JUST BE ABLE TO WIN.
I CAN WORK WITH THIS!!
HE CAN BE CHAIRMAN AND I'LL ASSIST HIM.
UM...I SAID SOME THINGS I SHOULDN'T HAVE...
FORGET ABOUT THE WANKING PART! THAT'S ALL!!
CLAP CLAP CLAP CLAP CLAP CLAP CLAP
CLAP CLAP CLAP CLAP CLAP CLAP CLAP CLAP

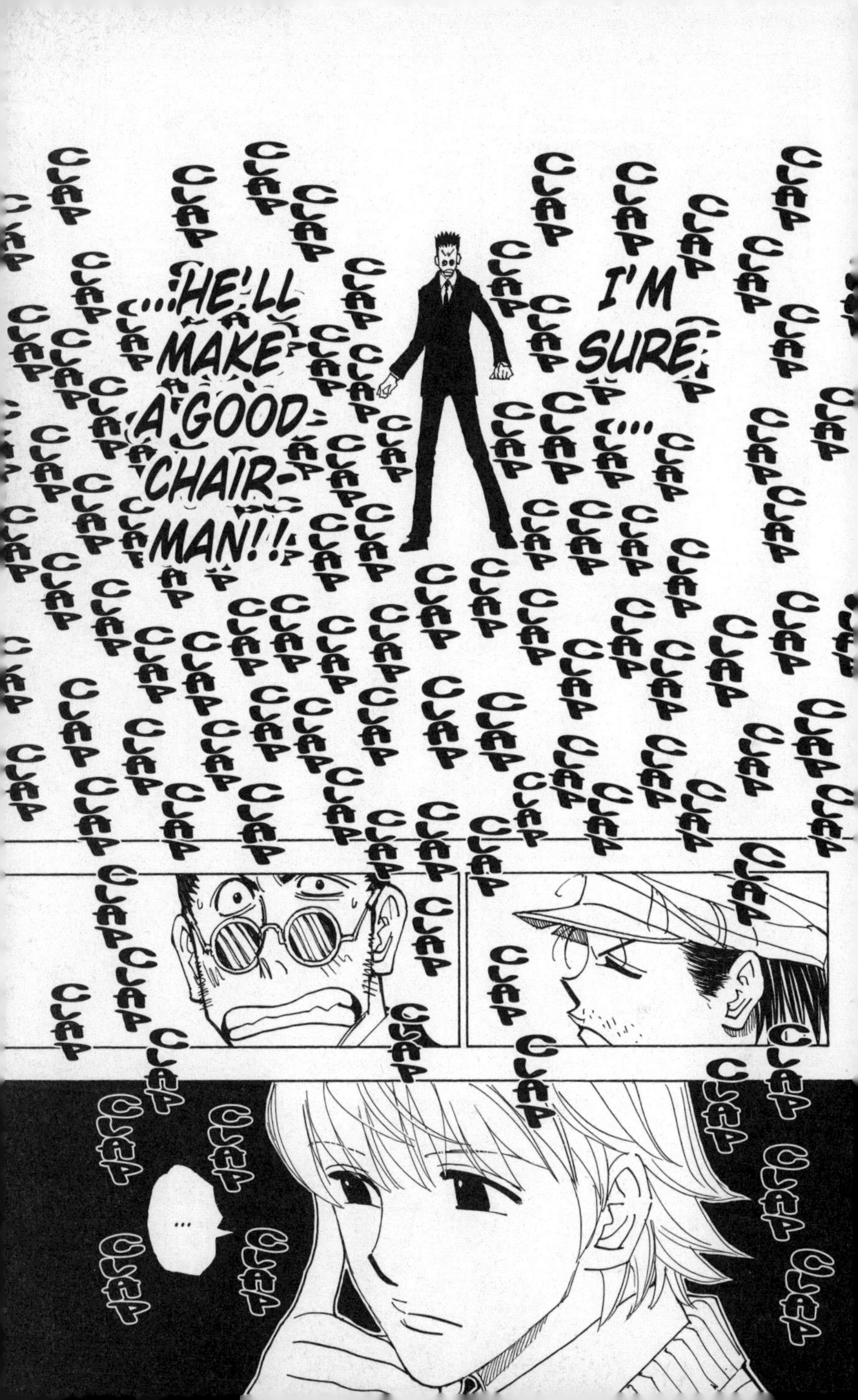
I'M SURE...
...HE'LL MAKE A GOOD CHAIRMAN!!
CLAP
...

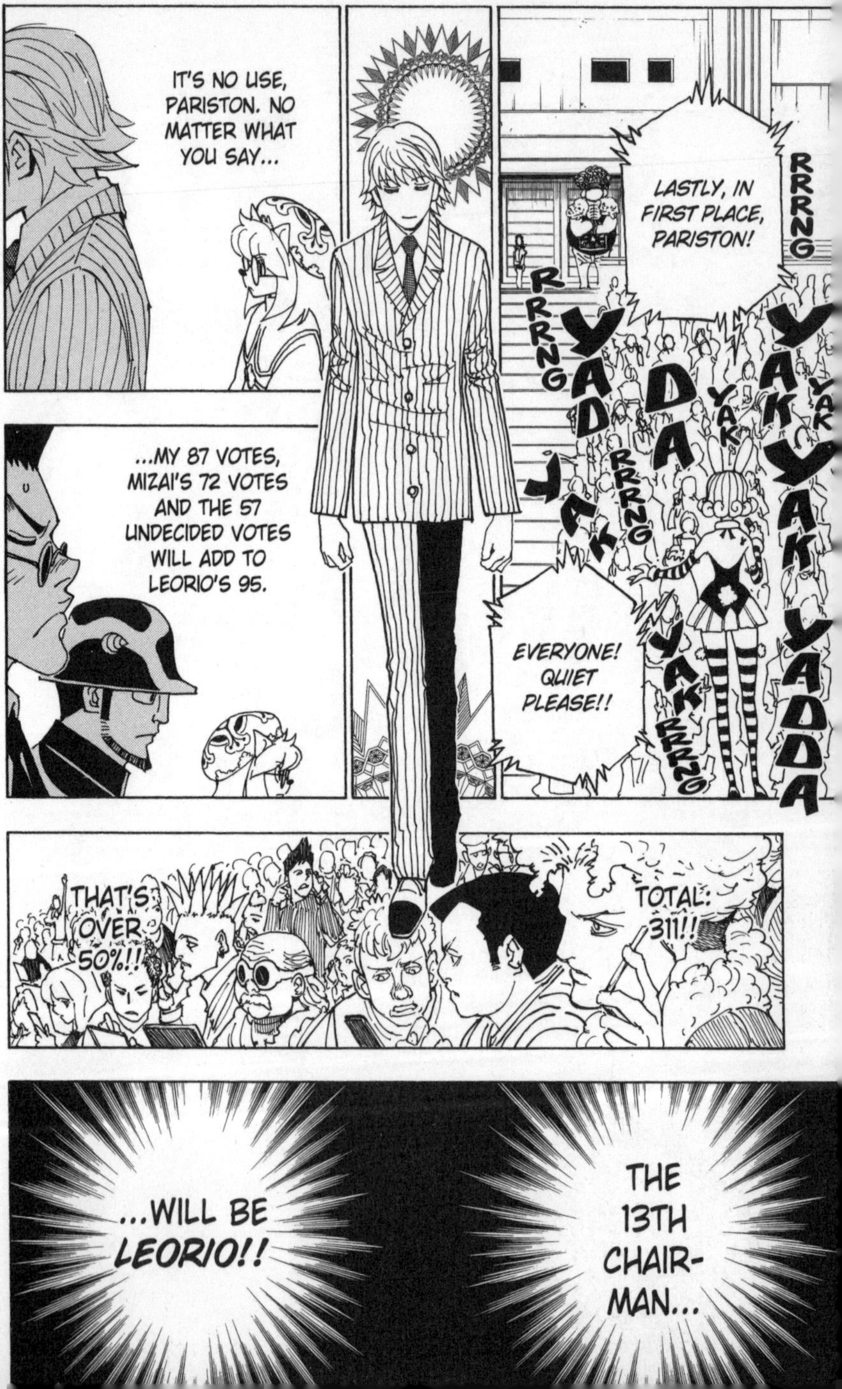
LASTLY, IN FIRST PLACE, PARISTON!
RRRNG
RRRNG
YADDA
YAK
YAK YAK
YAK YAK
YADDA
YAK
YAK
RRRNG
RRRNG
EVERYONE! QUIET PLEASE!!
RRRNG
IT'S NO USE, PARISTON. NO MATTER WHAT YOU SAY...
...MY 87 VOTES, MIZAI'S 72 VOTES AND THE 57 UNDECIDED VOTES WILL ADD TO LEORIO'S 95.
TOTAL: 311!!
THAT'S OVER 50%!!
THE 13TH CHAIR-MAN...
...WILL BE LEORIO!!

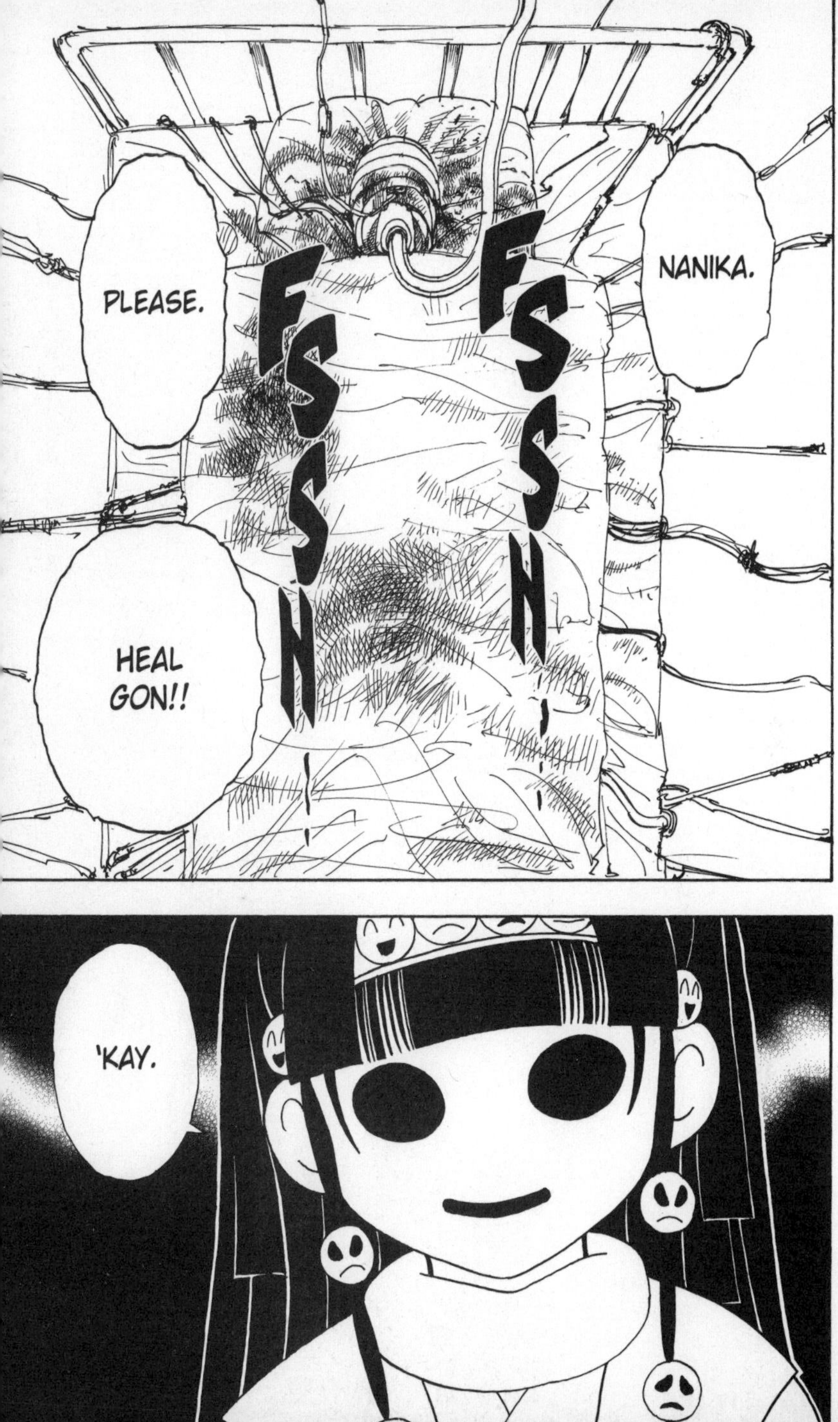
NANIKA.
PLEASE.
HEAL GON!!
FSSH!!
FSSH!!
'KAY.

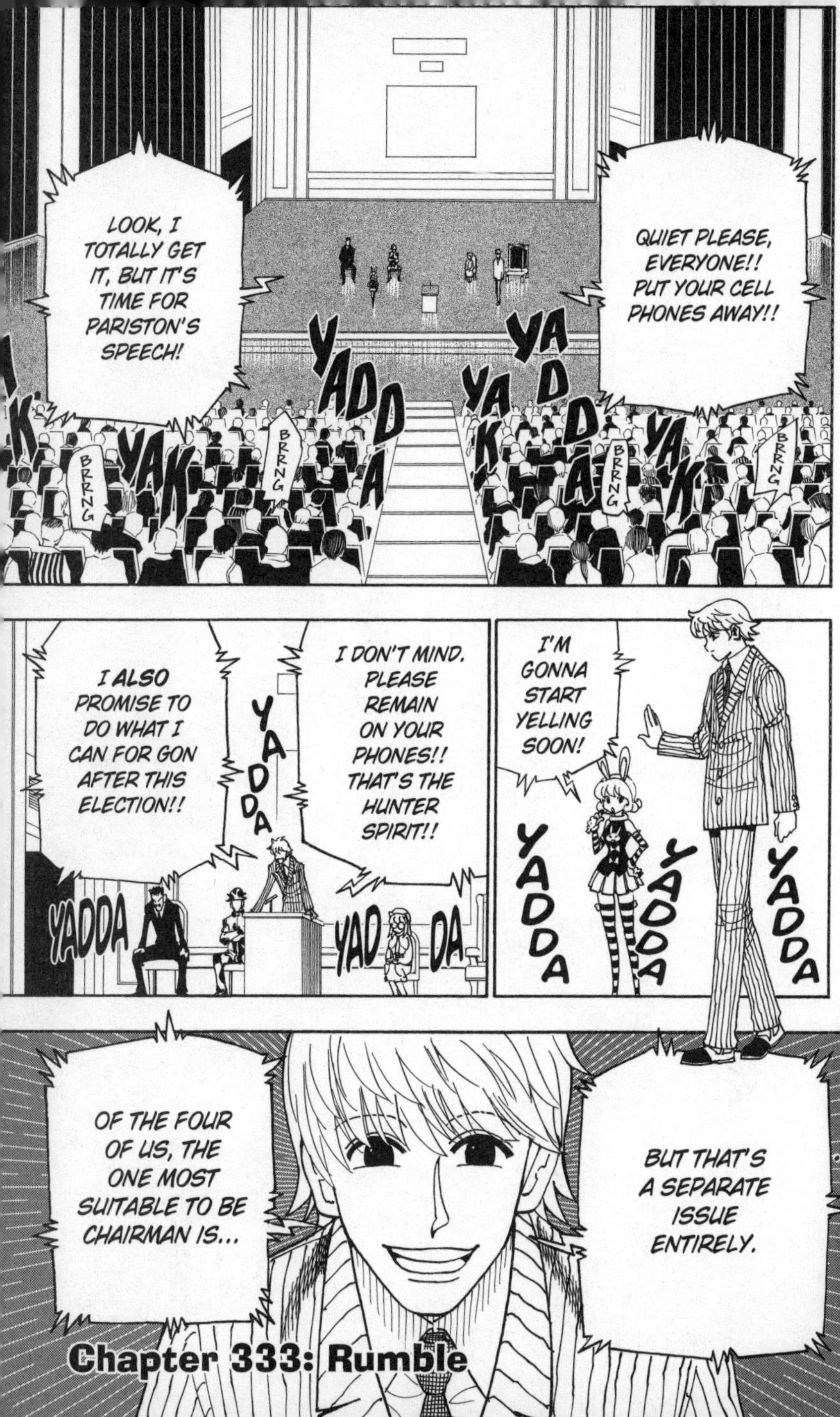
QUIET PLEASE, EVERYONE!! PUT YOUR CELL PHONES AWAY!!
LOOK, I TOTALLY GET IT, BUT IT'S TIME FOR PARISTON'S SPEECH!
BRRNG
YAK
YA YADDA
YADDA
BRRNG
YAK
BRRNG
YAK
I'M GONNA START YELLING SOON!
YADDA
YADDA
YADDA
I DON'T MIND. PLEASE REMAIN ON YOUR PHONES!! THAT'S THE HUNTER SPIRIT!!
I ALSO PROMISE TO DO WHAT I CAN FOR GON AFTER THIS ELECTION!!
YADDA
YAD DA
YADDA
BUT THAT'S A SEPARATE ISSUE ENTIRELY.
OF THE FOUR OF US, THE ONE MOST SUITABLE TO BE CHAIRMAN IS...

Chapter 333: Rumble

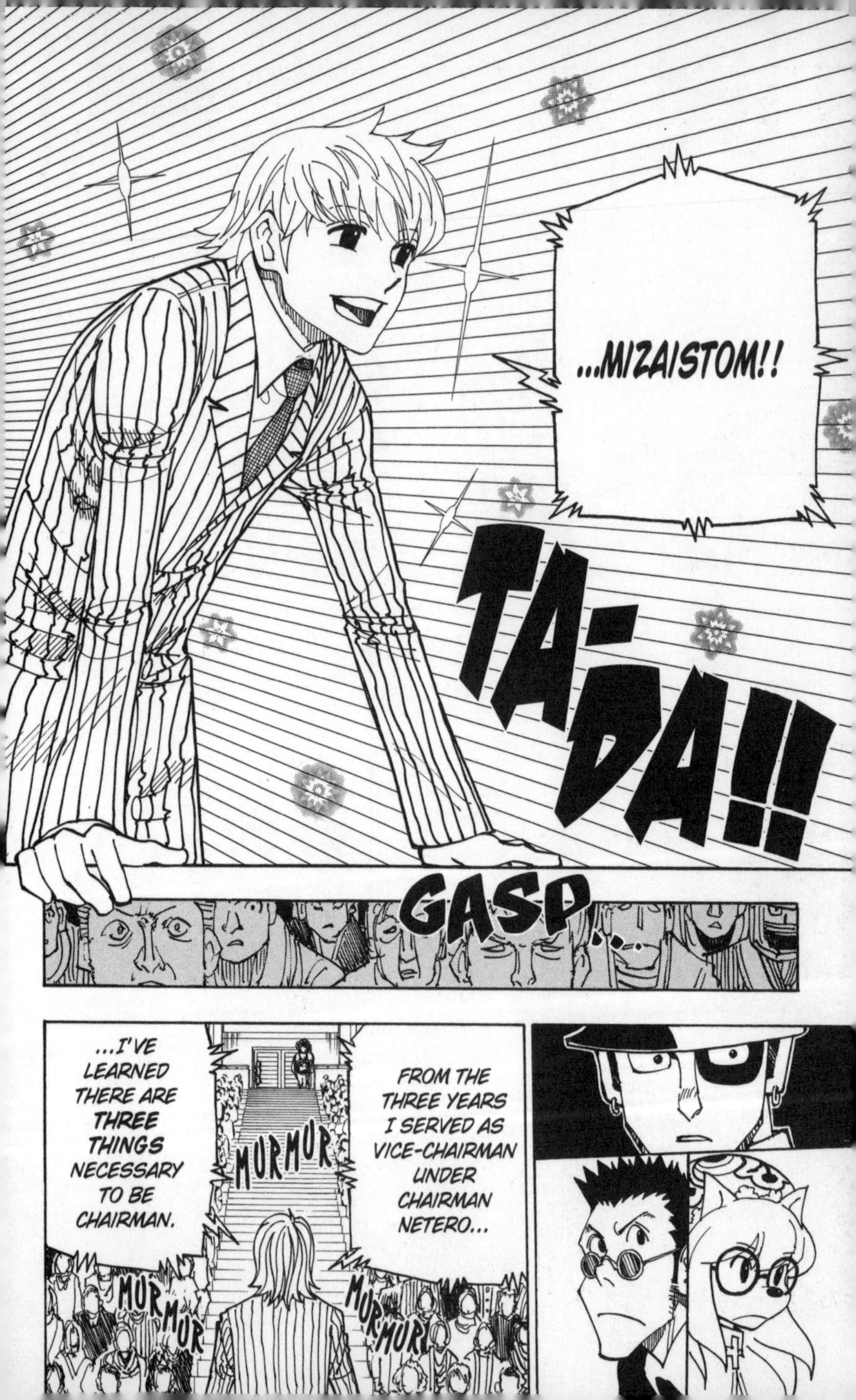
...MIZAISTOM!!
TA-DA!!
GASP...
MURMUR
FROM THE THREE YEARS I SERVED AS VICE-CHAIRMAN UNDER CHAIRMAN NETERO...
...I'VE LEARNED THERE ARE THREE THINGS NECESSARY TO BE CHAIRMAN.
MURMUR
MURMUR

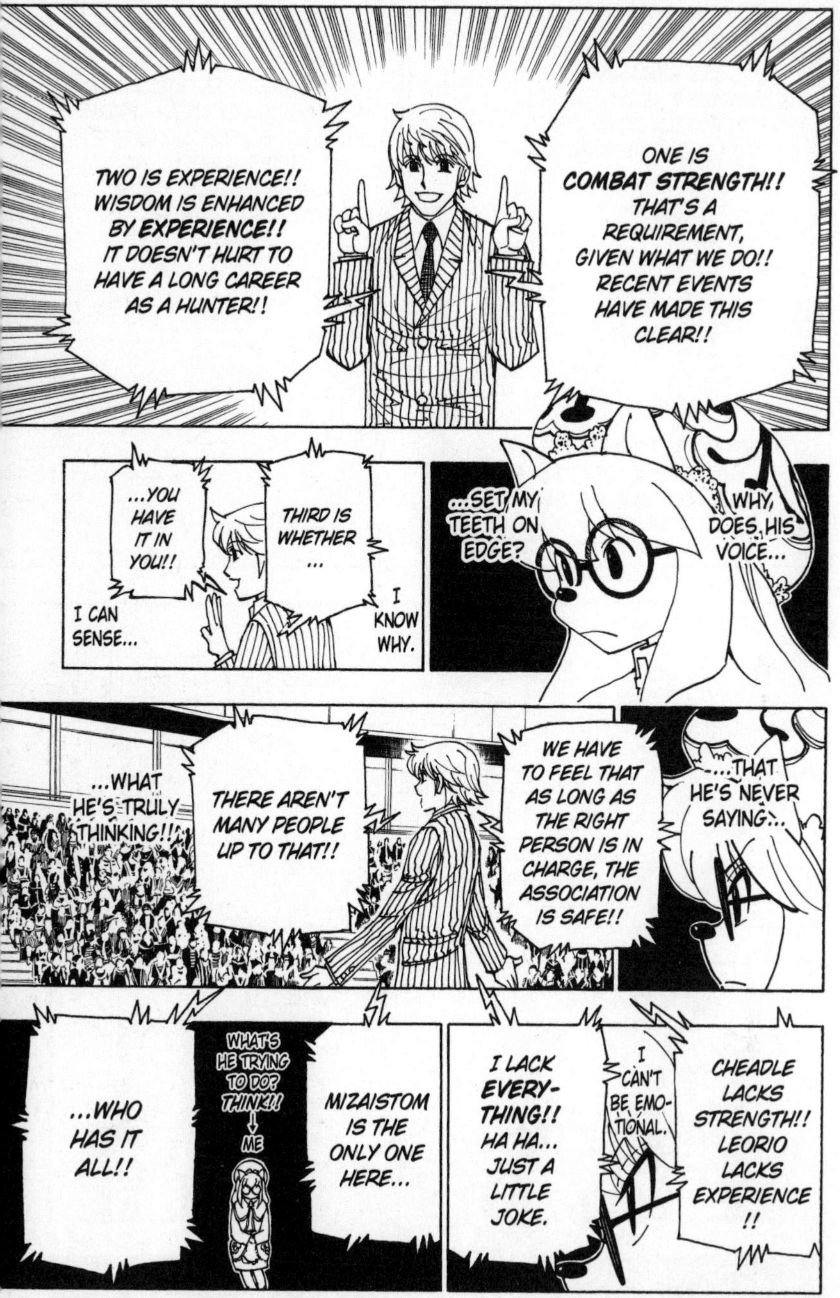
ONE IS COMBAT STRENGTH!! THAT'S A REQUIREMENT, GIVEN WHAT WE DO!! RECENT EVENTS HAVE MADE THIS CLEAR!!
TWO IS EXPERIENCE!! WISDOM IS ENHANCED BY EXPERIENCE!! IT DOESN'T HURT TO HAVE A LONG CAREER AS A HUNTER!!
WHY DOES HIS VOICE...
...SET MY TEETH ON EDGE?
THIRD IS WHETHER...
I KNOW WHY.
...YOU HAVE IT IN YOU!!
I CAN SENSE...
...THAT HE'S NEVER SAYING...
WE HAVE TO FEEL THAT AS LONG AS THE RIGHT PERSON IS IN CHARGE, THE ASSOCIATION IS SAFE!!
THERE AREN'T MANY PEOPLE UP TO THAT!!
...WHAT HE'S TRULY THINKING!!
CHEADLE LACKS STRENGTH!! LEORIO LACKS EXPERIENCE!!
I CAN'T BE EMOTIONAL.
I LACK EVERYTHING!! HA HA... JUST A LITTLE JOKE.
MIZAISTOM IS THE ONLY ONE HERE...
WHAT'S HE TRYING TO DO? THINK!!
ME
...WHO HAS IT ALL!!

THE REMAINING 140 VOTERS, HOWEVER, ARE MOSTLY UNDECIDED. THEY CAN BE **SWAYED**.

OUT OF PARISTON'S 290 VOTES, ABOUT 120 ARE FROM THE TEMPS AND 30 ARE FROM PARISTON'S PERSONAL STAFF. NO MATTER WHAT HE SAYS IN HIS SPEECHES, THOSE LOYALISTS GET THEIR OWN COMMANDS.

LET'S HAVE A Q&A!

OKAY, THANK YOU!

WITH PARISTON'S SPEECH, THE UNDECIDED VOTES THAT WOULD'VE ALL GONE TO LEORIO...

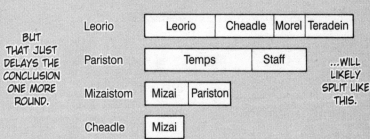

BUT THAT JUST DELAYS THE CONCLUSION ONE MORE ROUND.

Leorio	Leorio	Cheadle	Morel	Teradein
Pariston	Temps		Staff	
Mizaistom	Mizai	Pariston		
Cheadle	Mizai			

...WILL LIKELY SPLIT LIKE THIS.

...WITH THIS Q&A?

WHAT WILL CHANGE...

HM

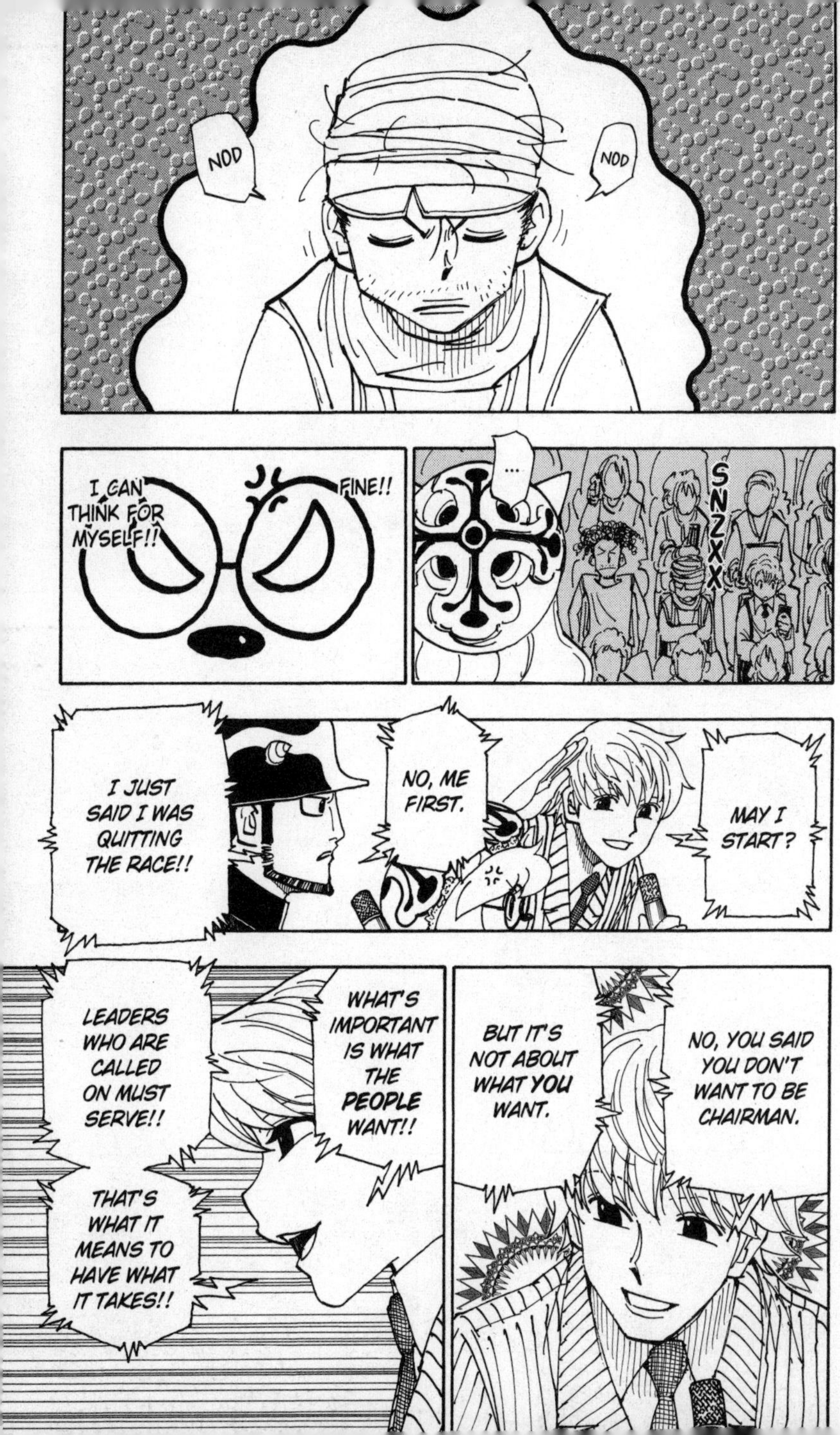
NOD
NOD
...
SNZXX
FINE!!
I CAN THINK FOR MYSELF!!
MAY I START?
NO, ME FIRST.
I JUST SAID I WAS QUITTING THE RACE!!
NO, YOU SAID YOU DON'T WANT TO BE CHAIRMAN.
BUT IT'S NOT ABOUT WHAT YOU WANT.
WHAT'S IMPORTANT IS WHAT THE PEOPLE WANT!!
LEADERS WHO ARE CALLED ON MUST SERVE!!
THAT'S WHAT IT MEANS TO HAVE WHAT IT TAKES!!

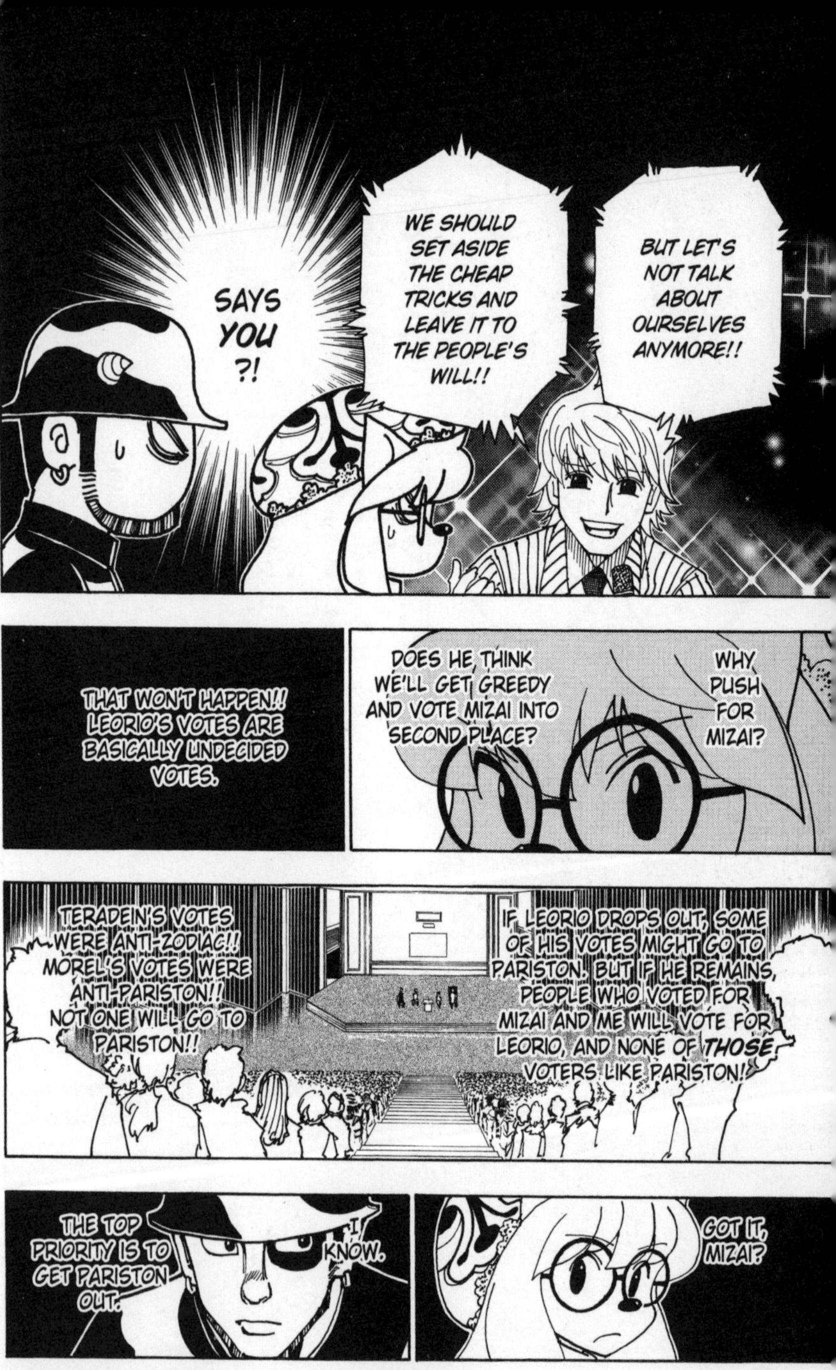
BUT LET'S NOT TALK ABOUT OURSELVES ANYMORE!!
WE SHOULD SET ASIDE THE CHEAP TRICKS AND LEAVE IT TO THE PEOPLE'S WILL!!
SAYS *YOU* ?!
WHY PUSH FOR MIZAI?
DOES HE THINK WE'LL GET GREEDY AND VOTE MIZAI INTO SECOND PLACE?
THAT WON'T HAPPEN!! LEORIO'S VOTES ARE BASICALLY UNDECIDED VOTES.
IF LEORIO DROPS OUT, SOME OF HIS VOTES MIGHT GO TO PARISTON. BUT IF HE REMAINS, PEOPLE WHO VOTED FOR MIZAI AND ME WILL VOTE FOR LEORIO, AND NONE OF *THOSE* VOTERS LIKE PARISTON!!
TERADEIN'S VOTES WERE ANTI-ZODIAC!! MOREL'S VOTES WERE ANTI-PARISTON!! NOT ONE WILL GO TO PARISTON!!
GOT IT, MIZAI?
I KNOW.
THE TOP PRIORITY IS TO GET PARISTON OUT.

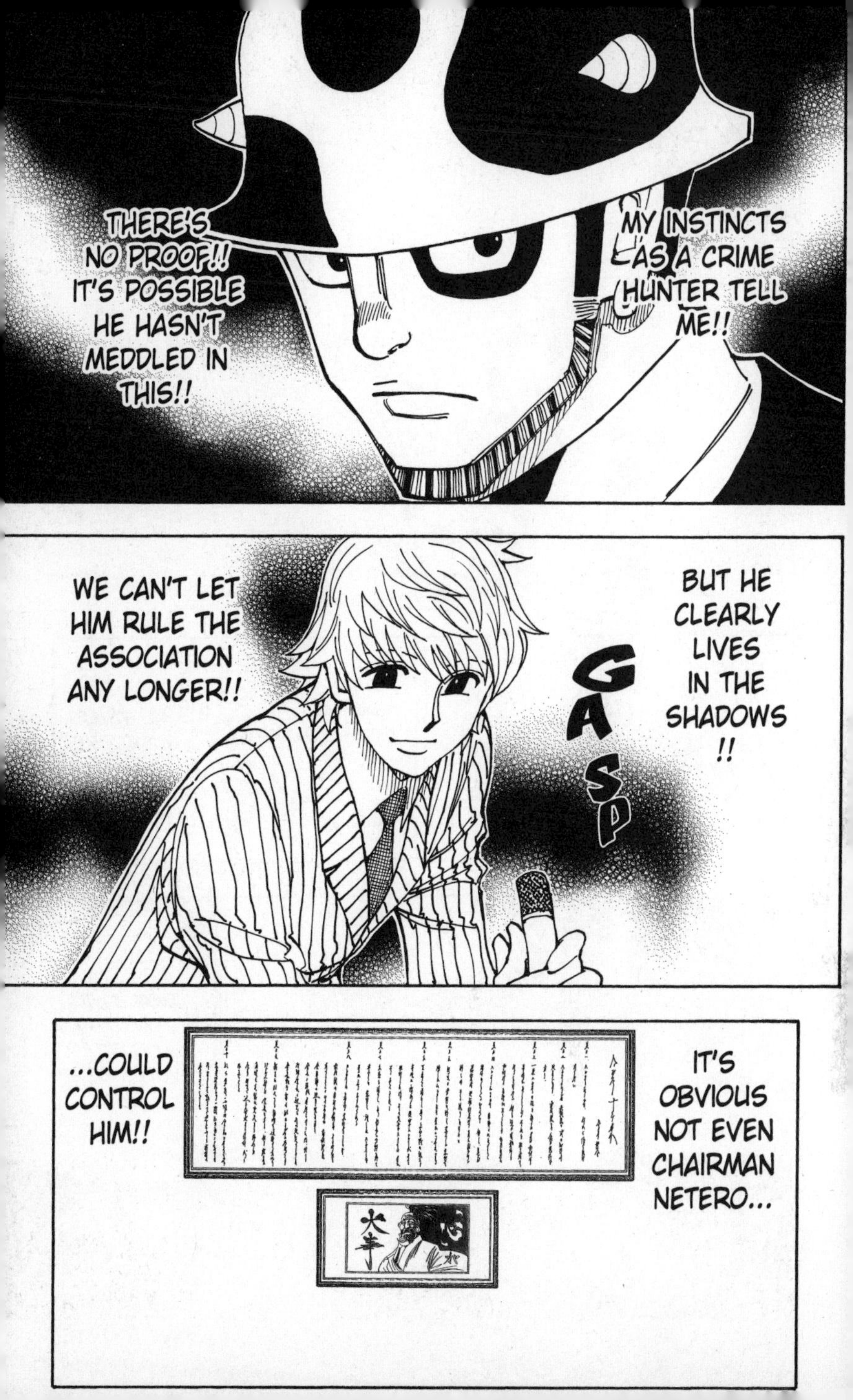
MY INSTINCTS AS A CRIME HUNTER TELL ME!!
THERE'S NO PROOF!! IT'S POSSIBLE HE HASN'T MEDDLED IN THIS!!
BUT HE CLEARLY LIVES IN THE SHADOWS !!
GASP
WE CAN'T LET HIM RULE THE ASSOCIATION ANY LONGER!!
IT'S OBVIOUS NOT EVEN CHAIRMAN NETERO...
...COULD CONTROL HIM!!

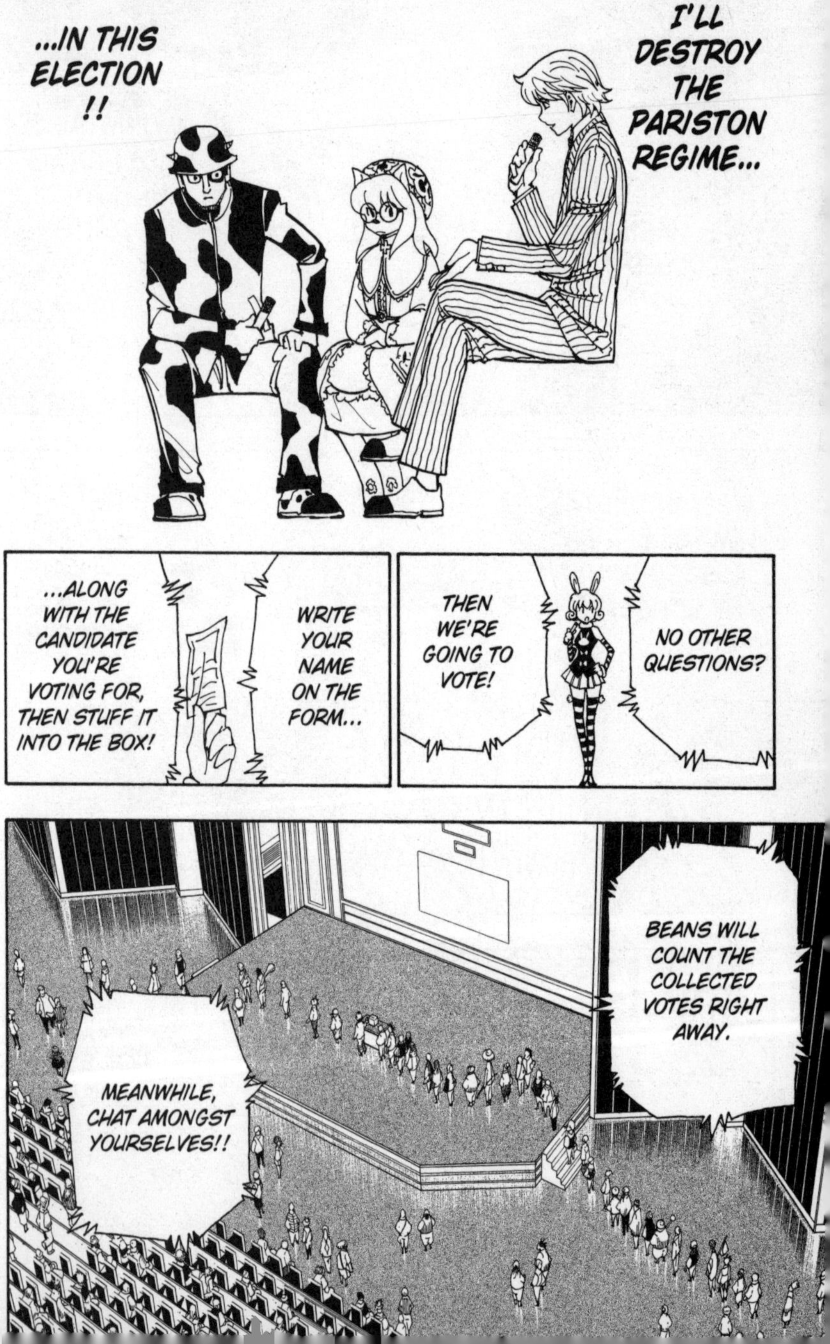
I'LL DESTROY THE PARISTON REGIME...
...IN THIS ELECTION !!
NO OTHER QUESTIONS?
THEN WE'RE GOING TO VOTE!
WRITE YOUR NAME ON THE FORM...
...ALONG WITH THE CANDIDATE YOU'RE VOTING FOR, THEN STUFF IT INTO THE BOX!
BEANS WILL COUNT THE COLLECTED VOTES RIGHT AWAY.
MEANWHILE, CHAT AMONGST YOURSELVES!!

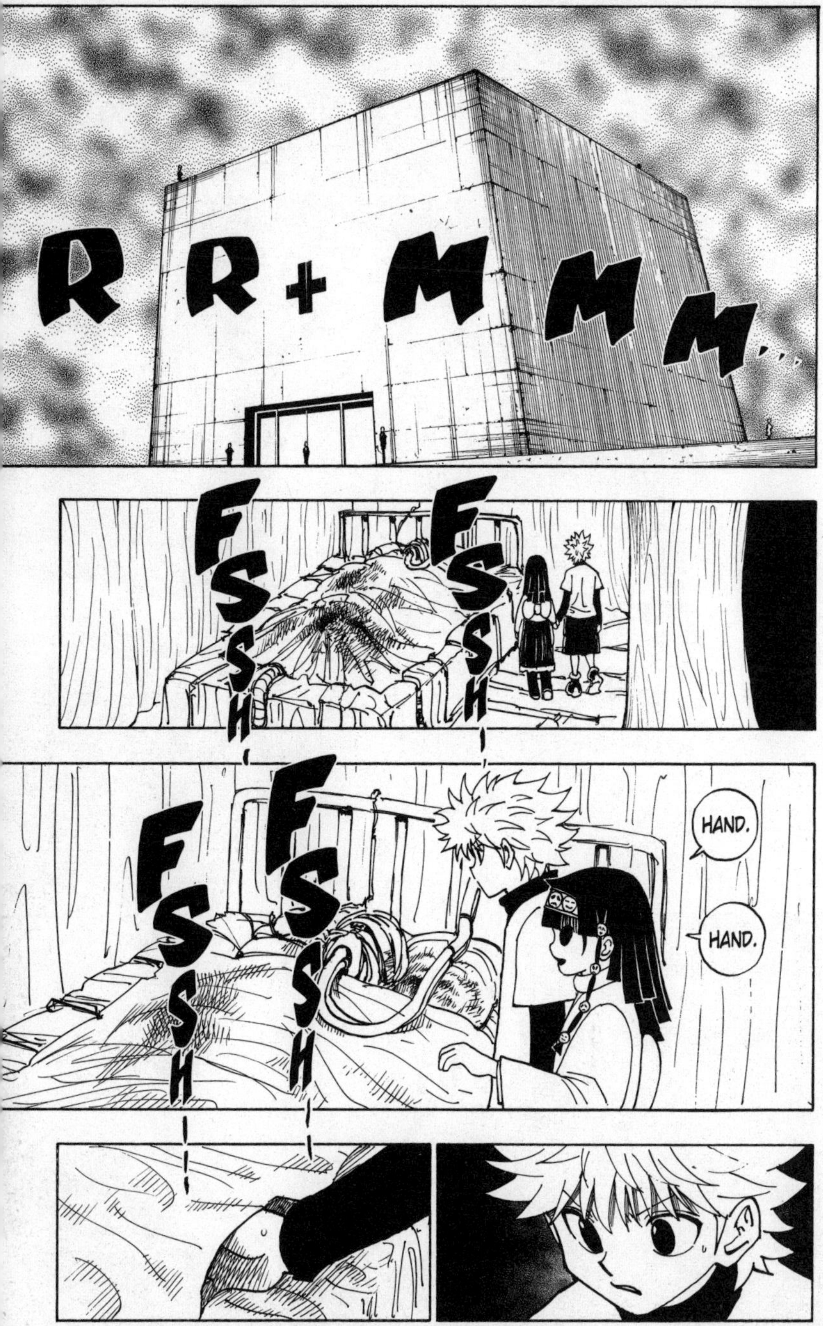
RRMMM...
FSSH!
FSSH!
HAND.
HAND.
FSSH!!
FSSH!!

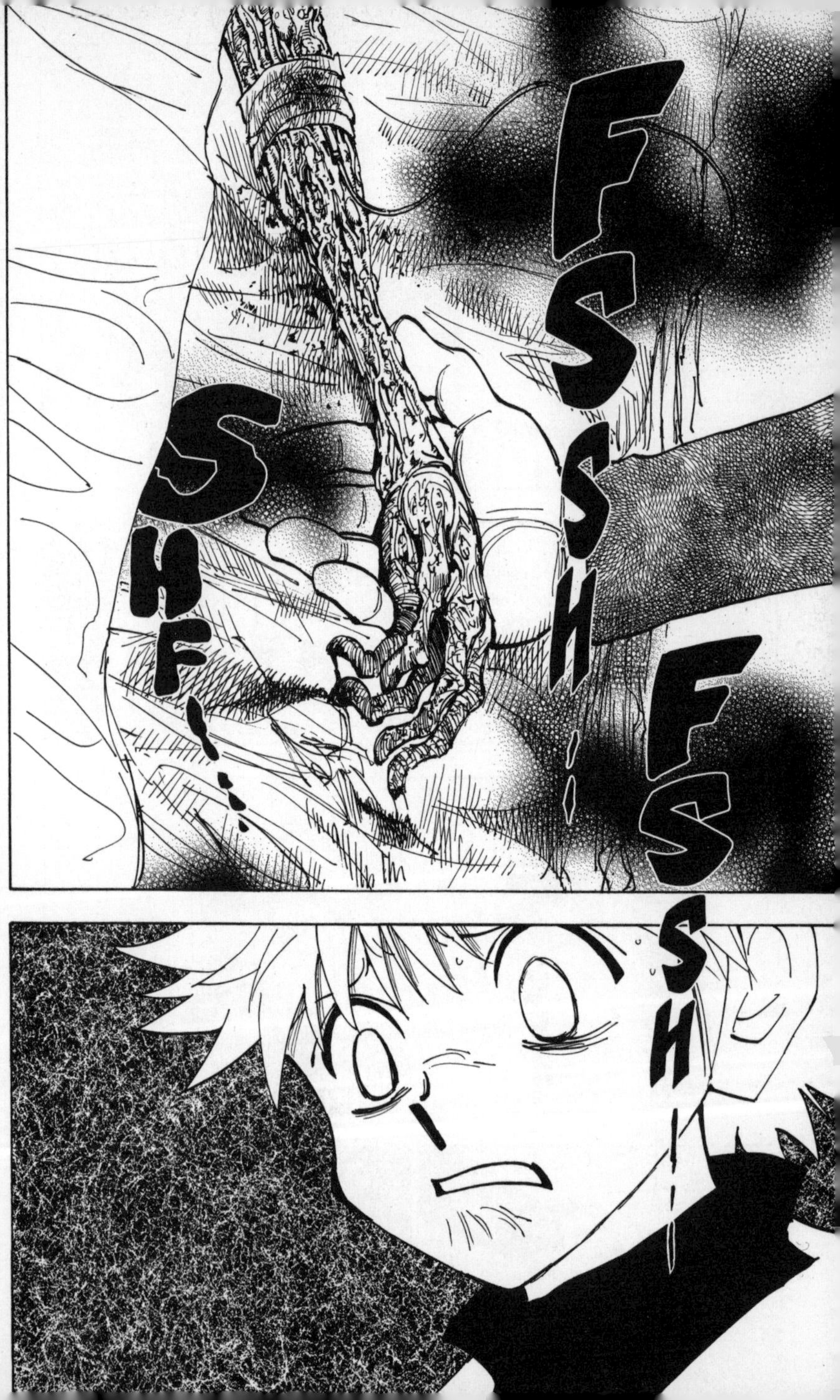
FSSSH!
SHF...
FSSH!

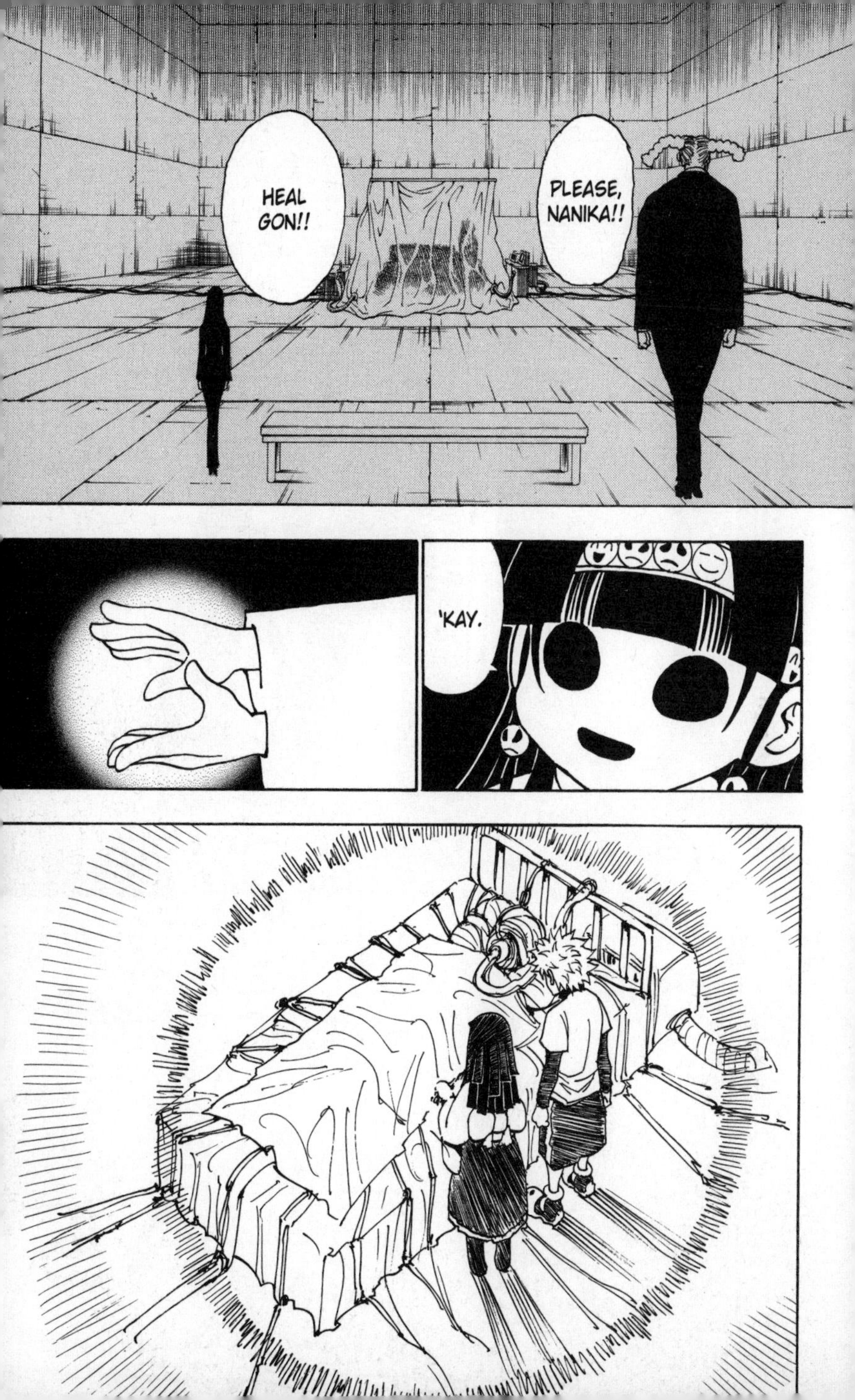
PLEASE, NANIKA!!
HEAL GON!!
'KAY.

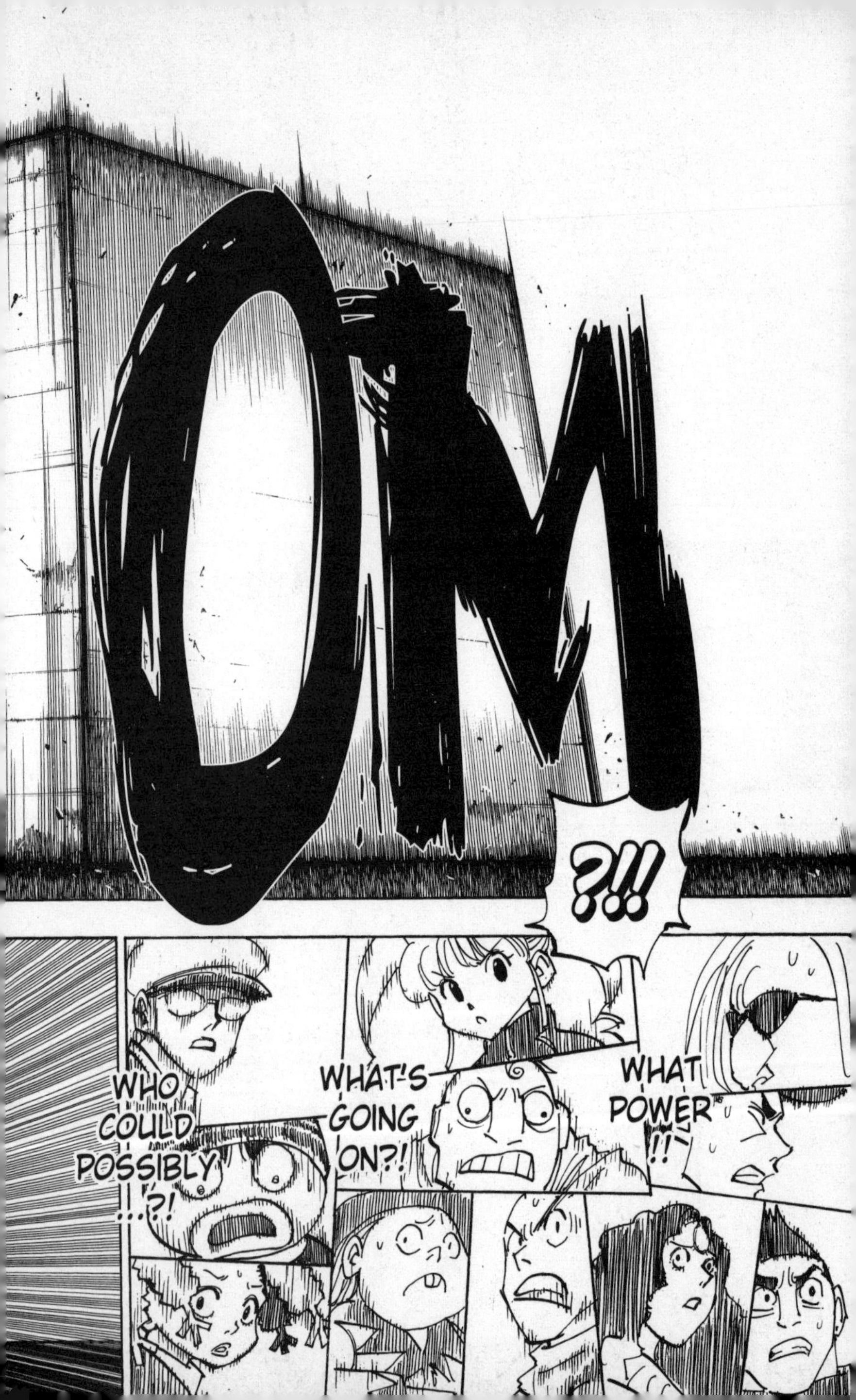
OM
?!!
WHAT POWER!!
WHAT'S GOING ON?!
WHO COULD POSSIBLY ...?!

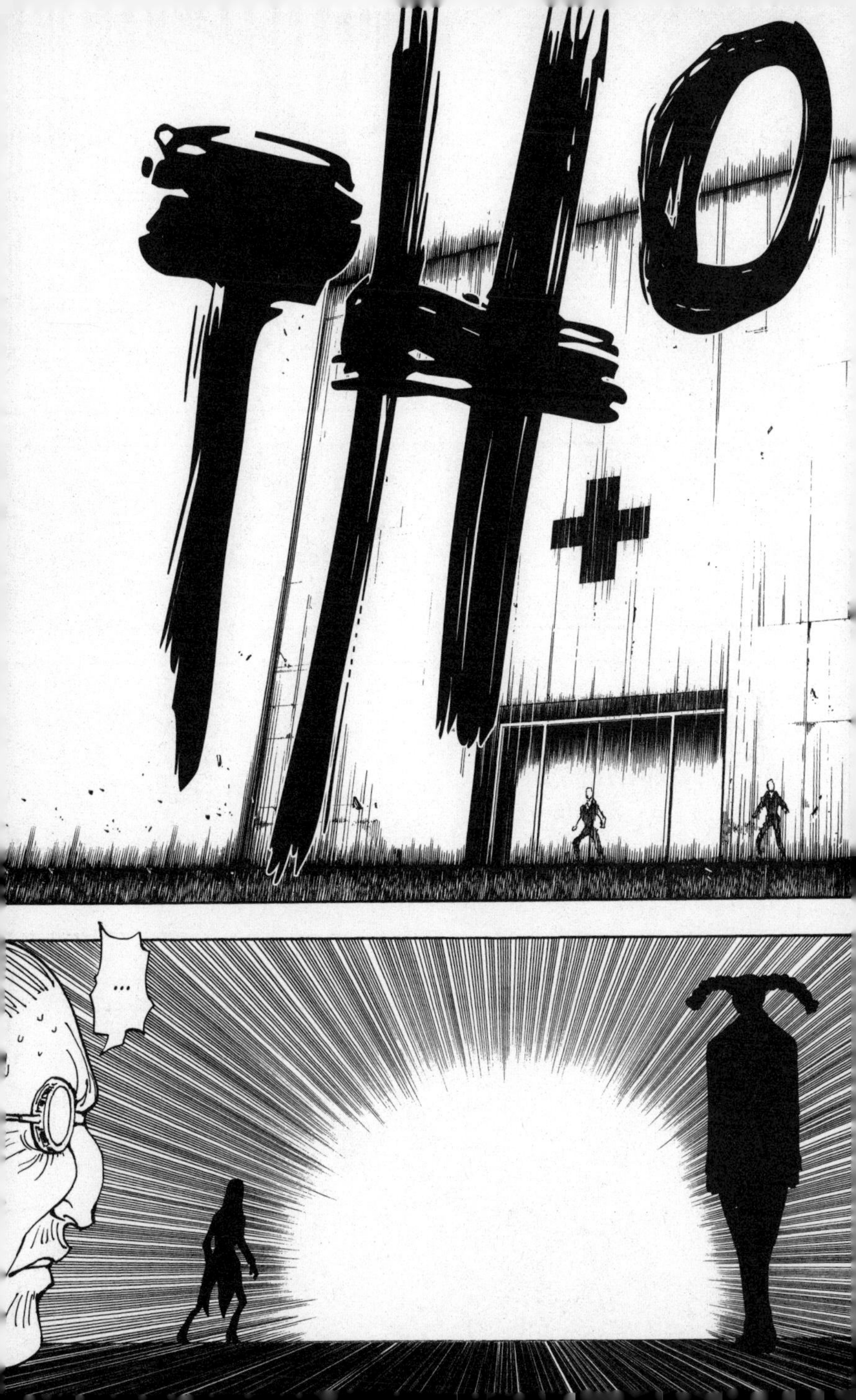
THO
...

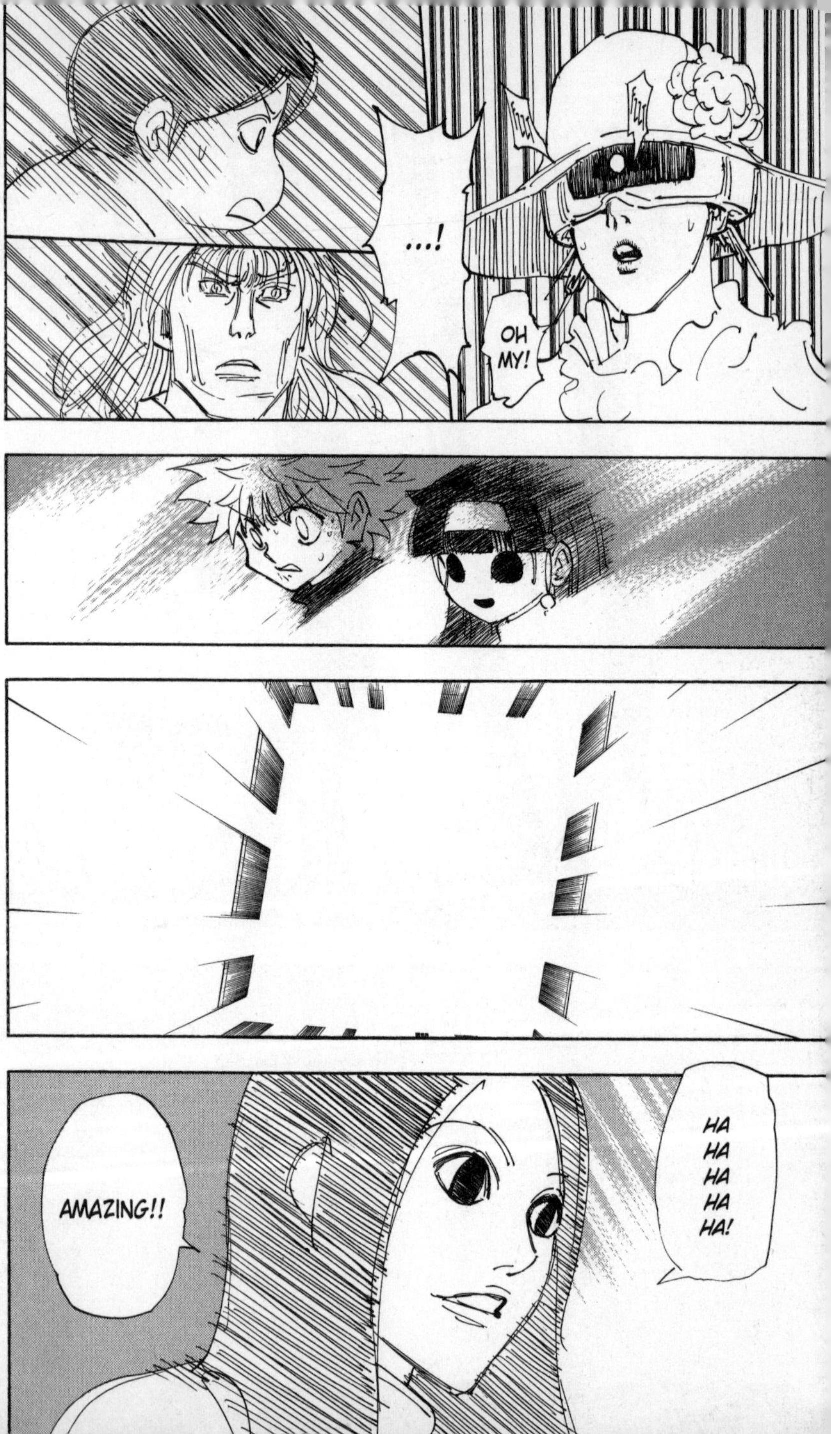
fzzz
OH MY!
...!
HA HA HA HA HA!
AMAZING!!

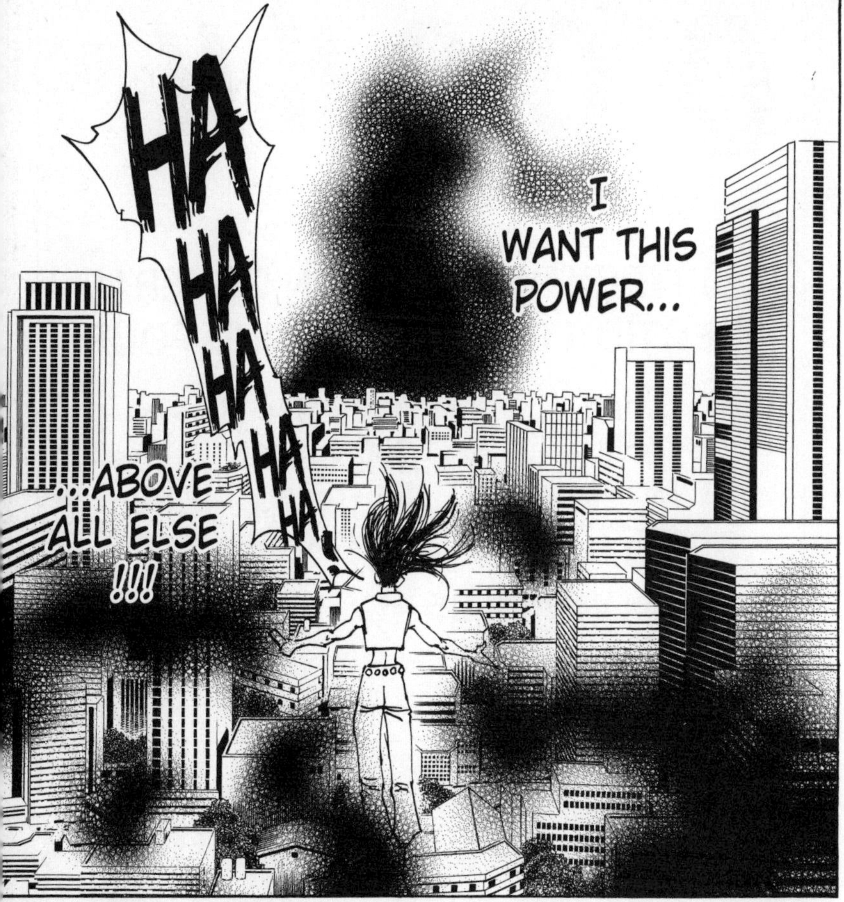
I WANT THIS POWER...
HA HA HA HA HA HA
...ABOVE ALL ELSE !!!
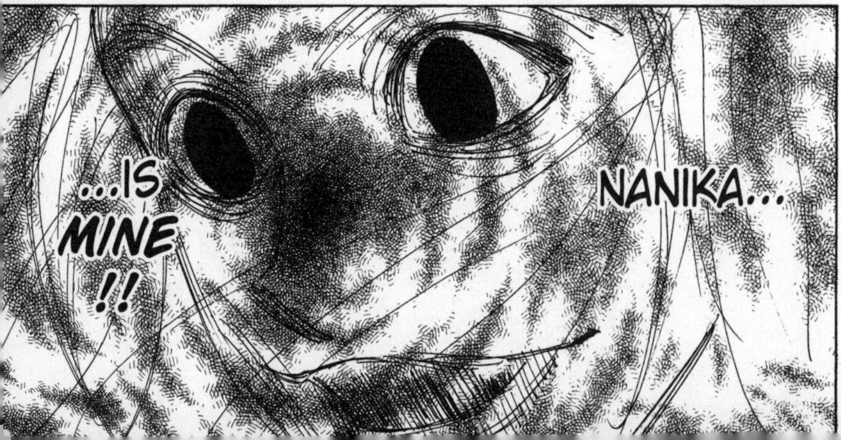
NANIKA...
...IS MINE !!

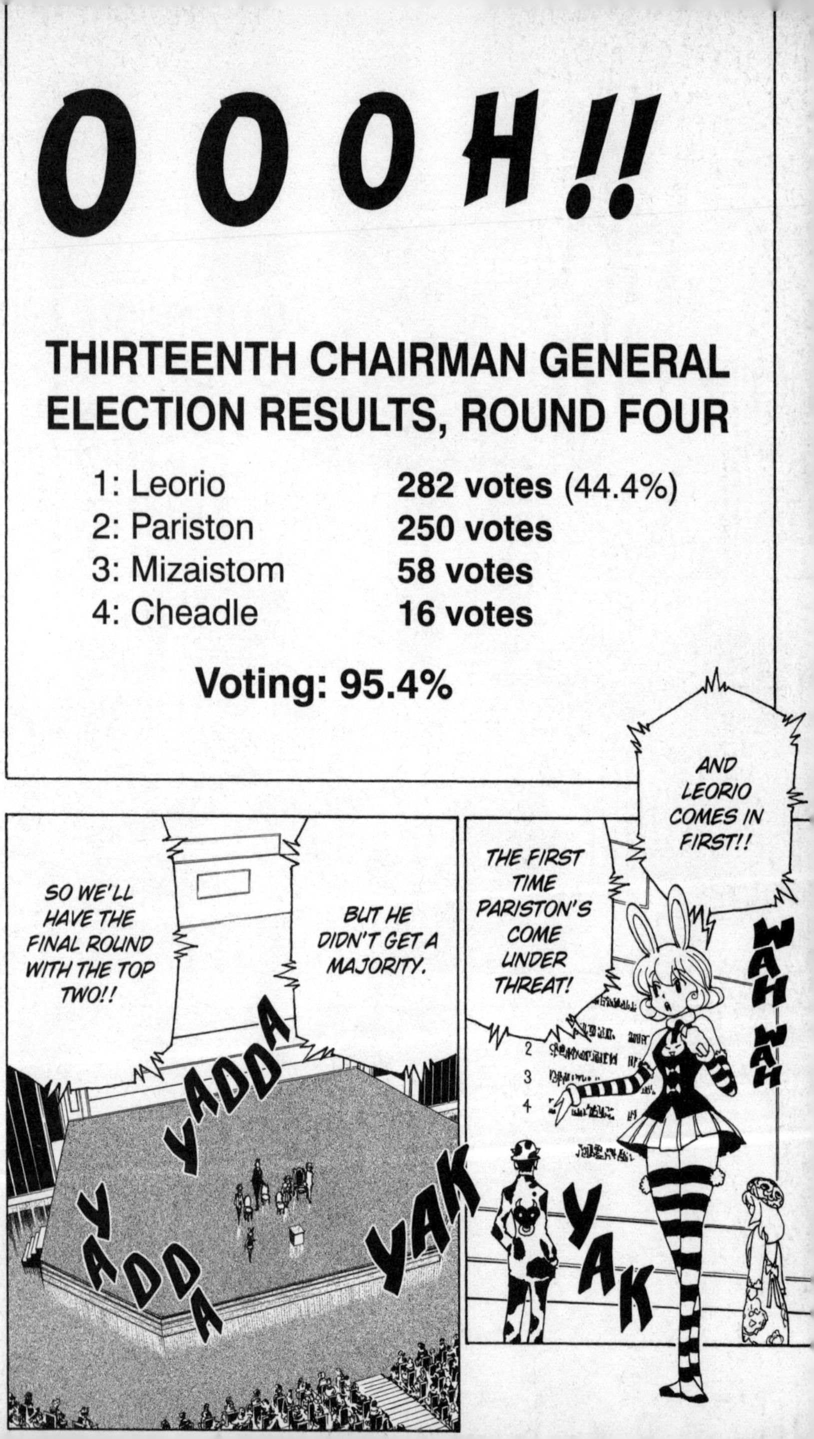
OOOH!!
THIRTEENTH CHAIRMAN GENERAL ELECTION RESULTS, ROUND FOUR
1: Leorio 282 votes (44.4%)
2: Pariston 250 votes
3: Mizaistom 58 votes
4: Cheadle 16 votes
Voting: 95.4%
AND LEORIO COMES IN FIRST!!
THE FIRST TIME PARISTON'S COME UNDER THREAT!
WAH WAH
YAK YAK
BUT HE DIDN'T GET A MAJORITY.
SO WE'LL HAVE THE FINAL ROUND WITH THE TOP TWO!!
YADDA YADDA
YADDA
YAK

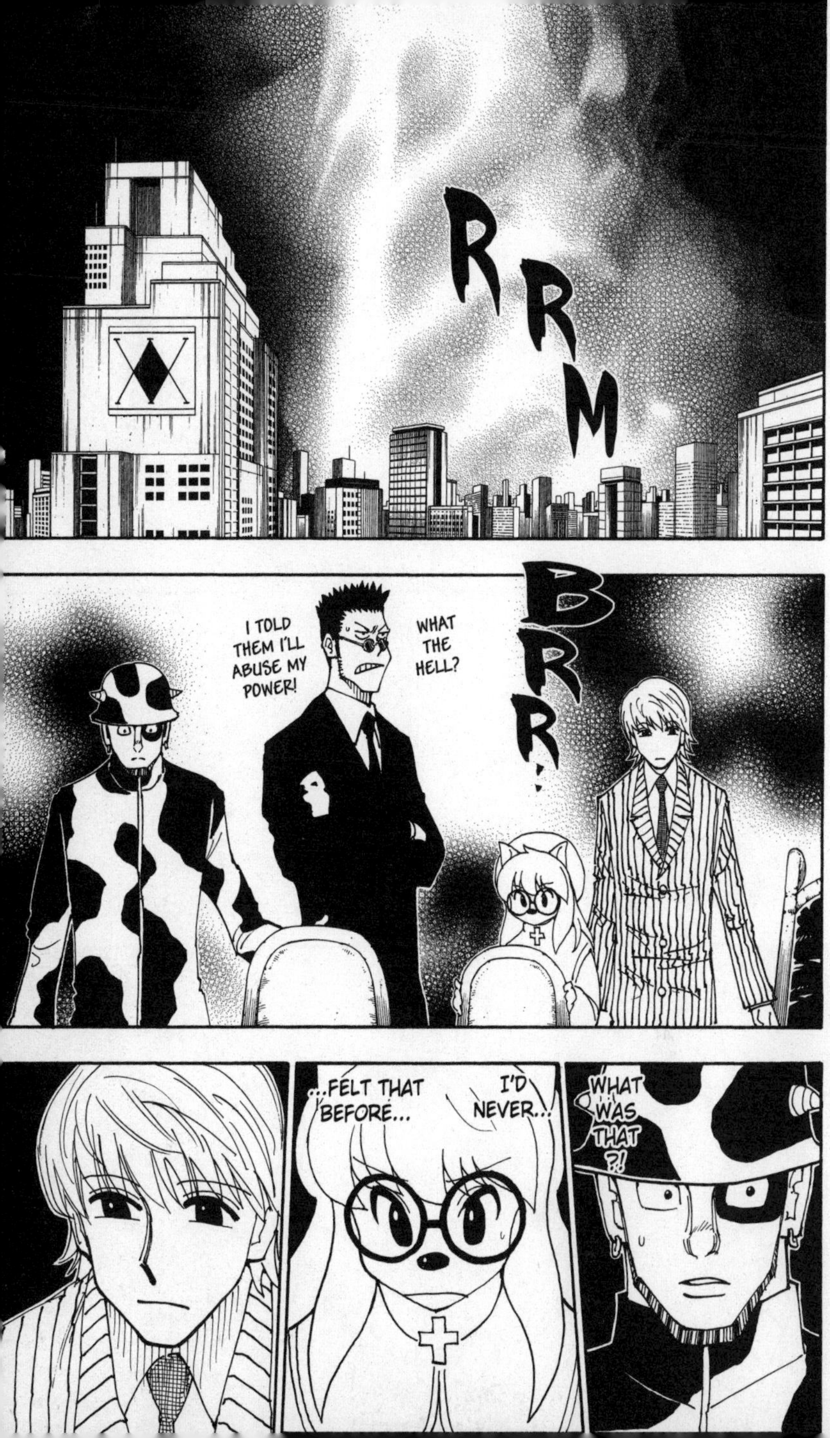
RRRM
BRRR
WHAT THE HELL?
I TOLD THEM I'LL ABUSE MY POWER!
WHAT WAS THAT ?!
I'D NEVER...
...FELT THAT BEFORE...

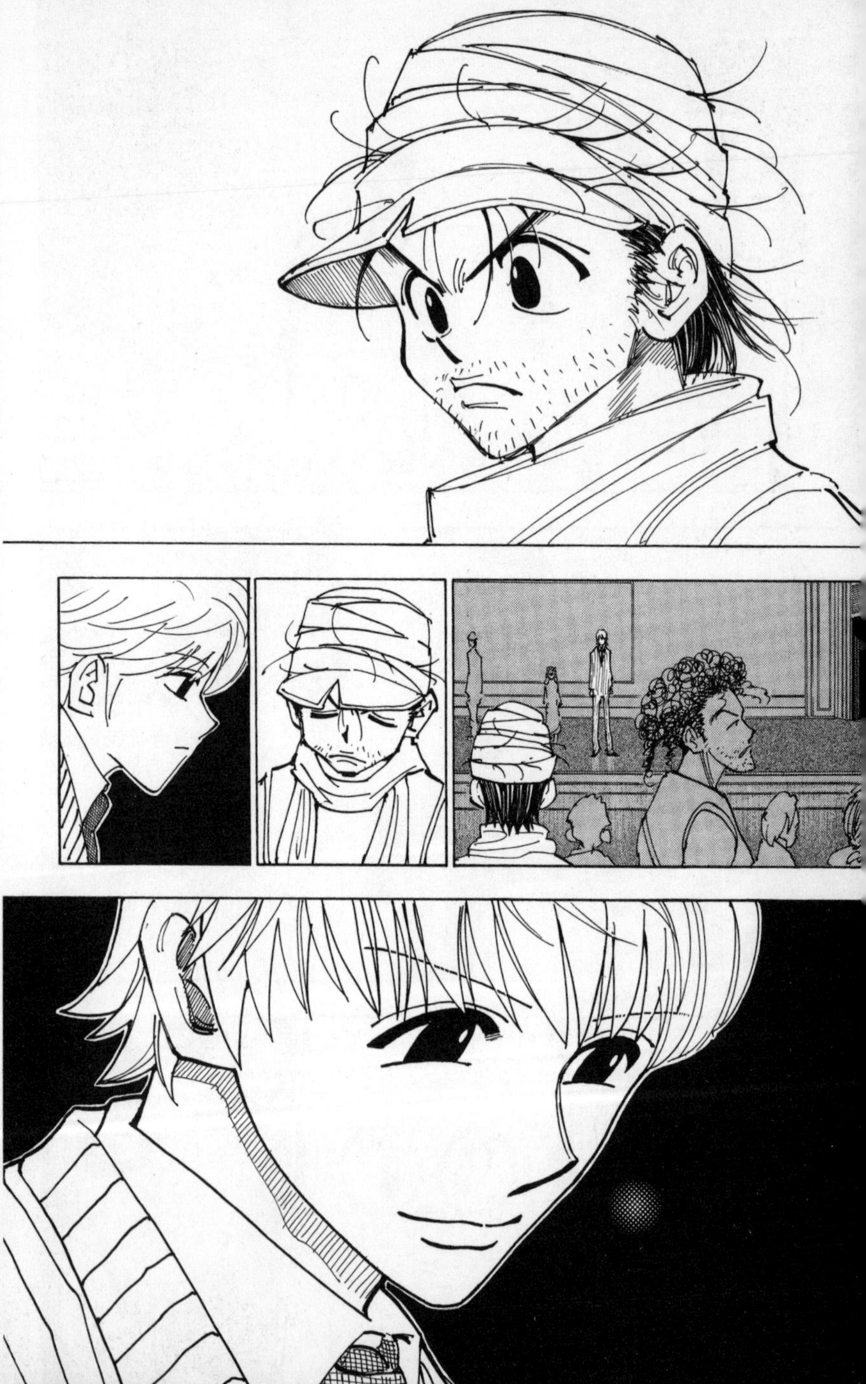

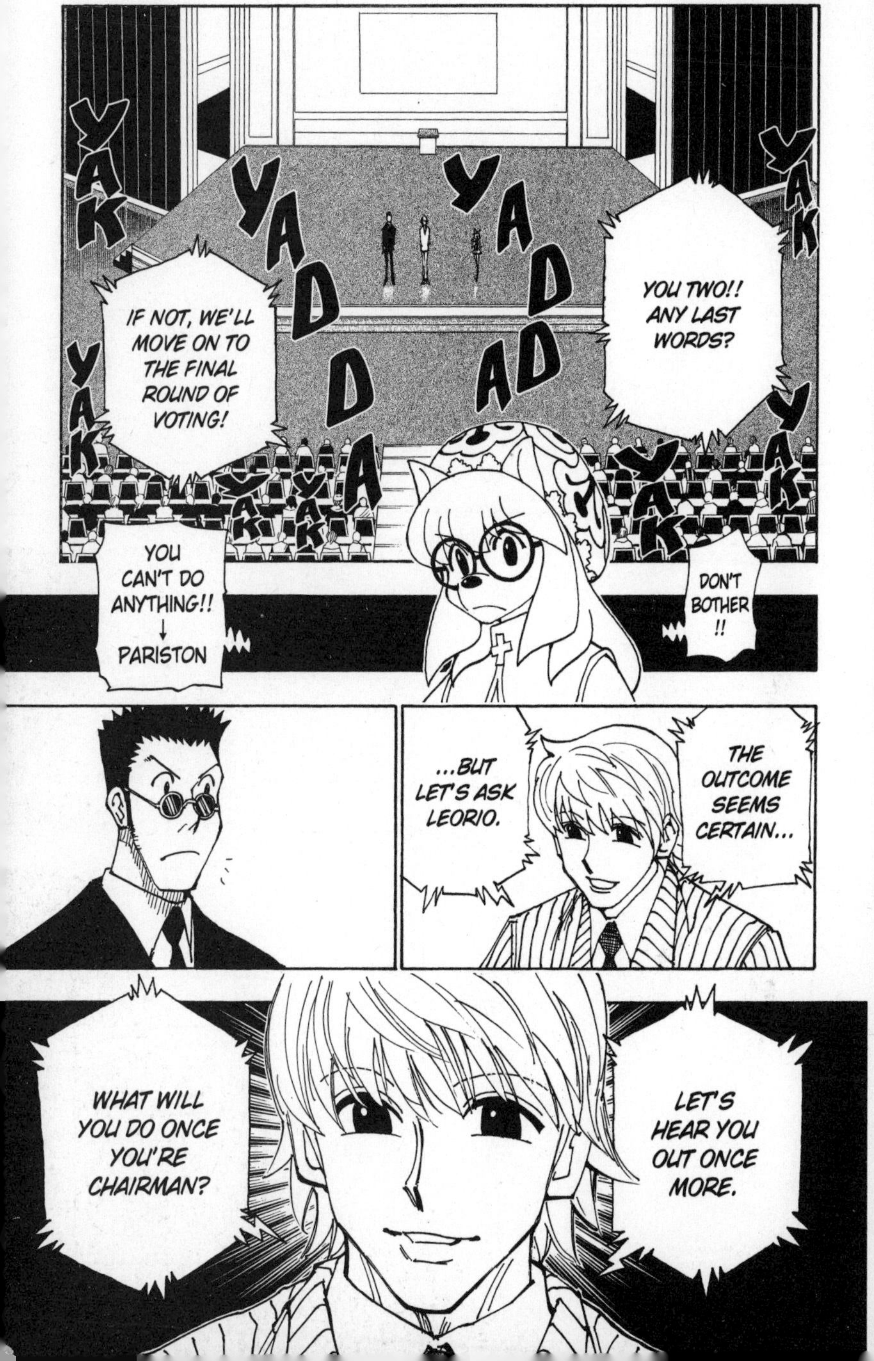
YAK YAK
YOU TWO!! ANY LAST WORDS?
YADDA YADDA
IF NOT, WE'LL MOVE ON TO THE FINAL ROUND OF VOTING!
YAK YAK
YAK YAK
YAK YAK
DON'T BOTHER!!
YOU CAN'T DO ANYTHING!! ↓ PARISTON
THE OUTCOME SEEMS CERTAIN...
...BUT LET'S ASK LEORIO.
LET'S HEAR YOU OUT ONCE MORE.
WHAT WILL YOU DO ONCE YOU'RE CHAIRMAN?

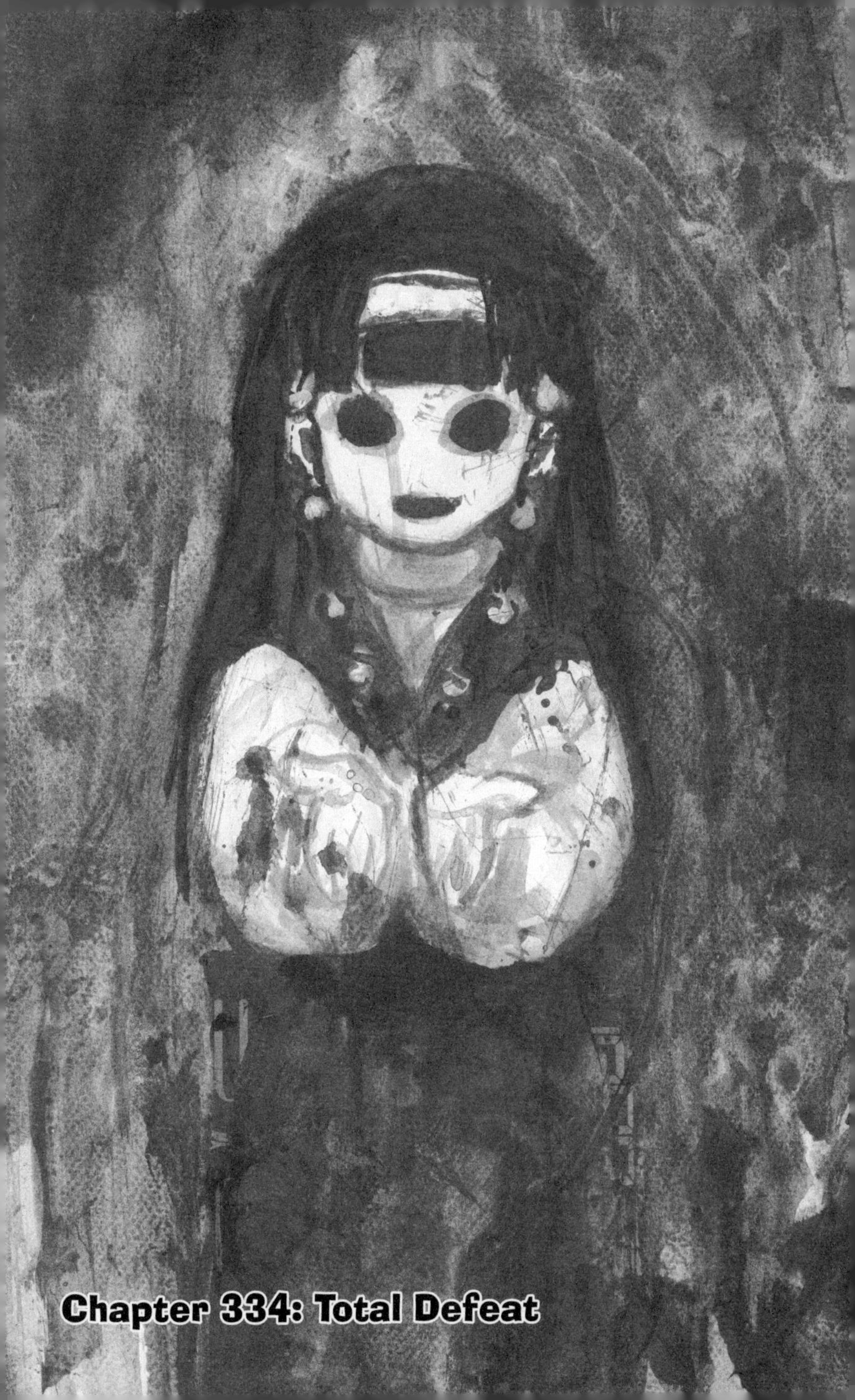

Chapter 334: Total Defeat

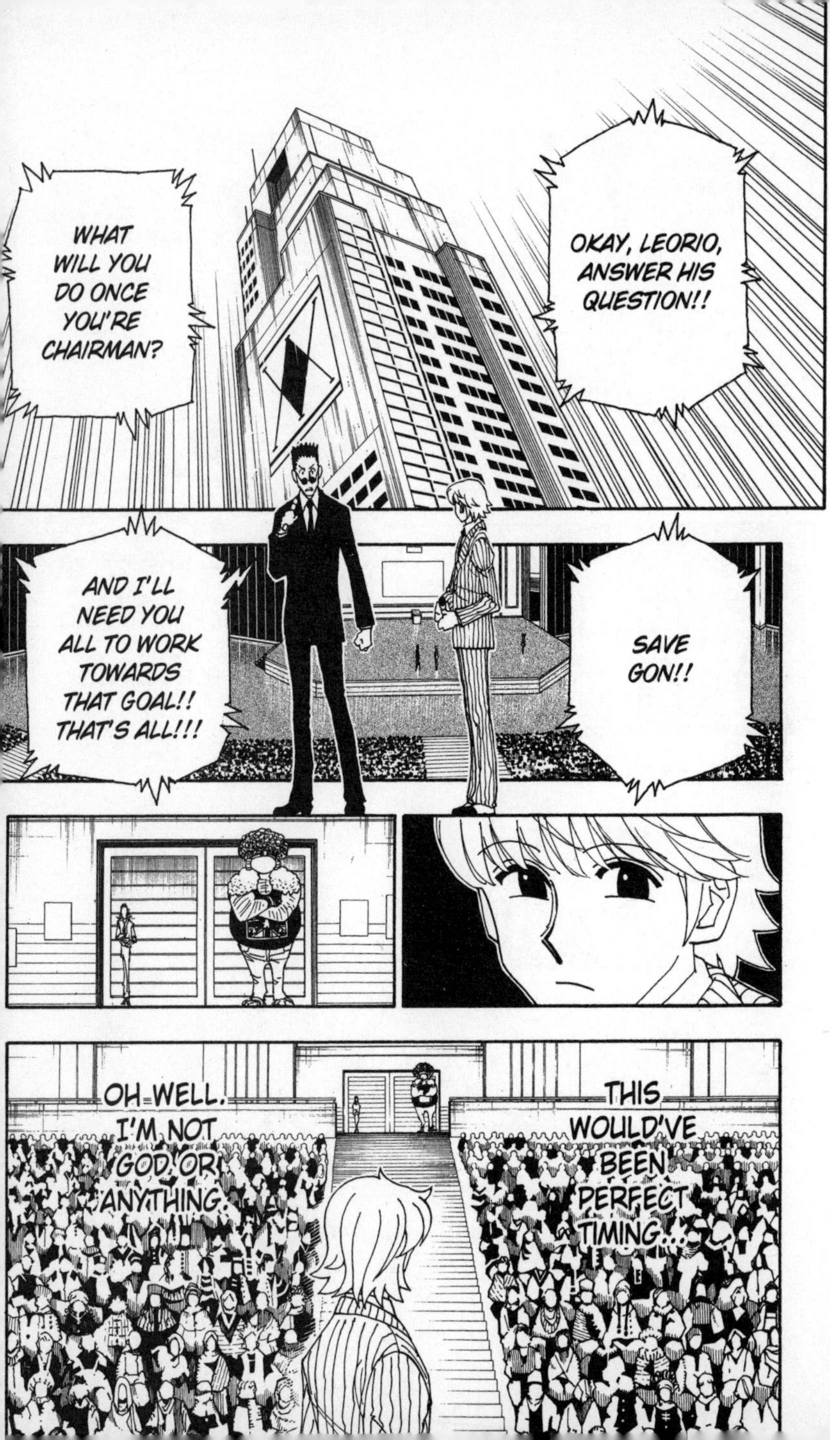
OKAY, LEORIO, ANSWER HIS QUESTION!!
WHAT WILL YOU DO ONCE YOU'RE CHAIRMAN?
SAVE GON!!
AND I'LL NEED YOU ALL TO WORK TOWARDS THAT GOAL!! THAT'S ALL!!!
THIS WOULD'VE BEEN PERFECT TIMING...
OH WELL. I'M NOT GOD OR ANYTHING.

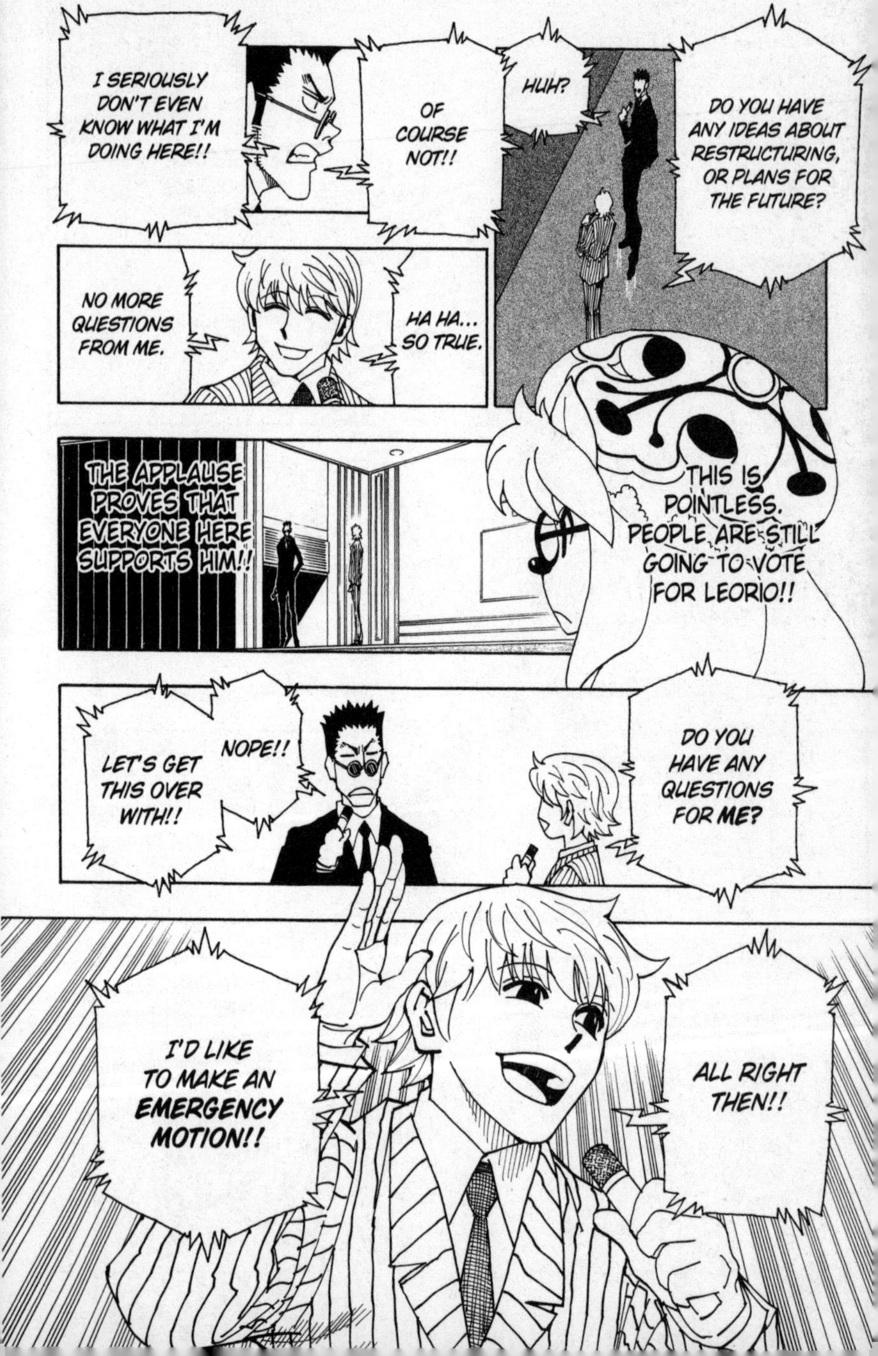
DO YOU HAVE ANY IDEAS ABOUT RESTRUCTURING, OR PLANS FOR THE FUTURE?
HUH?
OF COURSE NOT!!
I SERIOUSLY DON'T EVEN KNOW WHAT I'M DOING HERE!!
HA HA... SO TRUE.
NO MORE QUESTIONS FROM ME.
THIS IS POINTLESS. PEOPLE ARE STILL GOING TO VOTE FOR LEORIO!!
THE APPLAUSE PROVES THAT EVERYONE HERE SUPPORTS HIM!!
DO YOU HAVE ANY QUESTIONS FOR ME?
NOPE!!
LET'S GET THIS OVER WITH!!
ALL RIGHT THEN!!
I'D LIKE TO MAKE AN EMERGENCY MOTION!!

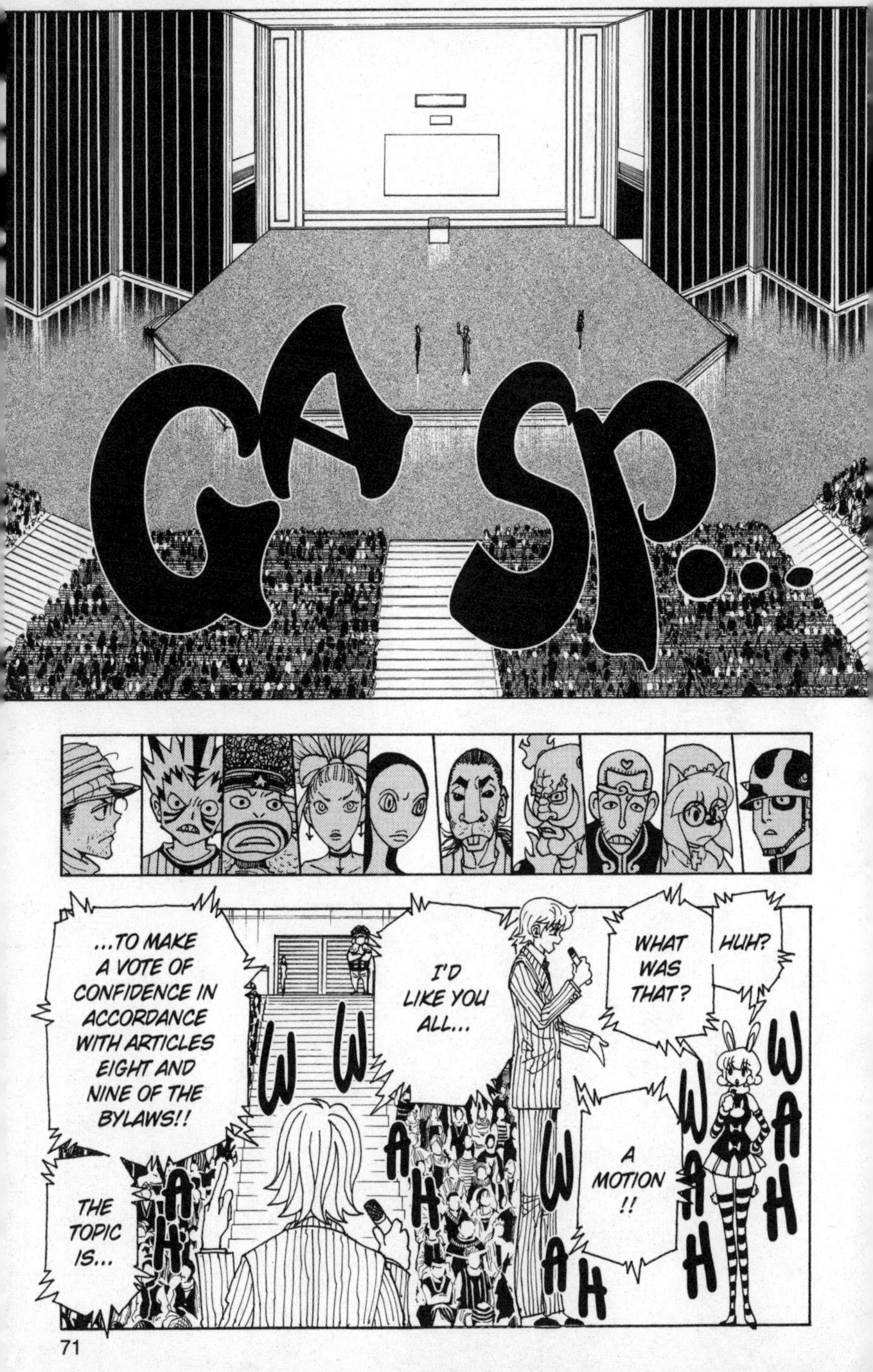
GASP...
HUH?
WHAT WAS THAT?
WAAH
I'D LIKE YOU ALL...
...TO MAKE A VOTE OF CONFIDENCE IN ACCORDANCE WITH ARTICLES EIGHT AND NINE OF THE BYLAWS!!
A MOTION!!
WAAH
WAAH
WAAH
THE TOPIC IS...

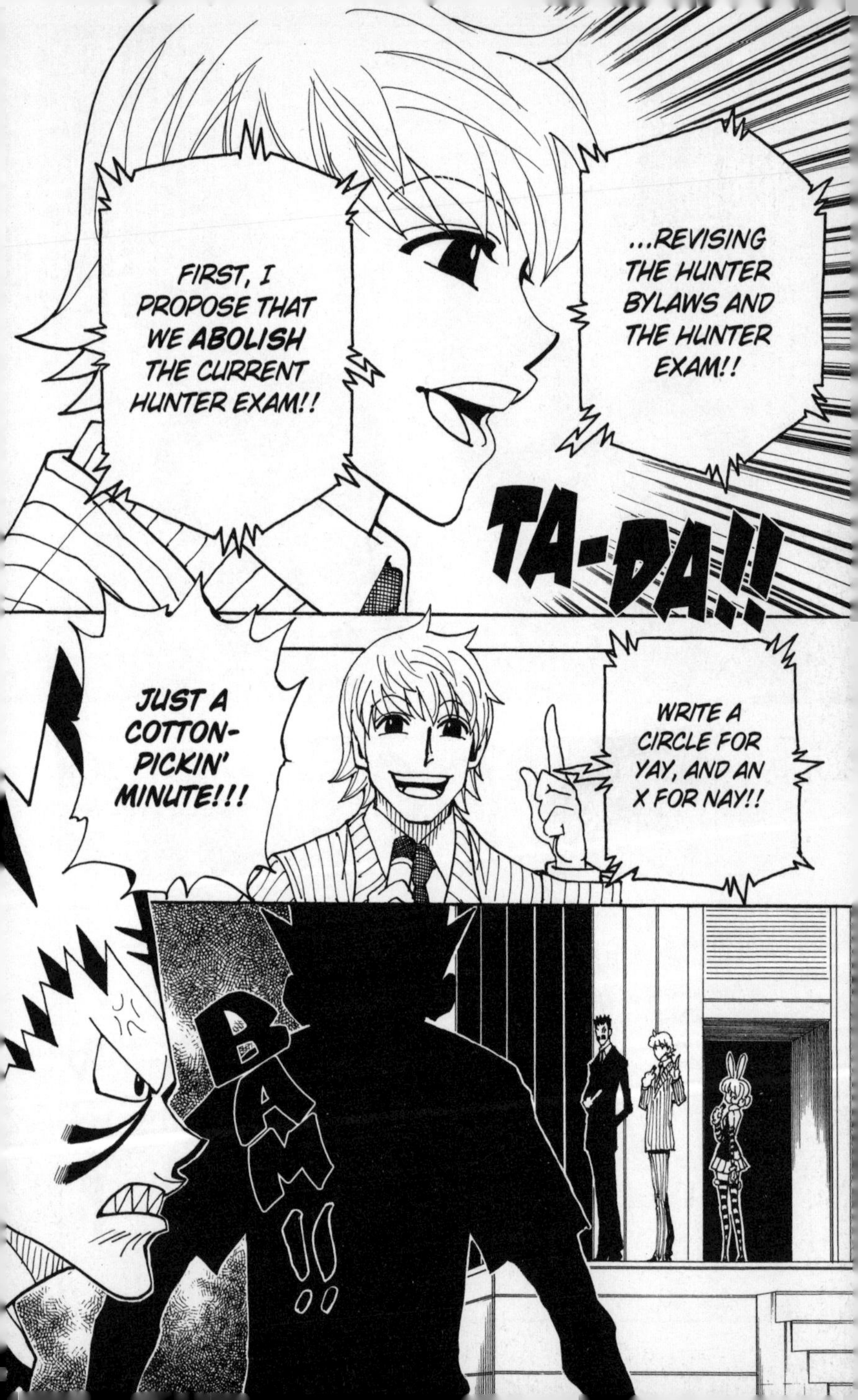
...REVISING THE HUNTER BYLAWS AND THE HUNTER EXAM!!
FIRST, I PROPOSE THAT WE ABOLISH THE CURRENT HUNTER EXAM!!
TA-DA!!
WRITE A CIRCLE FOR YAY, AND AN X FOR NAY!!
JUST A COTTON-PICKIN' MINUTE!!!
BAM!!

READ THIS WAY

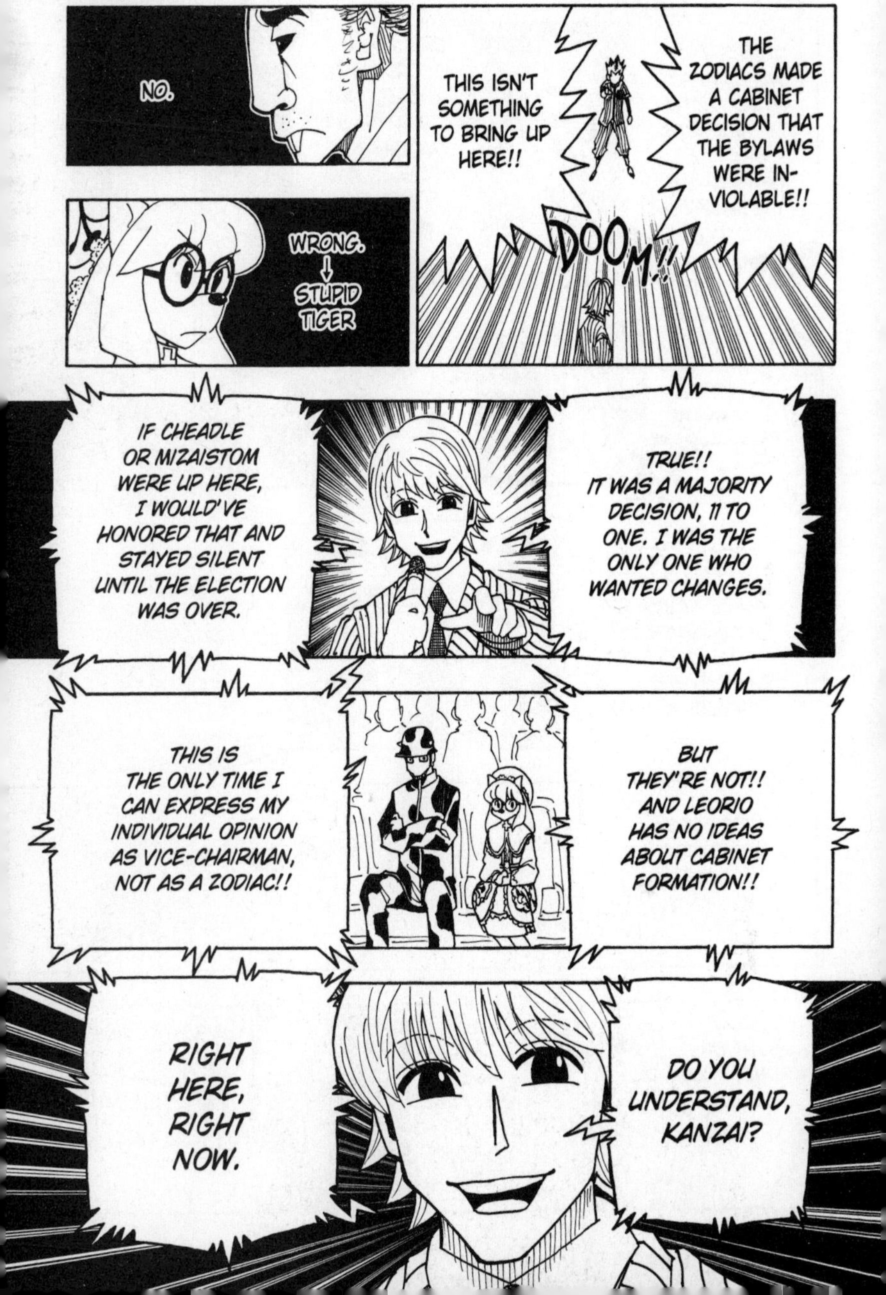
THE ZODIACS MADE A CABINET DECISION THAT THE BYLAWS WERE IN-VIOLABLE!!
THIS ISN'T SOMETHING TO BRING UP HERE!!
DOOM!!
NO.
WRONG. ↓ STUPID TIGER
TRUE!! IT WAS A MAJORITY DECISION, 11 TO ONE. I WAS THE ONLY ONE WHO WANTED CHANGES.
IF CHEADLE OR MIZAISTOM WERE UP HERE, I WOULD'VE HONORED THAT AND STAYED SILENT UNTIL THE ELECTION WAS OVER.
BUT THEY'RE NOT!! AND LEORIO HAS NO IDEAS ABOUT CABINET FORMATION!!
THIS IS THE ONLY TIME I CAN EXPRESS MY INDIVIDUAL OPINION AS VICE-CHAIRMAN, NOT AS A ZODIAC!!
DO YOU UNDERSTAND, KANZAI?
RIGHT HERE, RIGHT NOW.

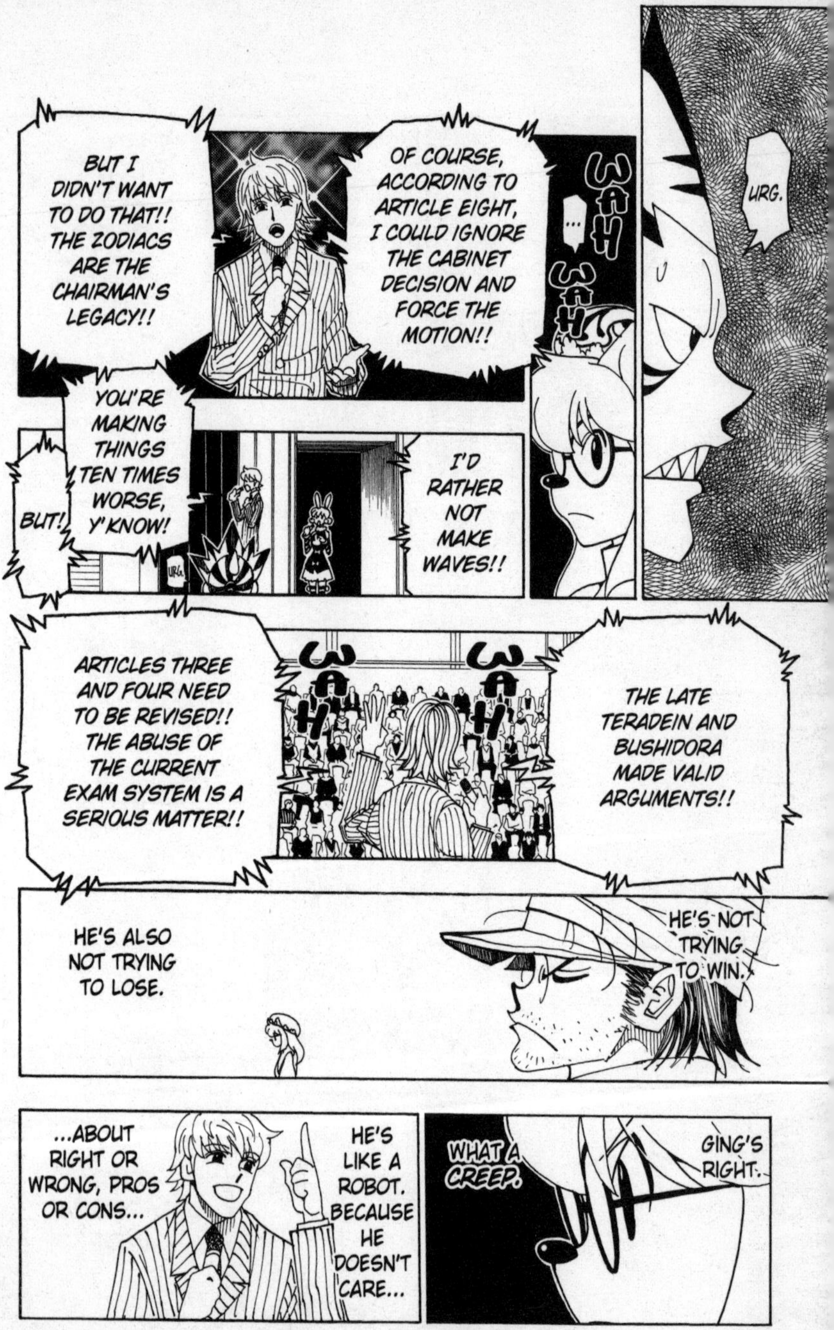
URG.
...
WAH WAH
OF COURSE, ACCORDING TO ARTICLE EIGHT, I COULD IGNORE THE CABINET DECISION AND FORCE THE MOTION!!
BUT I DIDN'T WANT TO DO THAT!! THE ZODIACS ARE THE CHAIRMAN'S LEGACY!!
I'D RATHER NOT MAKE WAVES!!
URG.
YOU'RE MAKING THINGS TEN TIMES WORSE, Y'KNOW!
BUT!
THE LATE TERADEIN AND BUSHIDORA MADE VALID ARGUMENTS!!
WAH WAH
ARTICLES THREE AND FOUR NEED TO BE REVISED!! THE ABUSE OF THE CURRENT EXAM SYSTEM IS A SERIOUS MATTER!!
HE'S NOT TRYING TO WIN.
HE'S ALSO NOT TRYING TO LOSE.
GING'S RIGHT.
WHAT A CREEP.
HE'S LIKE A ROBOT. BECAUSE HE DOESN'T CARE...
...ABOUT RIGHT OR WRONG, PROS OR CONS...

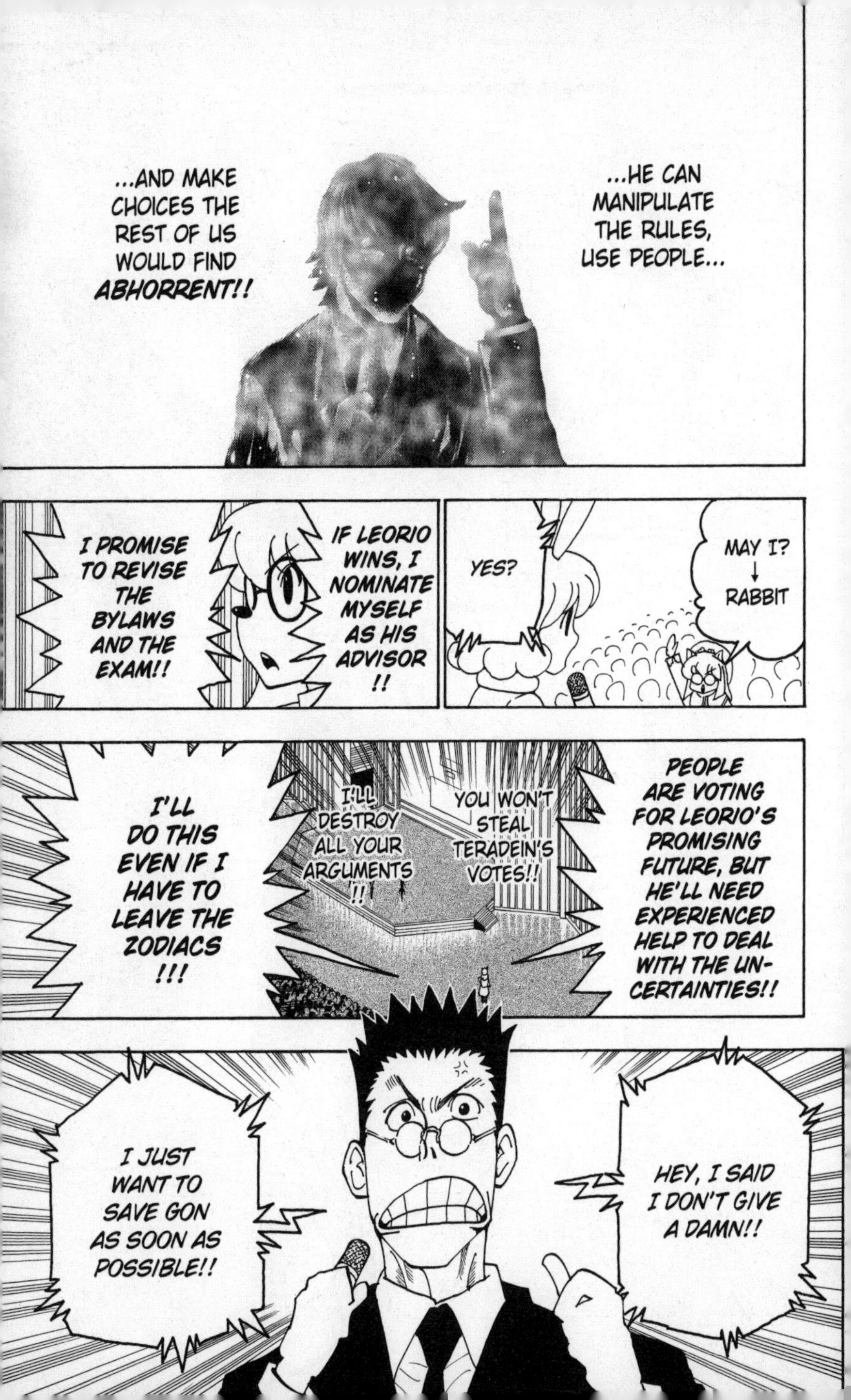
...HE CAN MANIPULATE THE RULES, USE PEOPLE...
...AND MAKE CHOICES THE REST OF US WOULD FIND ABHORRENT!!
MAY I? ↓ RABBIT
YES?
IF LEORIO WINS, I NOMINATE MYSELF AS HIS ADVISOR!!
I PROMISE TO REVISE THE BYLAWS AND THE EXAM!!
PEOPLE ARE VOTING FOR LEORIO'S PROMISING FUTURE, BUT HE'LL NEED EXPERIENCED HELP TO DEAL WITH THE UN-CERTAINTIES!!
YOU WON'T STEAL TERADEIN'S VOTES!!
I'LL DESTROY ALL YOUR ARGUMENTS!!
I'LL DO THIS EVEN IF I HAVE TO LEAVE THE ZODIACS!!!
HEY, I SAID I DON'T GIVE A DAMN!!
I JUST WANT TO SAVE GON AS SOON AS POSSIBLE!!

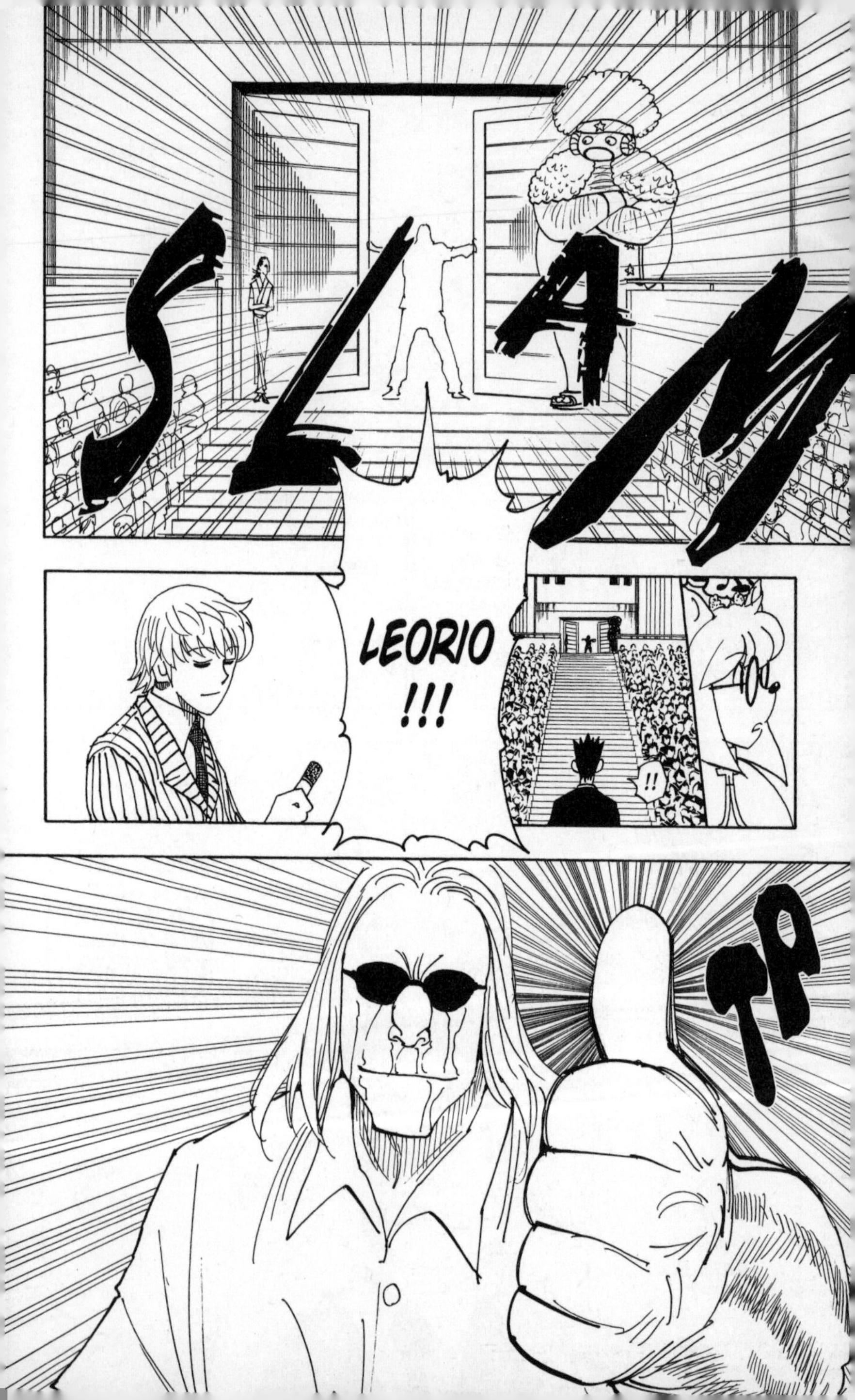
SLAM
LEORIO !!!
!!
TP

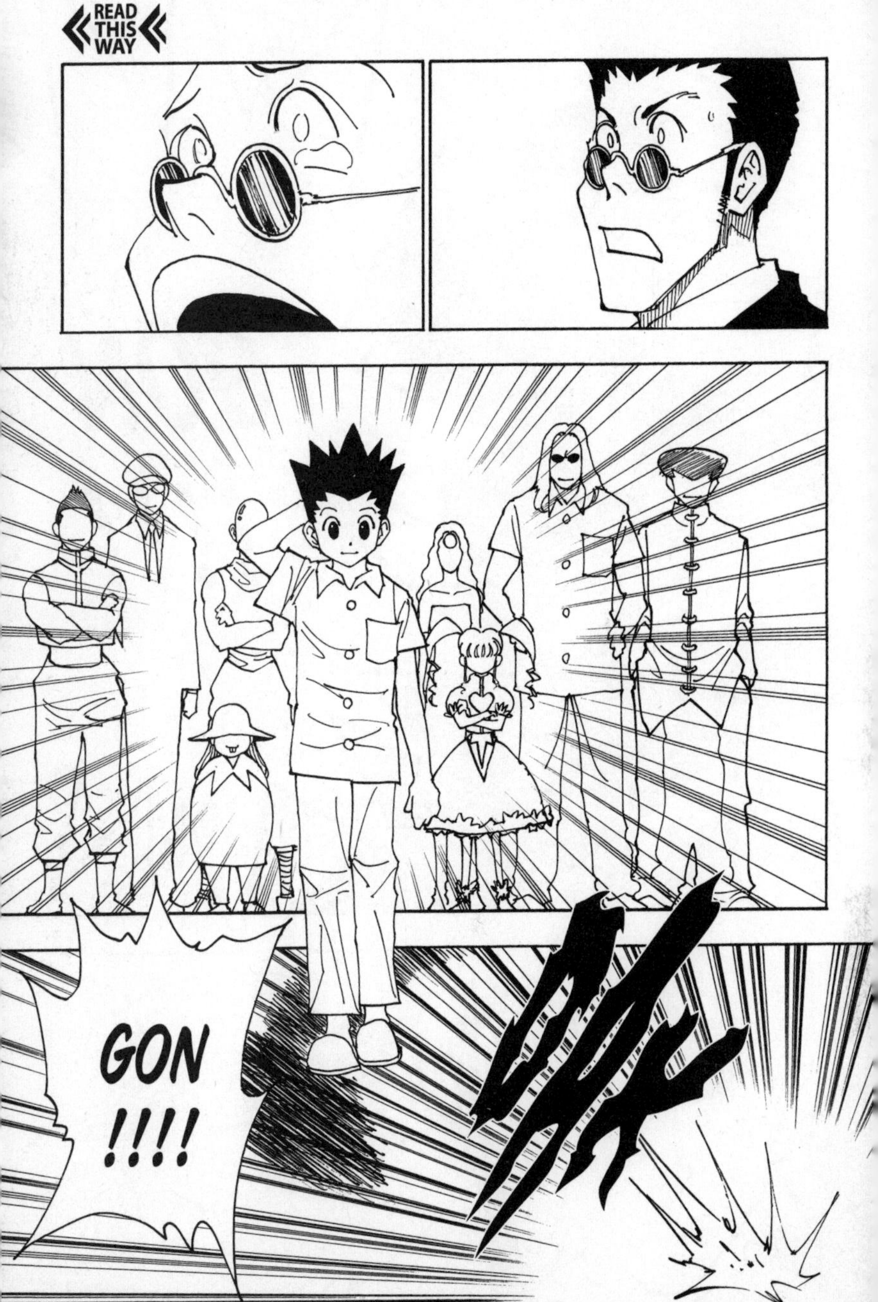
READ THIS WAY
GON !!!!

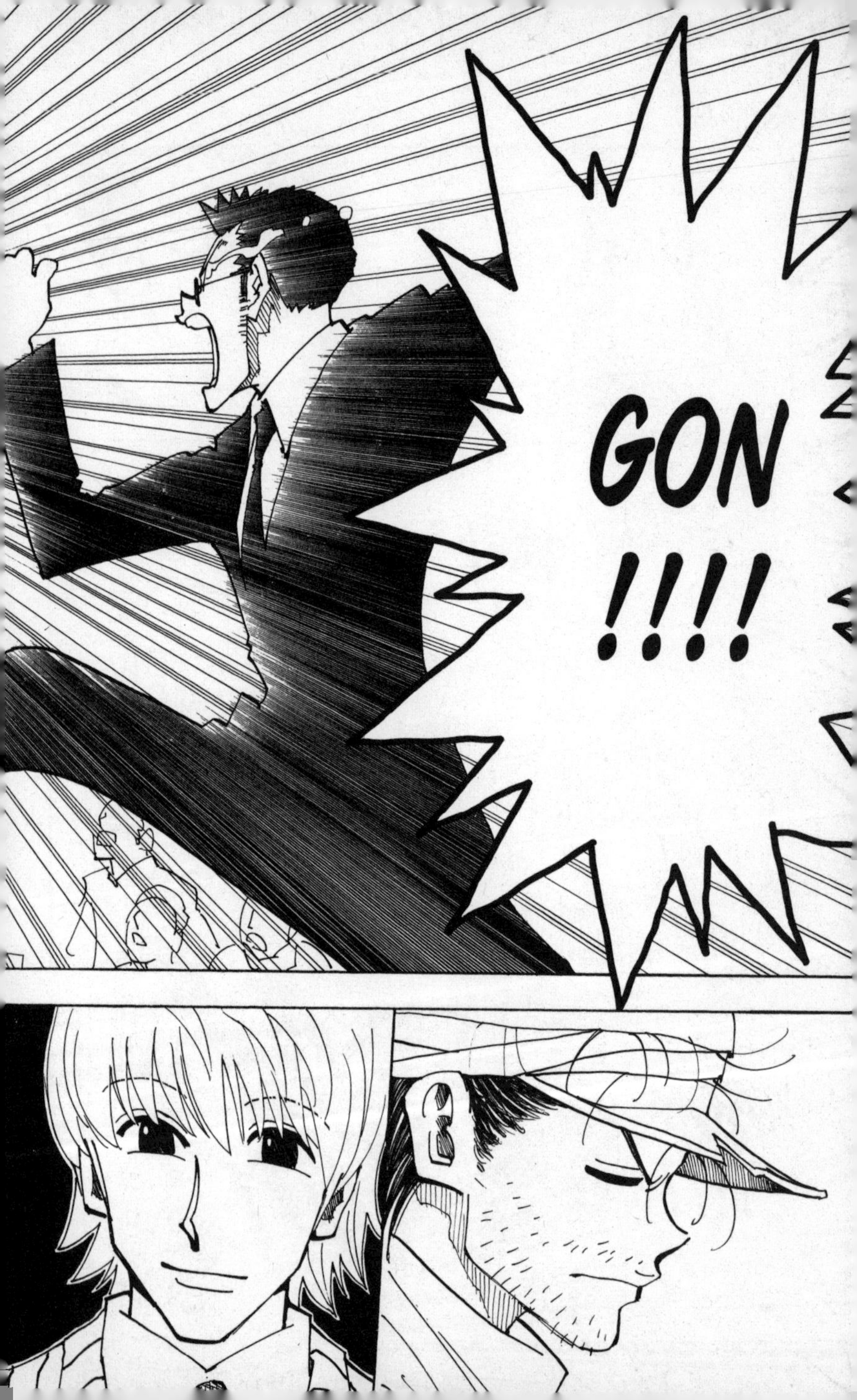
GON
!!!!

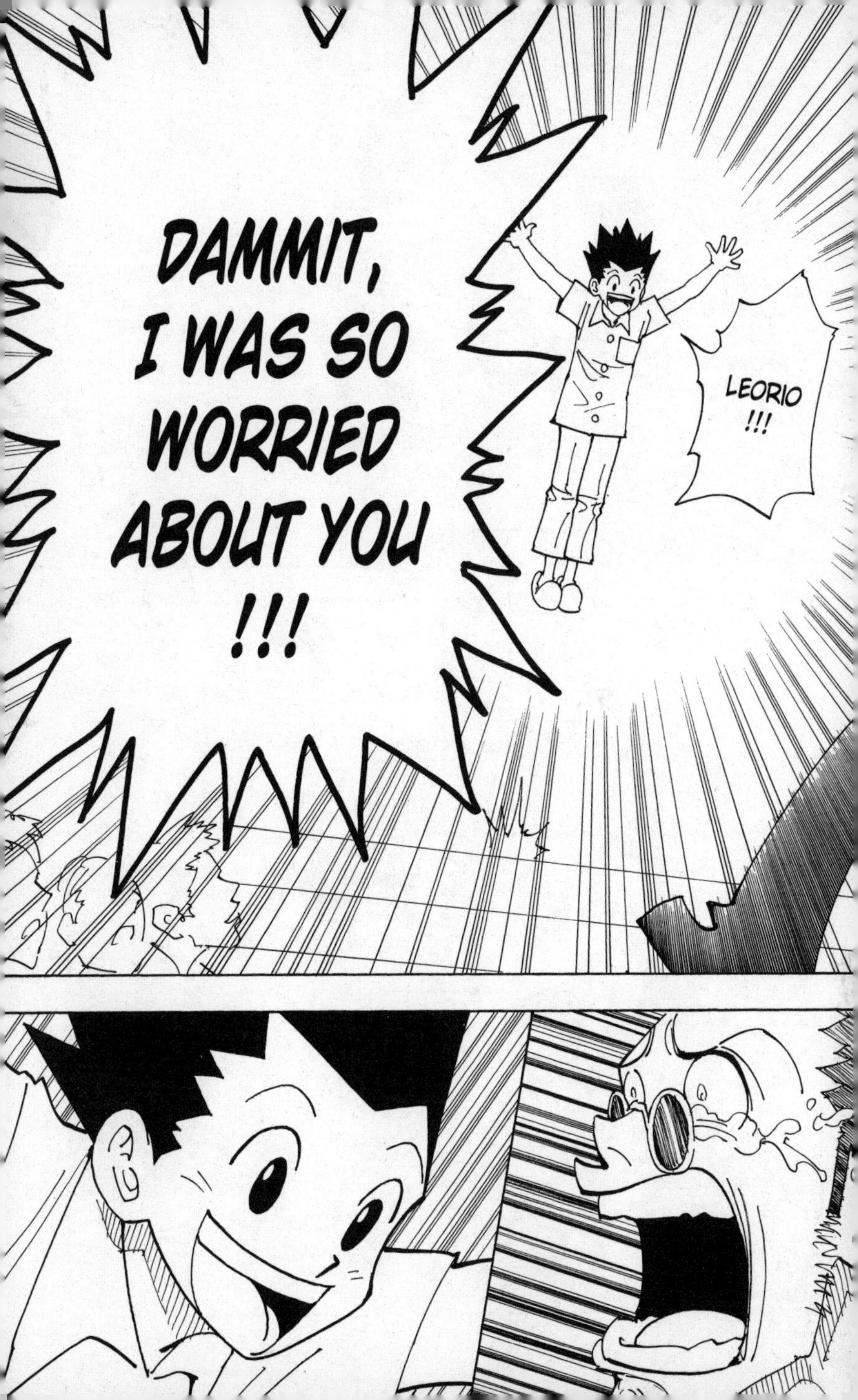
LEORIO !!!
DAMMIT, I WAS SO WORRIED ABOUT YOU !!!

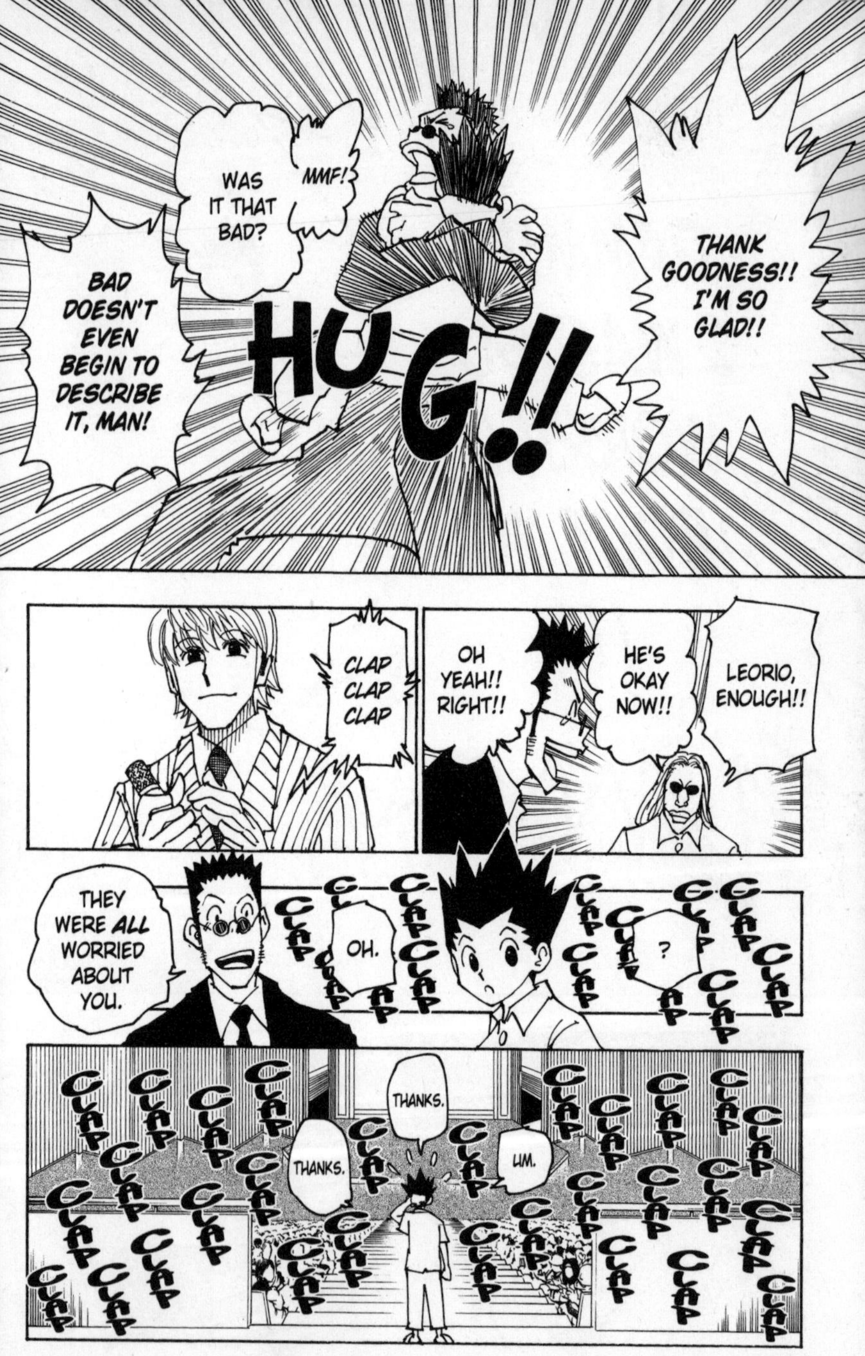
THANK GOODNESS!! I'M SO GLAD!!
HUG!!
MMF!
WAS IT THAT BAD?
BAD DOESN'T EVEN BEGIN TO DESCRIBE IT, MAN!
LEORIO, ENOUGH!!
HE'S OKAY NOW!!
OH YEAH!! RIGHT!!
CLAP CLAP CLAP
CLAP CLAP CLAP
?
OH.
CLAP CLAP CLAP
THEY WERE ALL WORRIED ABOUT YOU.
CLAP CLAP CLAP
UM.
THANKS.
THANKS.
CLAP CLAP CLAP

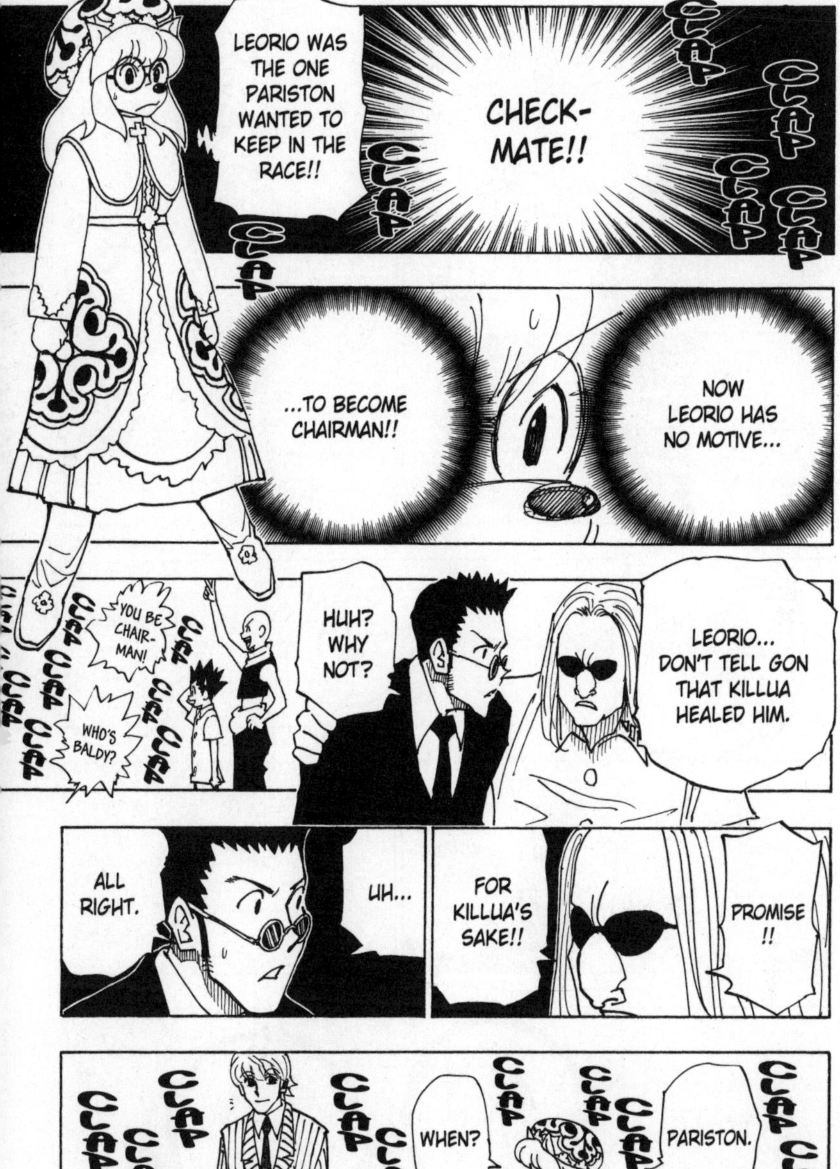
CLAP CLAP CLAP CLAP
CHECK-MATE!!
CLAP CLAP
LEORIO WAS THE ONE PARISTON WANTED TO KEEP IN THE RACE!!
NOW LEORIO HAS NO MOTIVE...
...TO BECOME CHAIRMAN!!
LEORIO... DON'T TELL GON THAT KILLUA HEALED HIM.
HUH? WHY NOT?
CLAP CLAP
YOU BE CHAIR-MAN!
WHO'S BALDY?
CLAP CLAP CLAP
PROMISE !!
FOR KILLUA'S SAKE!!
UH...
ALL RIGHT.
CLAP CLAP
PARISTON.
CLAP CLAP
WHEN?
CLAP CLAP CLAP CLAP CLAP

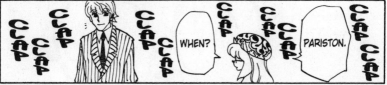

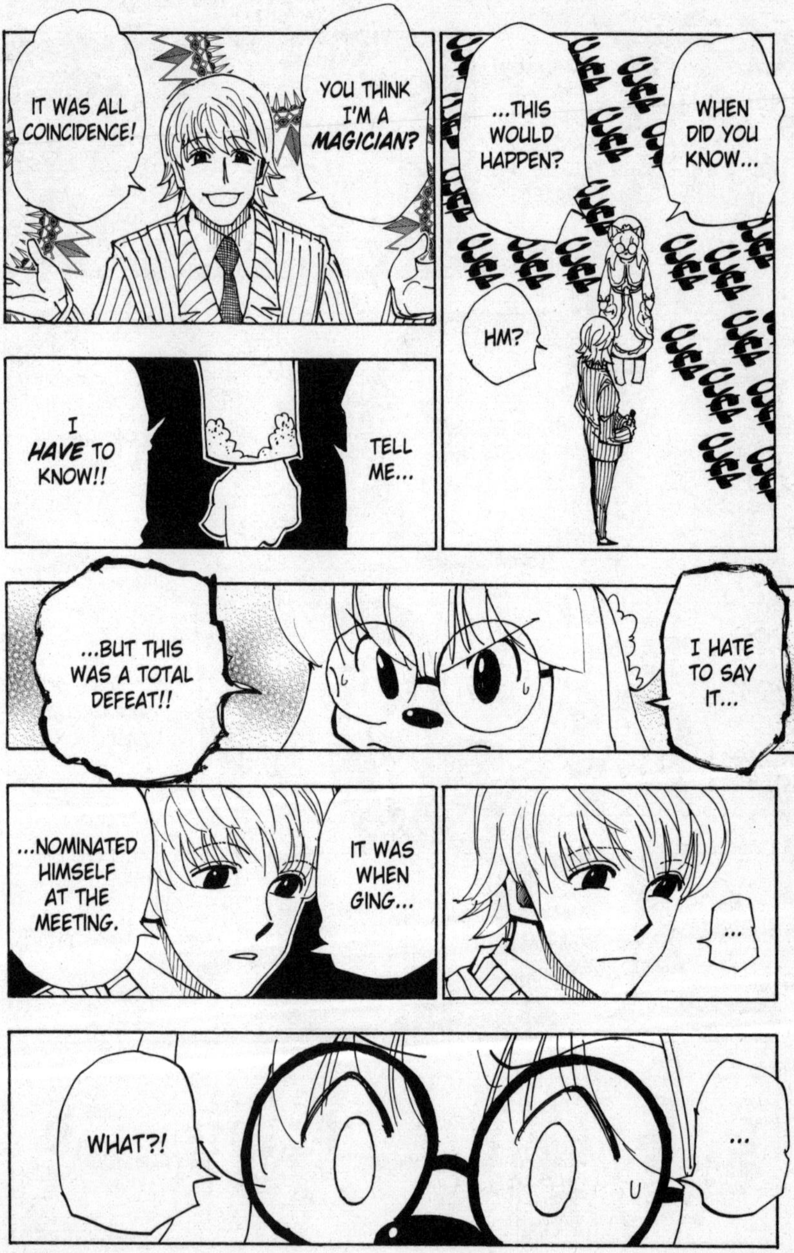
WHEN DID YOU KNOW...
...THIS WOULD HAPPEN?
CLAP CLAP CLAP CLAP
HM?
YOU THINK I'M A *MAGICIAN?*
IT WAS ALL COINCIDENCE!
TELL ME...
I *HAVE* TO KNOW!!
I HATE TO SAY IT...
...BUT THIS WAS A TOTAL DEFEAT!!
...
IT WAS WHEN GING...
...NOMINATED HIMSELF AT THE MEETING.
...
WHAT?!

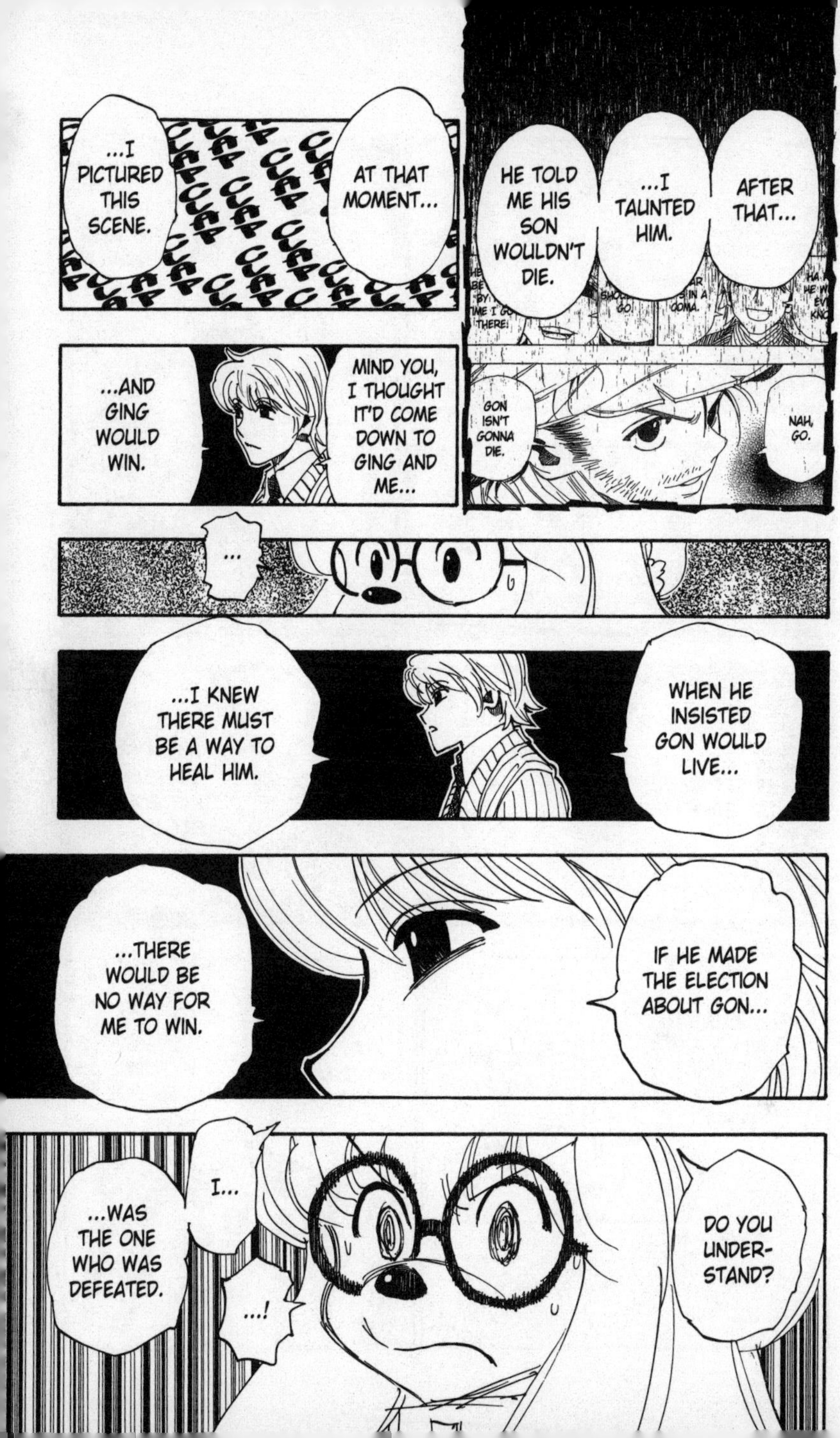
AFTER THAT...
...I TAUNTED HIM.
HE TOLD ME HIS SON WOULDN'T DIE.
NAH, GO.
GON ISN'T GONNA DIE.
AT THAT MOMENT...
...I PICTURED THIS SCENE.
CLAP CLAP CLAP CLAP
MIND YOU, I THOUGHT IT'D COME DOWN TO GING AND ME...
...AND GING WOULD WIN.
...
WHEN HE INSISTED GON WOULD LIVE...
...I KNEW THERE MUST BE A WAY TO HEAL HIM.
IF HE MADE THE ELECTION ABOUT GON...
...THERE WOULD BE NO WAY FOR ME TO WIN.
DO YOU UNDERSTAND?
I...
...!
...WAS THE ONE WHO WAS DEFEATED.

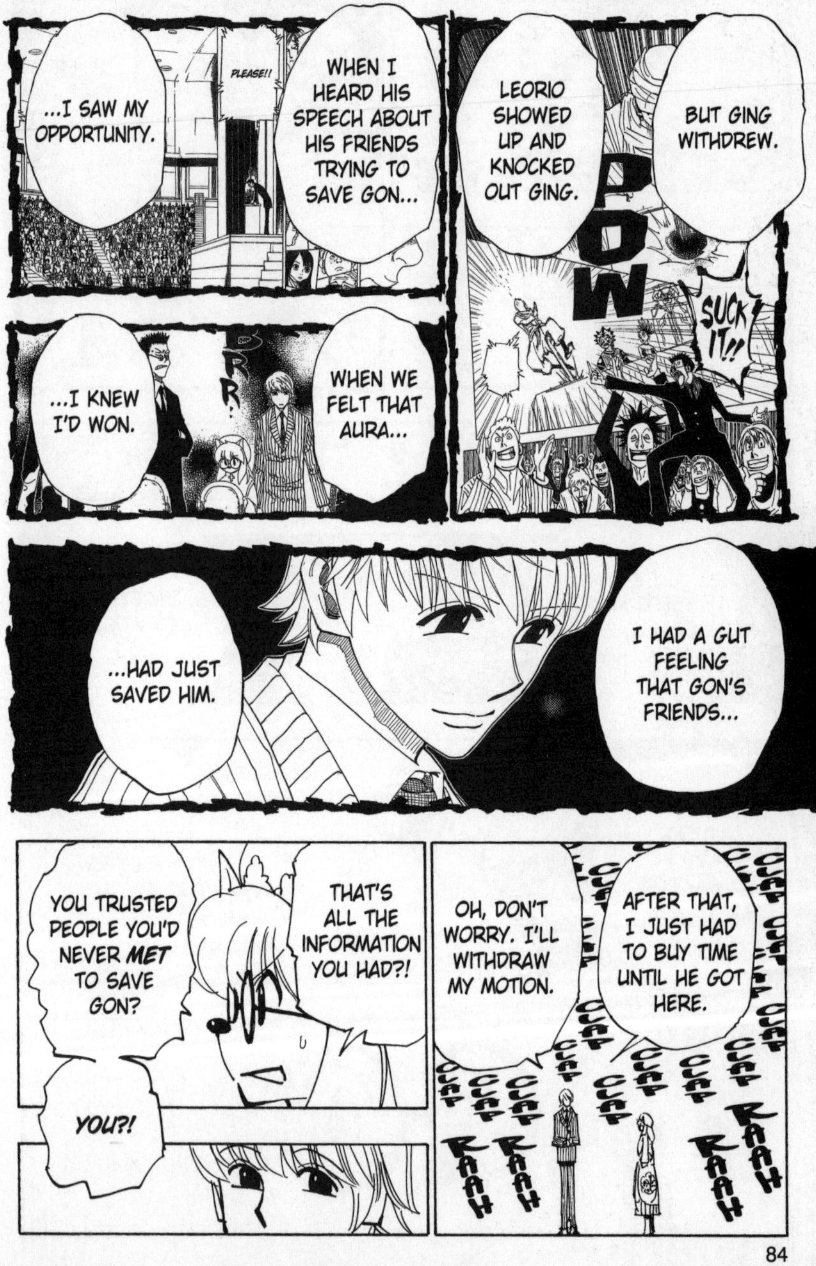

BUT GING WITHDREW.
LEORIO SHOWED UP AND KNOCKED OUT GING.
POW
SUCK IT!!
WHEN I HEARD HIS SPEECH ABOUT HIS FRIENDS TRYING TO SAVE GON...
PLEASE!!
...I SAW MY OPPORTUNITY.
WHEN WE FELT THAT AURA...
...I KNEW I'D WON.
I HAD A GUT FEELING THAT GON'S FRIENDS...
...HAD JUST SAVED HIM.
AFTER THAT, I JUST HAD TO BUY TIME UNTIL HE GOT HERE.
OH, DON'T WORRY. I'LL WITHDRAW MY MOTION.
CLAP CLAP CLAP
RAAAH
THAT'S ALL THE INFORMATION YOU HAD?!
YOU TRUSTED PEOPLE YOU'D NEVER *MET* TO SAVE GON?
YOU?!

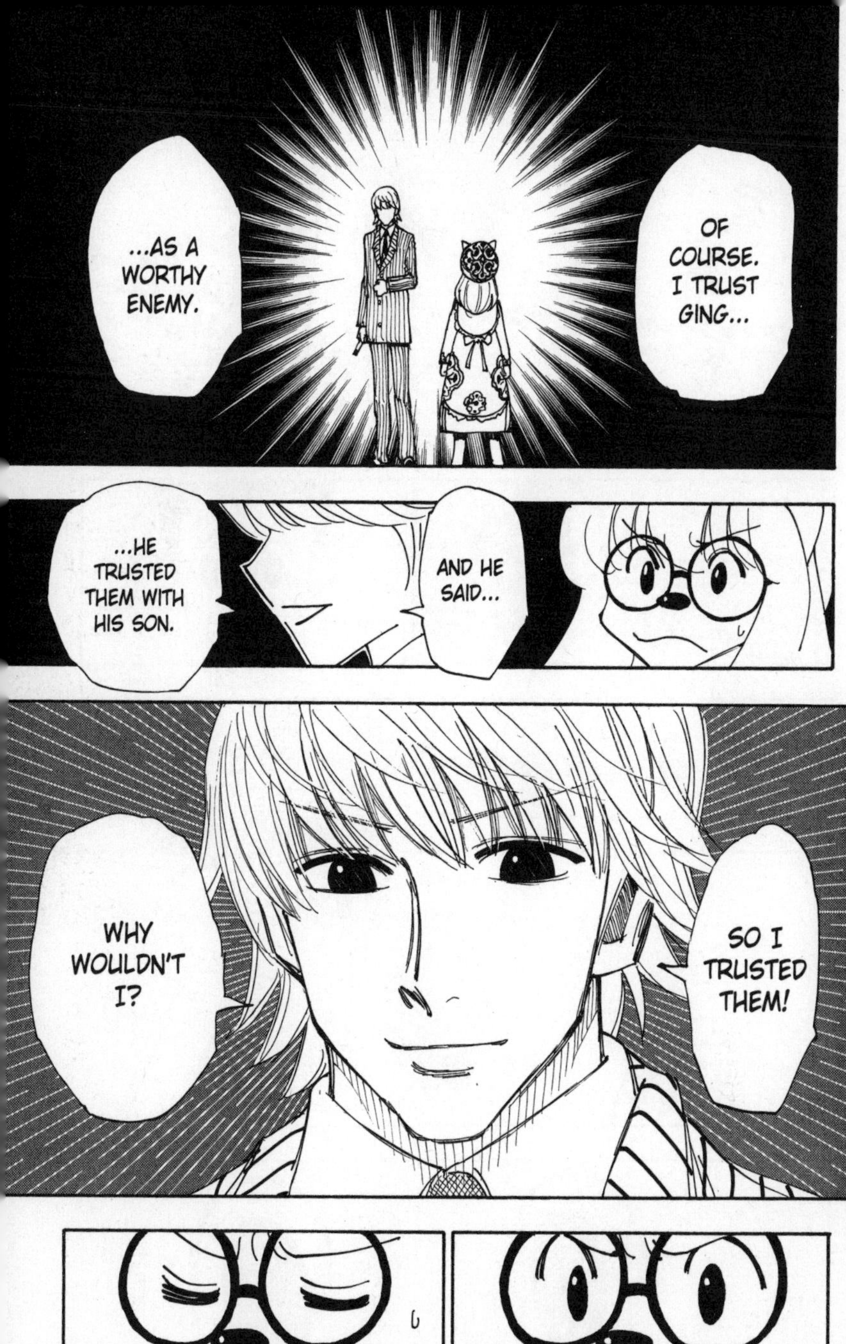
OF COURSE. I TRUST GING...
...AS A WORTHY ENEMY.
AND HE SAID...
...HE TRUSTED THEM WITH HIS SON.
SO I TRUSTED THEM!
WHY WOULDN'T I?

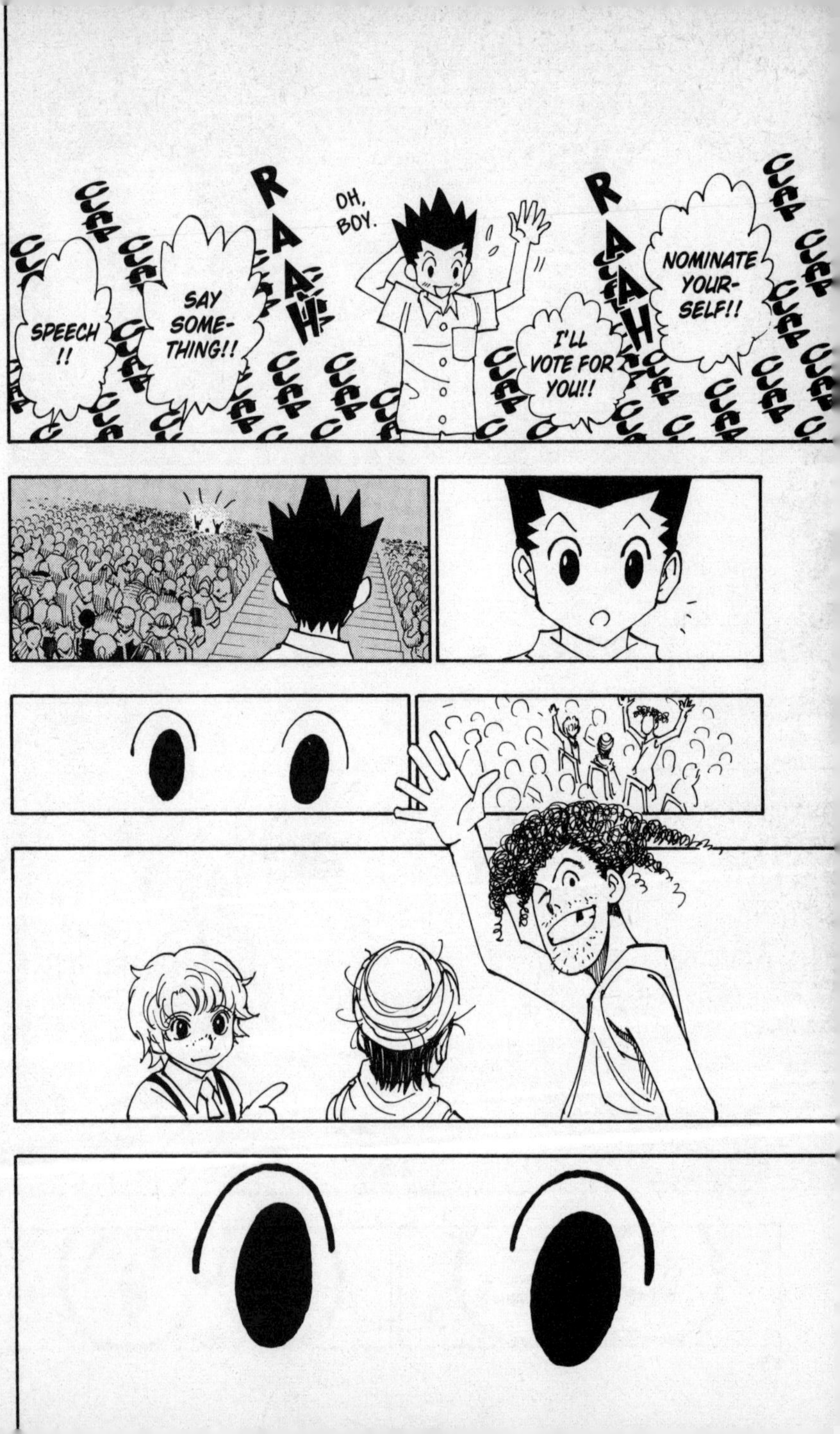
CLAP
NOMINATE YOURSELF!!
RAAH
I'LL VOTE FOR YOU!!
OH, BOY.
RAAH
SAY SOMETHING!!
SPEECH!!

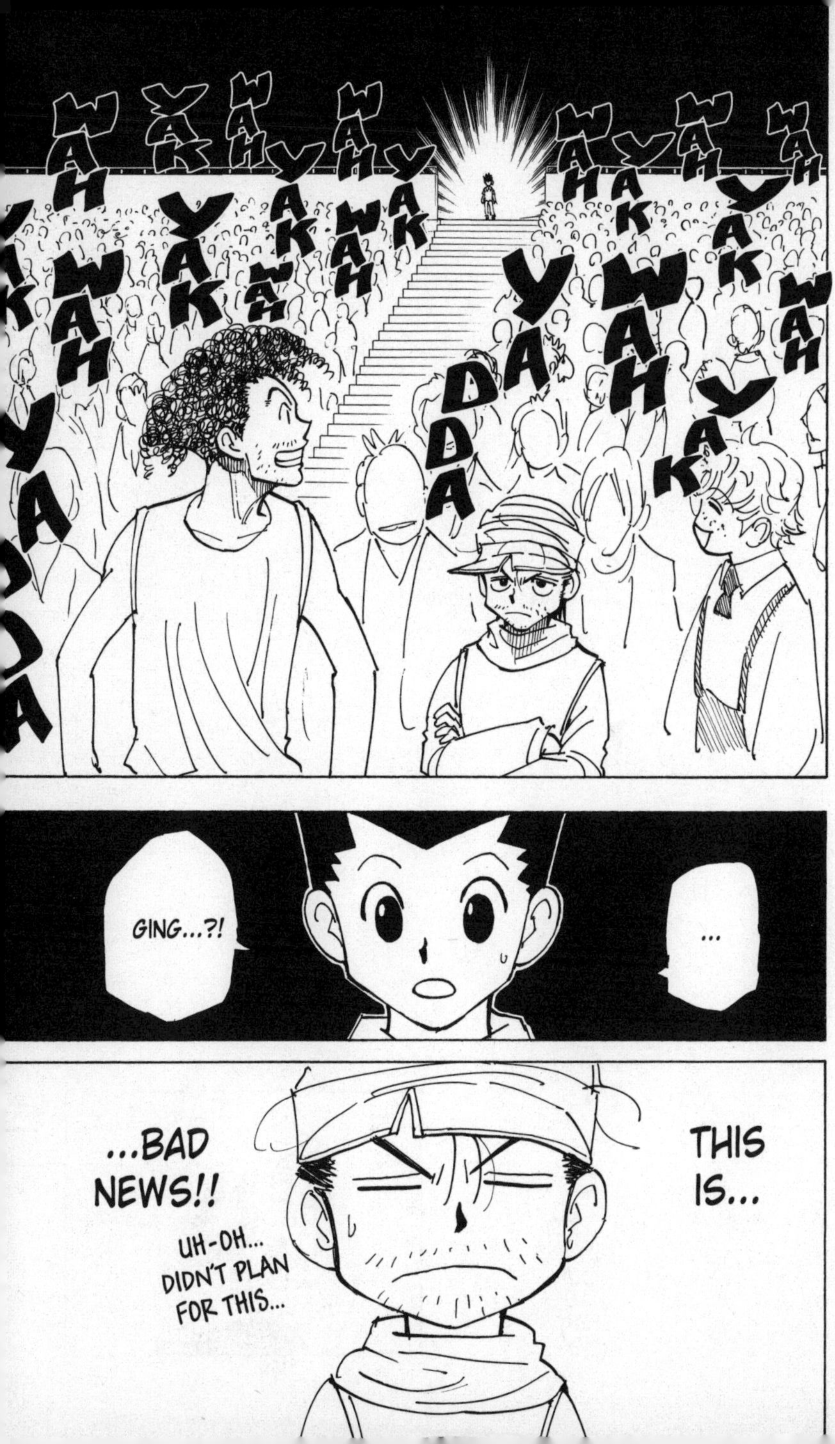
WAH WAH WAH
YAK YAK YAK
DA DA DA
...
GING...?!
THIS IS...
...BAD NEWS!!
UH-OH... DIDN'T PLAN FOR THIS...

Chapter 335: Decision

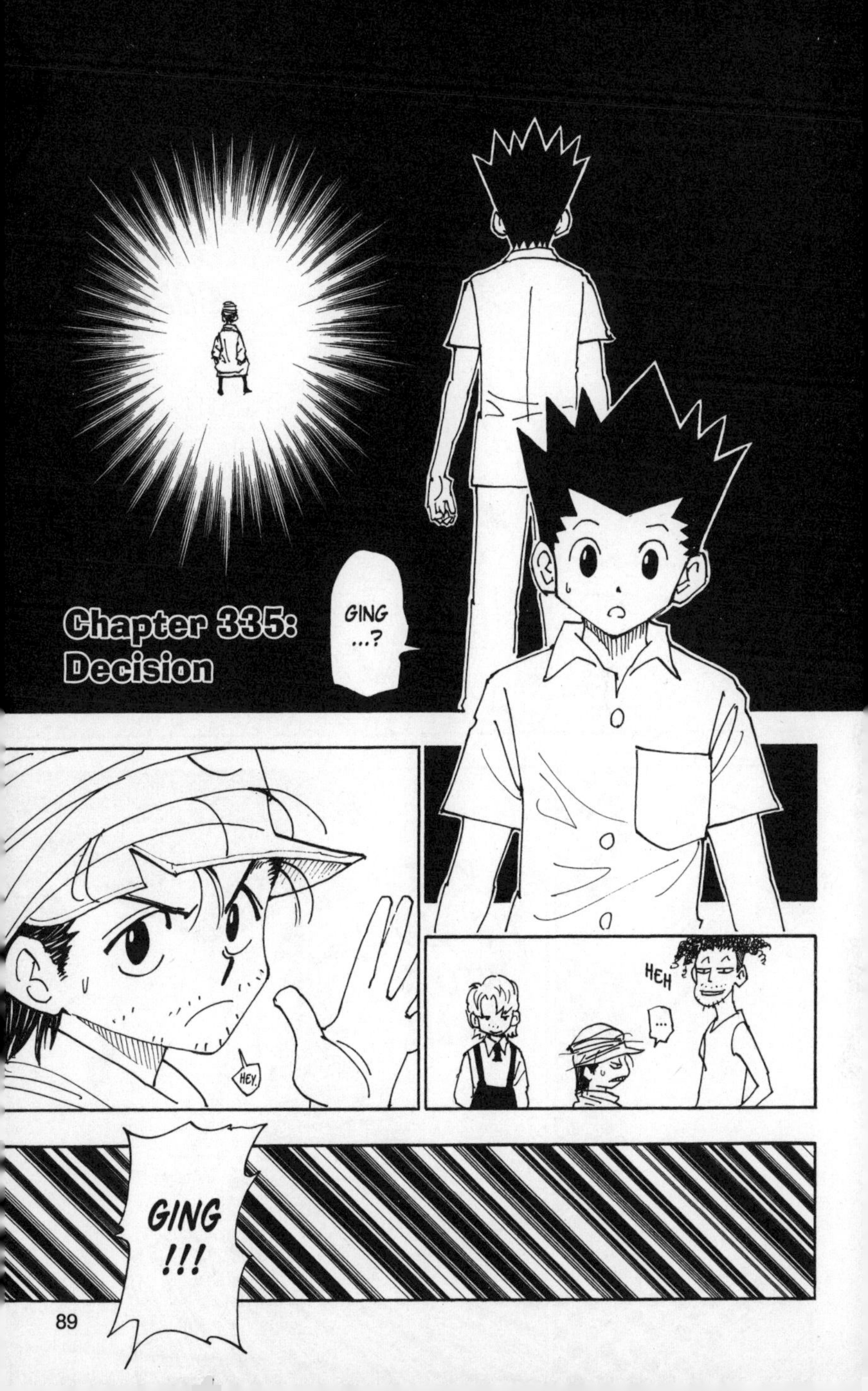
GING ...?
HEH
...
HEY.
GING !!!

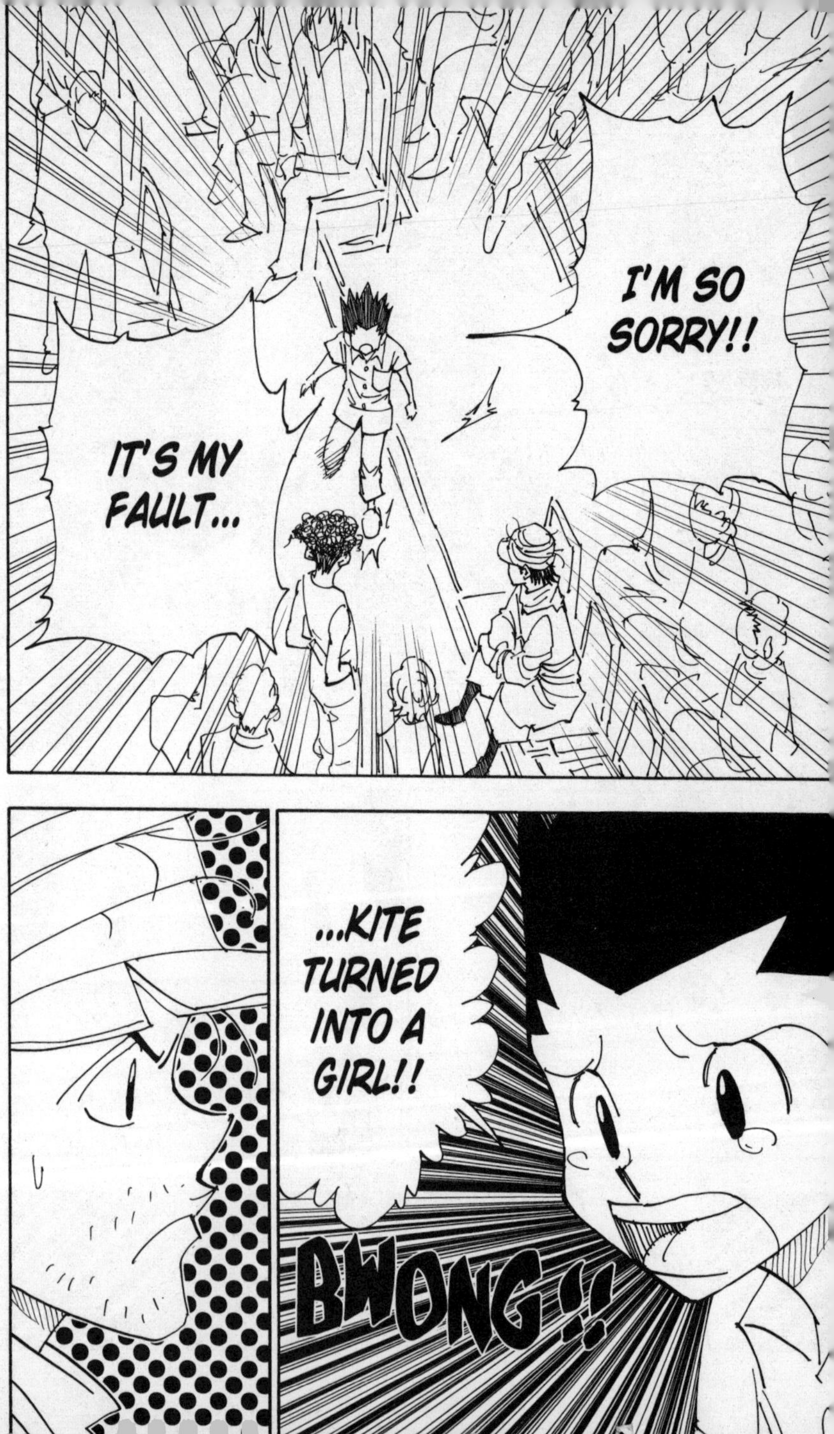
I'M SO SORRY!!
IT'S MY FAULT...
...KITE TURNED INTO A GIRL!!
BWONG!!

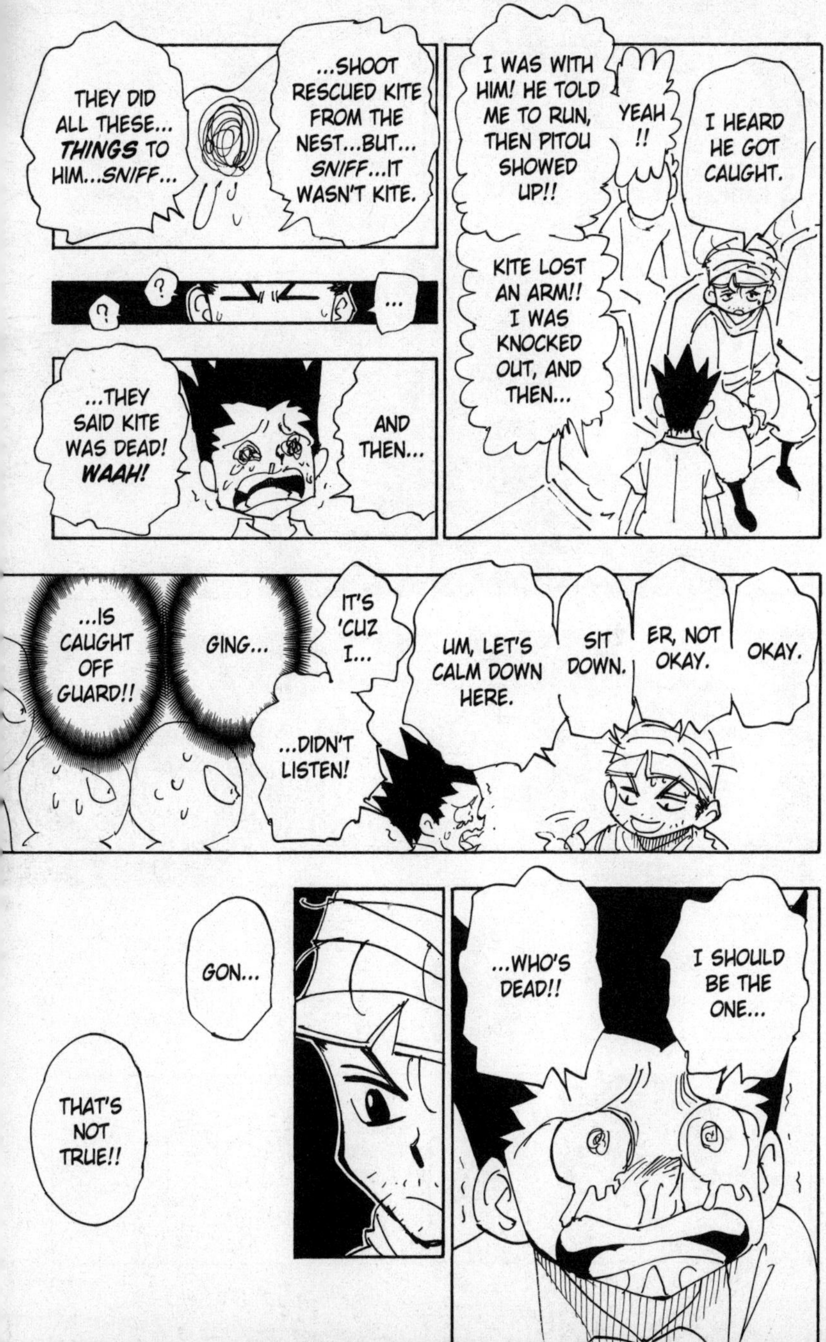
I HEARD HE GOT CAUGHT.
YEAH!!
I WAS WITH HIM! HE TOLD ME TO RUN, THEN PITOU SHOWED UP!!
KITE LOST AN ARM!! I WAS KNOCKED OUT, AND THEN...
...SHOOT RESCUED KITE FROM THE NEST...BUT... SNIFF...IT WASN'T KITE.
THEY DID ALL THESE... THINGS TO HIM...SNIFF...
...
?
?
AND THEN...
...THEY SAID KITE WAS DEAD! WAAH!
OKAY.
ER, NOT OKAY.
SIT DOWN.
UM, LET'S CALM DOWN HERE.
IT'S 'CUZ I...
...DIDN'T LISTEN!
GING...
...IS CAUGHT OFF GUARD!!
I SHOULD BE THE ONE...
...WHO'S DEAD!!
GON...
THAT'S NOT TRUE!!

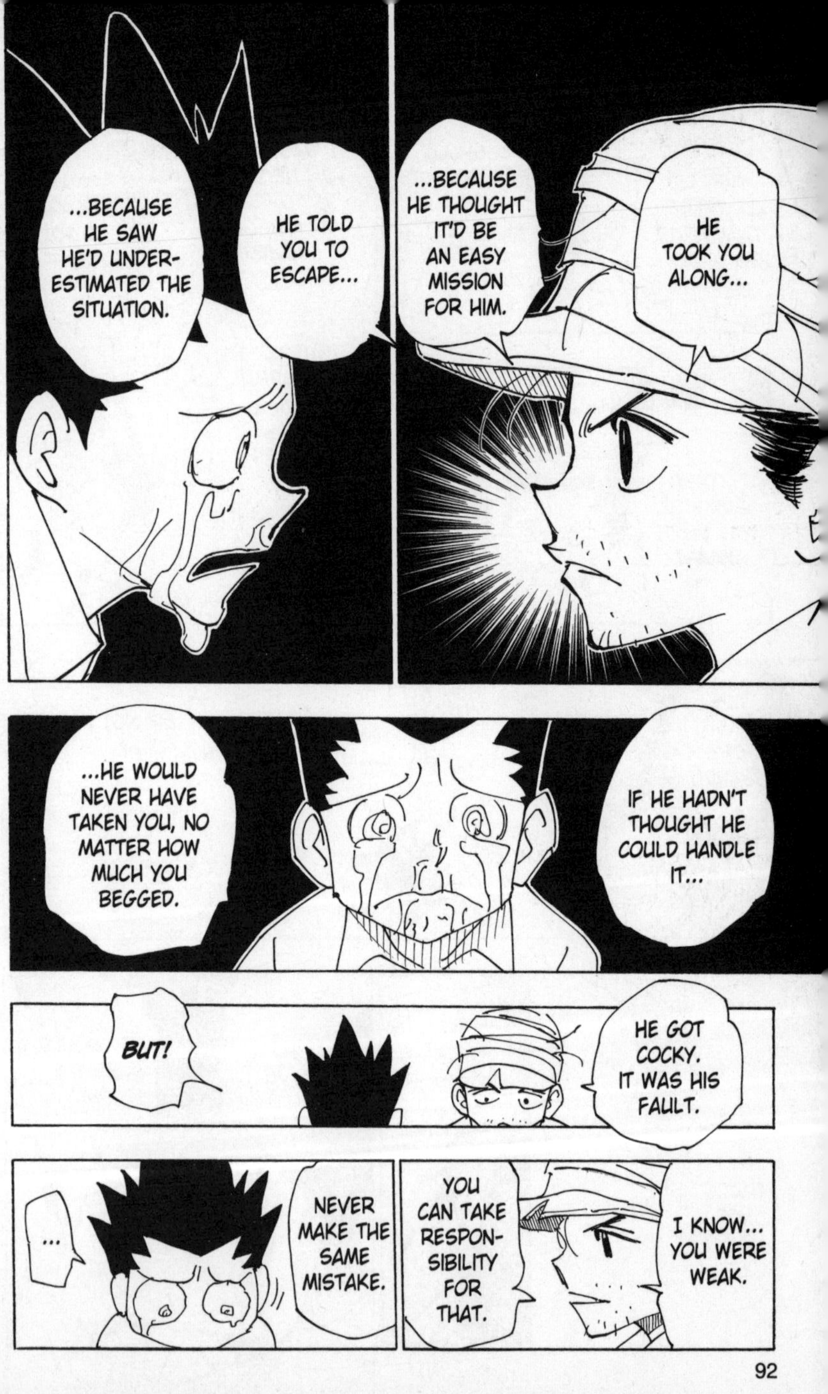
HE TOOK YOU ALONG...
...BECAUSE HE THOUGHT IT'D BE AN EASY MISSION FOR HIM.
HE TOLD YOU TO ESCAPE...
...BECAUSE HE SAW HE'D UNDER-ESTIMATED THE SITUATION.
IF HE HADN'T THOUGHT HE COULD HANDLE IT...
...HE WOULD NEVER HAVE TAKEN YOU, NO MATTER HOW MUCH YOU BEGGED.
HE GOT COCKY. IT WAS HIS FAULT.
BUT!
I KNOW... YOU WERE WEAK.
YOU CAN TAKE RESPON-SIBILITY FOR THAT.
NEVER MAKE THE SAME MISTAKE.
...

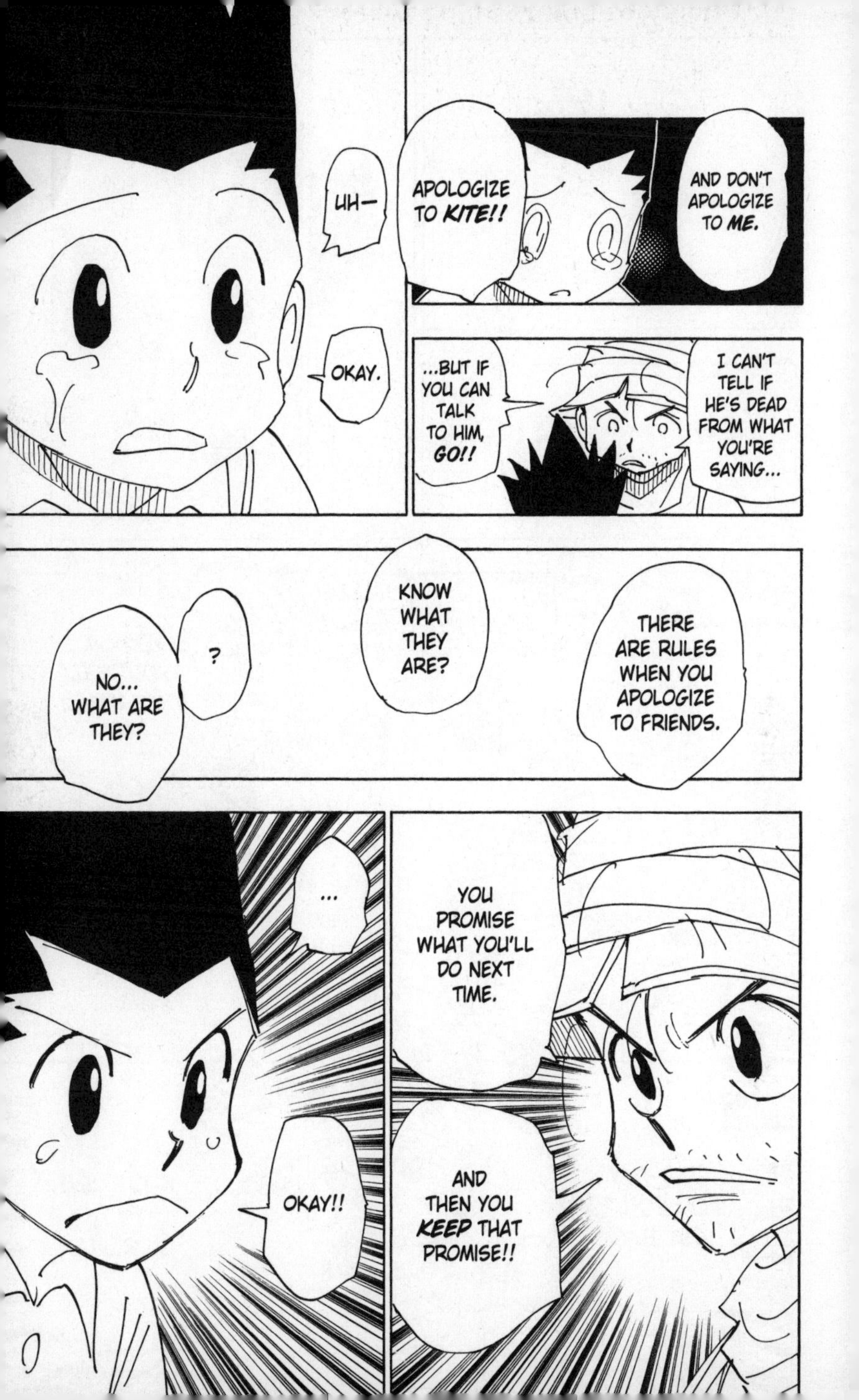
AND DON'T APOLOGIZE TO *ME.*
APOLOGIZE TO *KITE!!*
I CAN'T TELL IF HE'S DEAD FROM WHAT YOU'RE SAYING...
...BUT IF YOU CAN TALK TO HIM, *GO!!*
UH—
OKAY.
THERE ARE RULES WHEN YOU APOLOGIZE TO FRIENDS.
KNOW WHAT THEY ARE?
?
NO... WHAT ARE THEY?
YOU PROMISE WHAT YOU'LL DO NEXT TIME.
AND THEN YOU *KEEP* THAT PROMISE!!
...
OKAY!!

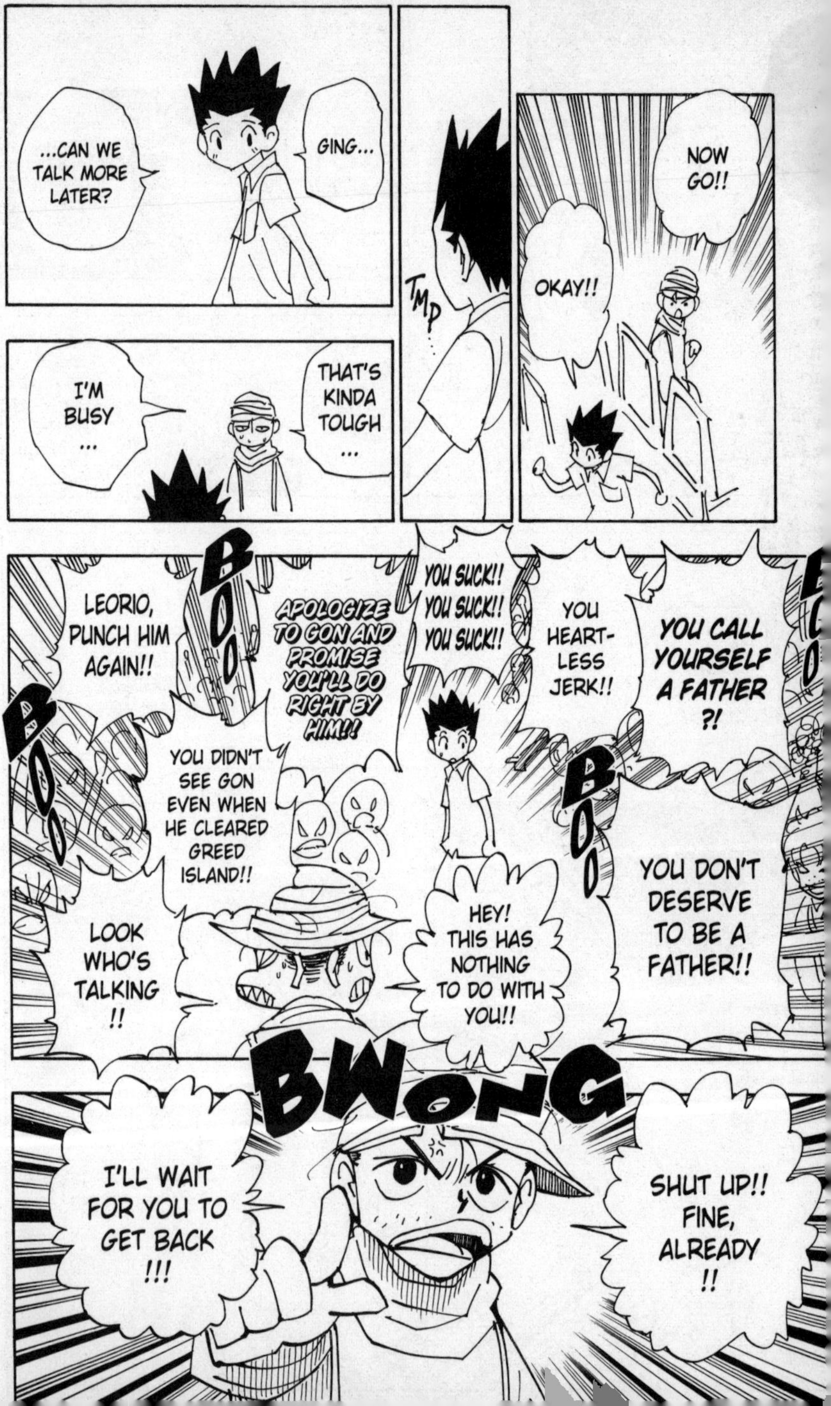
NOW GO!!
OKAY!!
TMP
GING...
...CAN WE TALK MORE LATER?
THAT'S KINDA TOUGH ...
I'M BUSY ...
YOU CALL YOURSELF A FATHER ?!
YOU HEART-LESS JERK!!
YOU SUCK!! YOU SUCK!! YOU SUCK!!
APOLOGIZE TO GON AND PROMISE YOU'LL DO RIGHT BY HIM!!
BOO
LEORIO, PUNCH HIM AGAIN!!
BOO
BOO
YOU DON'T DESERVE TO BE A FATHER!!
HEY! THIS HAS NOTHING TO DO WITH YOU!!
YOU DIDN'T SEE GON EVEN WHEN HE CLEARED GREED ISLAND!!
LOOK WHO'S TALKING !!
BWONG
SHUT UP!! FINE, ALREADY !!
I'LL WAIT FOR YOU TO GET BACK !!!

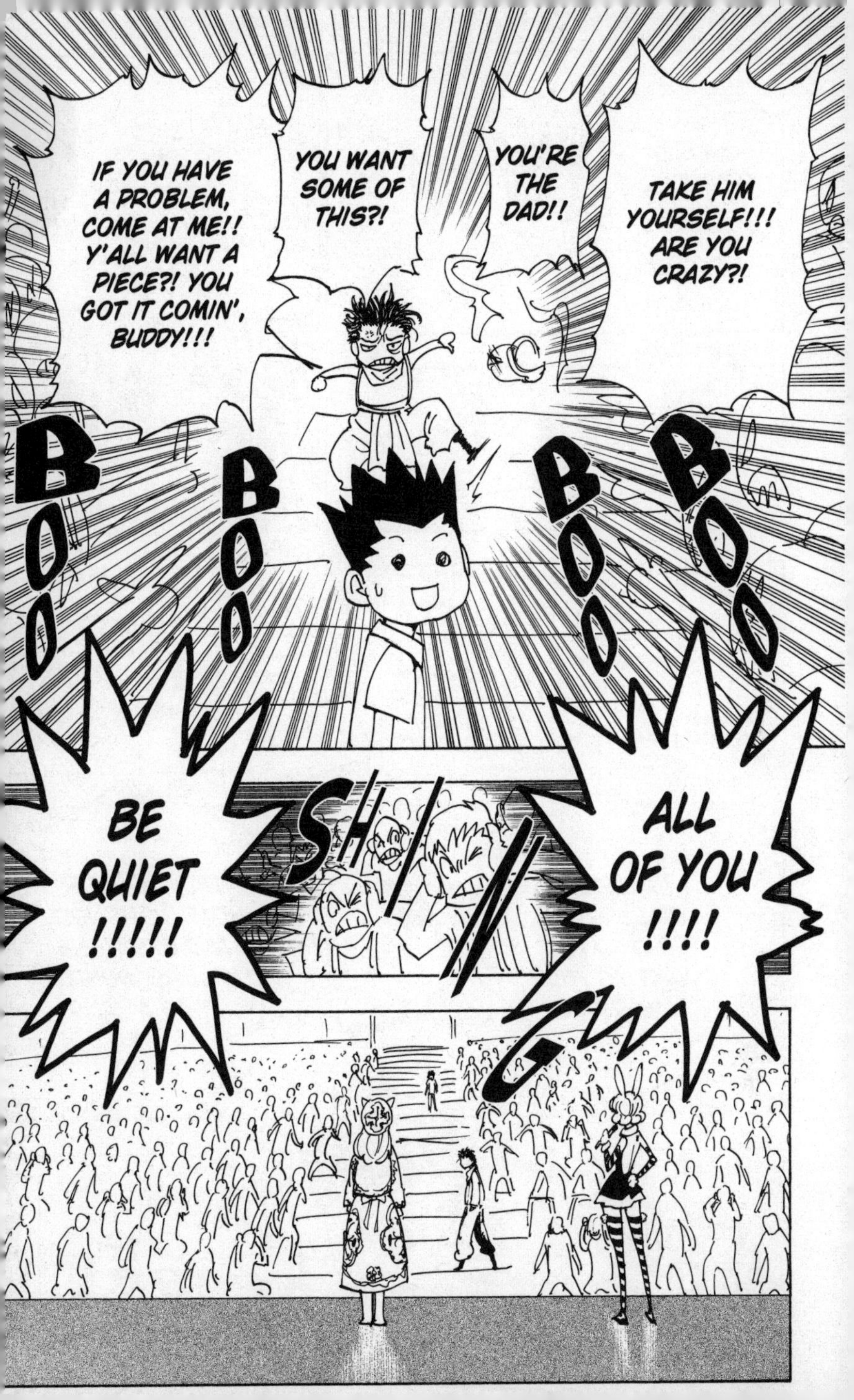
TAKE HIM YOURSELF!!! ARE YOU CRAZY?!
YOU'RE THE DAD!!
YOU WANT SOME OF THIS?!
IF YOU HAVE A PROBLEM, COME AT ME!! Y'ALL WANT A PIECE?! YOU GOT IT COMIN', BUDDY!!!
BOOO
BOOO
BOOO
BOOO
BE QUIET!!!!!
ALL OF YOU!!!!

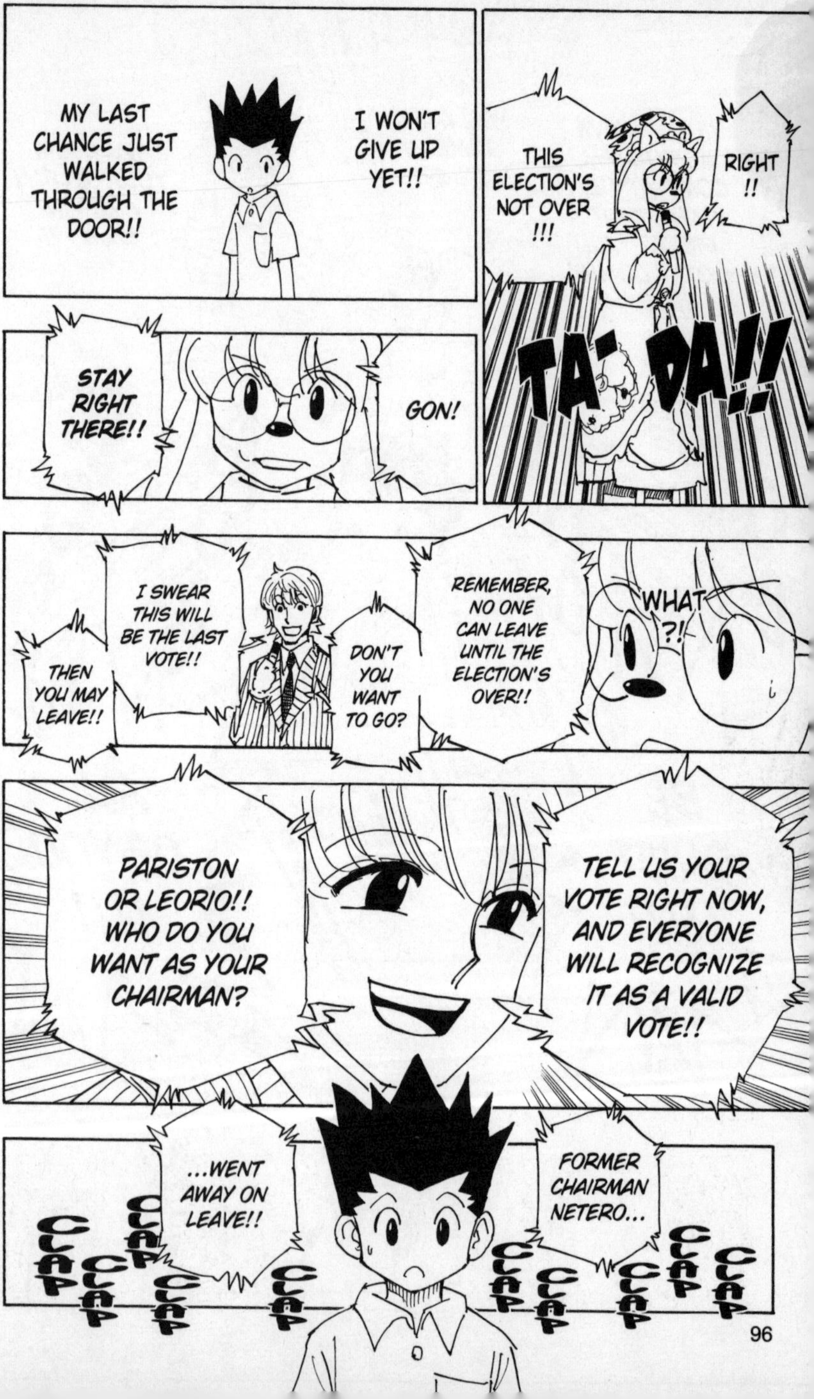
RIGHT !!
THIS ELECTION'S NOT OVER !!!
TA-DA!!
I WON'T GIVE UP YET!!
MY LAST CHANCE JUST WALKED THROUGH THE DOOR!!
GON!
STAY RIGHT THERE!!
WHAT?!
REMEMBER, NO ONE CAN LEAVE UNTIL THE ELECTION'S OVER!!
DON'T YOU WANT TO GO?
I SWEAR THIS WILL BE THE LAST VOTE!!
THEN YOU MAY LEAVE!!
TELL US YOUR VOTE RIGHT NOW, AND EVERYONE WILL RECOGNIZE IT AS A VALID VOTE!!
PARISTON OR LEORIO!! WHO DO YOU WANT AS YOUR CHAIRMAN?
FORMER CHAIRMAN NETERO...
...WENT AWAY ON LEAVE!!
CLAP CLAP CLAP

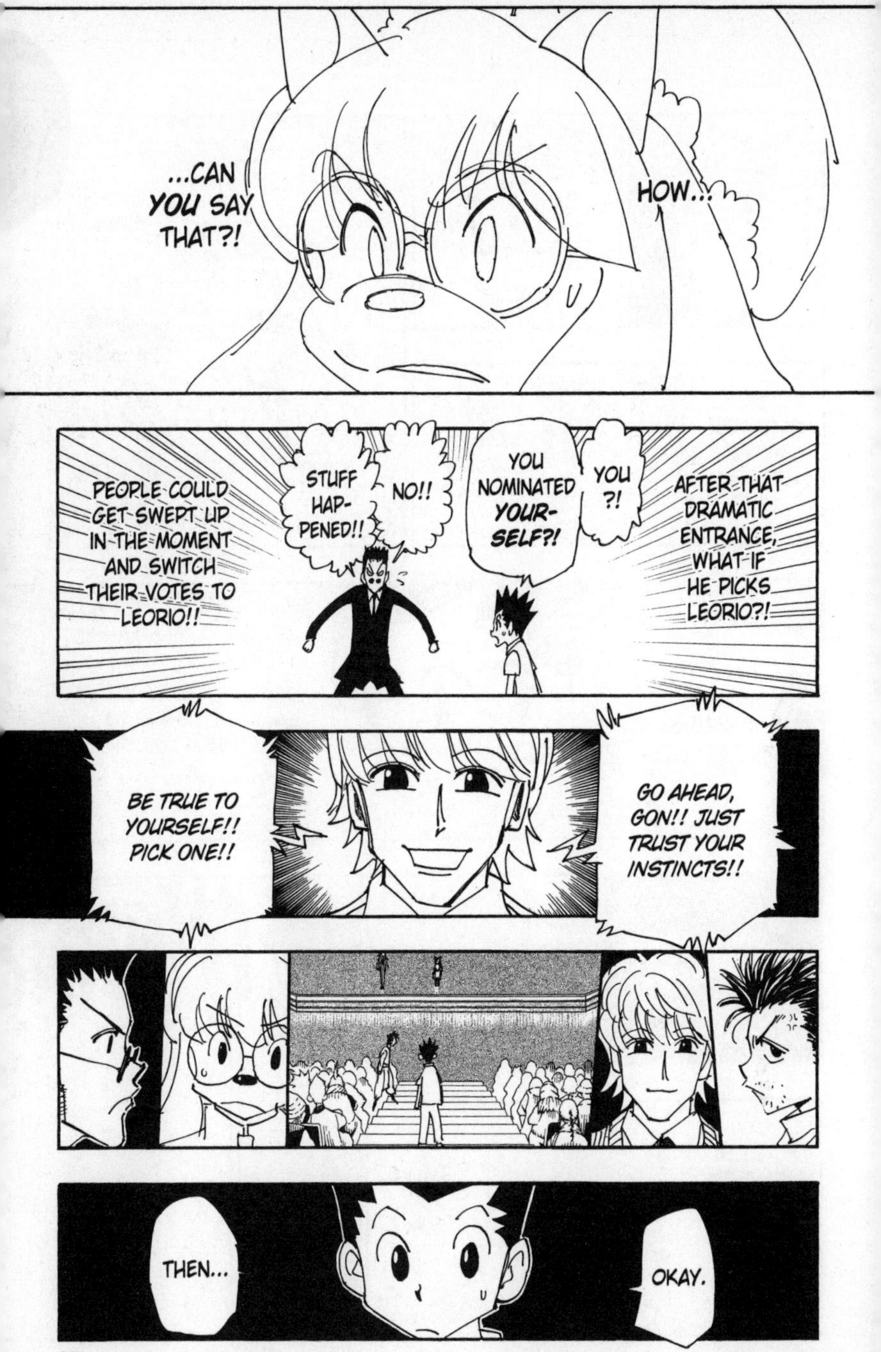
HOW...
...CAN YOU SAY THAT?!
AFTER THAT DRAMATIC ENTRANCE, WHAT IF HE PICKS LEORIO?!
YOU ?!
YOU NOMINATED YOURSELF?!
NO!!
STUFF HAPPENED!!
PEOPLE COULD GET SWEPT UP IN THE MOMENT AND SWITCH THEIR VOTES TO LEORIO!!
GO AHEAD, GON!! JUST TRUST YOUR INSTINCTS!!
BE TRUE TO YOURSELF!! PICK ONE!!
OKAY.
THEN...

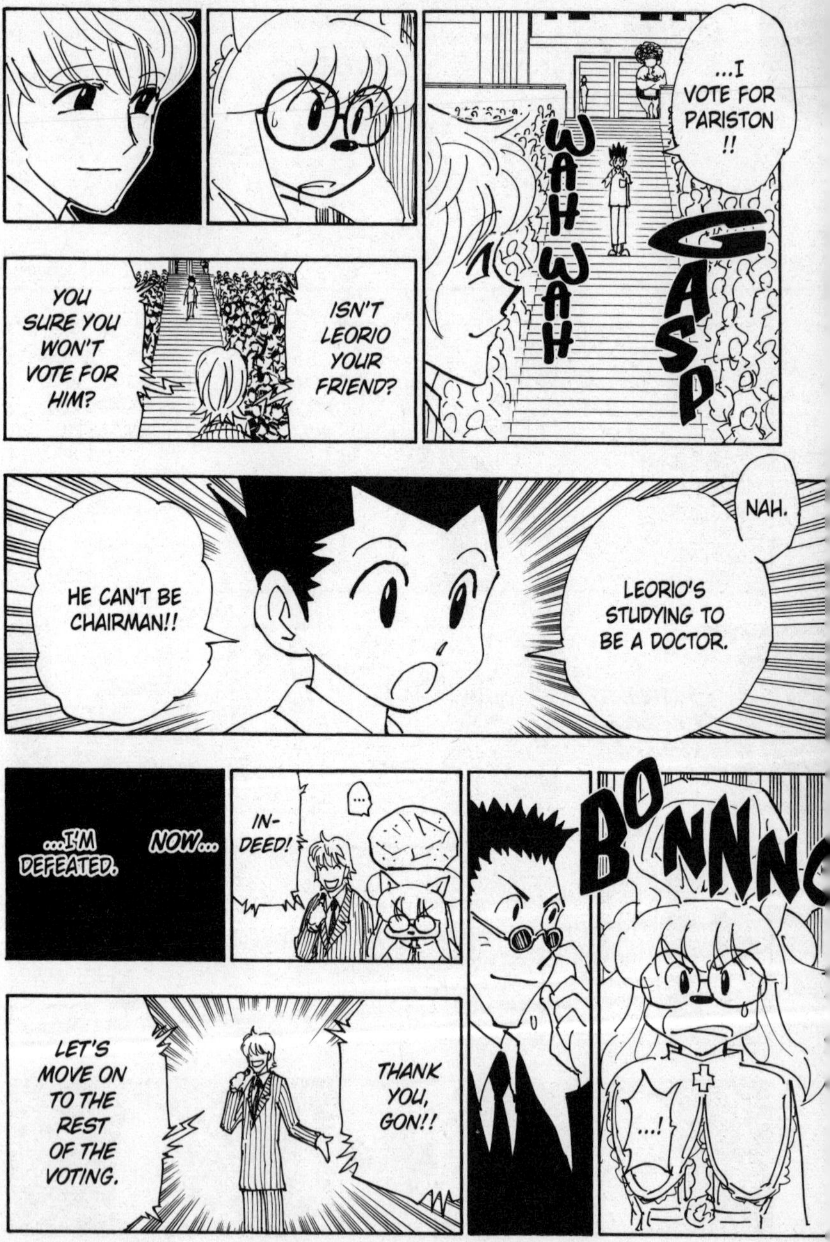
...I VOTE FOR PARISTON !!
GASP
WAH WAH
ISN'T LEORIO YOUR FRIEND?
YOU SURE YOU WON'T VOTE FOR HIM?
NAH.
LEORIO'S STUDYING TO BE A DOCTOR.
HE CAN'T BE CHAIRMAN!!
BONNN
...!
...
IN-DEED!
NOW...
...I'M DEFEATED.
THANK YOU, GON!!
LET'S MOVE ON TO THE REST OF THE VOTING.

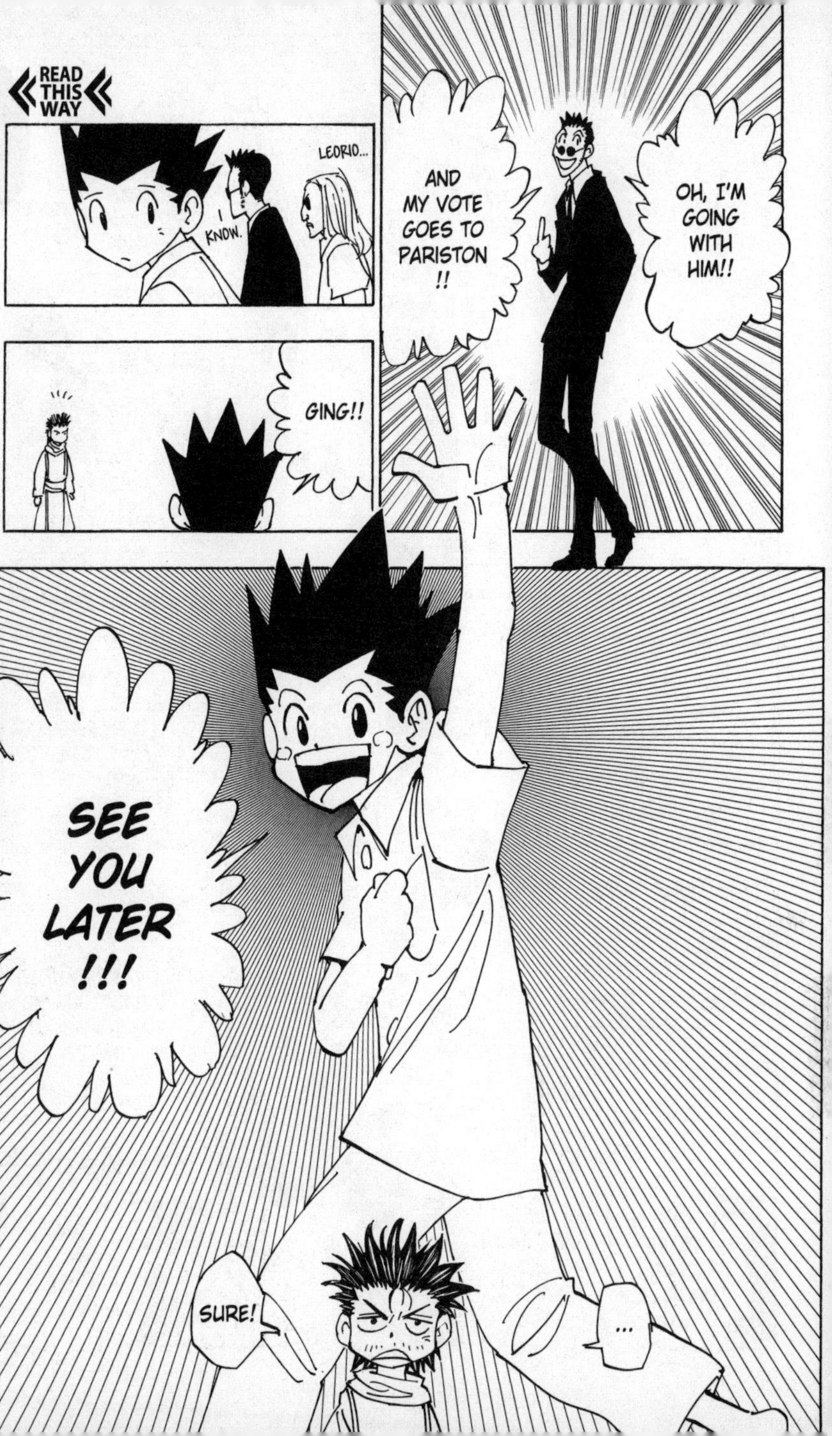
READ THIS WAY
OH, I'M GOING WITH HIM!!
AND MY VOTE GOES TO PARISTON !!
LEORIO...
I KNOW.
GING!!
SEE YOU LATER !!!
...
SURE!

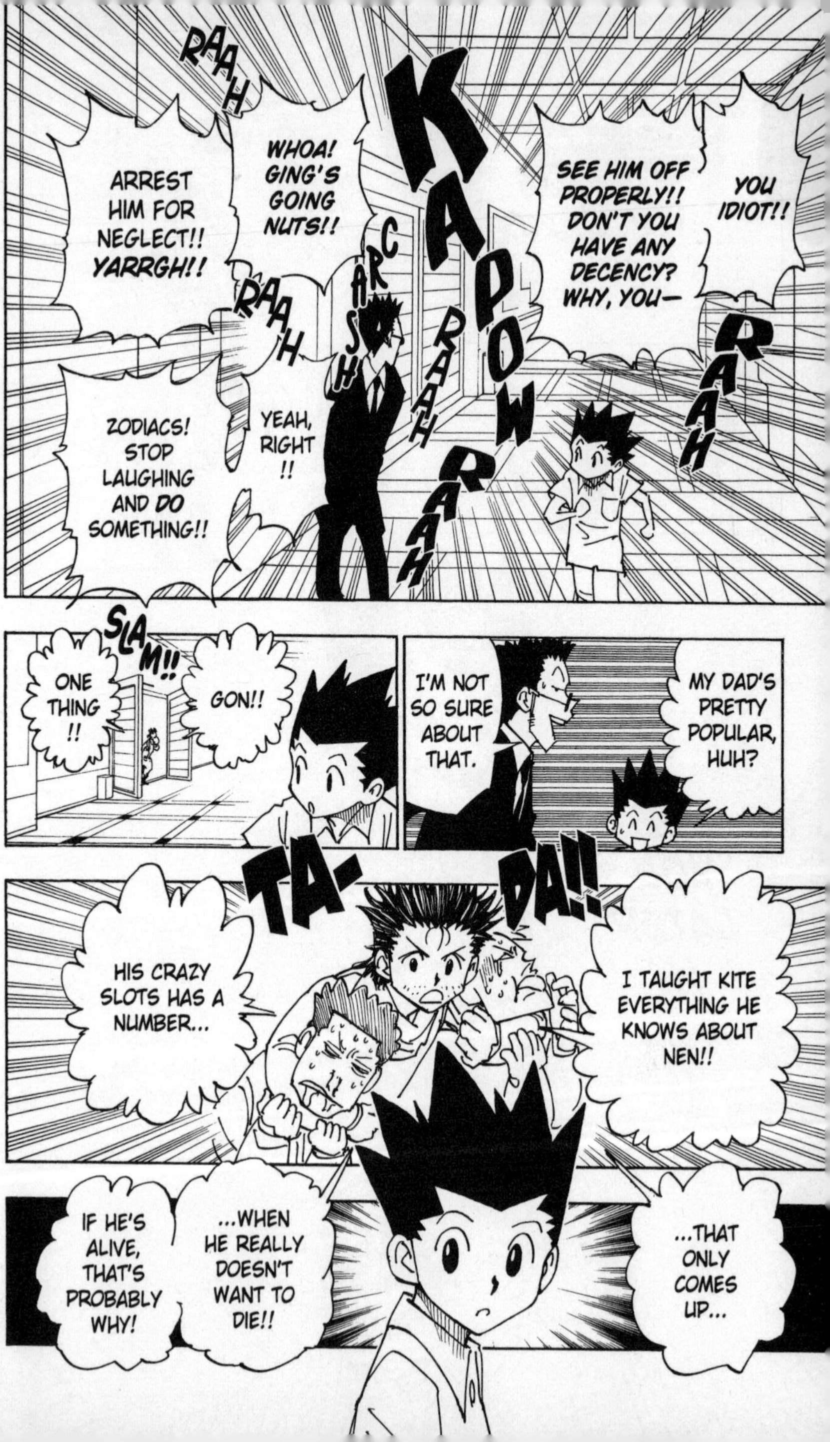

YOU IDIOT!!
SEE HIM OFF PROPERLY!! DON'T YOU HAVE ANY DECENCY? WHY, YOU—
RAAH
KAPOW
WHOA! GING'S GOING NUTS!!
RAAH
ARREST HIM FOR NEGLECT!! YARRGH!!
RAAH
RAAH
RAAH
YEAH, RIGHT!!
ZODIACS! STOP LAUGHING AND DO SOMETHING!!
MY DAD'S PRETTY POPULAR, HUH?
I'M NOT SO SURE ABOUT THAT.
SLAM!!
GON!!
ONE THING!!
TA-DA!!
I TAUGHT KITE EVERYTHING HE KNOWS ABOUT NEN!!
HIS CRAZY SLOTS HAS A NUMBER...
...THAT ONLY COMES UP...
...WHEN HE REALLY DOESN'T WANT TO DIE!!
IF HE'S ALIVE, THAT'S PROBABLY WHY!

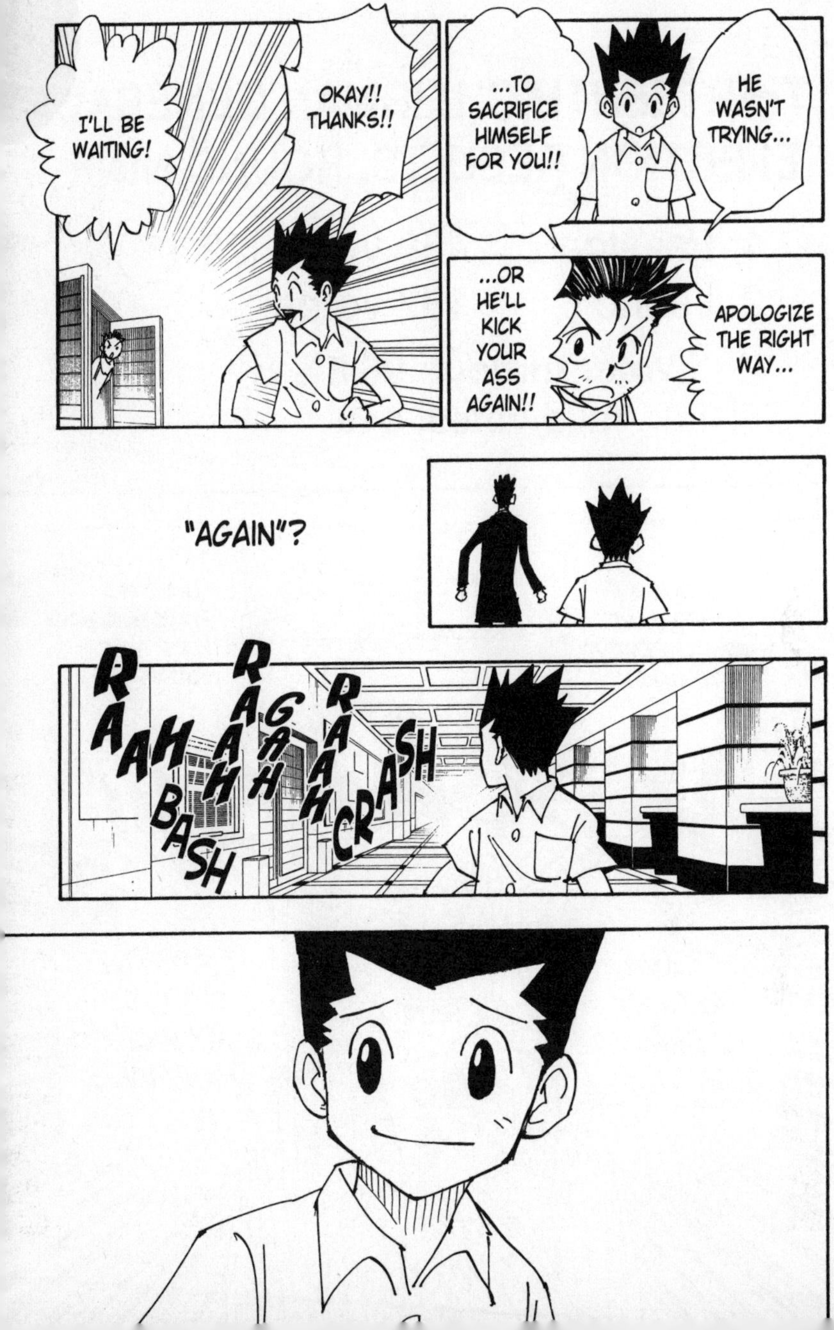
HE WASN'T TRYING...
...TO SACRIFICE HIMSELF FOR YOU!!
APOLOGIZE THE RIGHT WAY...
...OR HE'LL KICK YOUR ASS AGAIN!!
OKAY!! THANKS!!
I'LL BE WAITING!
"AGAIN"?
CRASH
RAAAH
GAAH
RAAAH
RAAAH
BASH

THIRTEENTH CHAIRMAN GENERAL ELECTION RESULTS, ROUND NINE

1: Pariston **458 votes** (72.1%)
2: Leorio **157 votes**

Voter turnout: 96.8%
Valid votes: 615

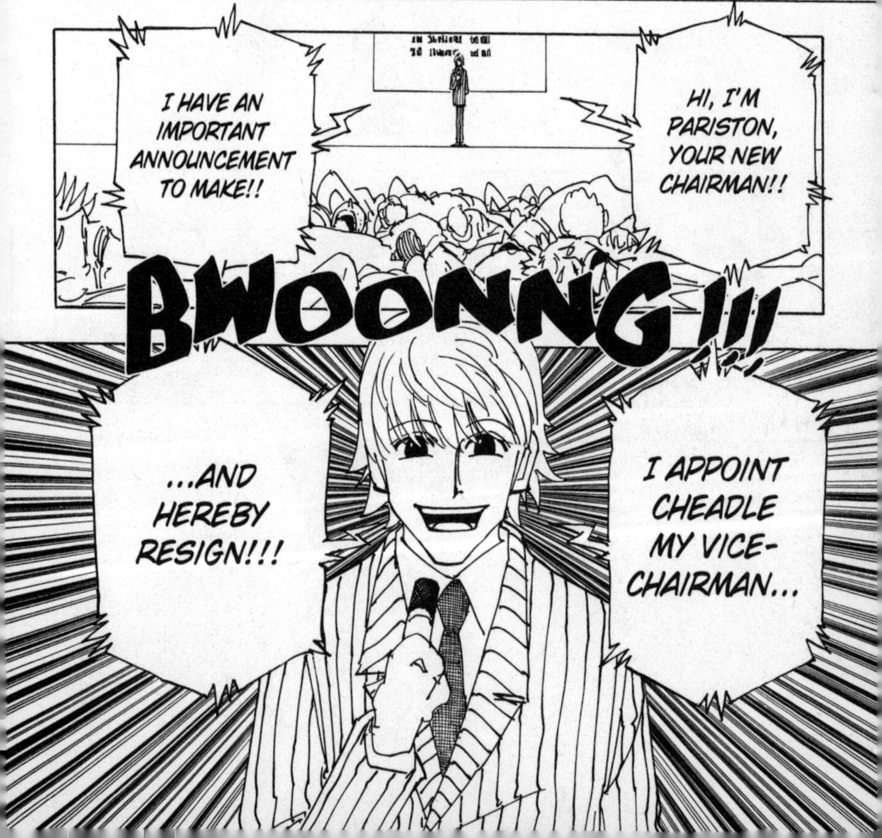
HI, I'M PARISTON, YOUR NEW CHAIRMAN!!
I HAVE AN IMPORTANT ANNOUNCEMENT TO MAKE!!
BWOONNG!!!
I APPOINT CHEADLE MY VICE-CHAIRMAN...
...AND HEREBY RESIGN!!!

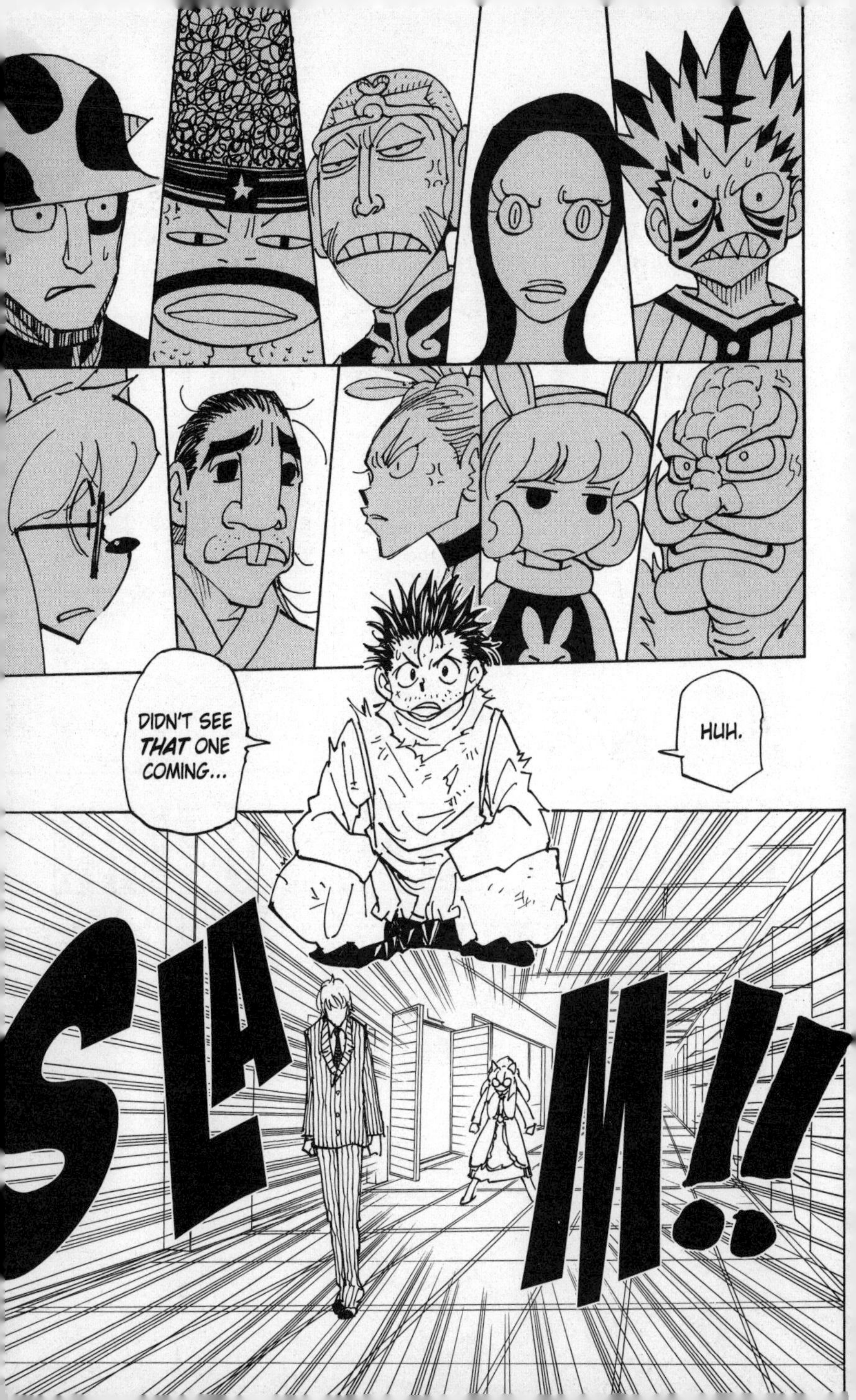
HUH.
DIDN'T SEE THAT ONE COMING...
SLAM!!

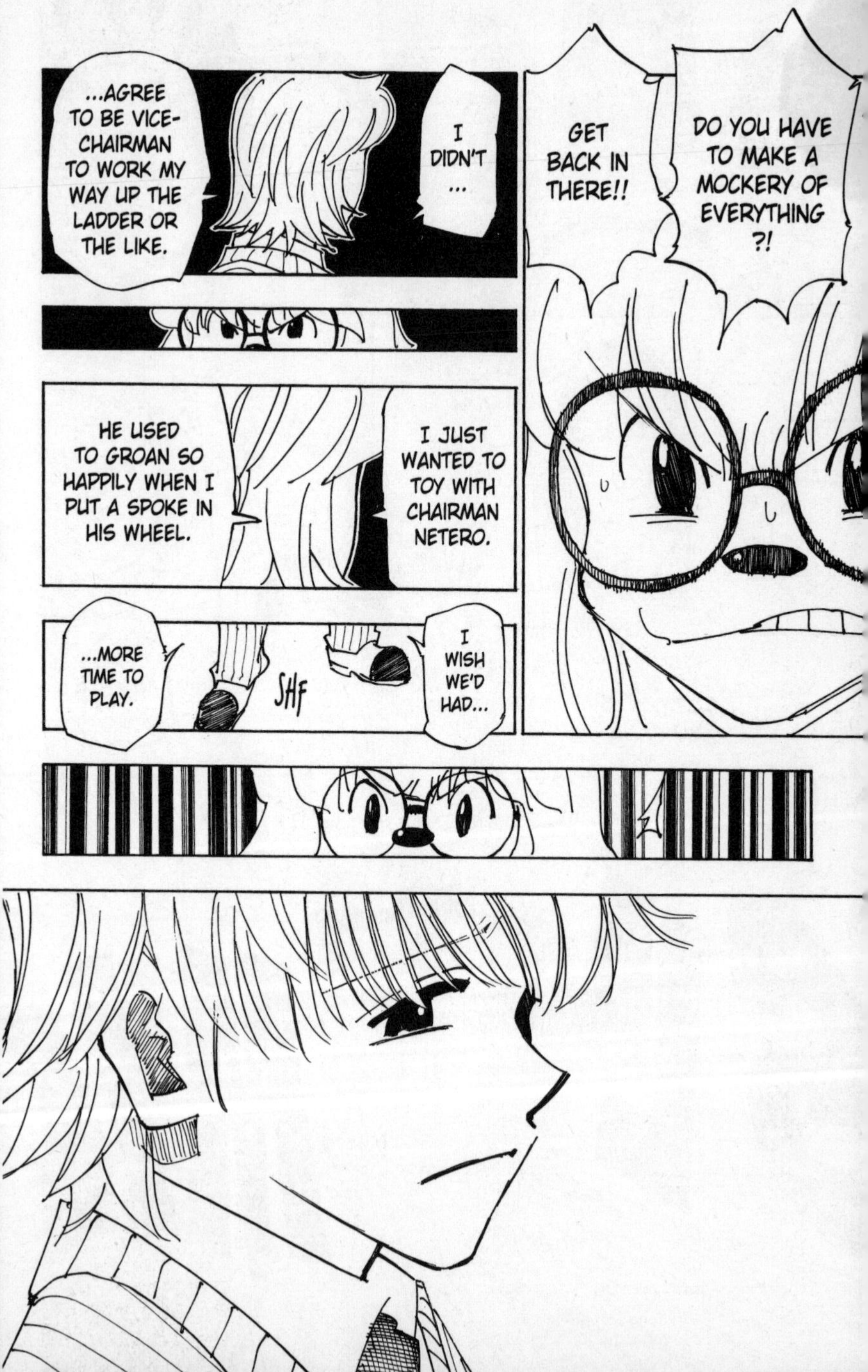
DO YOU HAVE TO MAKE A MOCKERY OF EVERYTHING ?!
GET BACK IN THERE!!
I DIDN'T ...
...AGREE TO BE VICE-CHAIRMAN TO WORK MY WAY UP THE LADDER OR THE LIKE.
I JUST WANTED TO TOY WITH CHAIRMAN NETERO.
HE USED TO GROAN SO HAPPILY WHEN I PUT A SPOKE IN HIS WHEEL.
I WISH WE'D HAD...
SHF
...MORE TIME TO PLAY.

READ THIS WAY

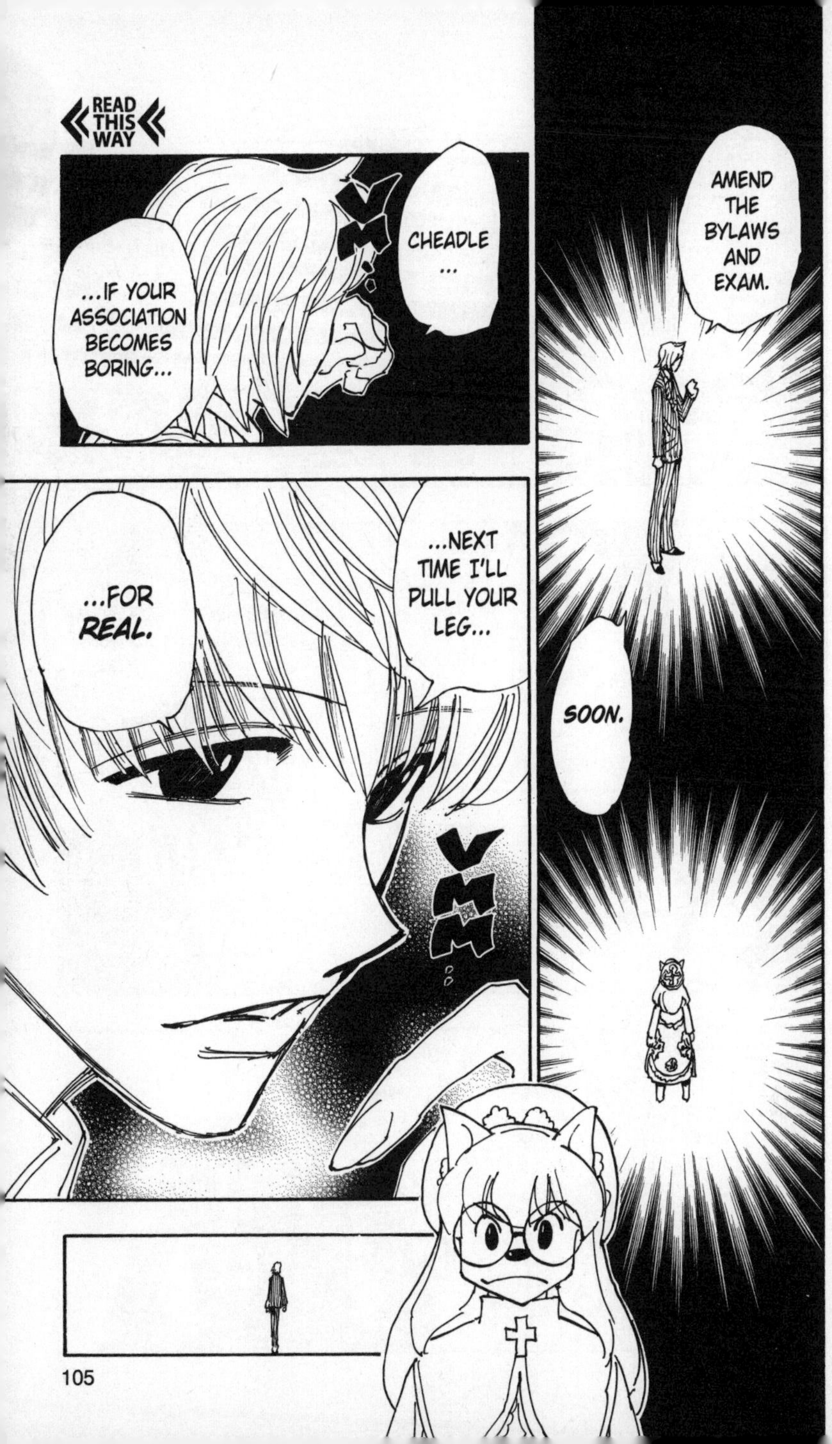

AMEND THE BYLAWS AND EXAM.
SOON.
CHEADLE ...
...IF YOUR ASSOCIATION BECOMES BORING...
...NEXT TIME I'LL PULL YOUR LEG...
...FOR REAL.
VMM

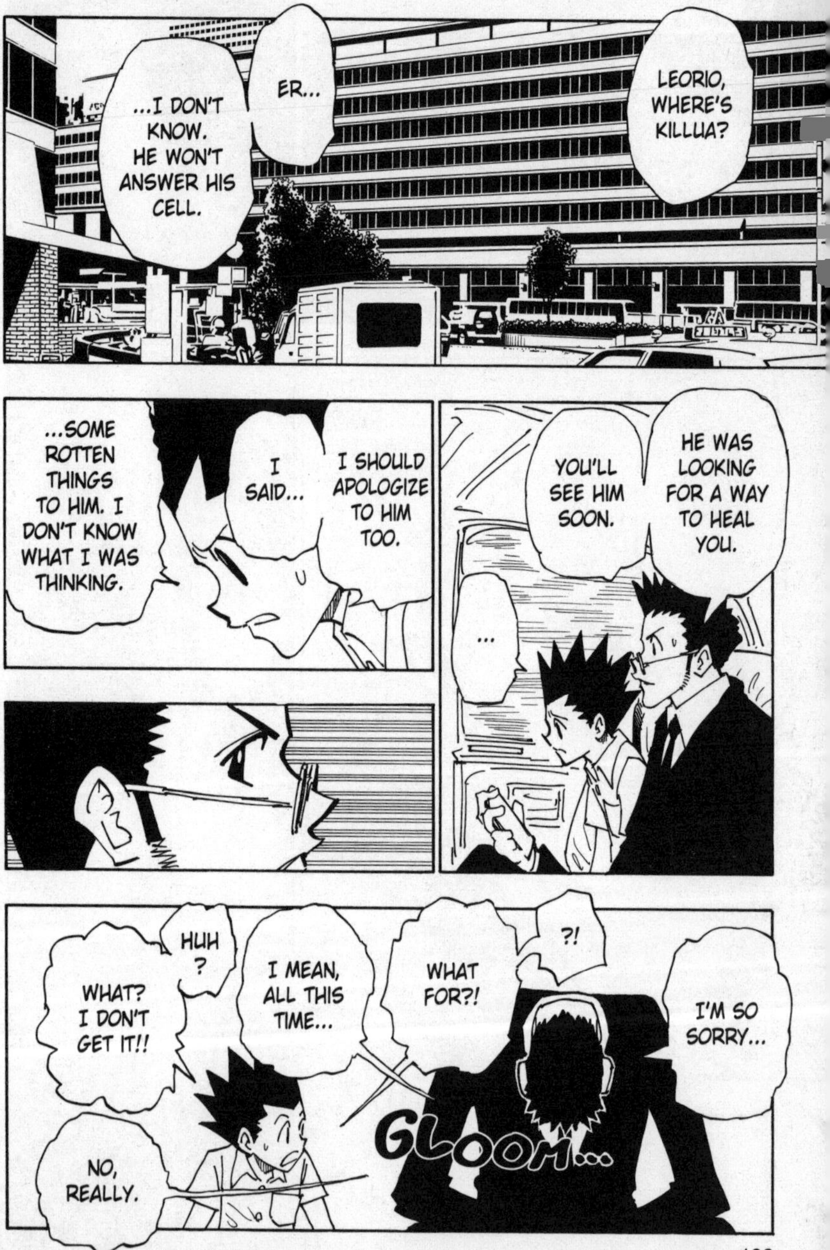
LEORIO, WHERE'S KILLUA?
ER...
...I DON'T KNOW. HE WON'T ANSWER HIS CELL.
HE WAS LOOKING FOR A WAY TO HEAL YOU.
YOU'LL SEE HIM SOON.
...
I SHOULD APOLOGIZE TO HIM TOO.
I SAID...
...SOME ROTTEN THINGS TO HIM. I DON'T KNOW WHAT I WAS THINKING.
I'M SO SORRY...
?!
WHAT FOR?!
I MEAN, ALL THIS TIME...
HUH?
WHAT? I DON'T GET IT!!
GLOOM...
NO, REALLY.

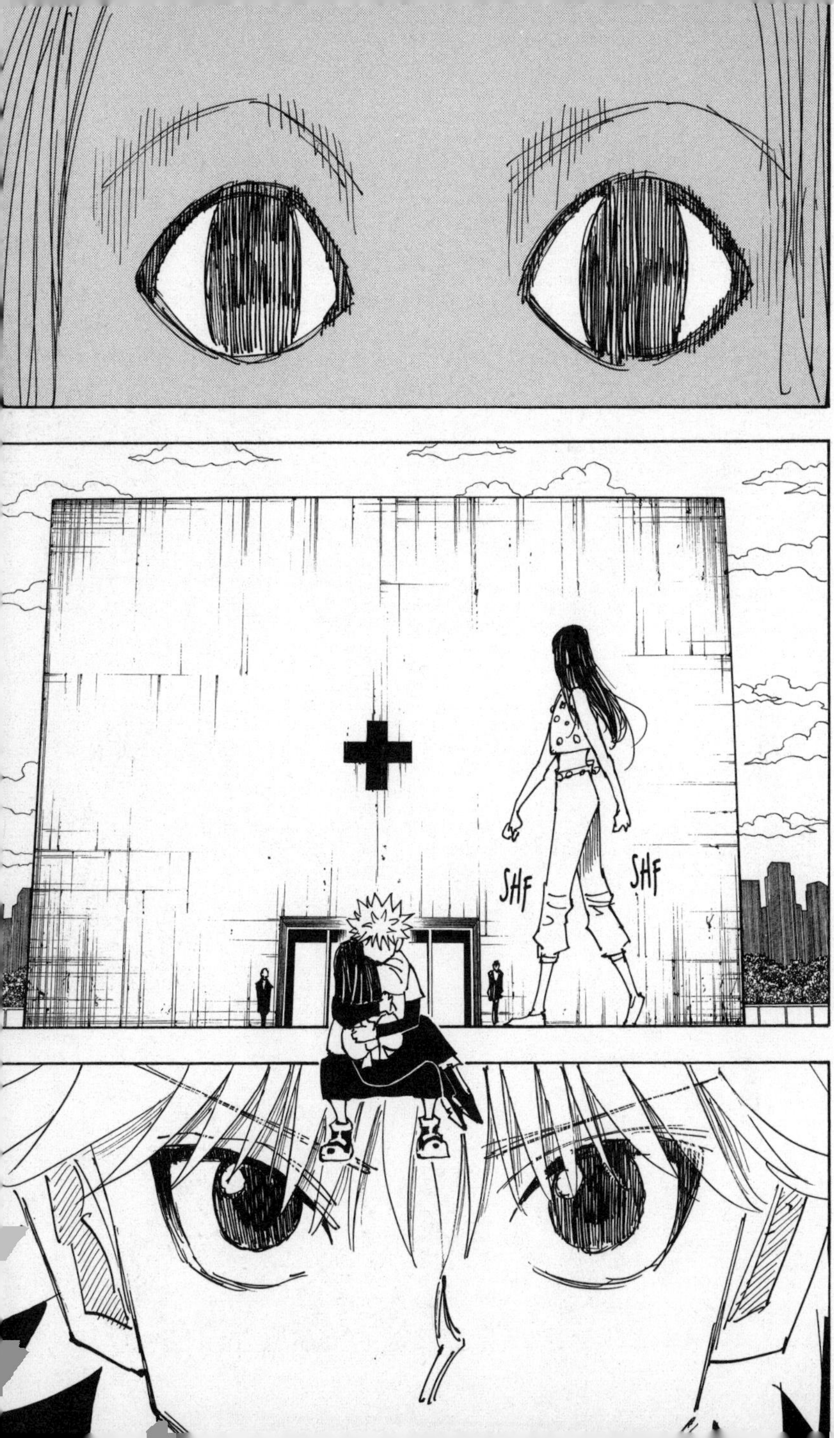
SHF
SHF

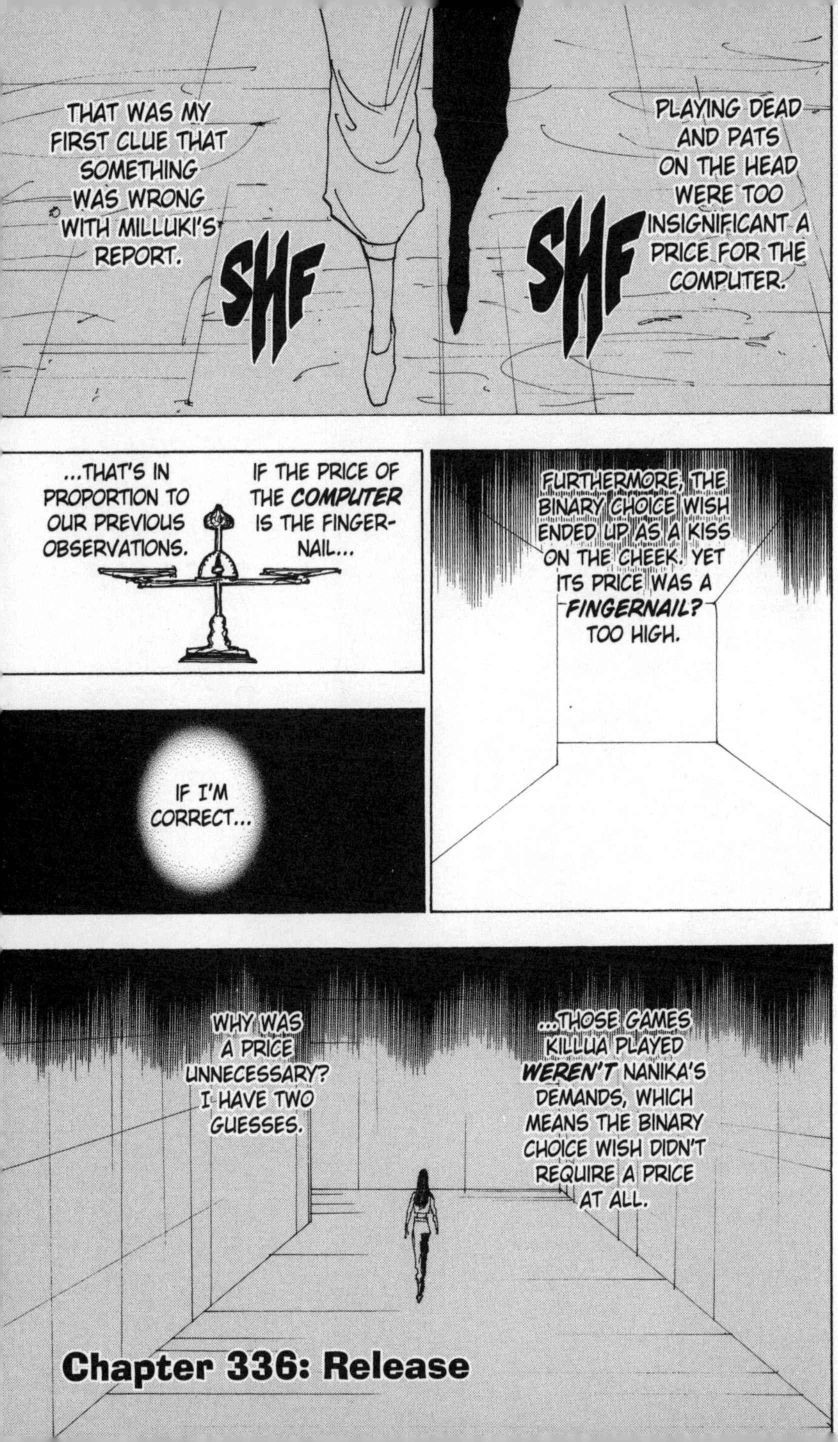
PLAYING DEAD AND PATS ON THE HEAD WERE TOO INSIGNIFICANT A PRICE FOR THE COMPUTER.
THAT WAS MY FIRST CLUE THAT SOMETHING WAS WRONG WITH MILLUKI'S REPORT.
SHF
SHF
FURTHERMORE, THE BINARY CHOICE WISH ENDED UP AS A KISS ON THE CHEEK. YET ITS PRICE WAS A *FINGERNAIL?* TOO HIGH.
IF THE PRICE OF THE *COMPUTER* IS THE FINGERNAIL...
...THAT'S IN PROPORTION TO OUR PREVIOUS OBSERVATIONS.
IF I'M CORRECT...
...THOSE GAMES KILLUA PLAYED *WEREN'T* NANIKA'S DEMANDS, WHICH MEANS THE BINARY CHOICE WISH DIDN'T REQUIRE A PRICE AT ALL.
WHY WAS A PRICE UNNECESSARY? I HAVE TWO GUESSES.
Chapter 336: Release

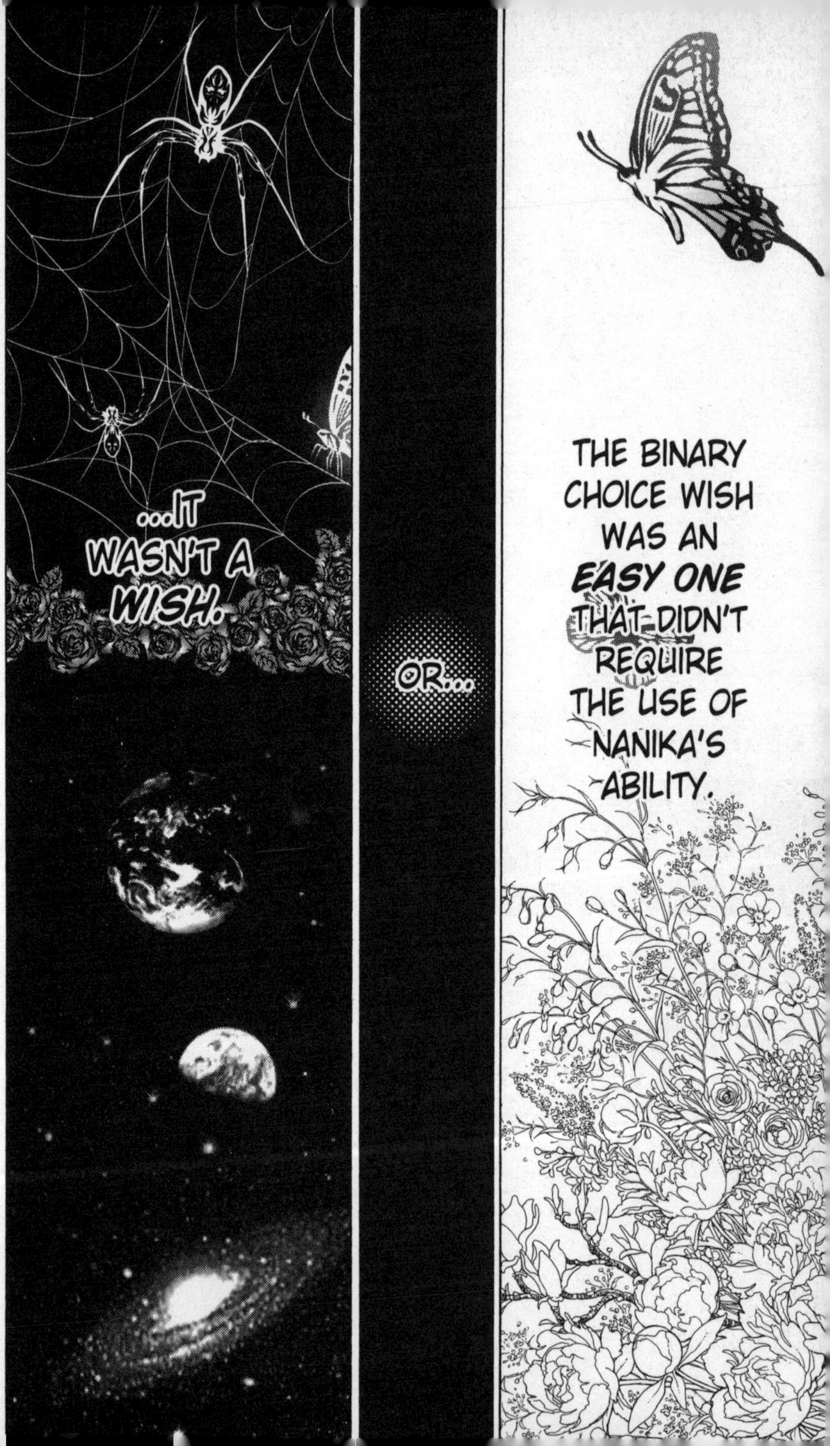
THE BINARY CHOICE WISH WAS AN *EASY ONE* THAT DIDN'T REQUIRE THE USE OF NANIKA'S ABILITY.
OR...
...IT WASN'T A WISH.

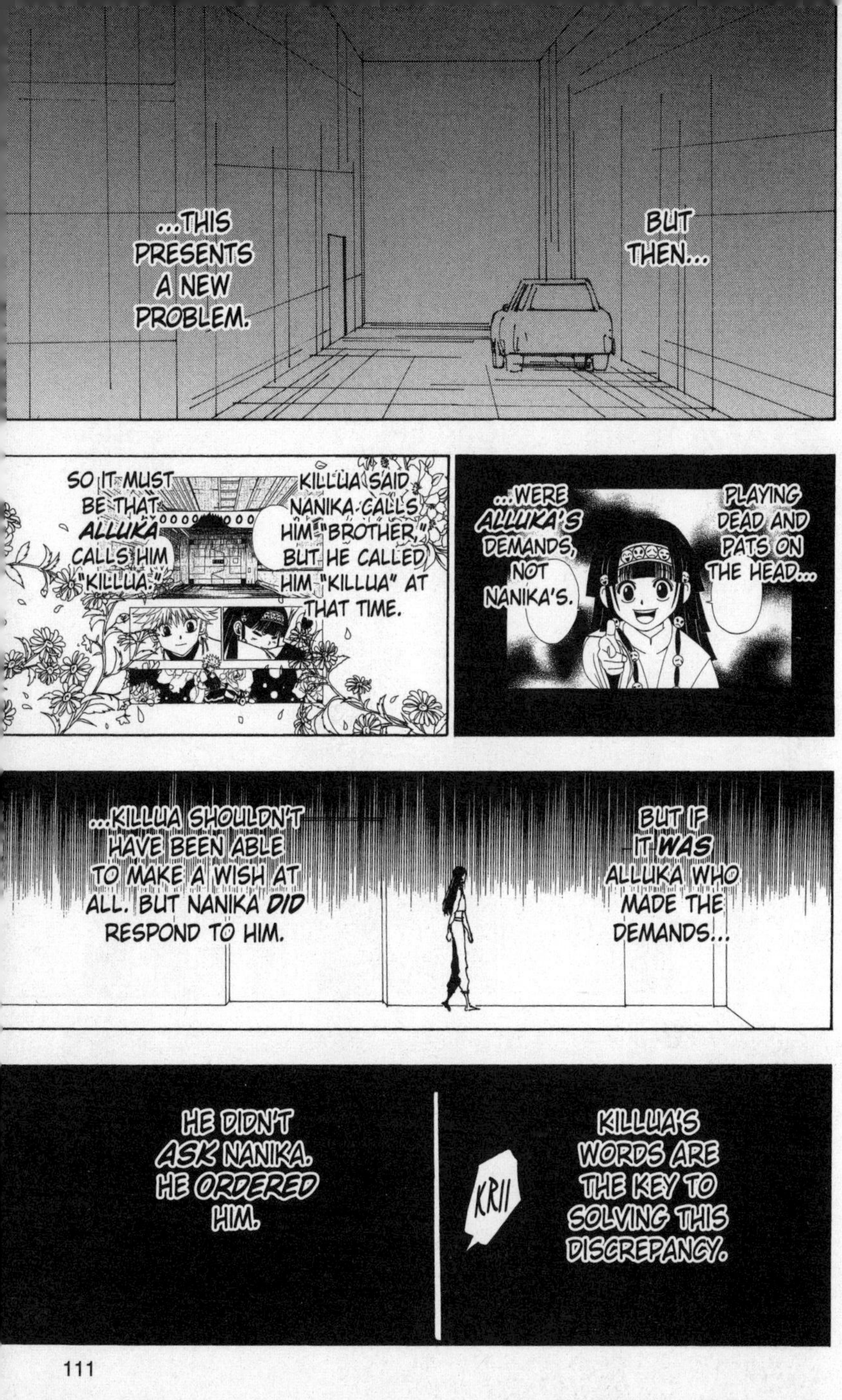
BUT THEN...
...THIS PRESENTS A NEW PROBLEM.
PLAYING DEAD AND PATS ON THE HEAD...
...WERE ALLUKA'S DEMANDS, NOT NANIKA'S.
KILLUA SAID NANIKA CALLS HIM "BROTHER," BUT HE CALLED HIM "KILLUA" AT THAT TIME.
SO IT MUST BE THAT ALLUKA CALLS HIM "KILLUA."
BUT IF IT WAS ALLUKA WHO MADE THE DEMANDS...
...KILLUA SHOULDN'T HAVE BEEN ABLE TO MAKE A WISH AT ALL. BUT NANIKA DID RESPOND TO HIM.
KILLUA'S WORDS ARE THE KEY TO SOLVING THIS DISCREPANCY.
KRII
HE DIDN'T ASK NANIKA. HE ORDERED HIM.

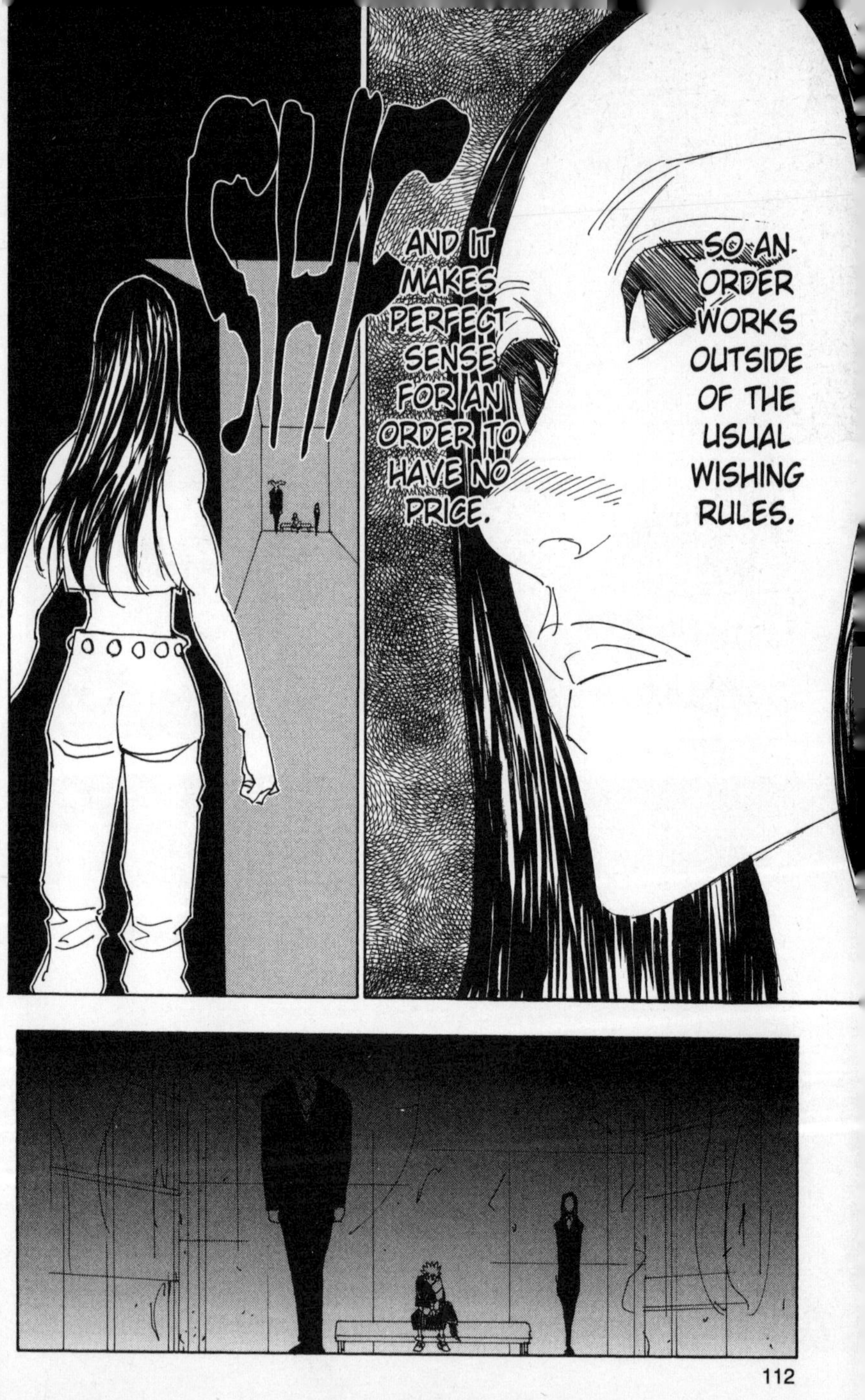
SO AN ORDER WORKS OUTSIDE OF THE USUAL WISHING RULES.
AND IT MAKES PERFECT SENSE FOR AN ORDER TO HAVE NO PRICE.

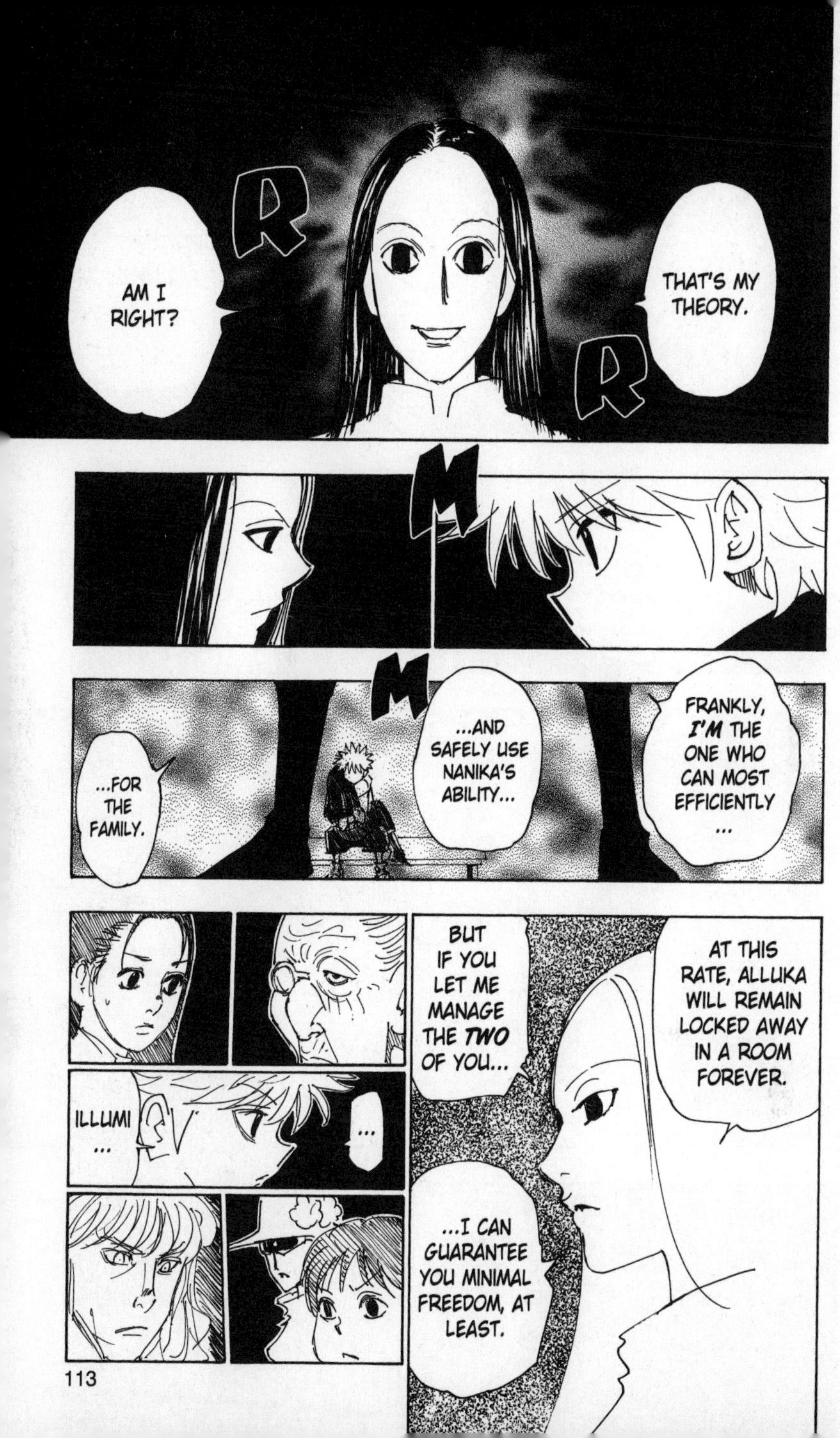
THAT'S MY THEORY.
R
R
AM I RIGHT?
M
FRANKLY, *I'M* THE ONE WHO CAN MOST EFFICIENTLY ...
...AND SAFELY USE NANIKA'S ABILITY...
M
...FOR THE FAMILY.
AT THIS RATE, ALLUKA WILL REMAIN LOCKED AWAY IN A ROOM FOREVER.
BUT IF YOU LET ME MANAGE THE *TWO* OF YOU...
...I CAN GUARANTEE YOU MINIMAL FREEDOM, AT LEAST.
...
ILLUMI ...

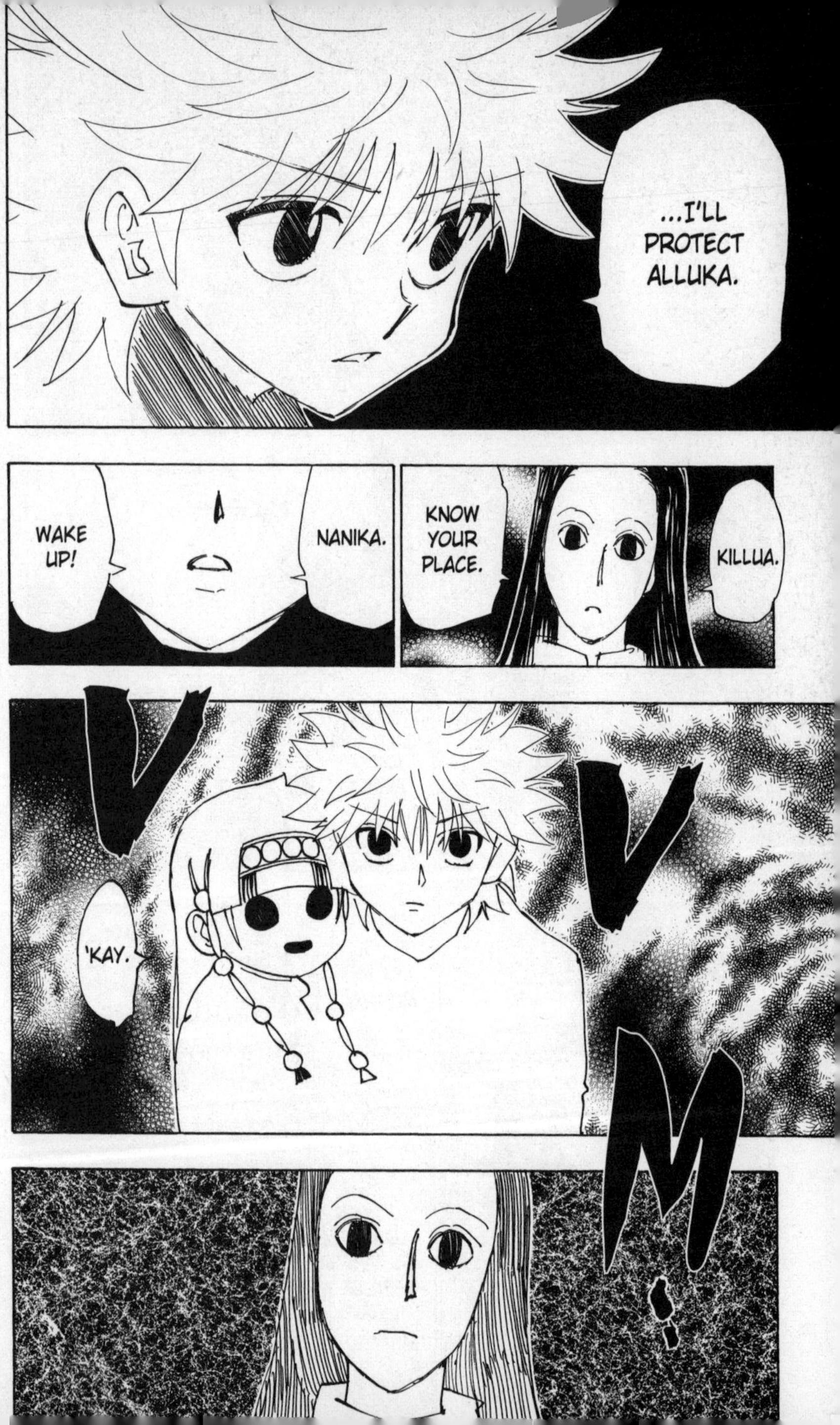
...I'LL PROTECT ALLUKA.
KILLUA.
KNOW YOUR PLACE.
NANIKA.
WAKE UP!
VVM
'KAY.

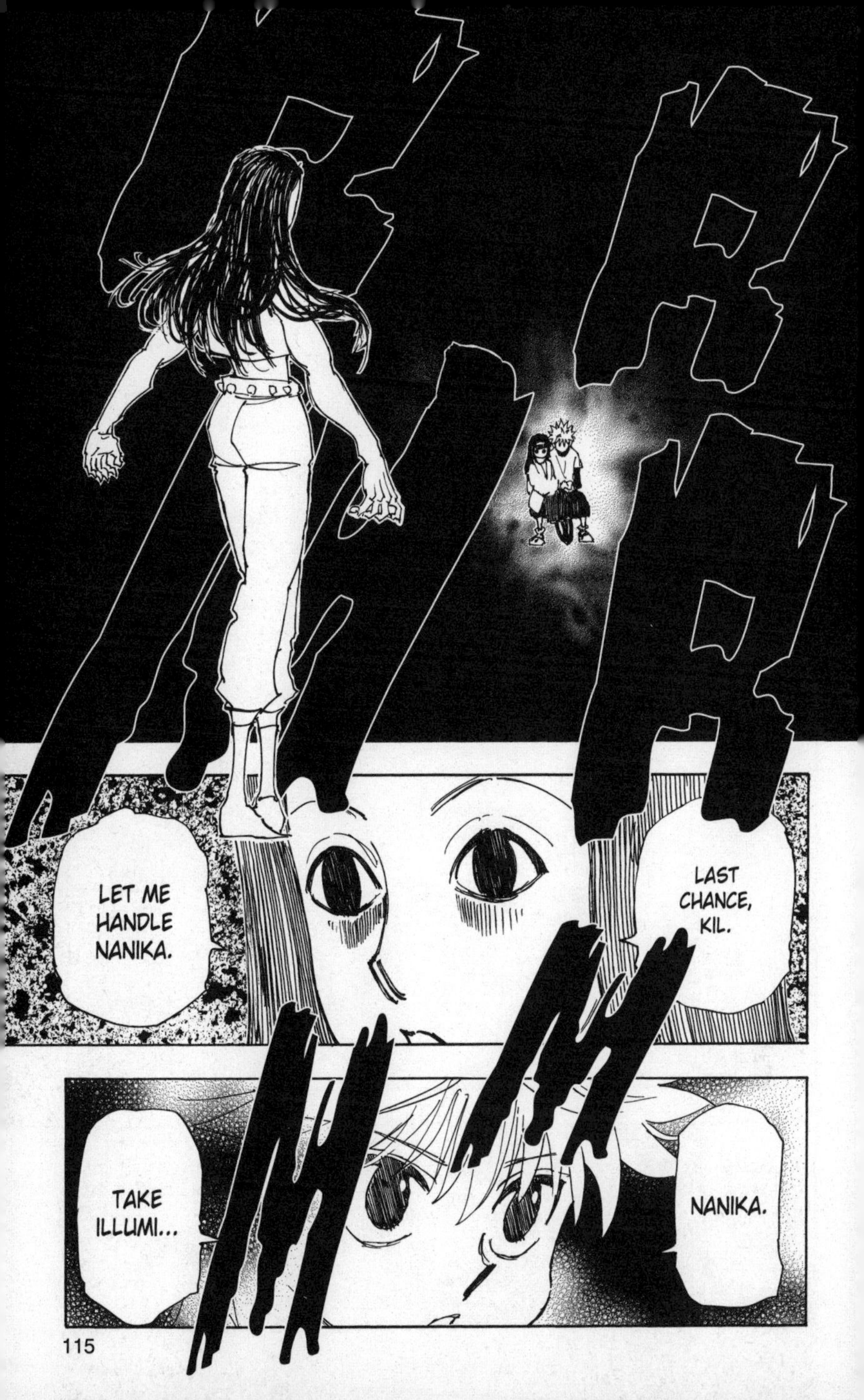
LAST CHANCE, KIL.
LET ME HANDLE NANIKA.
NANIKA.
TAKE ILLUMI...

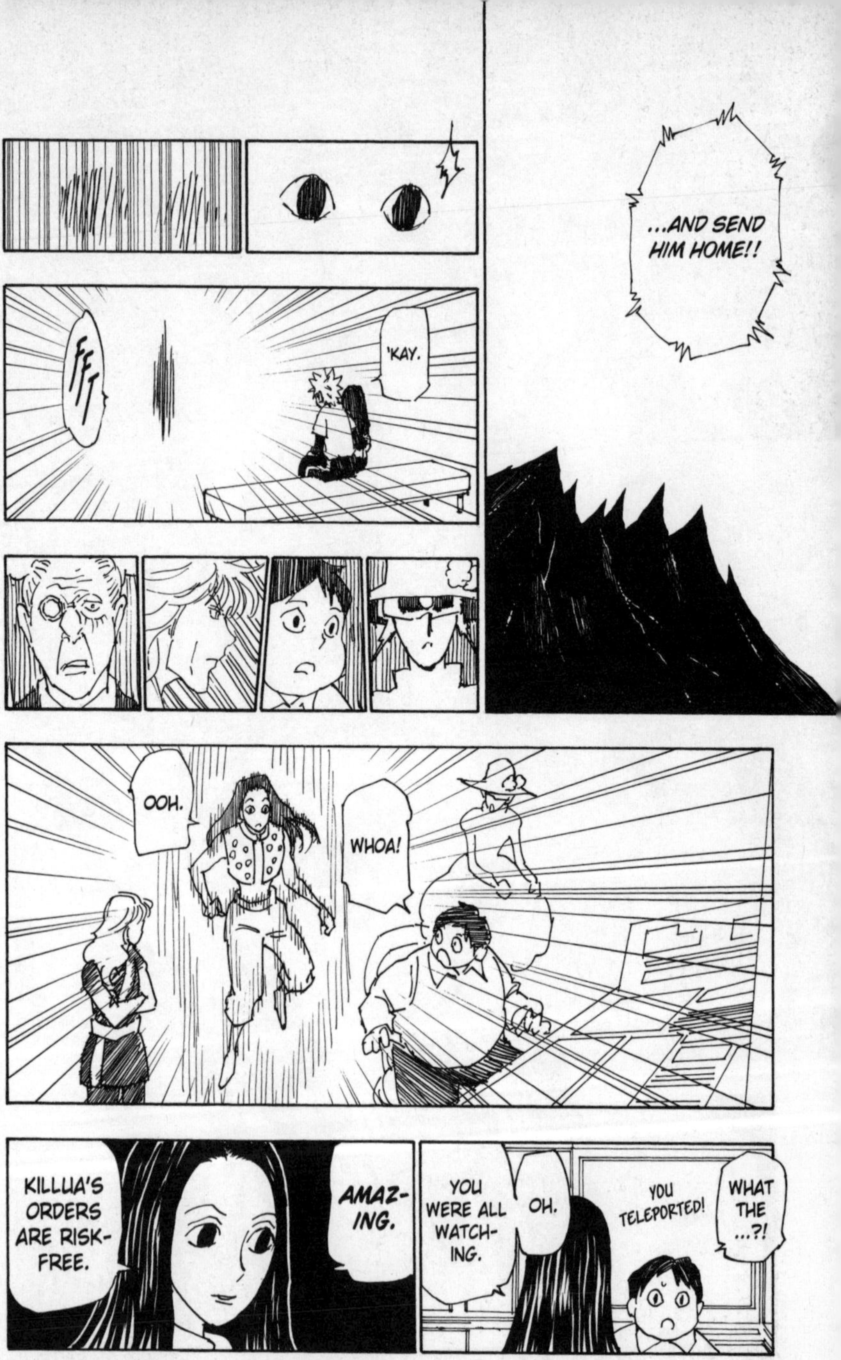
...AND SEND HIM HOME!!
'KAY.
FFT
WHOA!
OOH.
WHAT THE ...?!
YOU TELEPORTED!
OH.
YOU WERE ALL WATCH-ING.
AMAZ-ING.
KILLUA'S ORDERS ARE RISK-FREE.

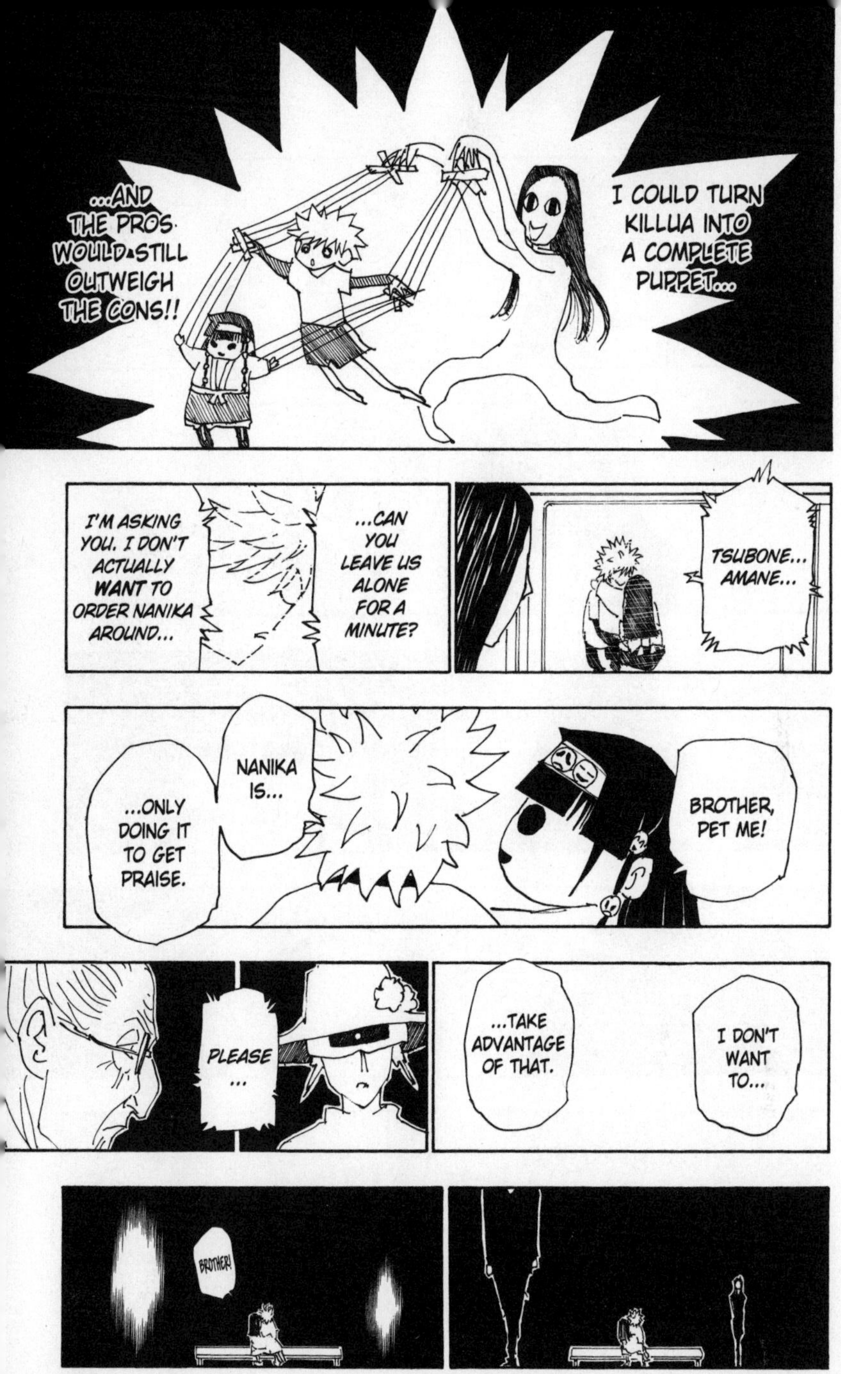
I COULD TURN KILLUA INTO A COMPLETE PUPPET...
...AND THE PROS WOULD STILL OUTWEIGH THE CONS!!
TSUBONE... AMANE...
...CAN YOU LEAVE US ALONE FOR A MINUTE?
I'M ASKING YOU. I DON'T ACTUALLY WANT TO ORDER NANIKA AROUND...
BROTHER, PET ME!
NANIKA IS...
...ONLY DOING IT TO GET PRAISE.
I DON'T WANT TO...
...TAKE ADVANTAGE OF THAT.
PLEASE ...
BROTHER!

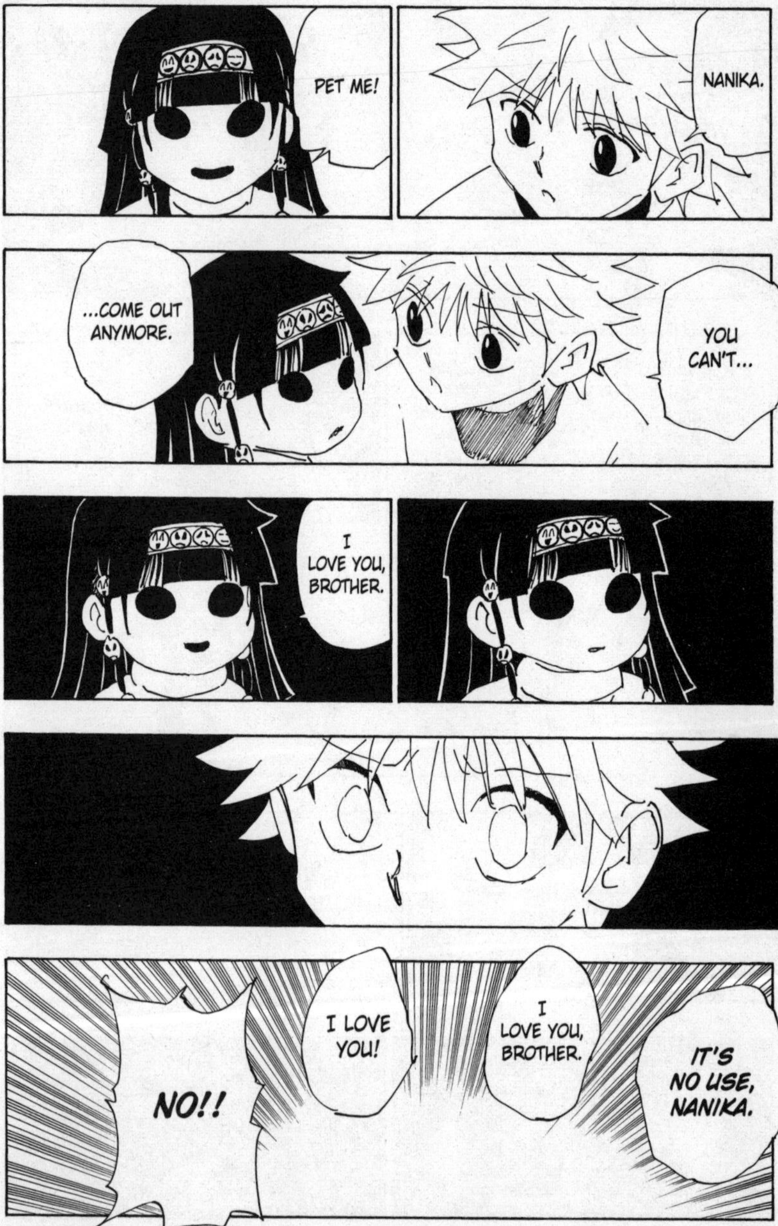
NANIKA.
PET ME!
YOU CAN'T...
...COME OUT ANYMORE.
I LOVE YOU, BROTHER.
IT'S NO USE, NANIKA.
I LOVE YOU, BROTHER.
I LOVE YOU!
NO!!

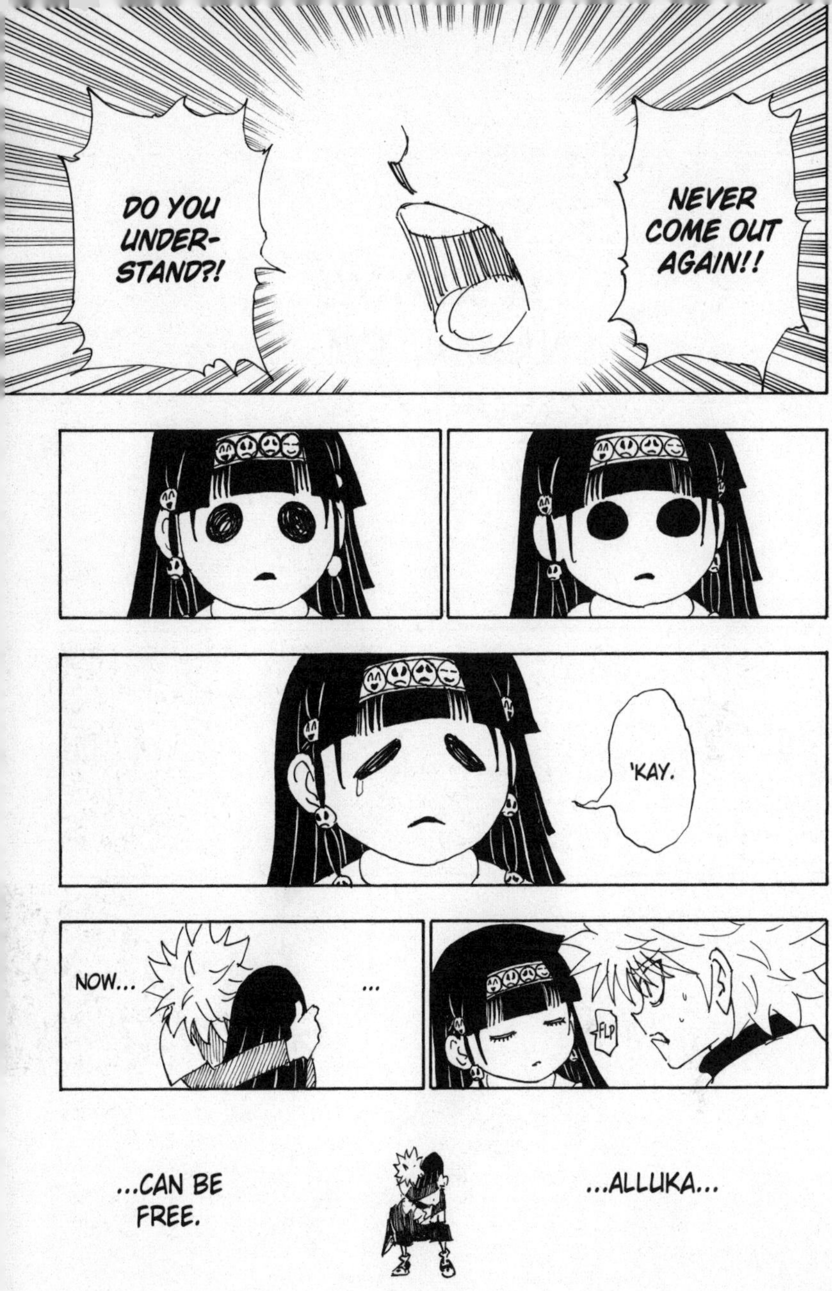
NEVER COME OUT AGAIN!!
DO YOU UNDER-STAND?!
'KAY.
FLP
...
NOW...
...ALLUKA...
...CAN BE FREE.

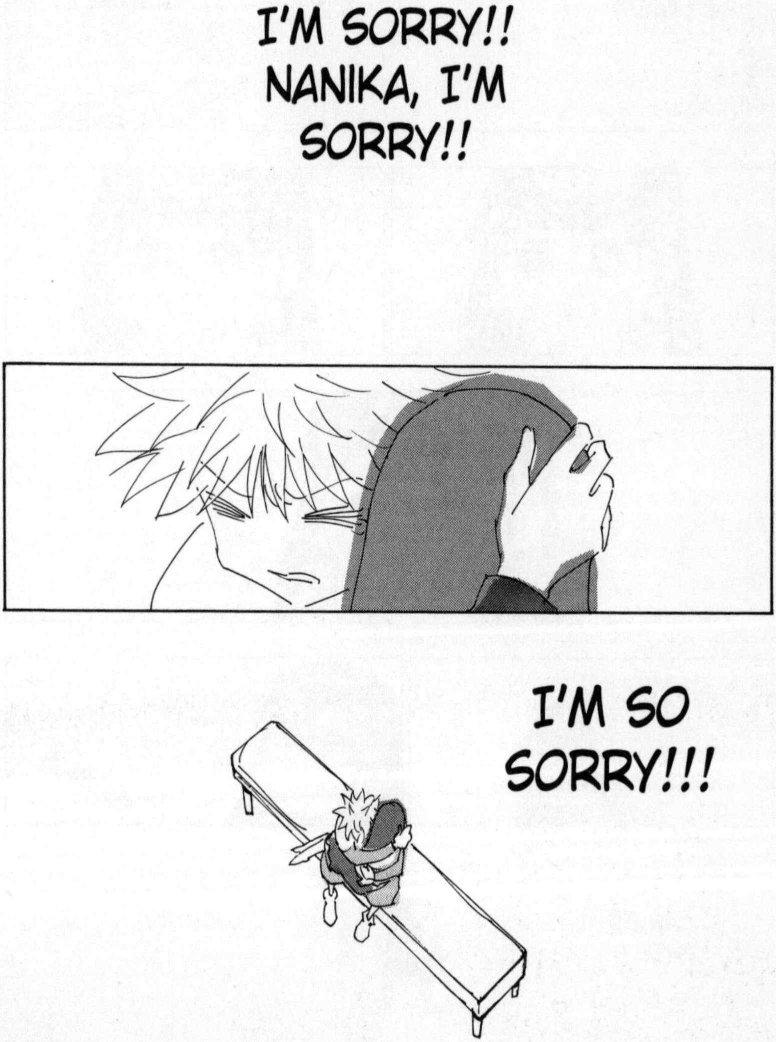
I'M SORRY!! NANIKA, I'M SORRY!!
I'M SO SORRY!!!

READ THIS WAY

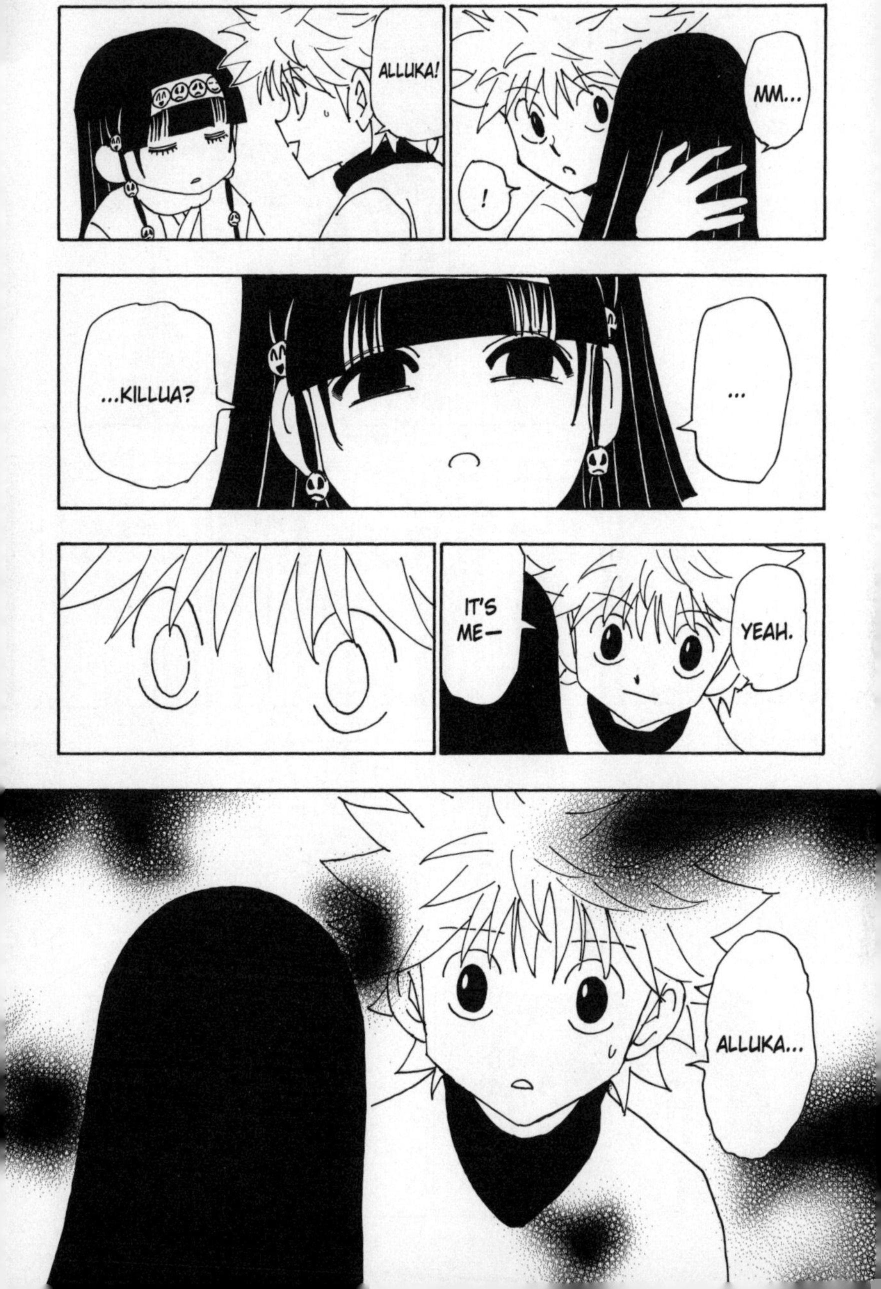
MM...
!
ALLUKA!
...
...KILLUA?
YEAH.
IT'S ME—
ALLUKA...

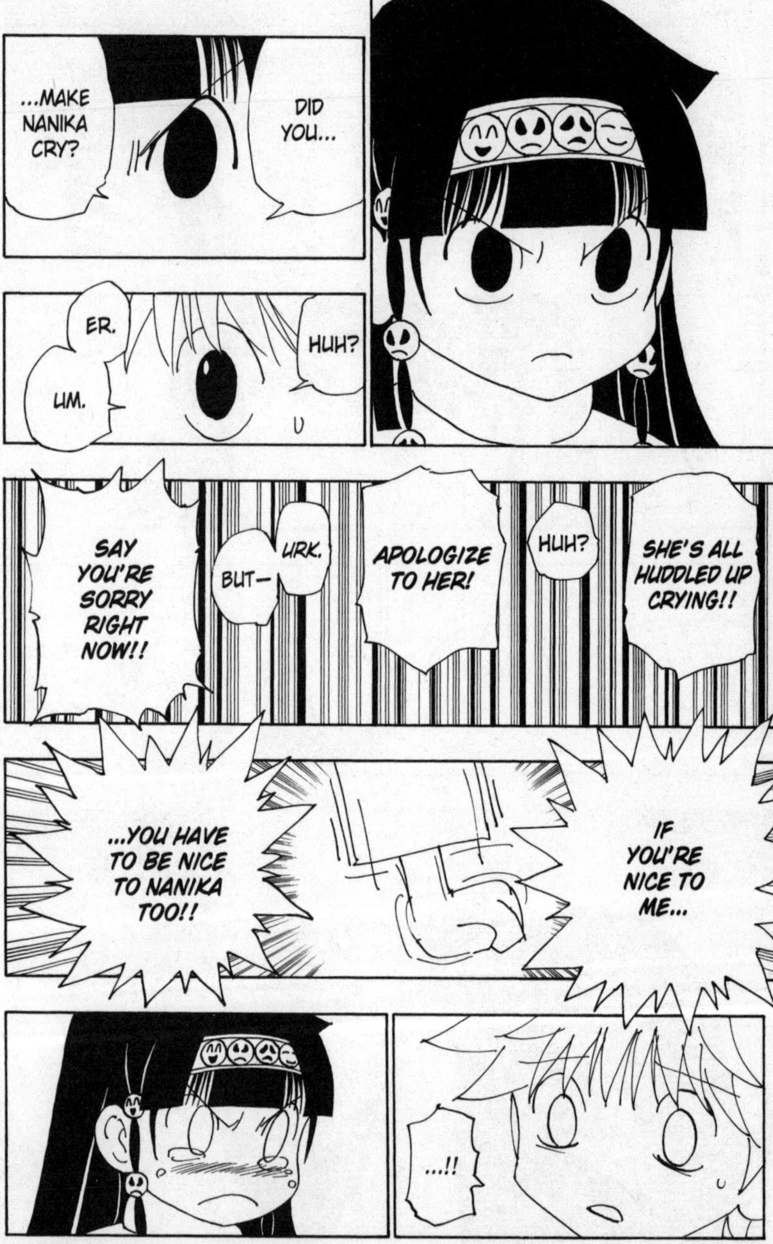
DID YOU...
...MAKE NANIKA CRY?
HUH?
ER.
UM.
SHE'S ALL HUDDLED UP CRYING!!
HUH?
APOLOGIZE TO HER!
URK.
BUT—
SAY YOU'RE SORRY RIGHT NOW!!
IF YOU'RE NICE TO ME...
...YOU HAVE TO BE NICE TO NANIKA TOO!!
...!!

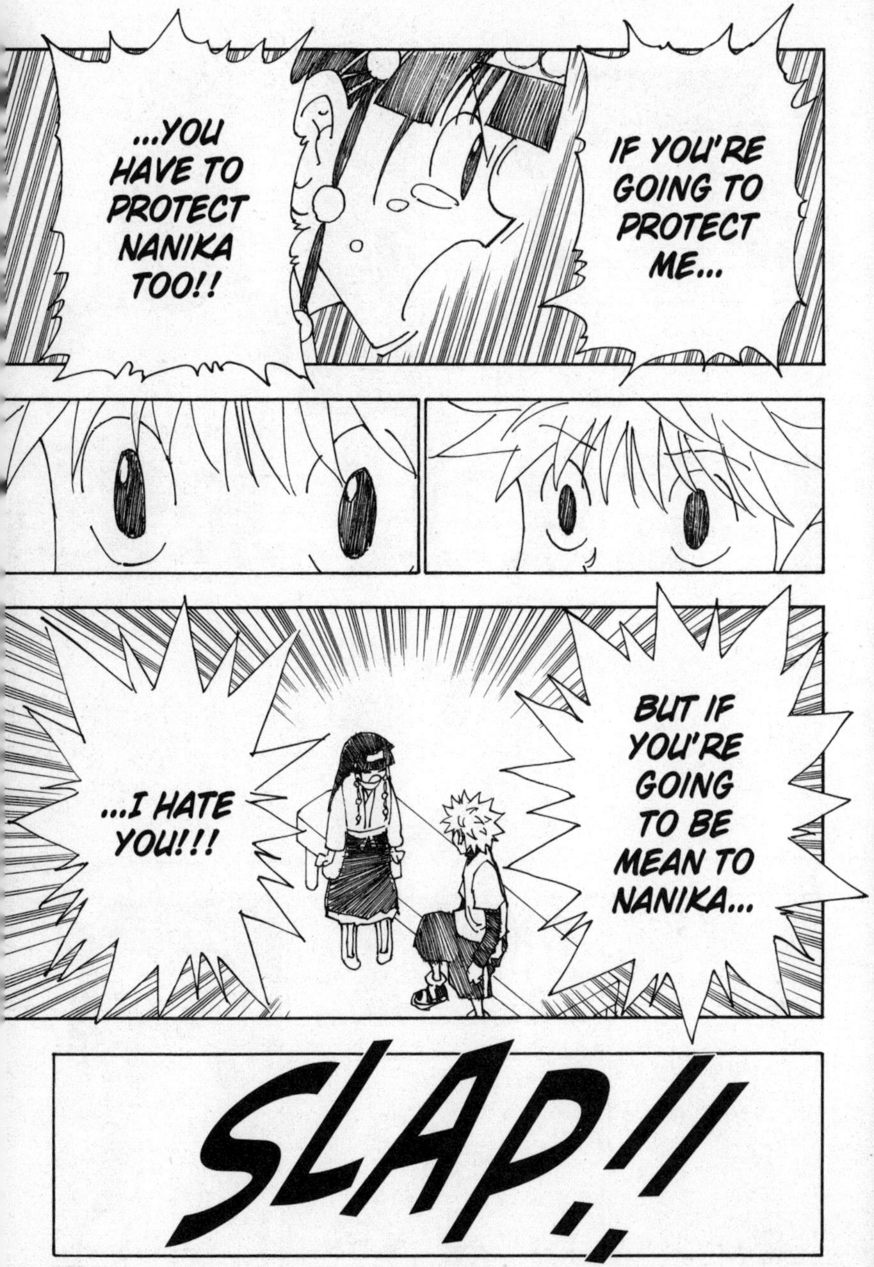
IF YOU'RE GOING TO PROTECT ME...
...YOU HAVE TO PROTECT NANIKA TOO!!
BUT IF YOU'RE GOING TO BE MEAN TO NANIKA...
...I HATE YOU!!!
SLAP!!

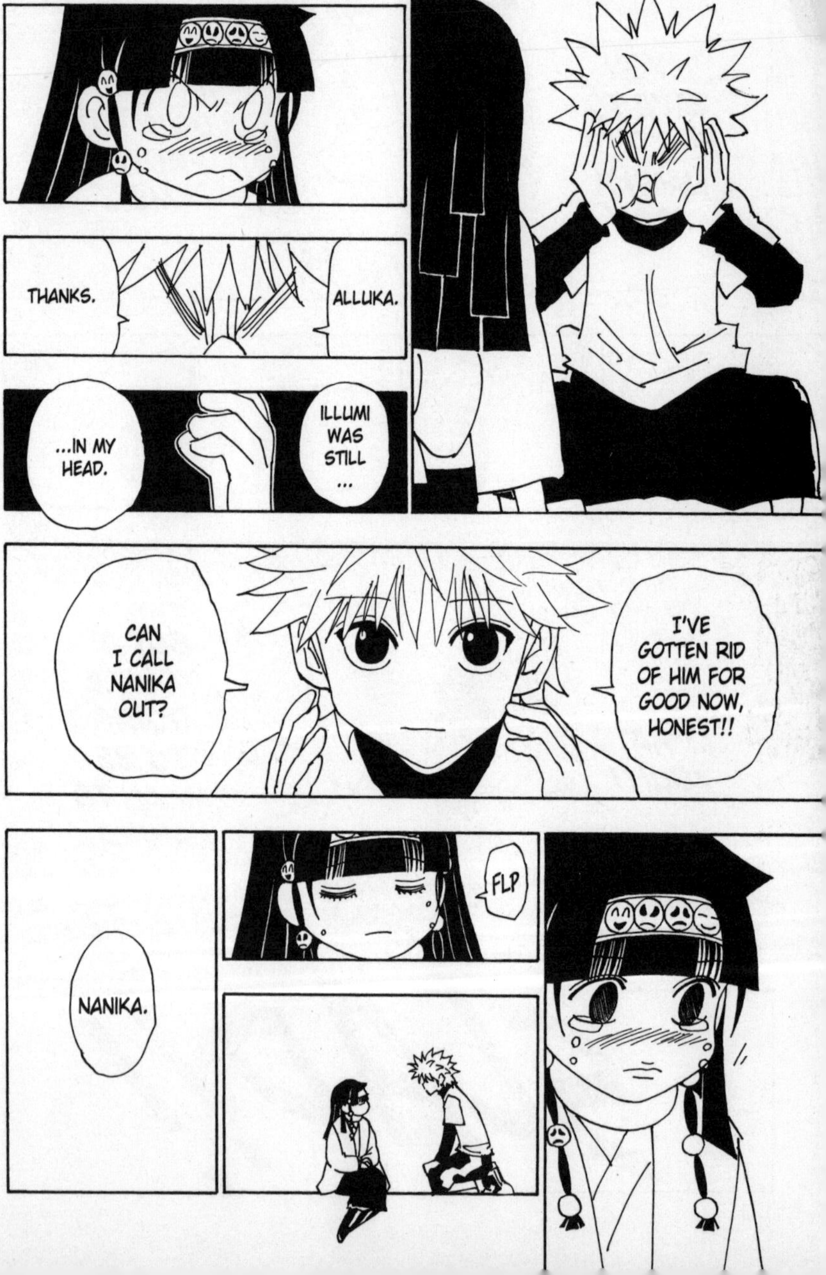
ALLUKA.
THANKS.
ILLUMI WAS STILL ...
...IN MY HEAD.
I'VE GOTTEN RID OF HIM FOR GOOD NOW, HONEST!!
CAN I CALL NANIKA OUT?
FLP
NANIKA.

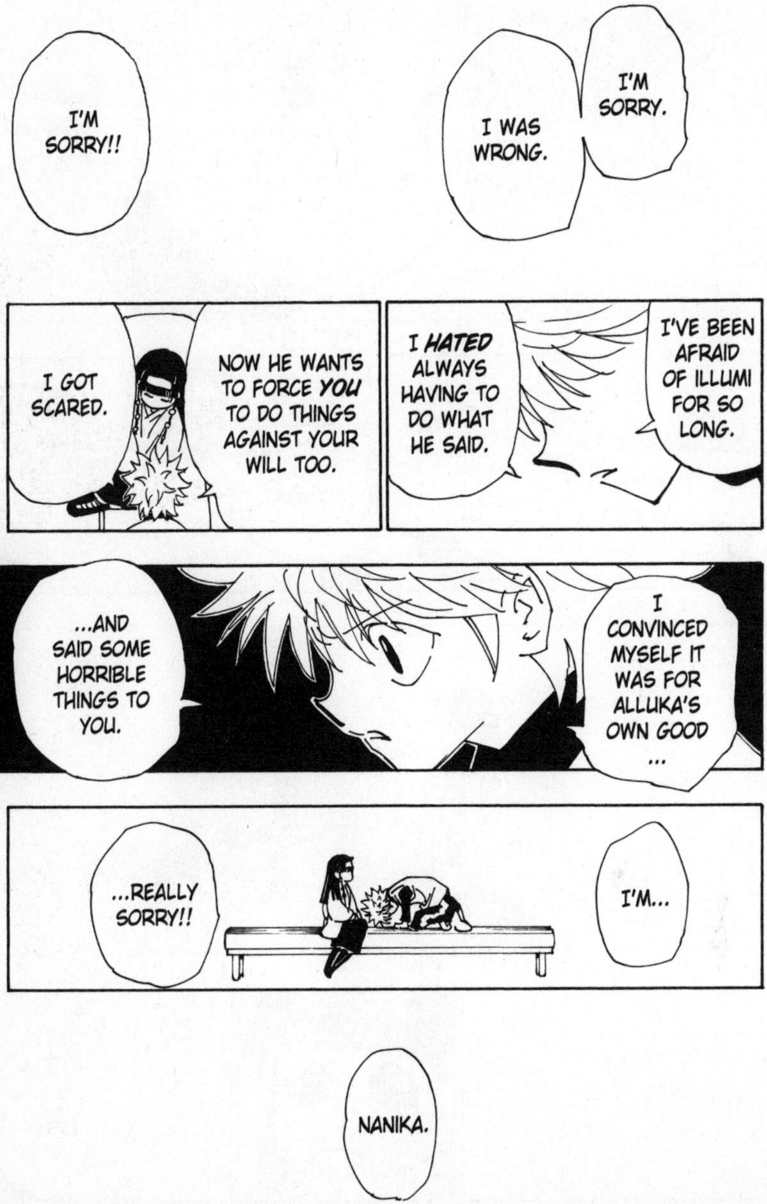
I'M SORRY.
I WAS WRONG.
I'M SORRY!!
I'VE BEEN AFRAID OF ILLUMI FOR SO LONG.
I *HATED* ALWAYS HAVING TO DO WHAT HE SAID.
NOW HE WANTS TO FORCE *YOU* TO DO THINGS AGAINST YOUR WILL TOO.
I GOT SCARED.
I CONVINCED MYSELF IT WAS FOR ALLUKA'S OWN GOOD ...
...AND SAID SOME HORRIBLE THINGS TO YOU.
I'M...
...REALLY SORRY!!
NANIKA.

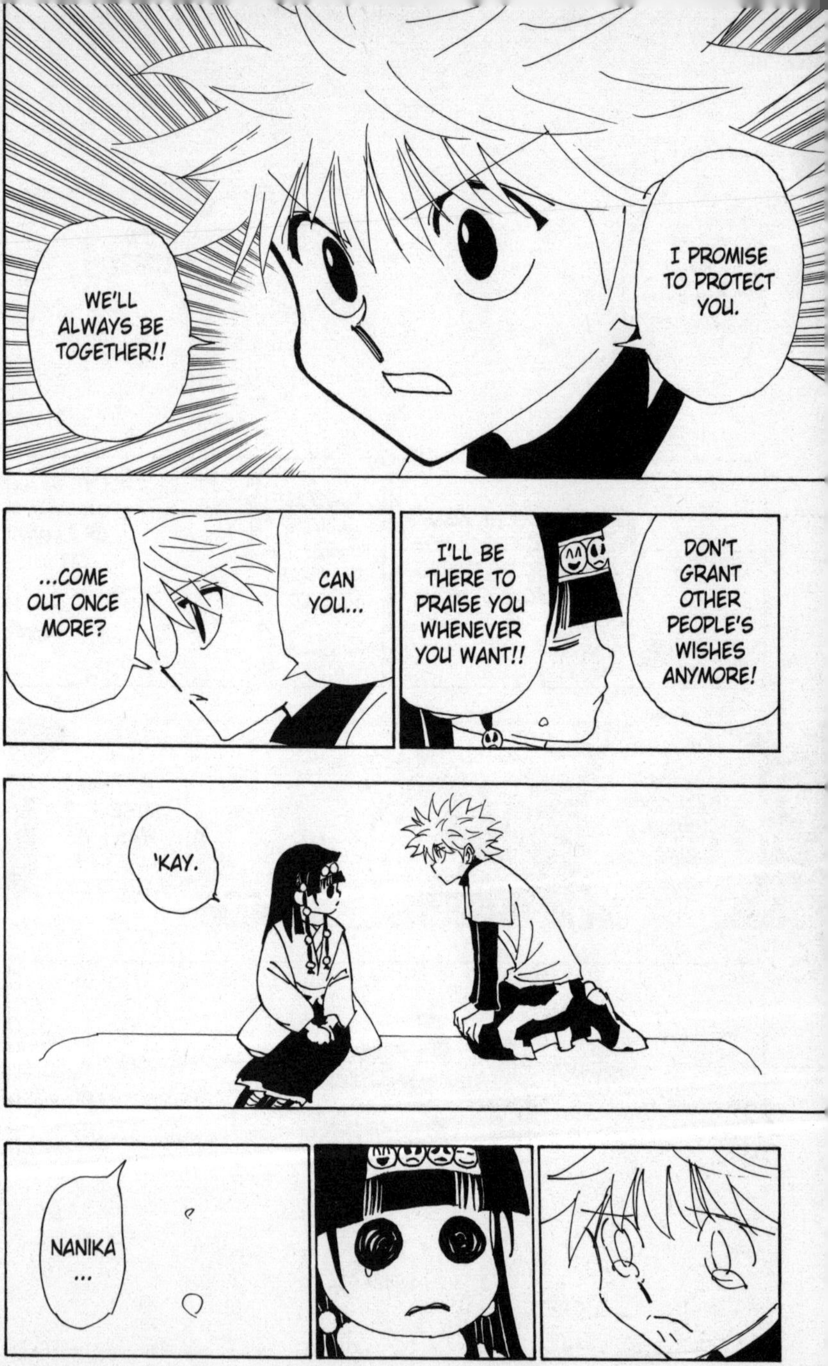
I PROMISE TO PROTECT YOU.
WE'LL ALWAYS BE TOGETHER!!
DON'T GRANT OTHER PEOPLE'S WISHES ANYMORE!
I'LL BE THERE TO PRAISE YOU WHENEVER YOU WANT!!
CAN YOU...
...COME OUT ONCE MORE?
'KAY.
NANIKA ...

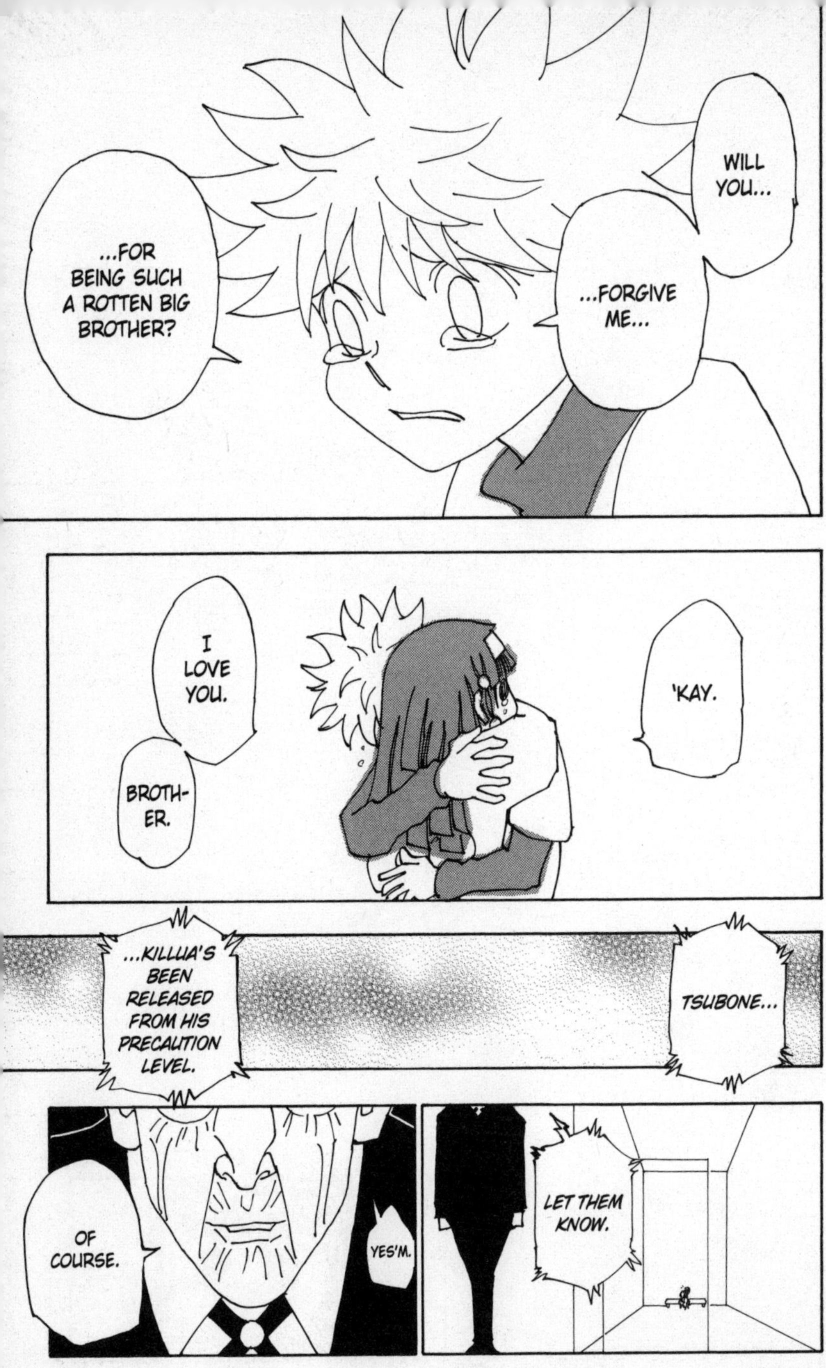
WILL YOU...
...FORGIVE ME...
...FOR BEING SUCH A ROTTEN BIG BROTHER?
'KAY.
I LOVE YOU.
BROTH-ER.
TSUBONE...
...KILLUA'S BEEN RELEASED FROM HIS PRECAUTION LEVEL.
LET THEM KNOW.
YES'M.
OF COURSE.

Chapter 337: Repentance

...JUST LIKE YOU.

SHE WAS A REDHEAD...

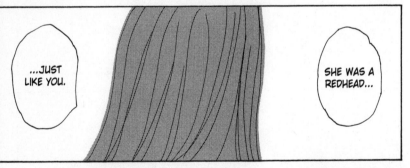

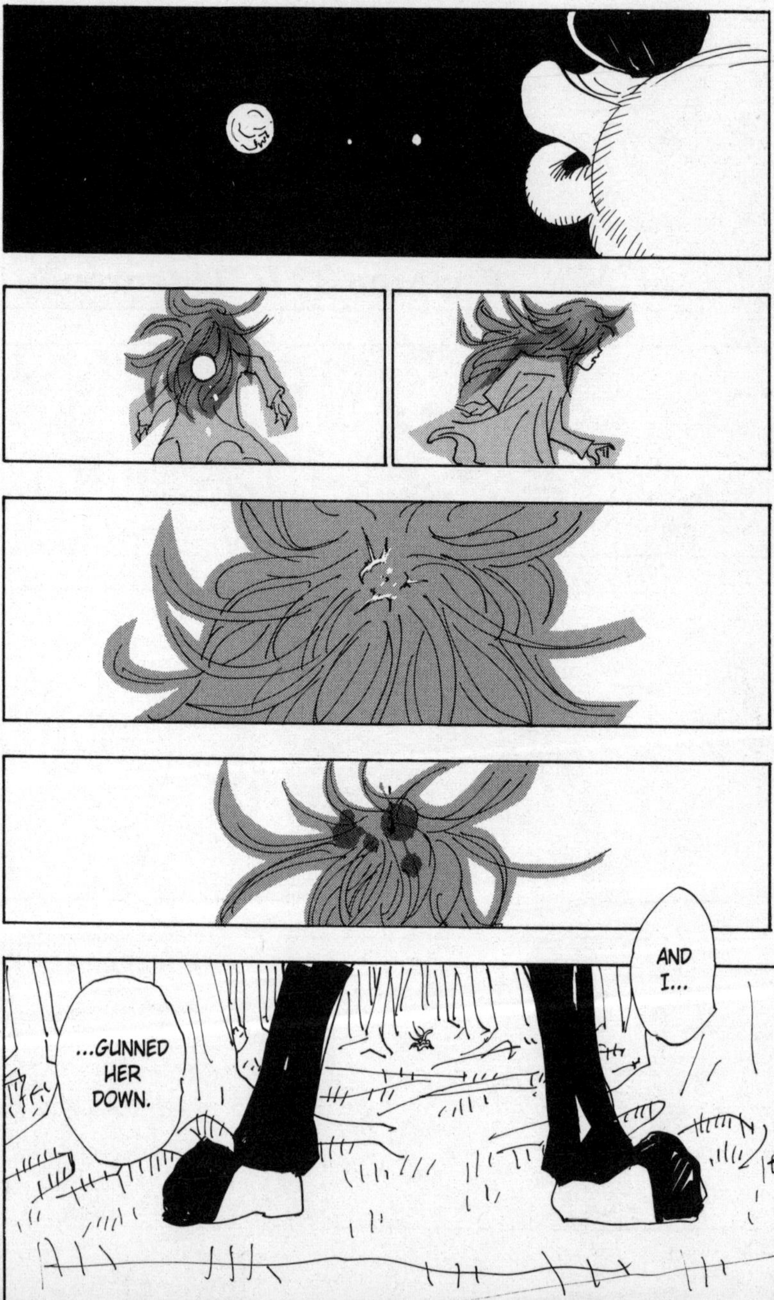
AND I...
...GUNNED HER DOWN.

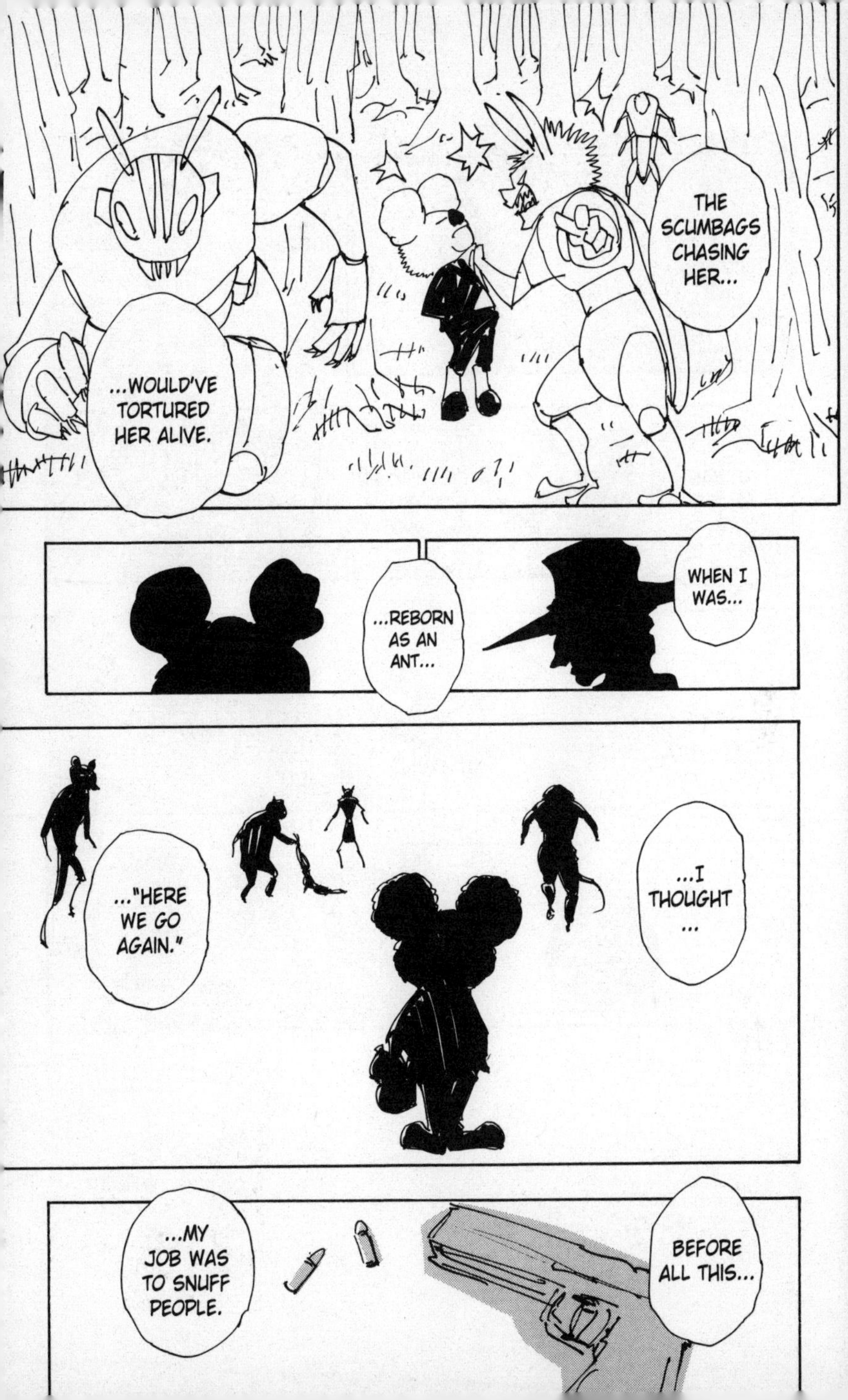
THE SCUMBAGS CHASING HER...
...WOULD'VE TORTURED HER ALIVE.
WHEN I WAS...
...REBORN AS AN ANT...
...I THOUGHT ...
..."HERE WE GO AGAIN."
BEFORE ALL THIS...
...MY JOB WAS TO SNUFF PEOPLE.

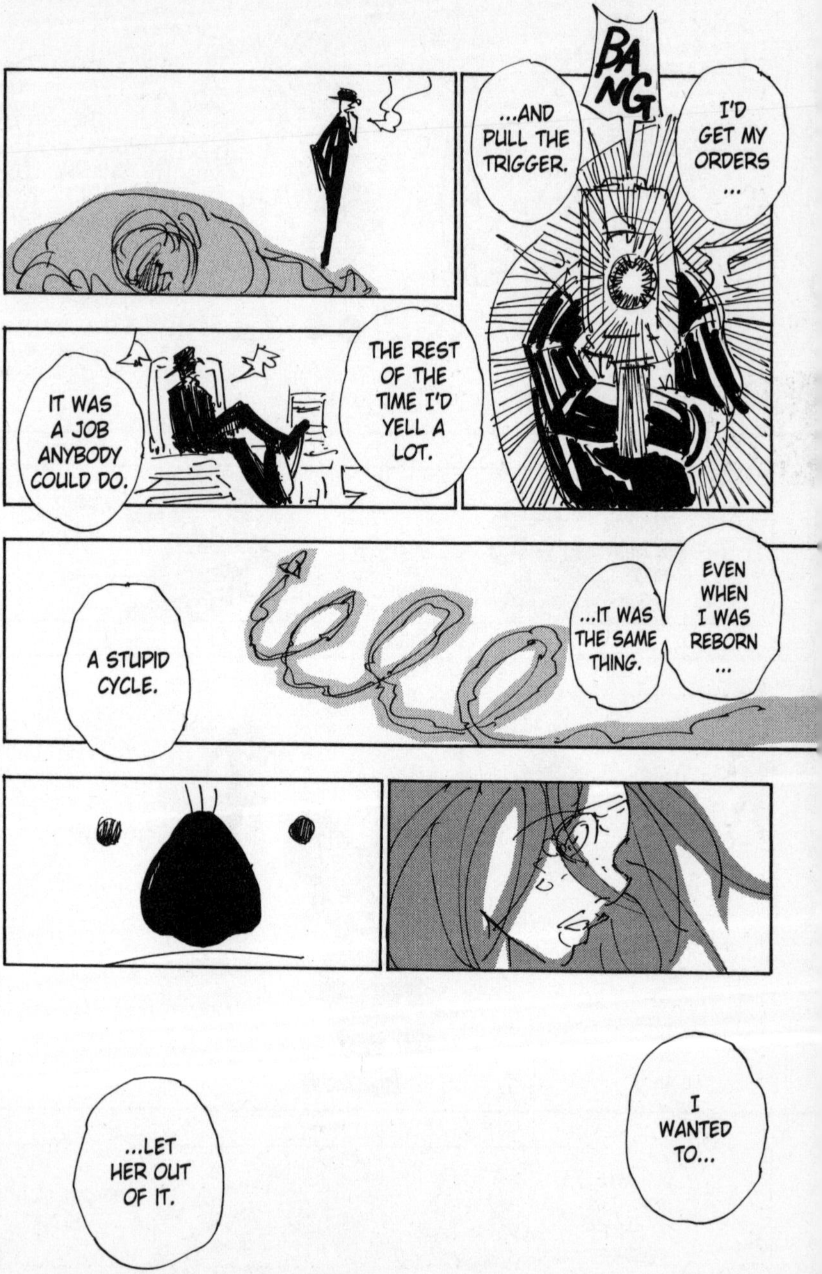
I'D GET MY ORDERS ...
BANG
...AND PULL THE TRIGGER.
THE REST OF THE TIME I'D YELL A LOT.
IT WAS A JOB ANYBODY COULD DO.
EVEN WHEN I WAS REBORN ...
...IT WAS THE SAME THING.
A STUPID CYCLE.
I WANTED TO...
...LET HER OUT OF IT.

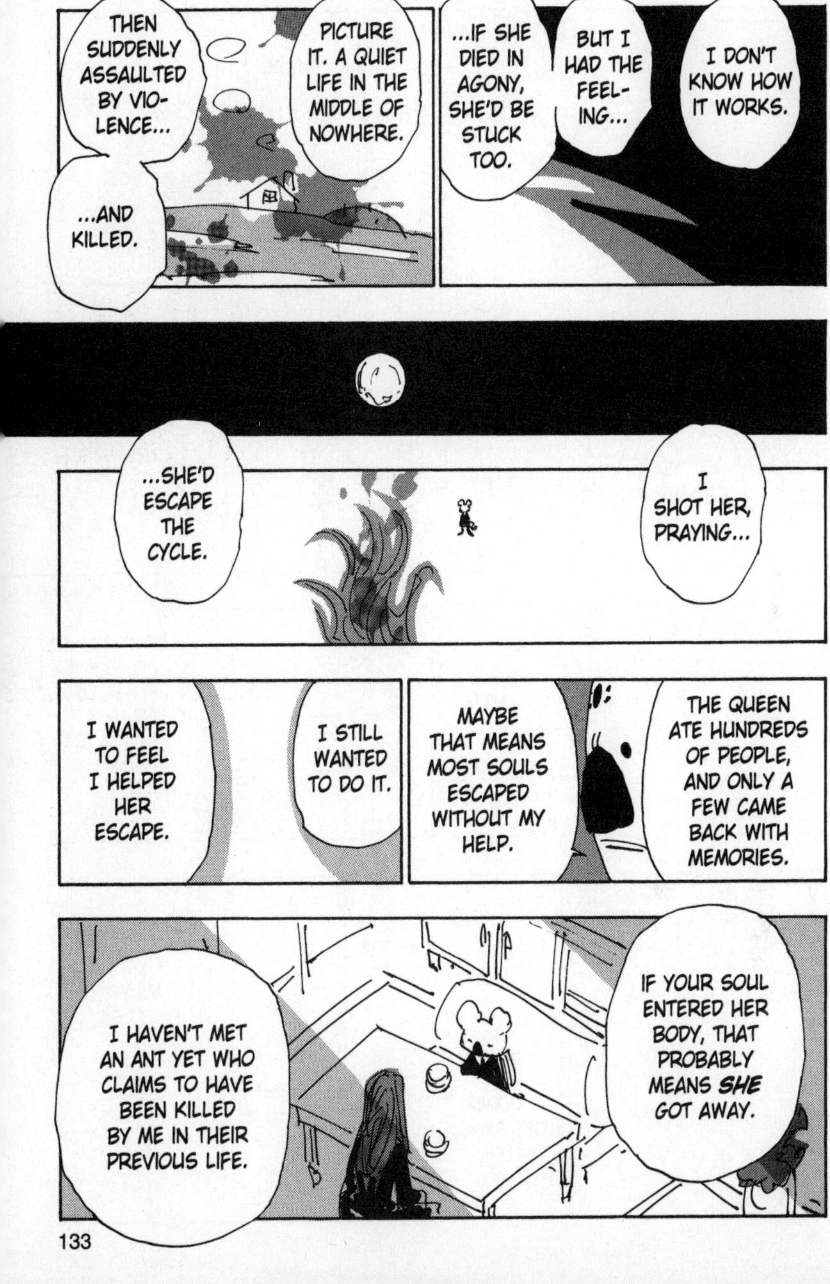
I DON'T KNOW HOW IT WORKS.
BUT I HAD THE FEELING...
...IF SHE DIED IN AGONY, SHE'D BE STUCK TOO.
PICTURE IT. A QUIET LIFE IN THE MIDDLE OF NOWHERE.
THEN SUDDENLY ASSAULTED BY VIOLENCE...
...AND KILLED.
I SHOT HER, PRAYING...
...SHE'D ESCAPE THE CYCLE.
THE QUEEN ATE HUNDREDS OF PEOPLE, AND ONLY A FEW CAME BACK WITH MEMORIES.
MAYBE THAT MEANS MOST SOULS ESCAPED WITHOUT MY HELP.
I STILL WANTED TO DO IT.
I WANTED TO FEEL I HELPED HER ESCAPE.
IF YOUR SOUL ENTERED HER BODY, THAT PROBABLY MEANS *SHE* GOT AWAY.
I HAVEN'T MET AN ANT YET WHO CLAIMS TO HAVE BEEN KILLED BY ME IN THEIR PREVIOUS LIFE.

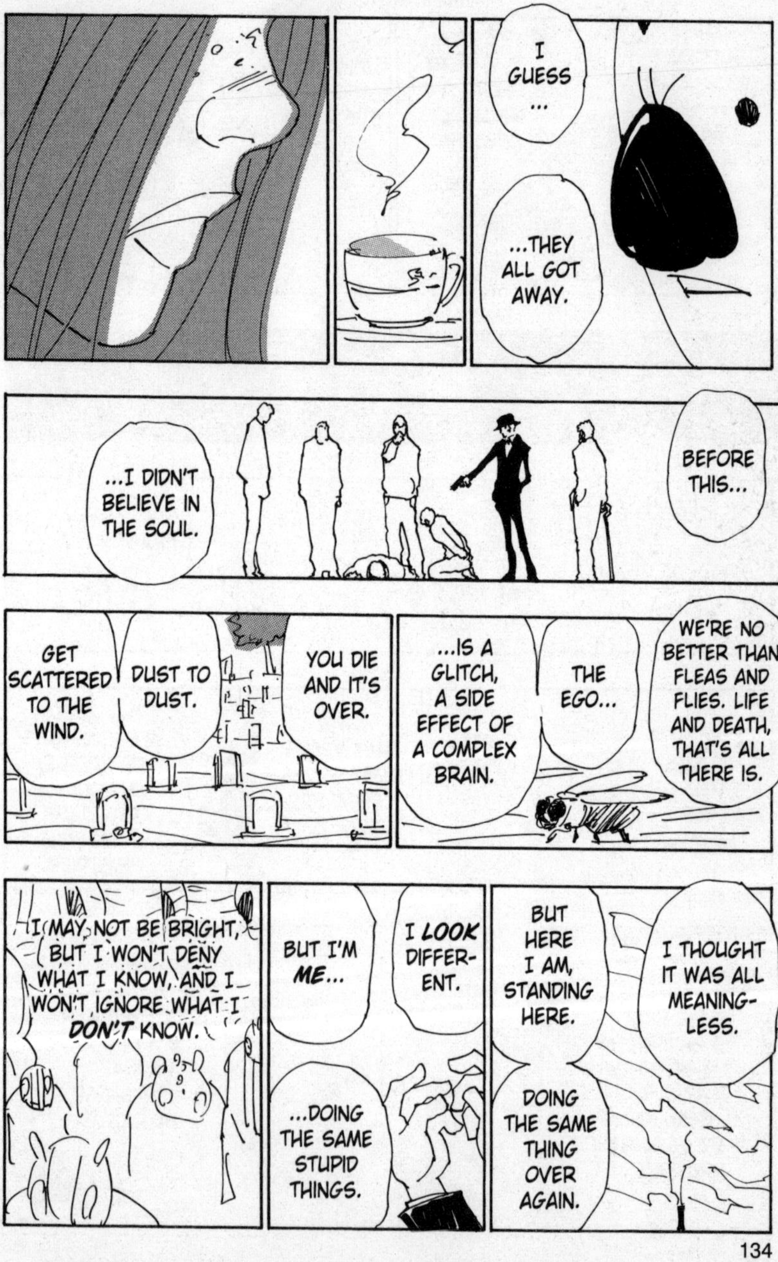
I GUESS...
...THEY ALL GOT AWAY.
BEFORE THIS...
...I DIDN'T BELIEVE IN THE SOUL.
WE'RE NO BETTER THAN FLEAS AND FLIES. LIFE AND DEATH, THAT'S ALL THERE IS.
THE EGO...
...IS A GLITCH, A SIDE EFFECT OF A COMPLEX BRAIN.
YOU DIE AND IT'S OVER.
DUST TO DUST.
GET SCATTERED TO THE WIND.
I THOUGHT IT WAS ALL MEANINGLESS.
BUT HERE I AM, STANDING HERE.
DOING THE SAME THING OVER AGAIN.
I *LOOK* DIFFERENT.
BUT I'M *ME*...
...DOING THE SAME STUPID THINGS.
I MAY NOT BE BRIGHT, BUT I WON'T DENY WHAT I KNOW, AND I WON'T IGNORE WHAT I *DON'T* KNOW.

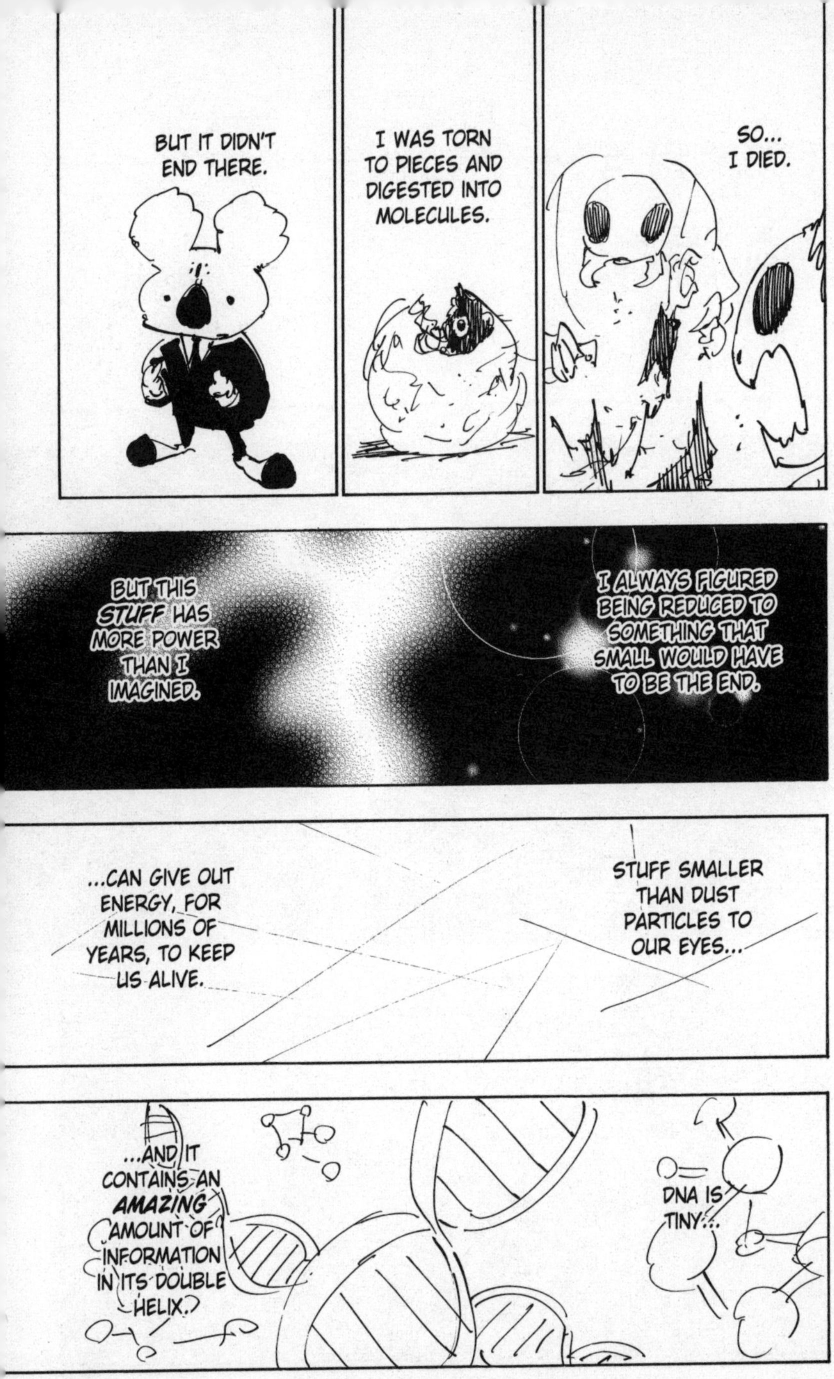
SO... I DIED.
I WAS TORN TO PIECES AND DIGESTED INTO MOLECULES.
BUT IT DIDN'T END THERE.
I ALWAYS FIGURED BEING REDUCED TO SOMETHING THAT SMALL WOULD HAVE TO BE THE END.
BUT THIS *STUFF* HAS MORE POWER THAN I IMAGINED.
STUFF SMALLER THAN DUST PARTICLES TO OUR EYES...
...CAN GIVE OUT ENERGY, FOR MILLIONS OF YEARS, TO KEEP US ALIVE.
DNA IS TINY...
...AND IT CONTAINS AN ***AMAZING*** AMOUNT OF INFORMATION IN ITS DOUBLE HELIX.

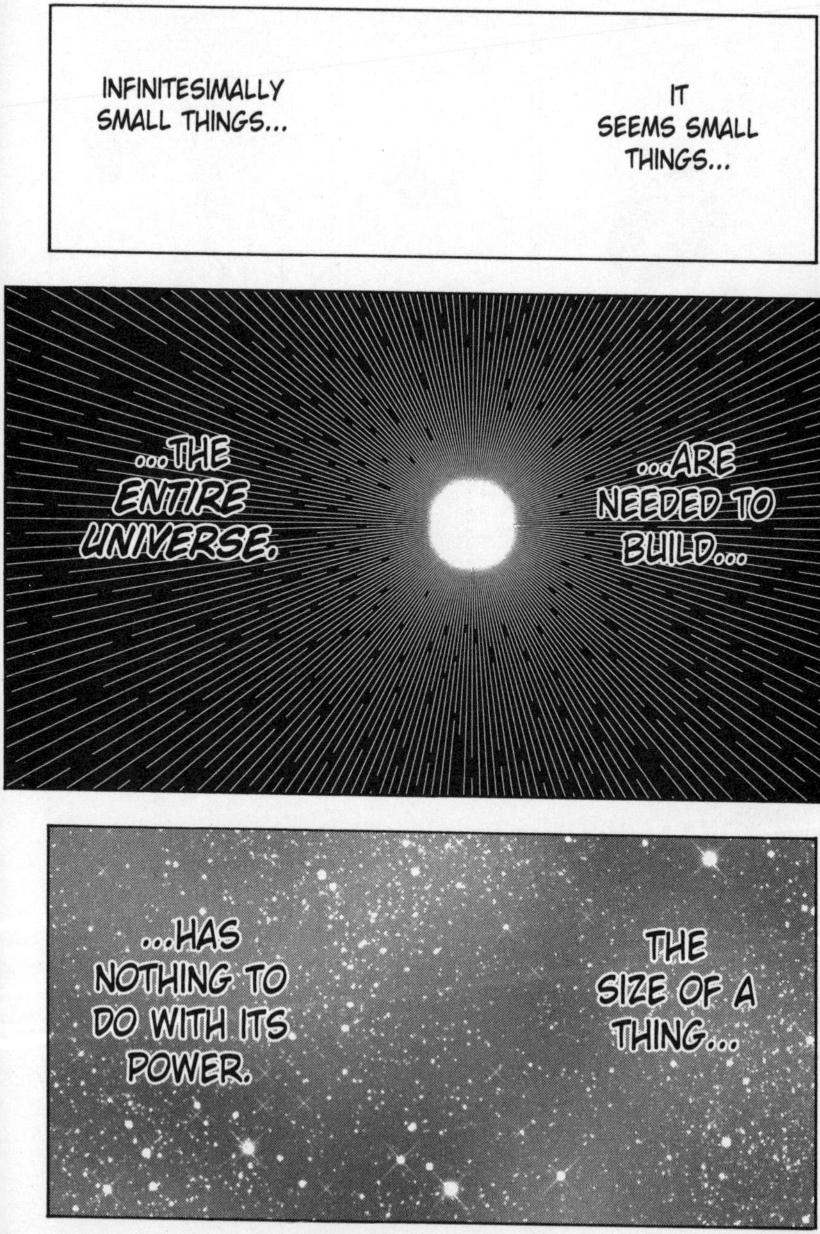
IT SEEMS SMALL THINGS...
INFINITESIMALLY SMALL THINGS...
...ARE NEEDED TO BUILD...
...THE ENTIRE UNIVERSE.
THE SIZE OF A THING...
...HAS NOTHING TO DO WITH ITS POWER.

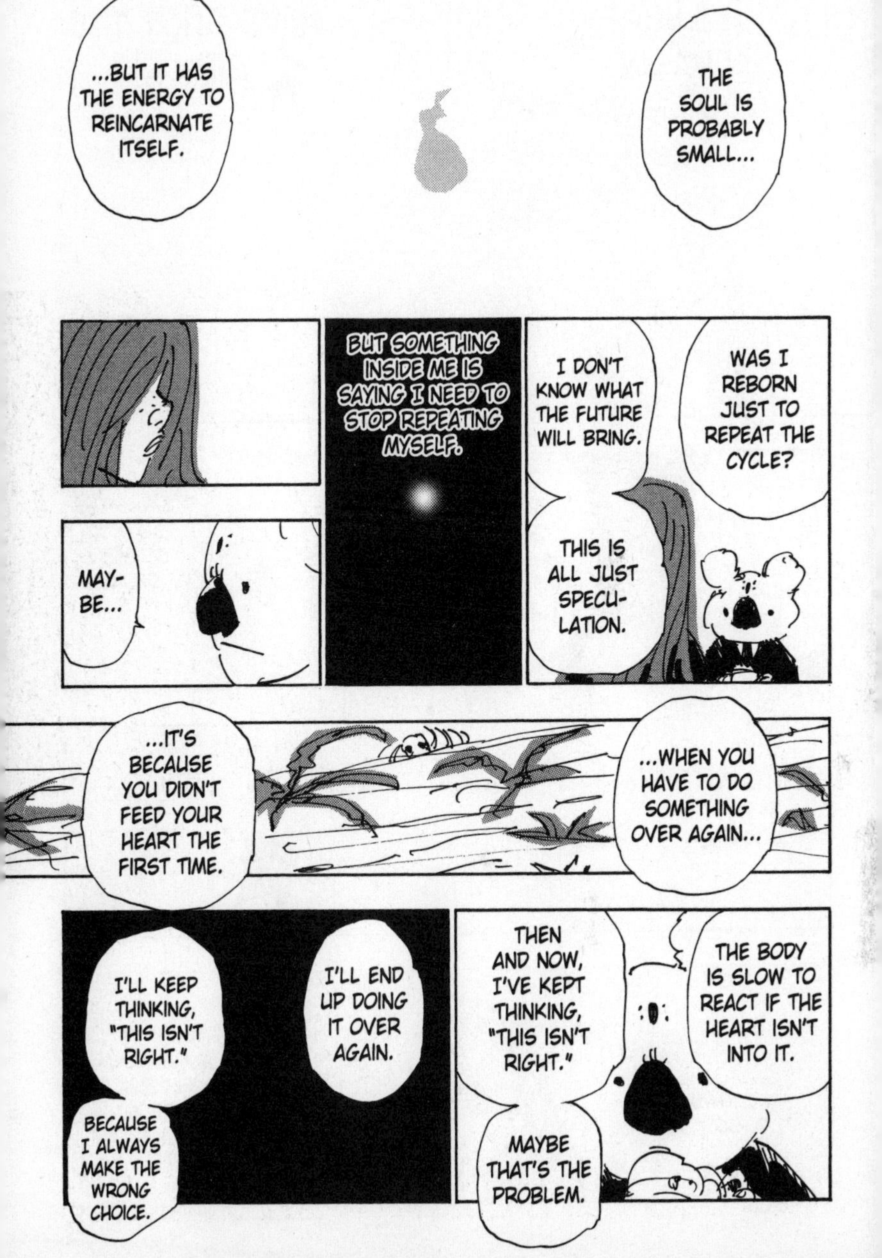
THE SOUL IS PROBABLY SMALL...
...BUT IT HAS THE ENERGY TO REINCARNATE ITSELF.
WAS I REBORN JUST TO REPEAT THE CYCLE?
I DON'T KNOW WHAT THE FUTURE WILL BRING.
THIS IS ALL JUST SPECU-LATION.
BUT SOMETHING INSIDE ME IS SAYING I NEED TO STOP REPEATING MYSELF.
MAY-BE...
...WHEN YOU HAVE TO DO SOMETHING OVER AGAIN...
...IT'S BECAUSE YOU DIDN'T FEED YOUR HEART THE FIRST TIME.
THE BODY IS SLOW TO REACT IF THE HEART ISN'T INTO IT.
THEN AND NOW, I'VE KEPT THINKING, "THIS ISN'T RIGHT."
MAYBE THAT'S THE PROBLEM.
I'LL END UP DOING IT OVER AGAIN.
I'LL KEEP THINKING, "THIS ISN'T RIGHT."
BECAUSE I ALWAYS MAKE THE WRONG CHOICE.

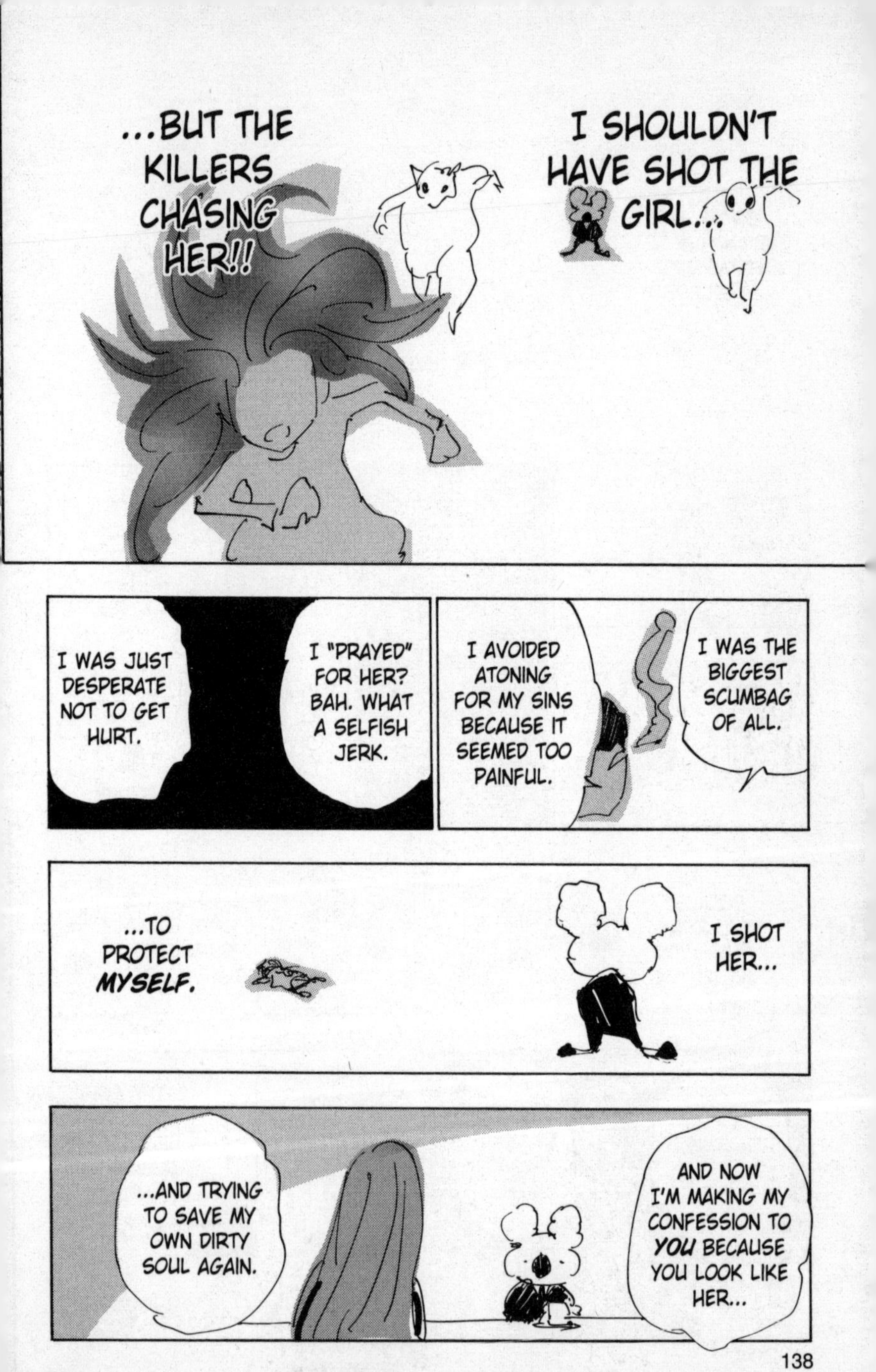
I SHOULDN'T HAVE SHOT THE GIRL...
...BUT THE KILLERS CHASING HER!!
I WAS THE BIGGEST SCUMBAG OF ALL.
I AVOIDED ATONING FOR MY SINS BECAUSE IT SEEMED TOO PAINFUL.
I "PRAYED" FOR HER? BAH. WHAT A SELFISH JERK.
I WAS JUST DESPERATE NOT TO GET HURT.
I SHOT HER...
...TO PROTECT *MYSELF.*
AND NOW I'M MAKING MY CONFESSION TO *YOU* BECAUSE YOU LOOK LIKE HER...
...AND TRYING TO SAVE MY OWN DIRTY SOUL AGAIN.

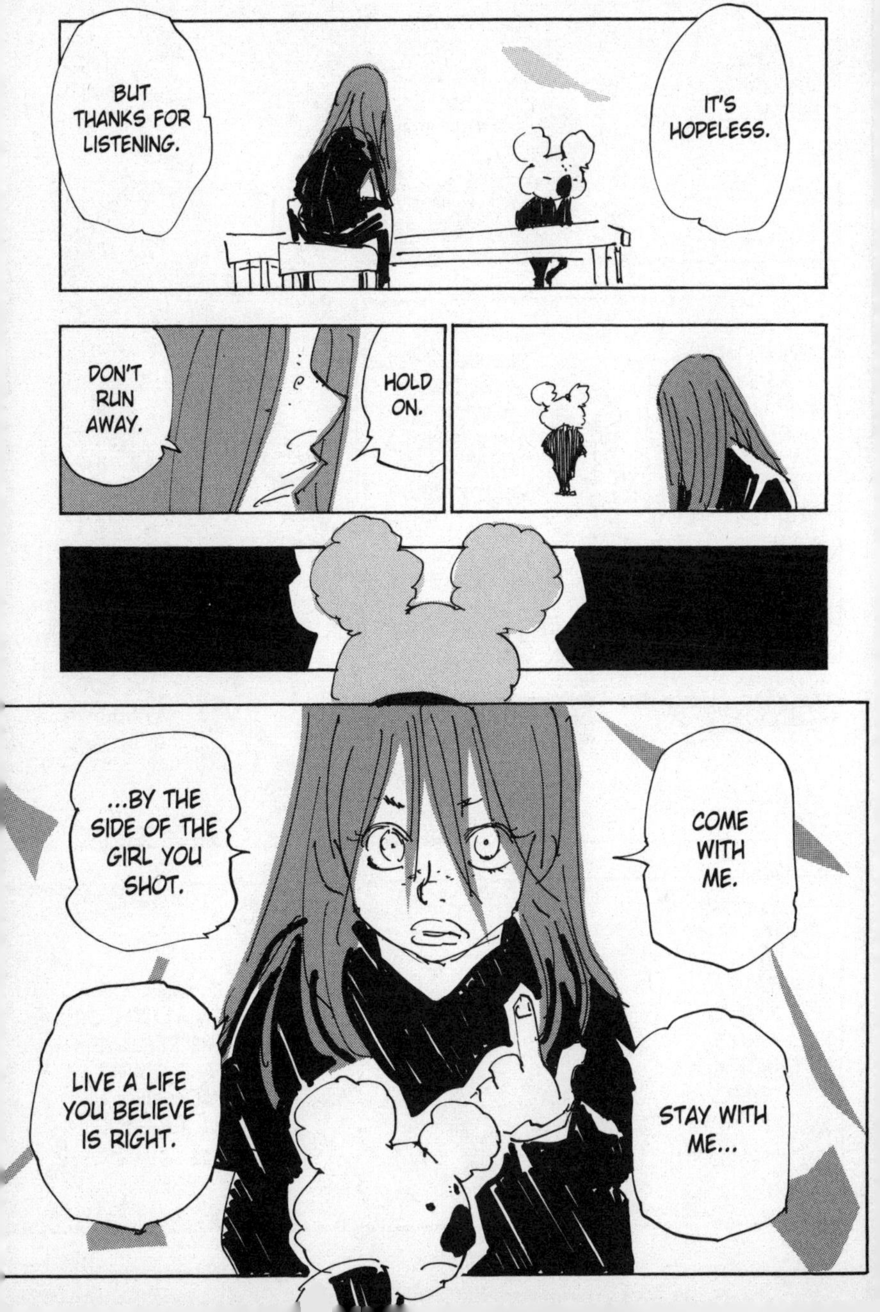
IT'S HOPELESS.
BUT THANKS FOR LISTENING.
HOLD ON.
DON'T RUN AWAY.
COME WITH ME.
...BY THE SIDE OF THE GIRL YOU SHOT.
STAY WITH ME...
LIVE A LIFE YOU BELIEVE IS RIGHT.

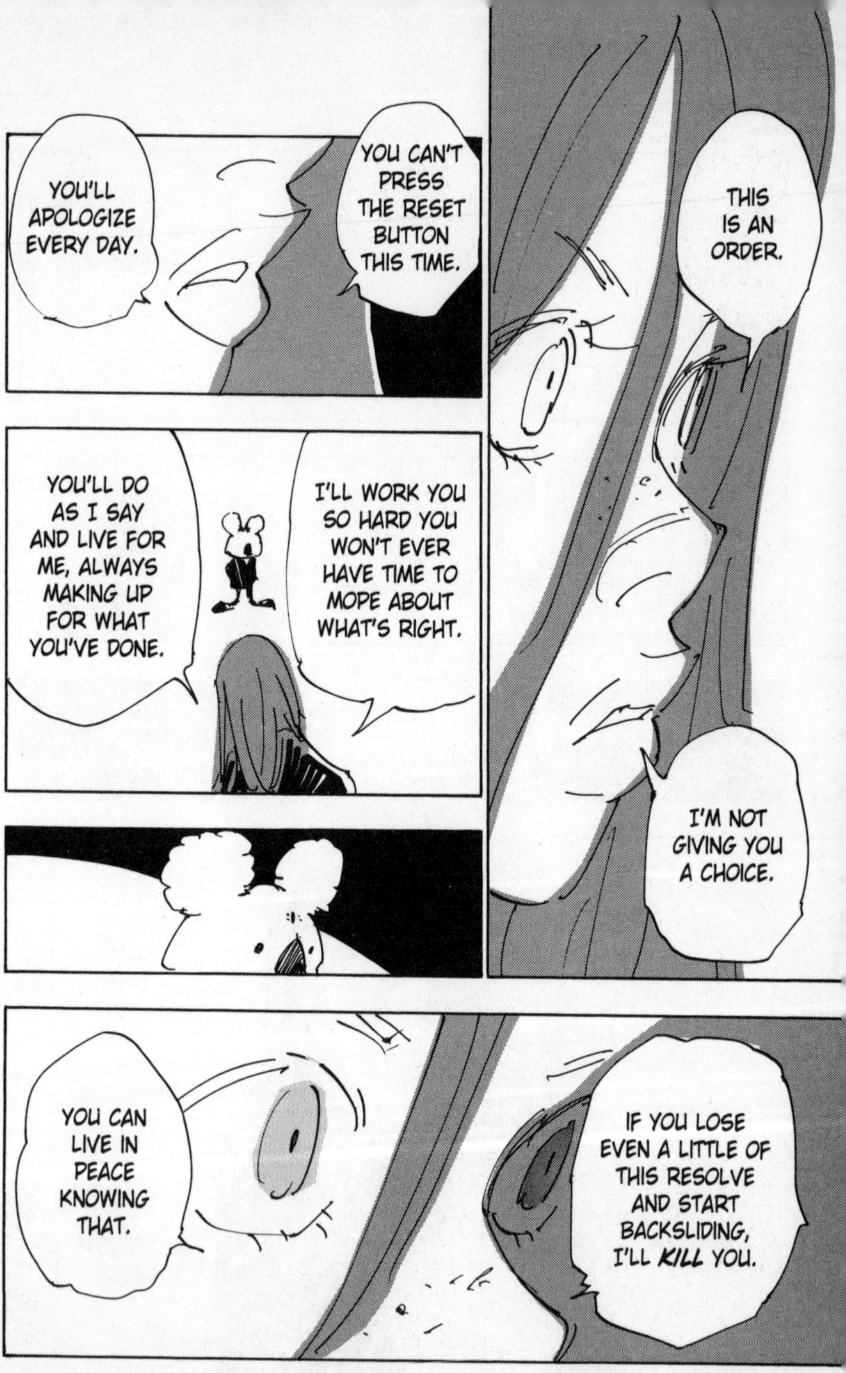
THIS IS AN ORDER.
I'M NOT GIVING YOU A CHOICE.
YOU CAN'T PRESS THE RESET BUTTON THIS TIME.
YOU'LL APOLOGIZE EVERY DAY.
I'LL WORK YOU SO HARD YOU WON'T EVER HAVE TIME TO MOPE ABOUT WHAT'S RIGHT.
YOU'LL DO AS I SAY AND LIVE FOR ME, ALWAYS MAKING UP FOR WHAT YOU'VE DONE.
IF YOU LOSE EVEN A LITTLE OF THIS RESOLVE AND START BACKSLIDING, I'LL *KILL* YOU.
YOU CAN LIVE IN PEACE KNOWING THAT.

READ THIS WAY

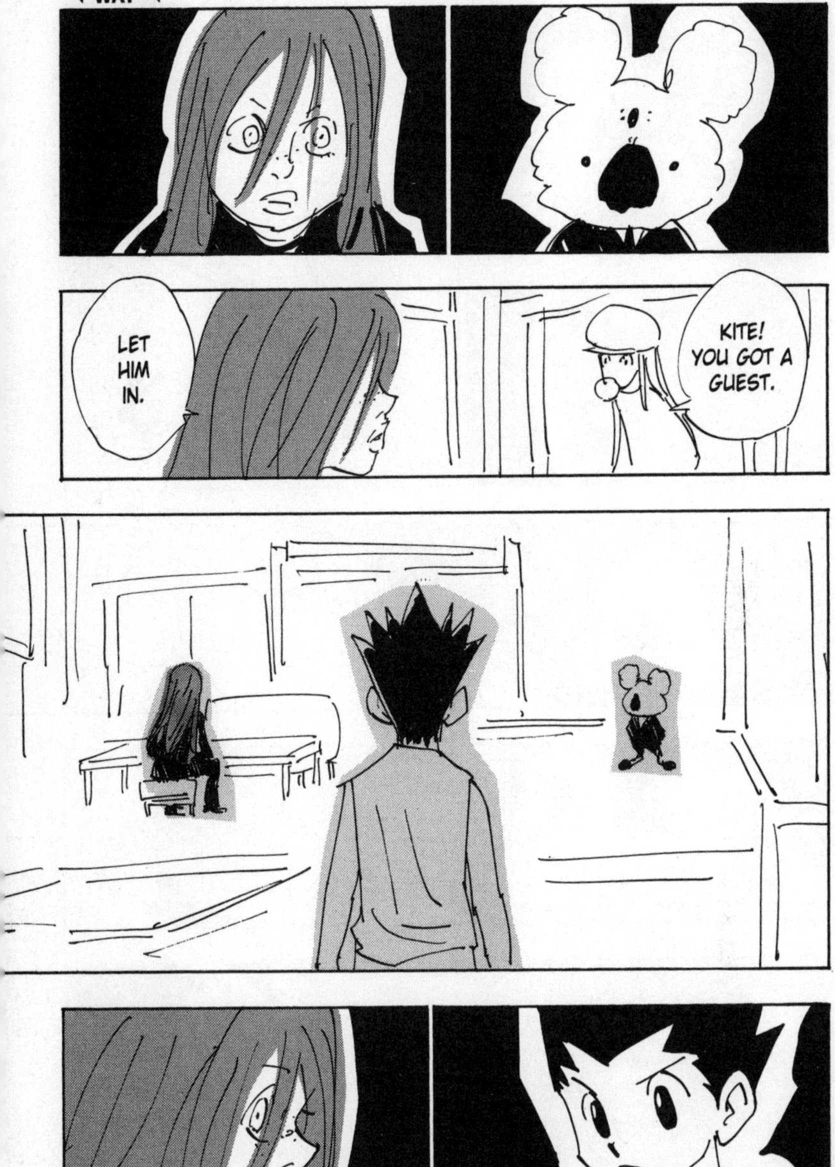

KITE! YOU GOT A GUEST.
LET HIM IN.

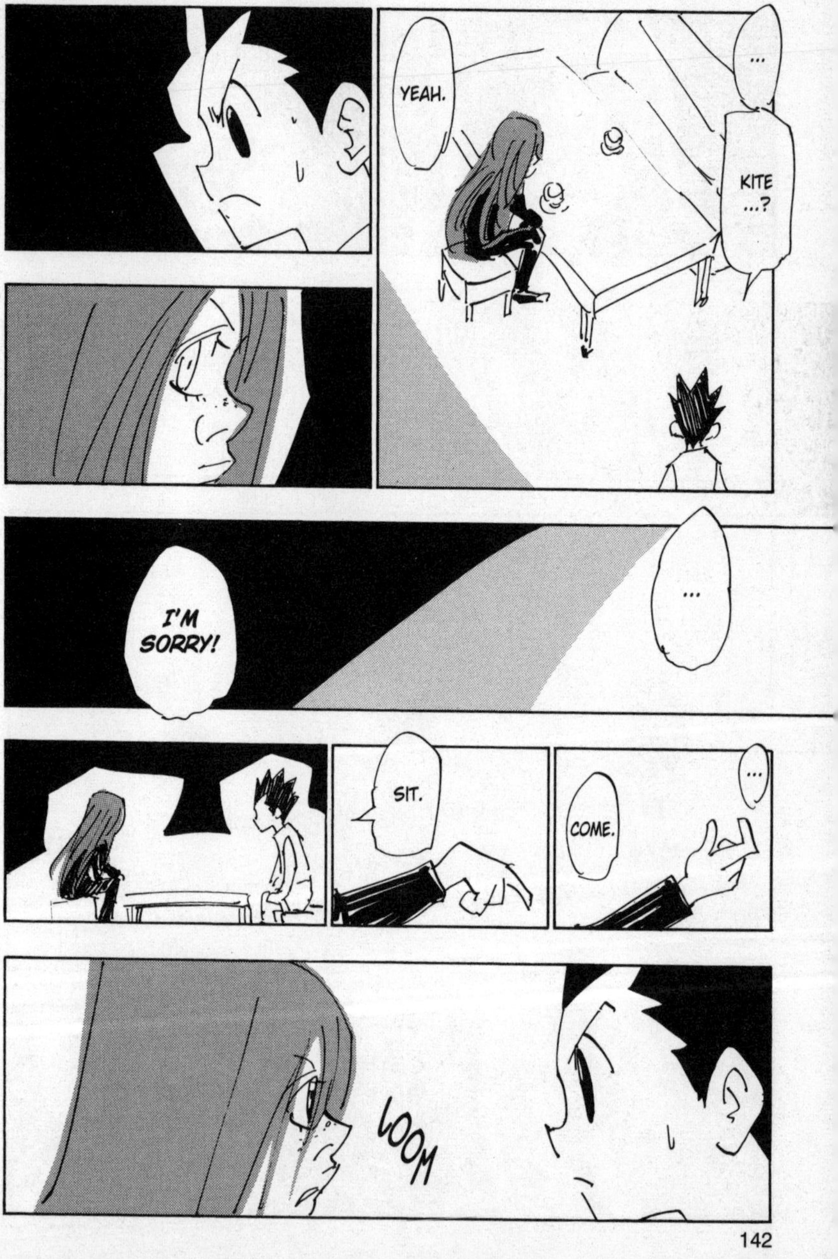
...
KITE ...?
YEAH.
...
I'M SORRY!
...
COME.
SIT.
VOOM

READ THIS WAY

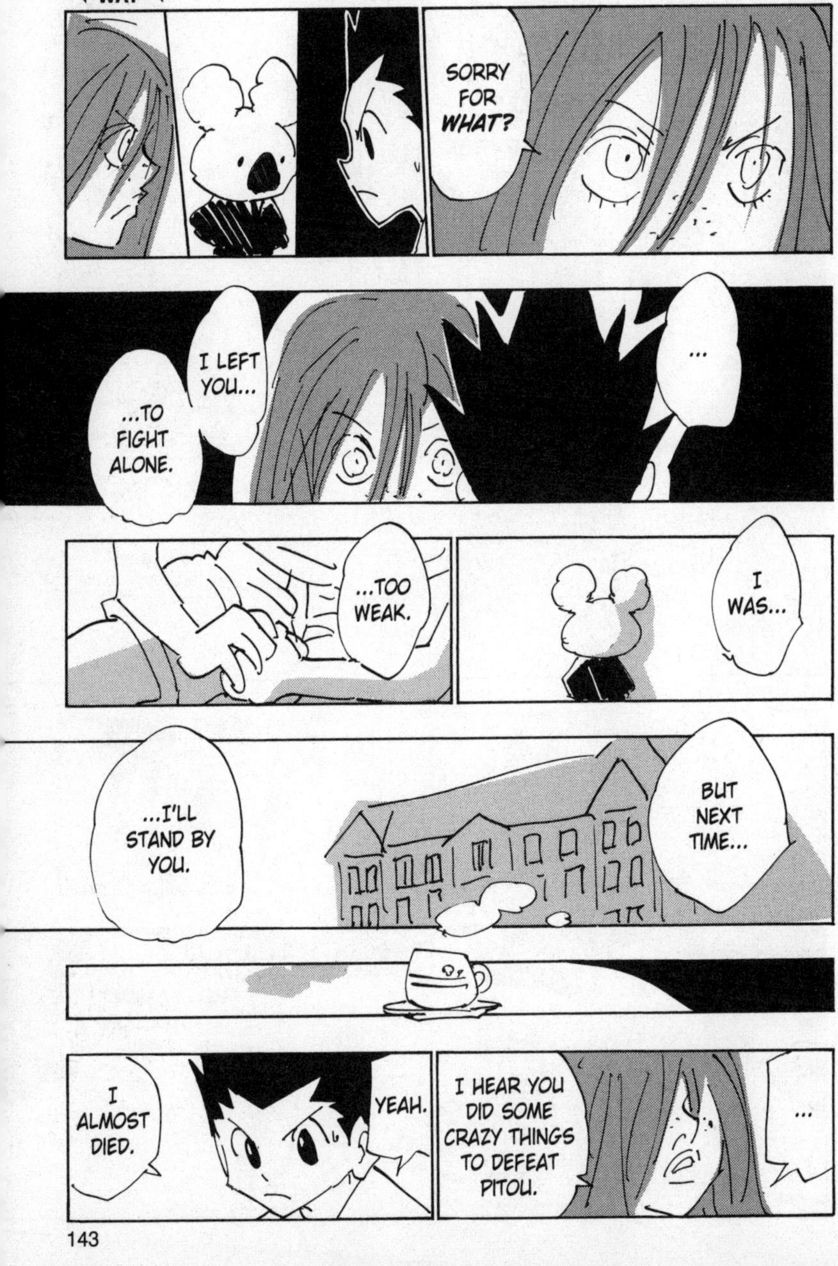

SORRY FOR WHAT?
...
I LEFT YOU...
...TO FIGHT ALONE.
I WAS...
...TOO WEAK.
BUT NEXT TIME...
...I'LL STAND BY YOU.
...
I HEAR YOU DID SOME CRAZY THINGS TO DEFEAT PITOU.
YEAH.
I ALMOST DIED.

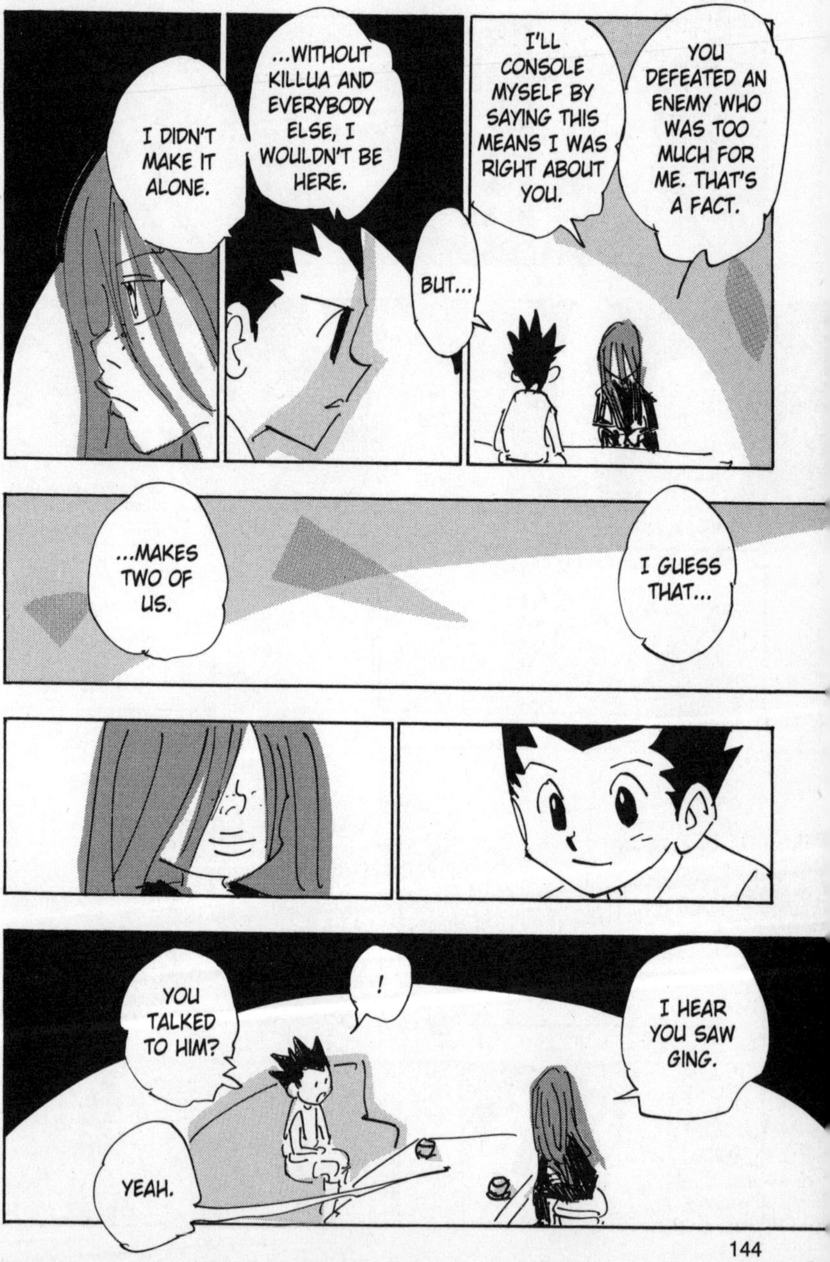
YOU DEFEATED AN ENEMY WHO WAS TOO MUCH FOR ME. THAT'S A FACT.
I'LL CONSOLE MYSELF BY SAYING THIS MEANS I WAS RIGHT ABOUT YOU.
BUT...
...WITHOUT KILLUA AND EVERYBODY ELSE, I WOULDN'T BE HERE.
I DIDN'T MAKE IT ALONE.
I GUESS THAT...
...MAKES TWO OF US.
I HEAR YOU SAW GING.
!
YOU TALKED TO HIM?
YEAH.

READ THIS WAY

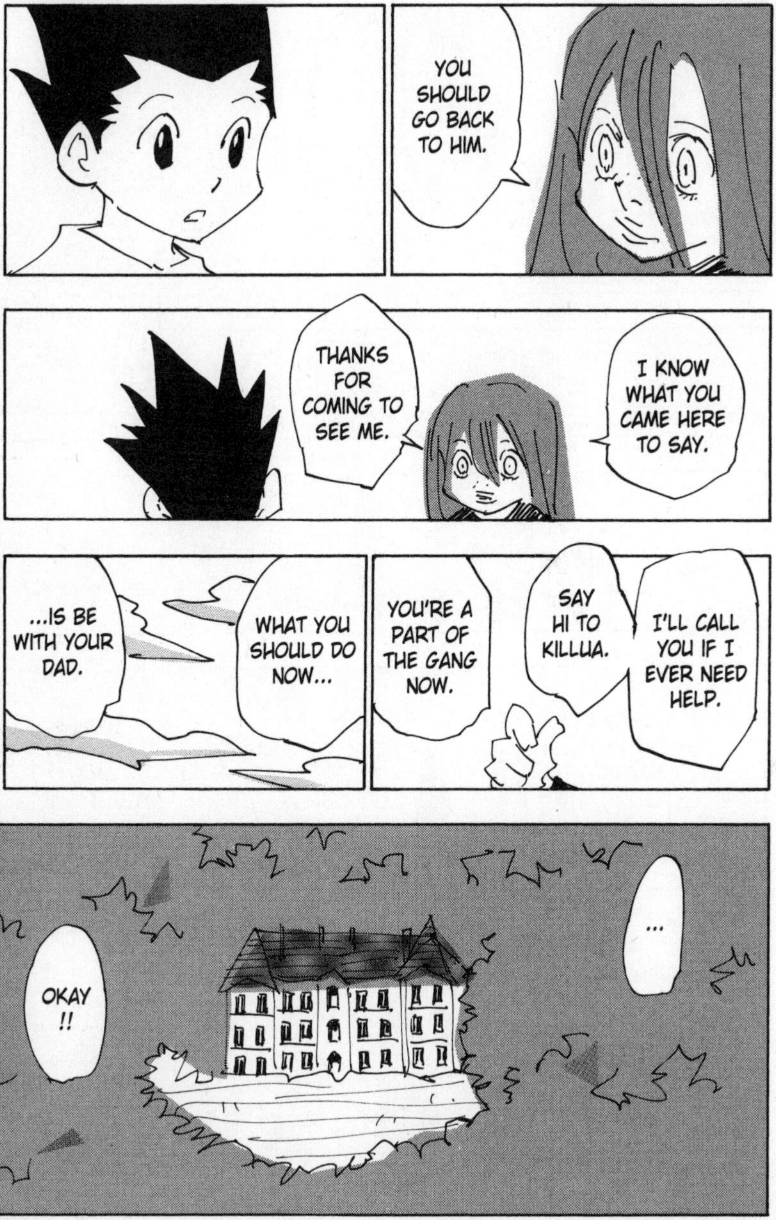
YOU SHOULD GO BACK TO HIM.
I KNOW WHAT YOU CAME HERE TO SAY.
THANKS FOR COMING TO SEE ME.
I'LL CALL YOU IF I EVER NEED HELP.
SAY HI TO KILLUA.
YOU'RE A PART OF THE GANG NOW.
WHAT YOU SHOULD DO NOW...
...IS BE WITH YOUR DAD.
...
OKAY !!

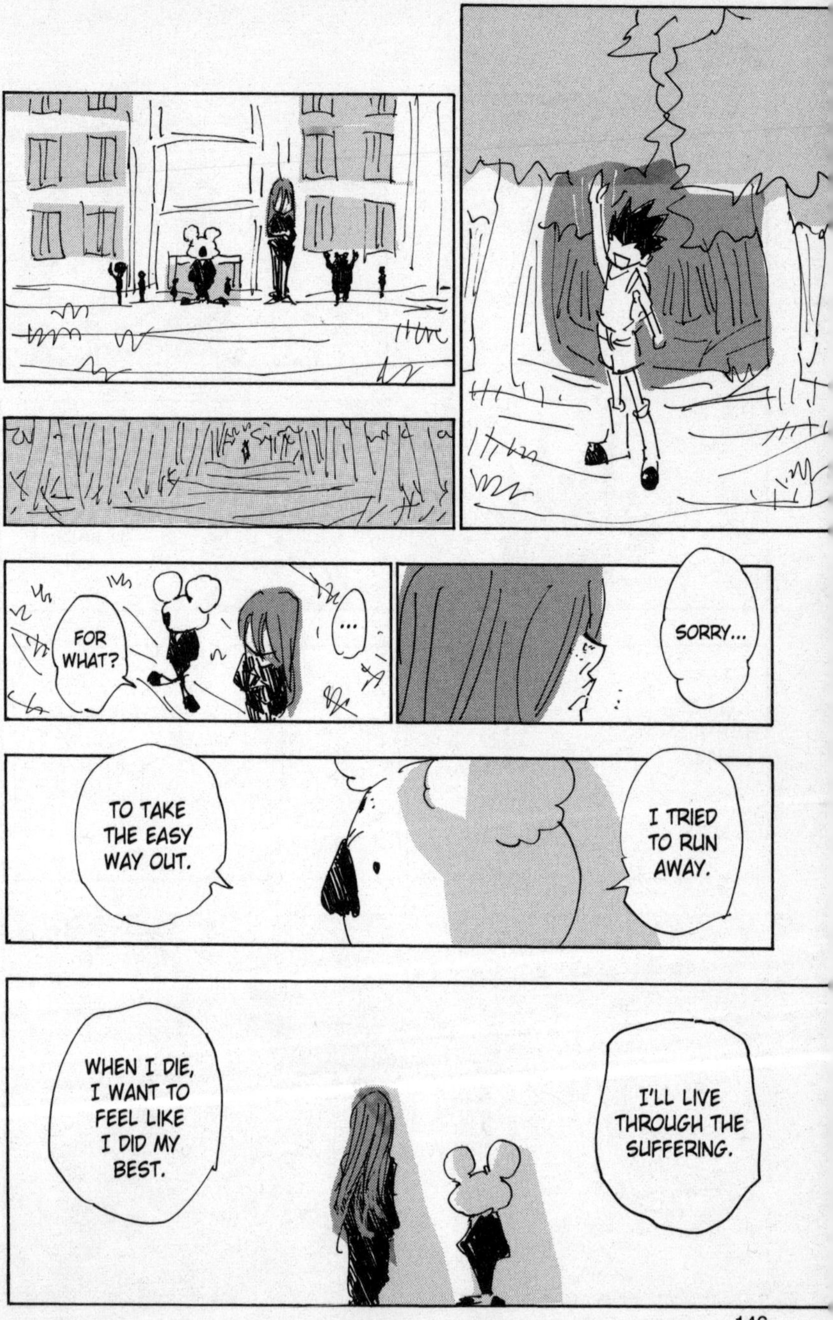
SORRY...
...
FOR WHAT?
I TRIED TO RUN AWAY.
TO TAKE THE EASY WAY OUT.
I'LL LIVE THROUGH THE SUFFERING.
WHEN I DIE, I WANT TO FEEL LIKE I DID MY BEST.

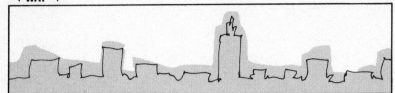

I'LL BE WAITING ON TOP OF THE WORLD TREE.

I TRIED TO STOP HIM...

...

...HE NEVER SAID HE'D BE WAITING *HERE*...

IT'S TRUE...

HUNTER×HUNTER the Movie: PHANTOM ROUGE
PROMO COMIC STRIP

PROMO ONE

OUR NEXT GUEST IS GON, STAR OF HUNTER X HUNTER!
CLAP CLAP CLAP
I'M HERE TO PROMOTE MY MOVIE!!
PLEASE WATCH IT!! THANKS!!
TA~ ~DA
I DID MY JOB!
NEXT QUESTION!!
AT LEAST PUT YOUR HAND ON THE BUZZER...
2500
0
12

Chapter 338: Atop a Tree

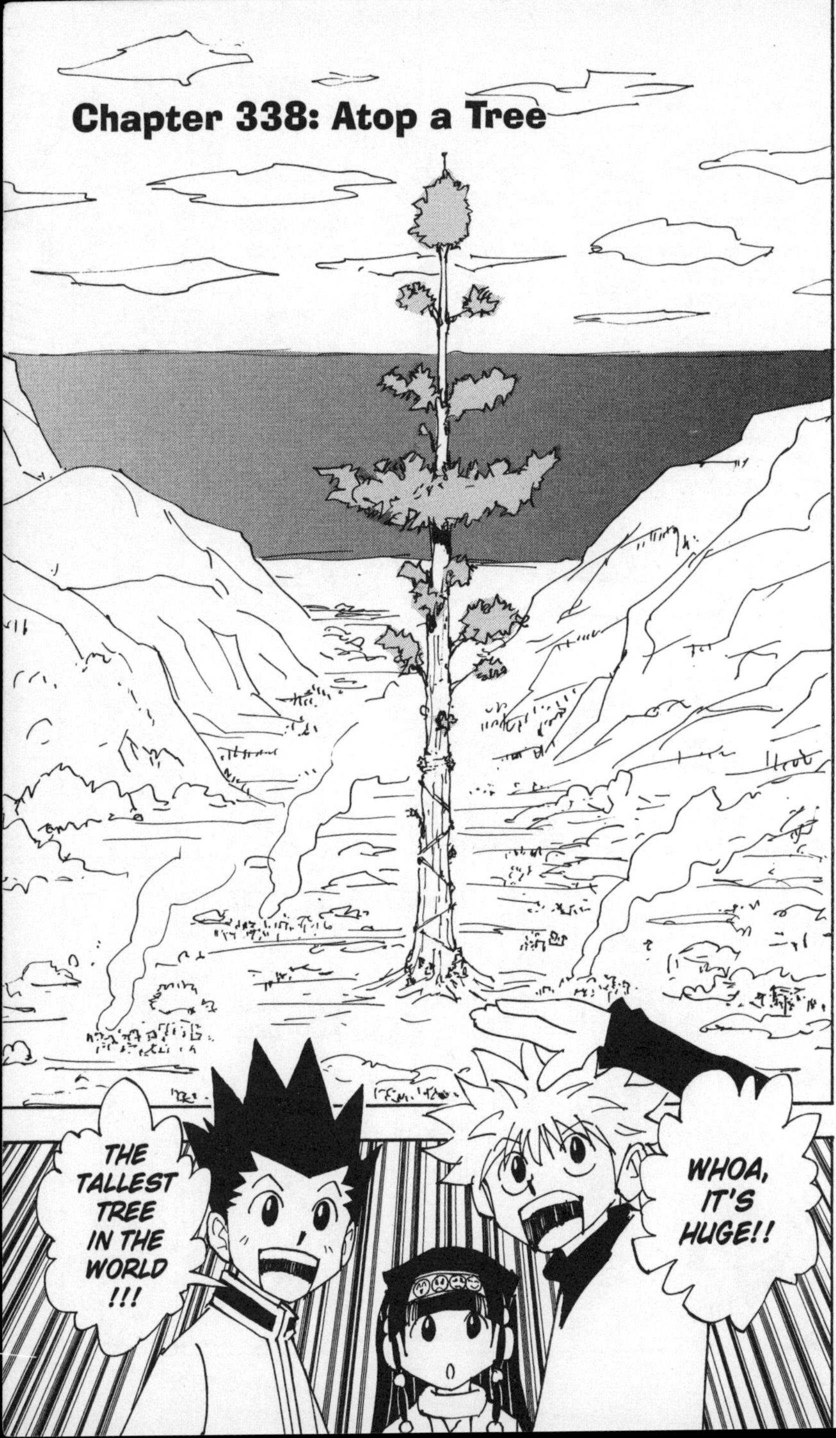
WHOA, IT'S HUGE!!
THE TALLEST TREE IN THE WORLD !!!

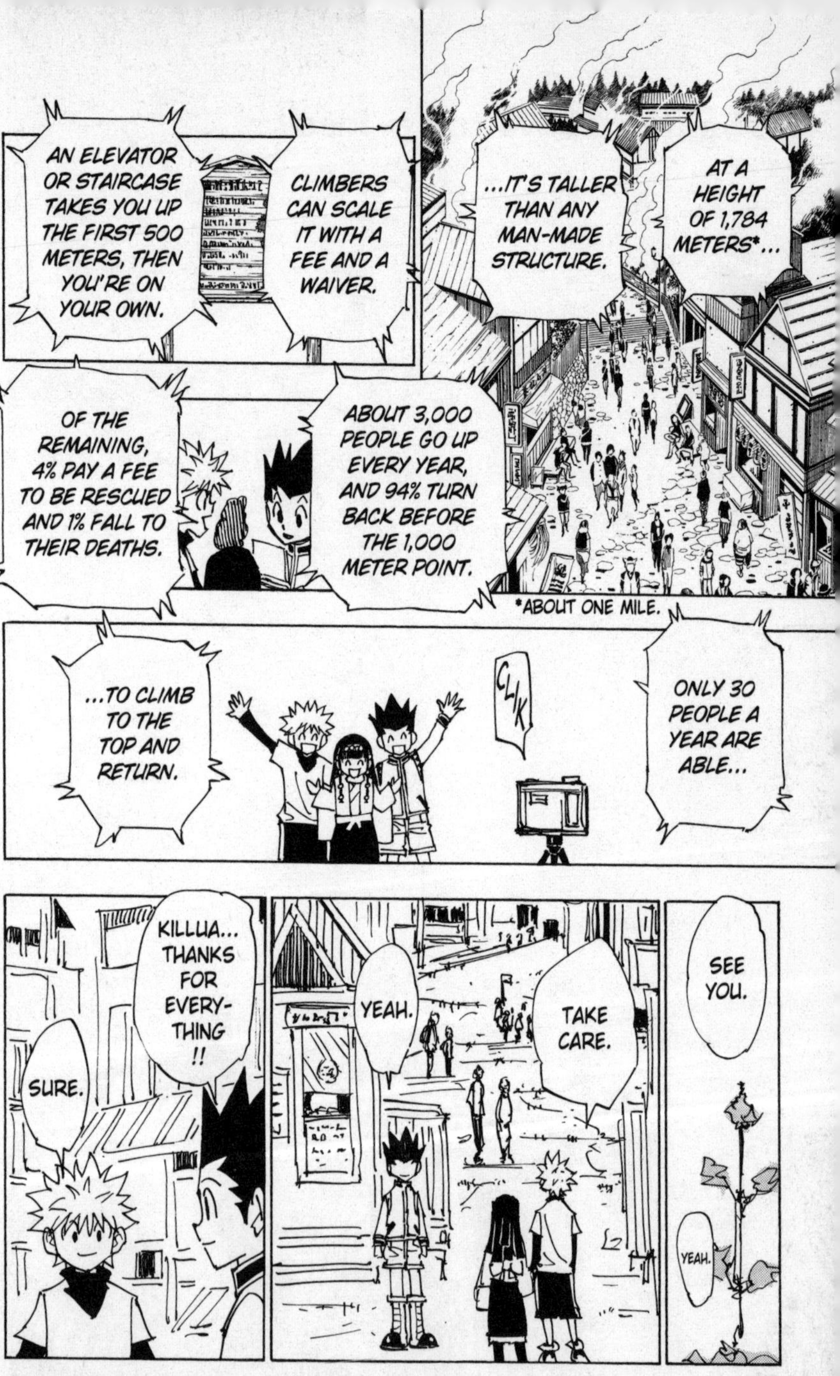
AT A HEIGHT OF 1,784 METERS*...
...IT'S TALLER THAN ANY MAN-MADE STRUCTURE.
*ABOUT ONE MILE.
CLIMBERS CAN SCALE IT WITH A FEE AND A WAIVER.
AN ELEVATOR OR STAIRCASE TAKES YOU UP THE FIRST 500 METERS, THEN YOU'RE ON YOUR OWN.
ABOUT 3,000 PEOPLE GO UP EVERY YEAR, AND 94% TURN BACK BEFORE THE 1,000 METER POINT.
OF THE REMAINING, 4% PAY A FEE TO BE RESCUED AND 1% FALL TO THEIR DEATHS.
ONLY 30 PEOPLE A YEAR ARE ABLE...
CLIK
...TO CLIMB TO THE TOP AND RETURN.
SEE YOU.
YEAH.
TAKE CARE.
YEAH.
KILLUA... THANKS FOR EVERYTHING!!
SURE.

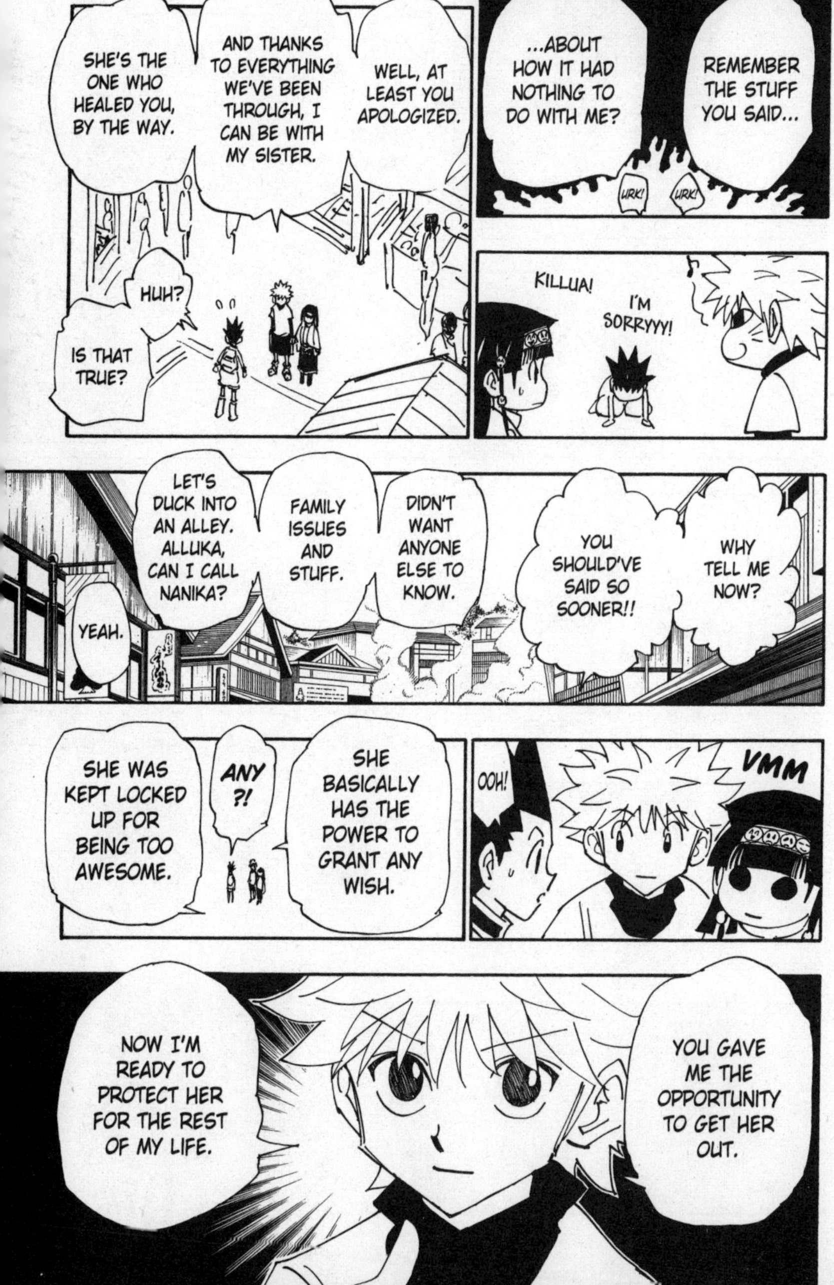
REMEMBER THE STUFF YOU SAID...
...ABOUT HOW IT HAD NOTHING TO DO WITH ME?
URK!
URK!
KILLUA!
I'M SORRYYY!
WELL, AT LEAST YOU APOLOGIZED.
AND THANKS TO EVERYTHING WE'VE BEEN THROUGH, I CAN BE WITH MY SISTER.
SHE'S THE ONE WHO HEALED YOU, BY THE WAY.
HUH?
IS THAT TRUE?
WHY TELL ME NOW?
YOU SHOULD'VE SAID SO SOONER!!
DIDN'T WANT ANYONE ELSE TO KNOW.
FAMILY ISSUES AND STUFF.
LET'S DUCK INTO AN ALLEY. ALLUKA, CAN I CALL NANIKA?
YEAH.
VMM
OOH!
SHE BASICALLY HAS THE POWER TO GRANT ANY WISH.
ANY ?!
SHE WAS KEPT LOCKED UP FOR BEING TOO AWESOME.
YOU GAVE ME THE OPPORTUNITY TO GET HER OUT.
NOW I'M READY TO PROTECT HER FOR THE REST OF MY LIFE.

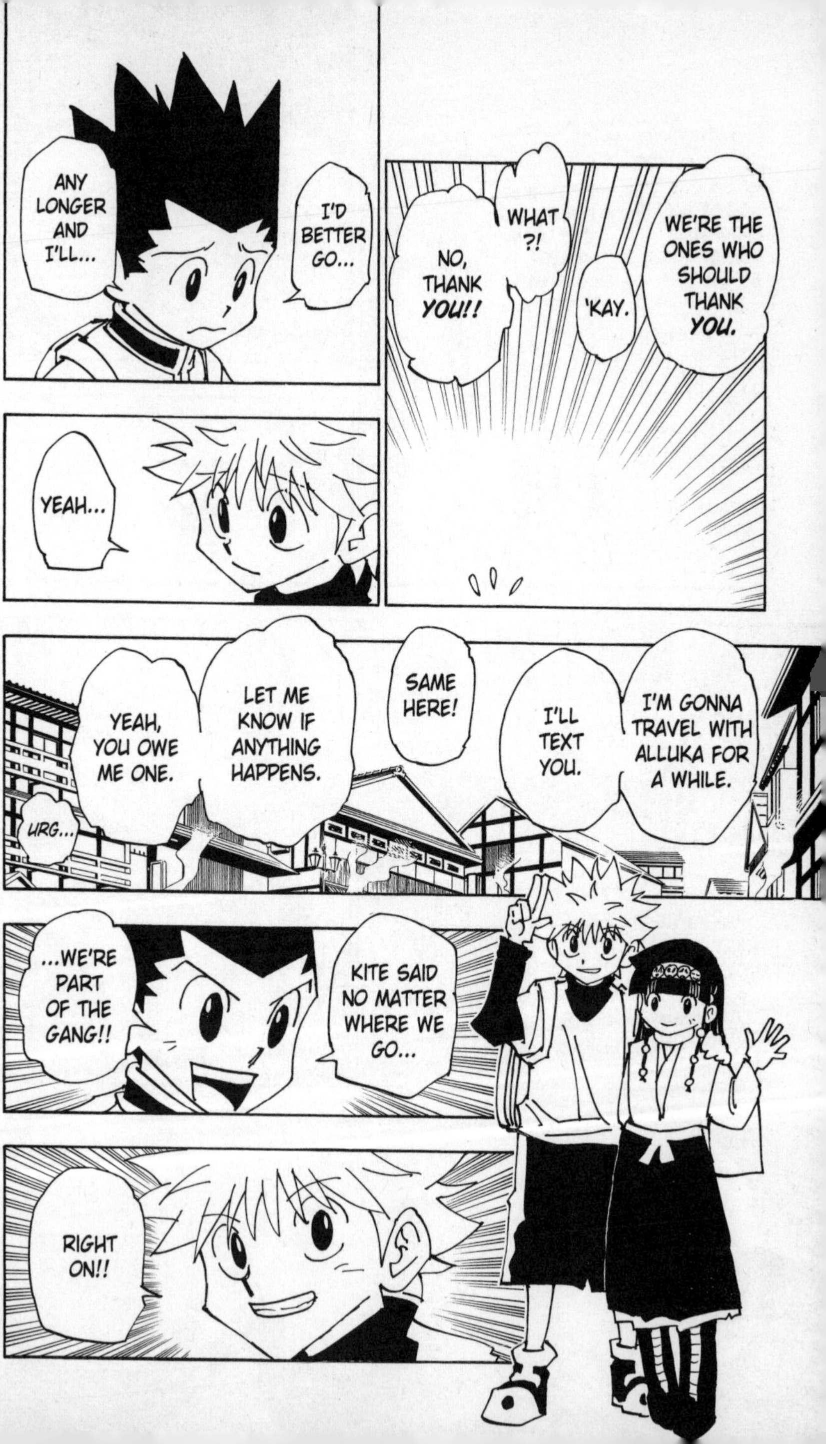
WE'RE THE ONES WHO SHOULD THANK YOU.
'KAY.
WHAT ?!
NO, THANK YOU!!
I'D BETTER GO...
ANY LONGER AND I'LL...
YEAH...
I'M GONNA TRAVEL WITH ALLUKA FOR A WHILE.
I'LL TEXT YOU.
SAME HERE!
LET ME KNOW IF ANYTHING HAPPENS.
YEAH, YOU OWE ME ONE.
URG...
KITE SAID NO MATTER WHERE WE GO...
...WE'RE PART OF THE GANG!!
RIGHT ON!!

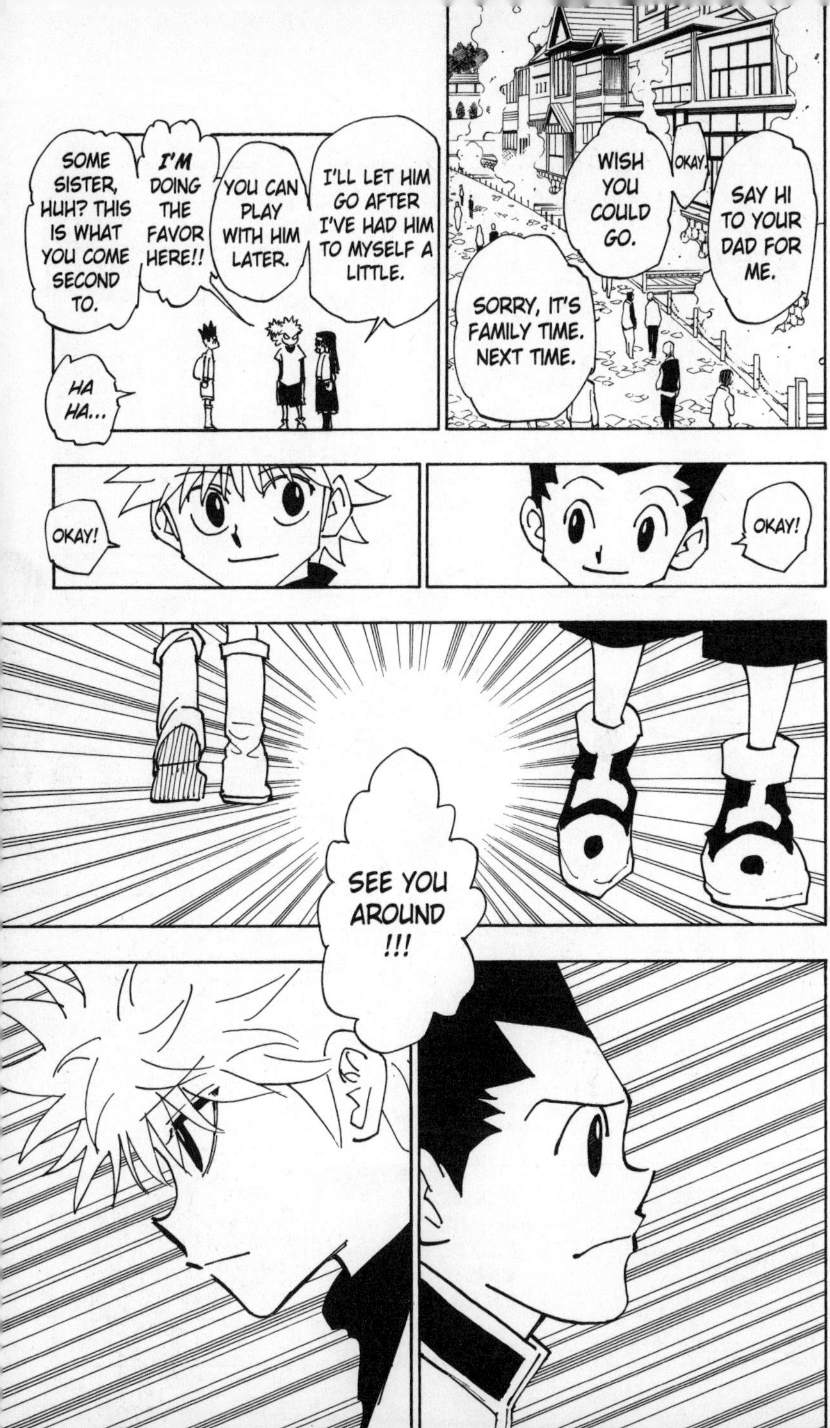
SAY HI TO YOUR DAD FOR ME.
OKAY.
WISH YOU COULD GO.
SORRY, IT'S FAMILY TIME. NEXT TIME.
I'LL LET HIM GO AFTER I'VE HAD HIM TO MYSELF A LITTLE.
YOU CAN PLAY WITH HIM LATER.
I'M DOING THE FAVOR HERE!!
SOME SISTER, HUH? THIS IS WHAT YOU COME SECOND TO.
HA HA...
OKAY!
OKAY!
SEE YOU AROUND !!!

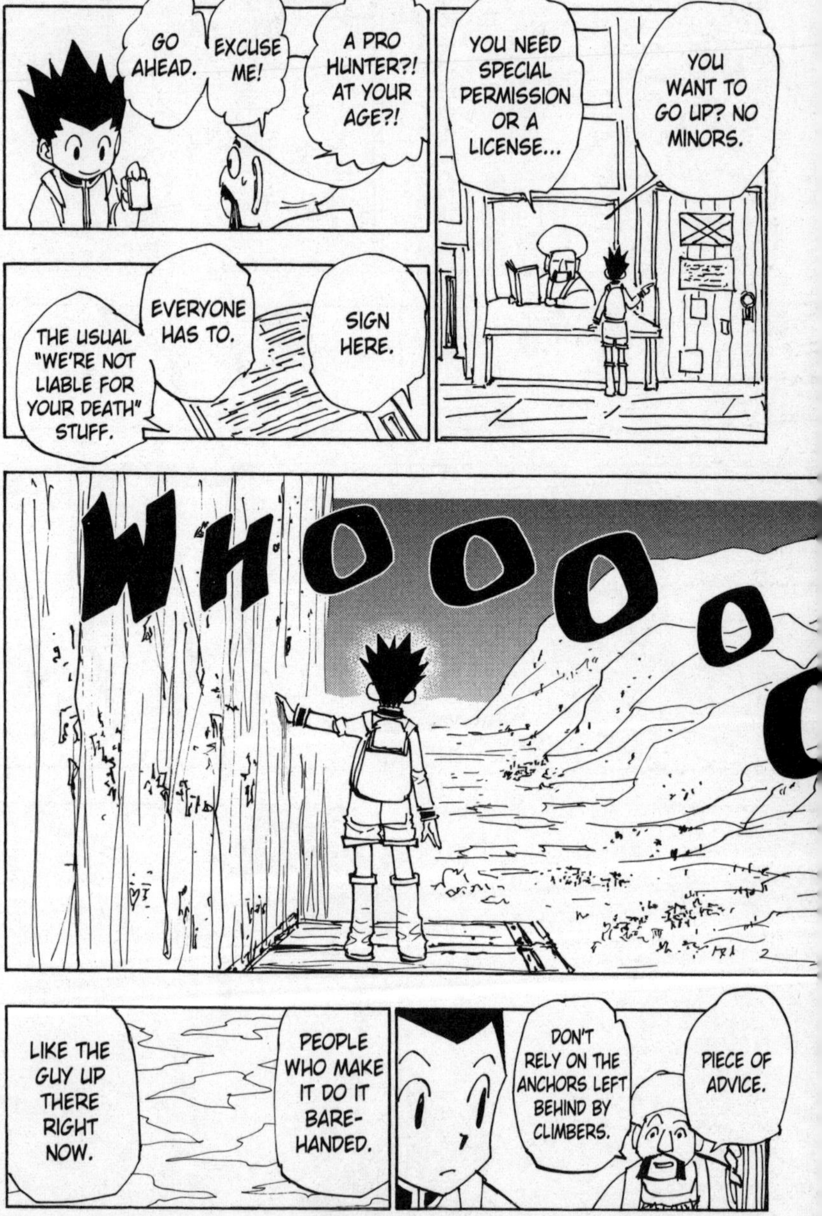
YOU WANT TO GO UP? NO MINORS.
YOU NEED SPECIAL PERMISSION OR A LICENSE...
A PRO HUNTER?! AT YOUR AGE?!
EXCUSE ME!
GO AHEAD.
SIGN HERE.
EVERYONE HAS TO.
THE USUAL "WE'RE NOT LIABLE FOR YOUR DEATH" STUFF.
WHOOOOO
PIECE OF ADVICE.
DON'T RELY ON THE ANCHORS LEFT BEHIND BY CLIMBERS.
PEOPLE WHO MAKE IT DO IT BARE-HANDED.
LIKE THE GUY UP THERE RIGHT NOW.

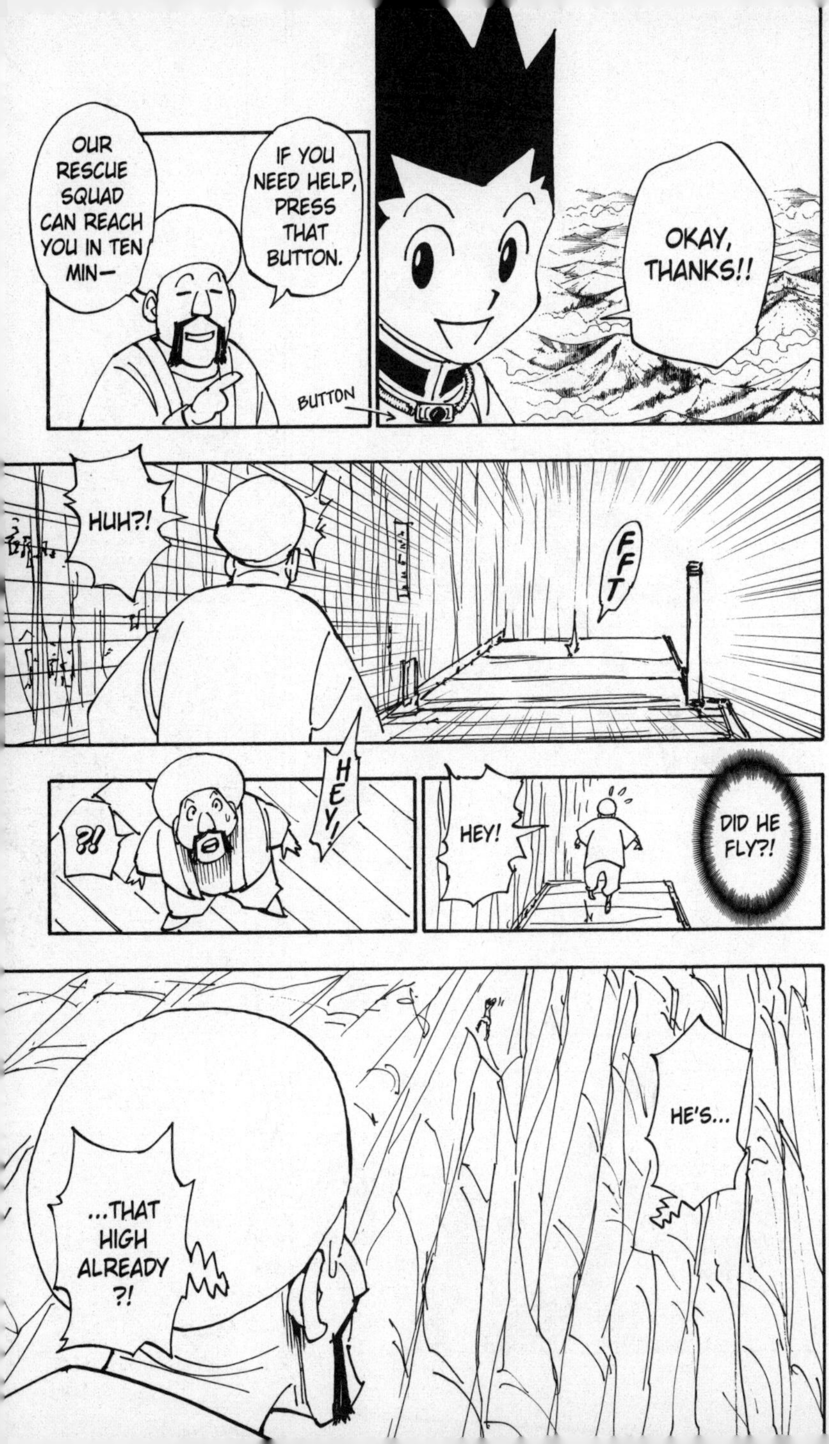
OKAY, THANKS!!
BUTTON
IF YOU NEED HELP, PRESS THAT BUTTON.
OUR RESCUE SQUAD CAN REACH YOU IN TEN MIN—
FFT
HUH?!
DID HE FLY?!
HEY!
HEY!
?!
HE'S...
...THAT HIGH ALREADY ?!

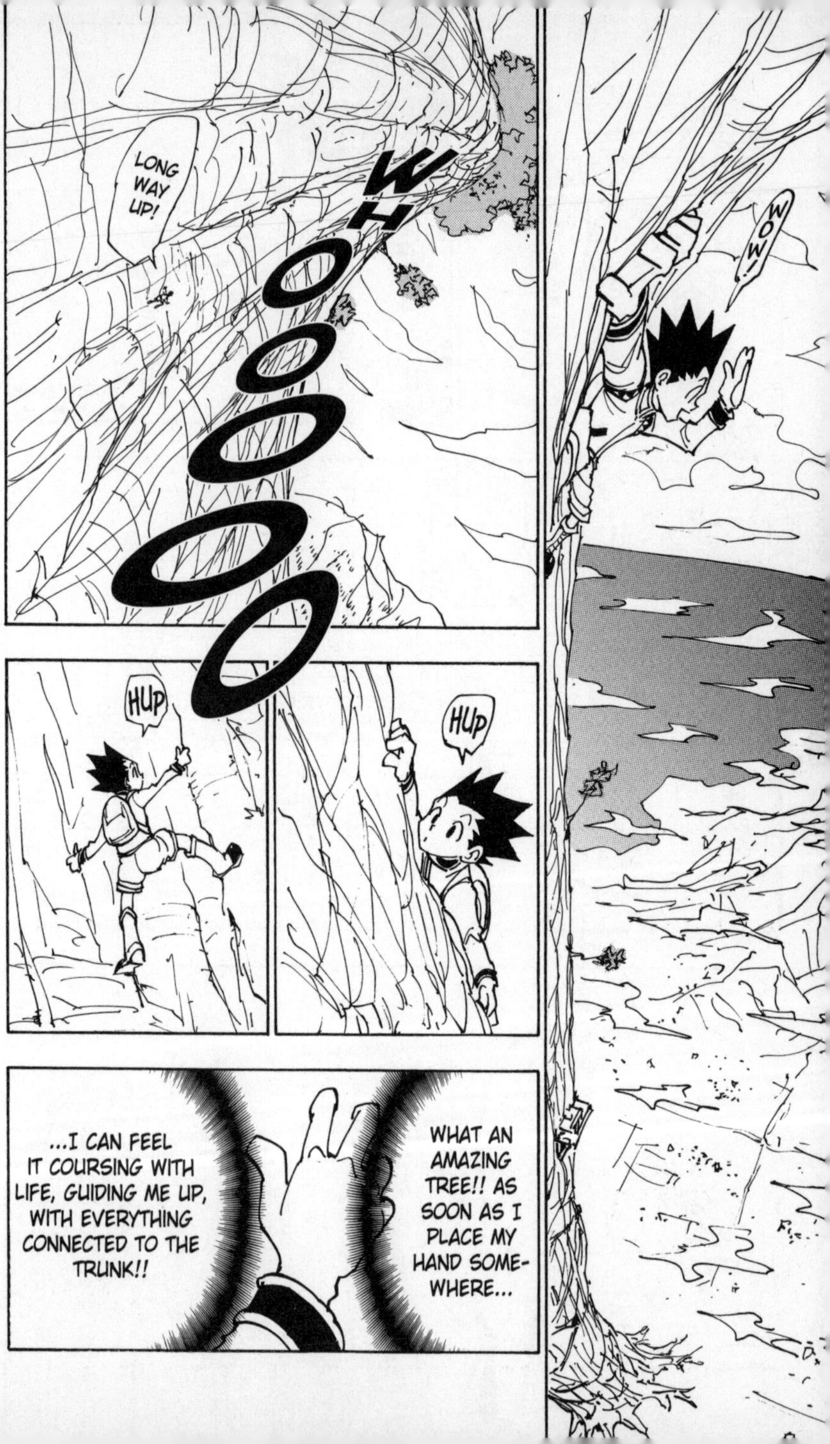
WOW!
LONG WAY UP!
WHOOOOOO
HUP
HUP
WHAT AN AMAZING TREE!! AS SOON AS I PLACE MY HAND SOME-WHERE...
...I CAN FEEL IT COURSING WITH LIFE, GUIDING ME UP, WITH EVERYTHING CONNECTED TO THE TRUNK!!

READ THIS WAY

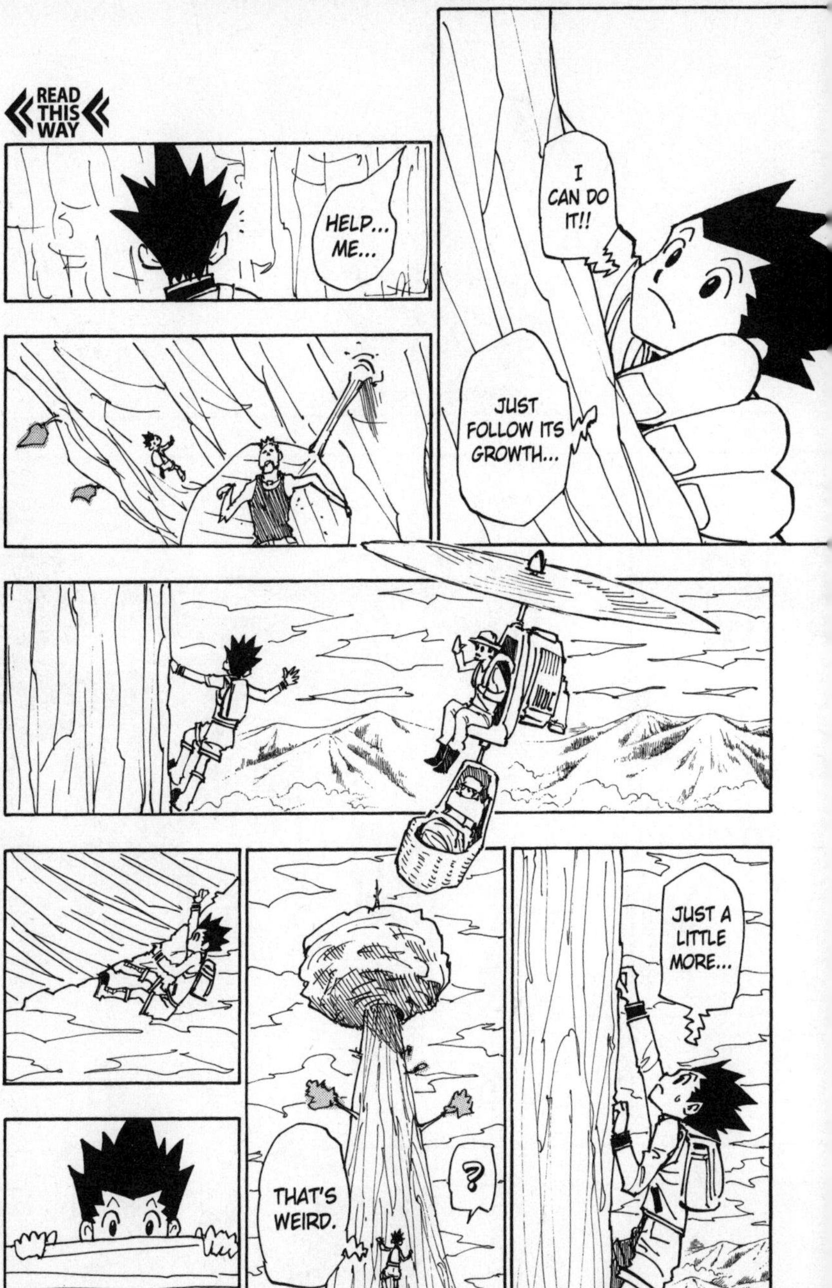
I CAN DO IT!!
JUST FOLLOW ITS GROWTH...
HELP... ME...
JUST A LITTLE MORE...
?
THAT'S WEIRD.

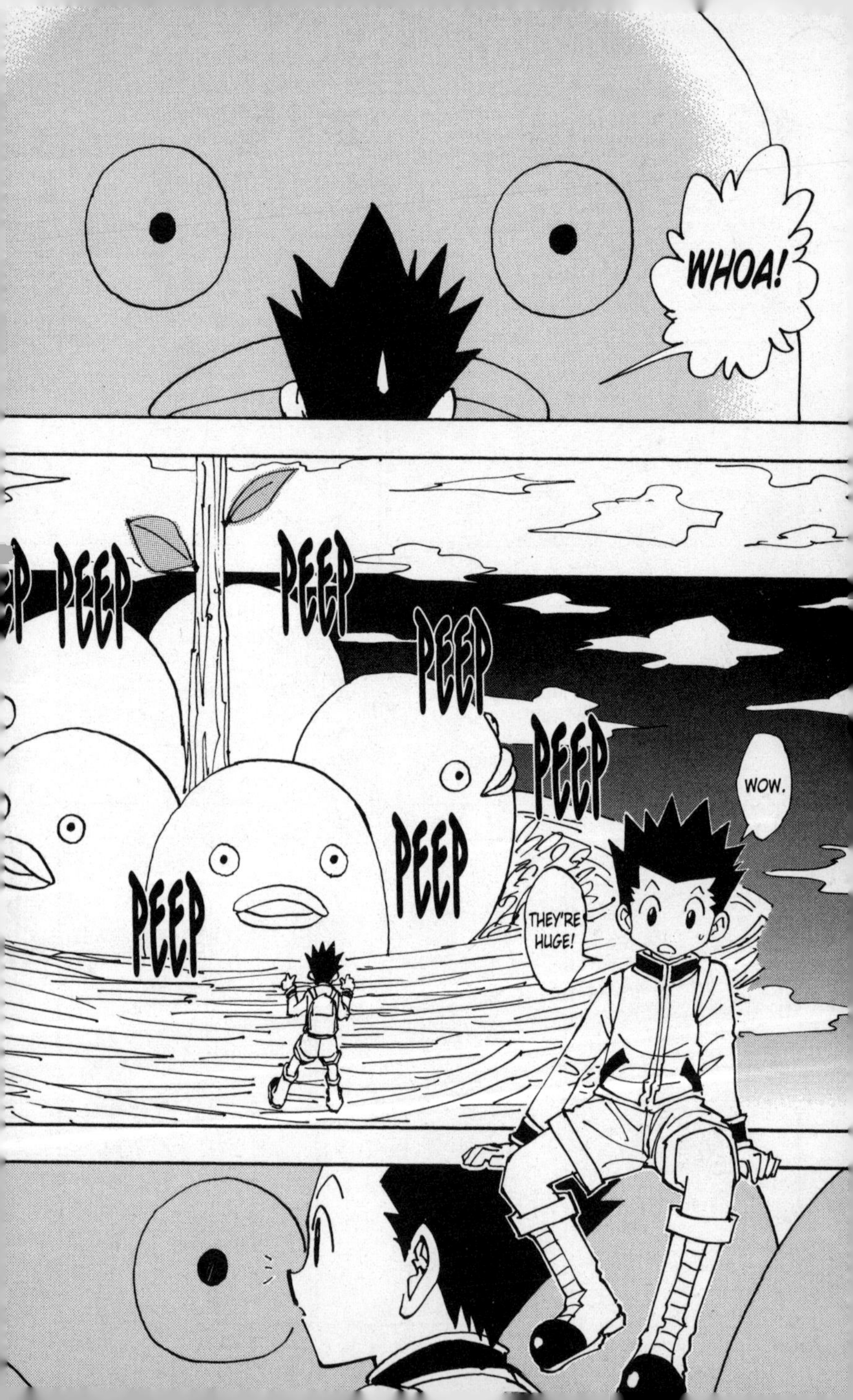
WHOA!
PEEP
PEEP
PEEP
WOW.
PEEP
THEY'RE HUGE!
PEEP
PEEP

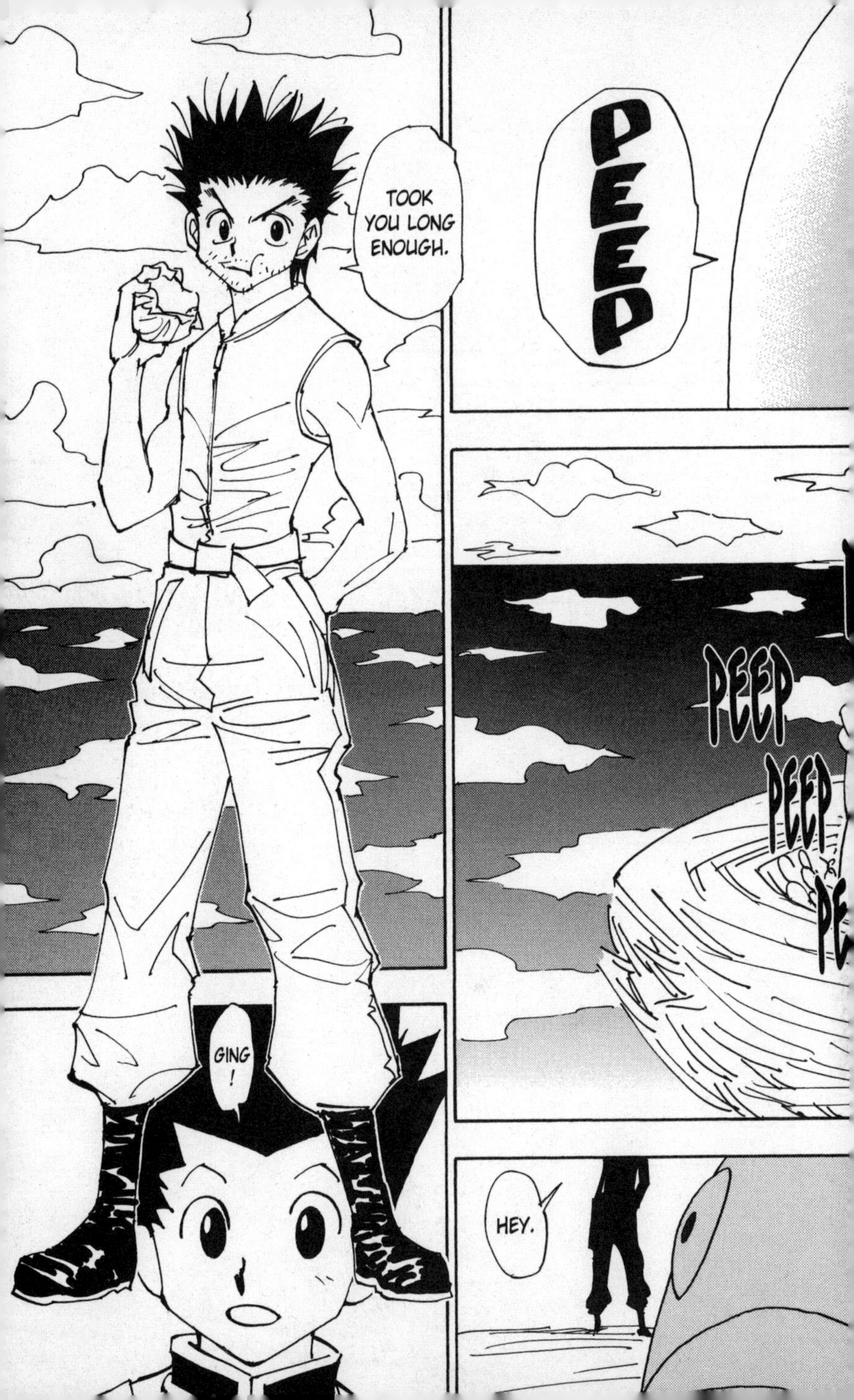
PEEP
PEEP
PEEP
HEY.
TOOK YOU LONG ENOUGH.
GING!

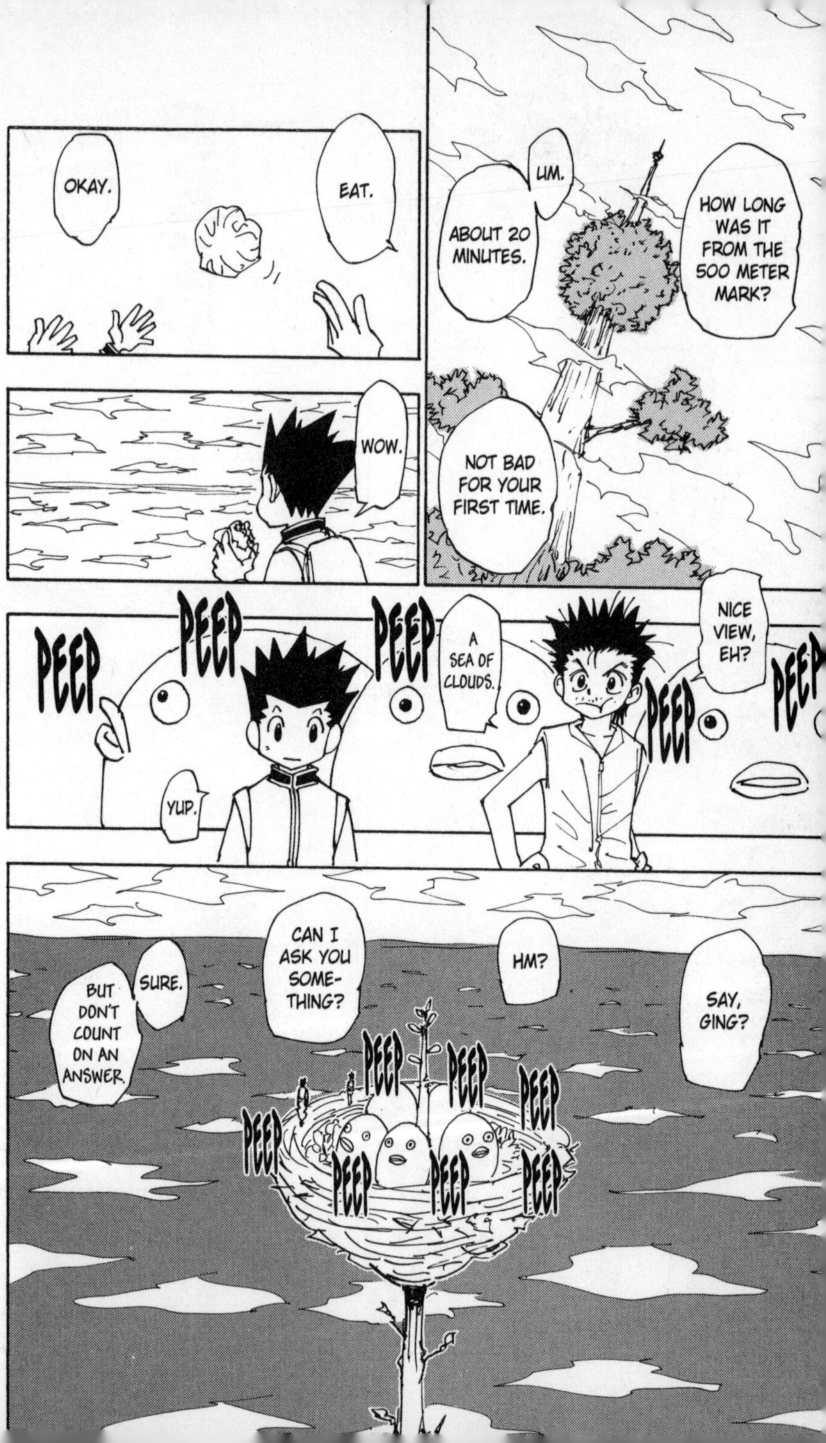
HOW LONG WAS IT FROM THE 500 METER MARK?
UM.
ABOUT 20 MINUTES.
NOT BAD FOR YOUR FIRST TIME.
EAT.
OKAY.
WOW.
PEEP
PEEP
NICE VIEW, EH?
A SEA OF CLOUDS.
PEEP
PEEP
PEEP
YUP.
SAY, GING?
HM?
CAN I ASK YOU SOME-THING?
SURE.
BUT DON'T COUNT ON AN ANSWER.
PEEP
PEEP
PEEP
PEEP
PEEP
PEEP
PEEP

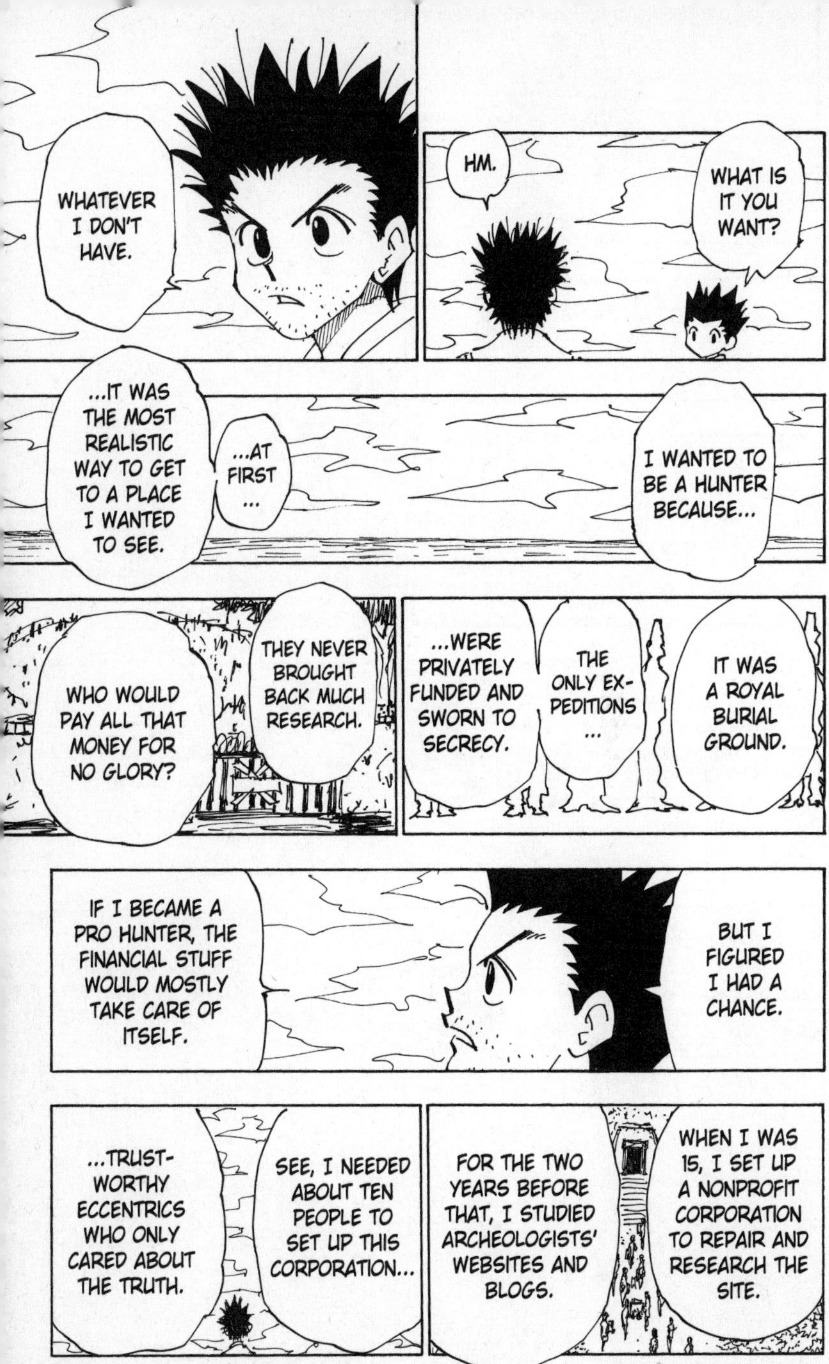
WHAT IS IT YOU WANT?
HM.
WHATEVER I DON'T HAVE.
I WANTED TO BE A HUNTER BECAUSE...
...AT FIRST ...
...IT WAS THE MOST REALISTIC WAY TO GET TO A PLACE I WANTED TO SEE.
IT WAS A ROYAL BURIAL GROUND.
THE ONLY EX-PEDITIONS ...
...WERE PRIVATELY FUNDED AND SWORN TO SECRECY.
THEY NEVER BROUGHT BACK MUCH RESEARCH.
WHO WOULD PAY ALL THAT MONEY FOR NO GLORY?
BUT I FIGURED I HAD A CHANCE.
IF I BECAME A PRO HUNTER, THE FINANCIAL STUFF WOULD MOSTLY TAKE CARE OF ITSELF.
WHEN I WAS 15, I SET UP A NONPROFIT CORPORATION TO REPAIR AND RESEARCH THE SITE.
FOR THE TWO YEARS BEFORE THAT, I STUDIED ARCHEOLOGISTS' WEBSITES AND BLOGS.
SEE, I NEEDED ABOUT TEN PEOPLE TO SET UP THIS CORPORATION...
...TRUST-WORTHY ECCENTRICS WHO ONLY CARED ABOUT THE TRUTH.

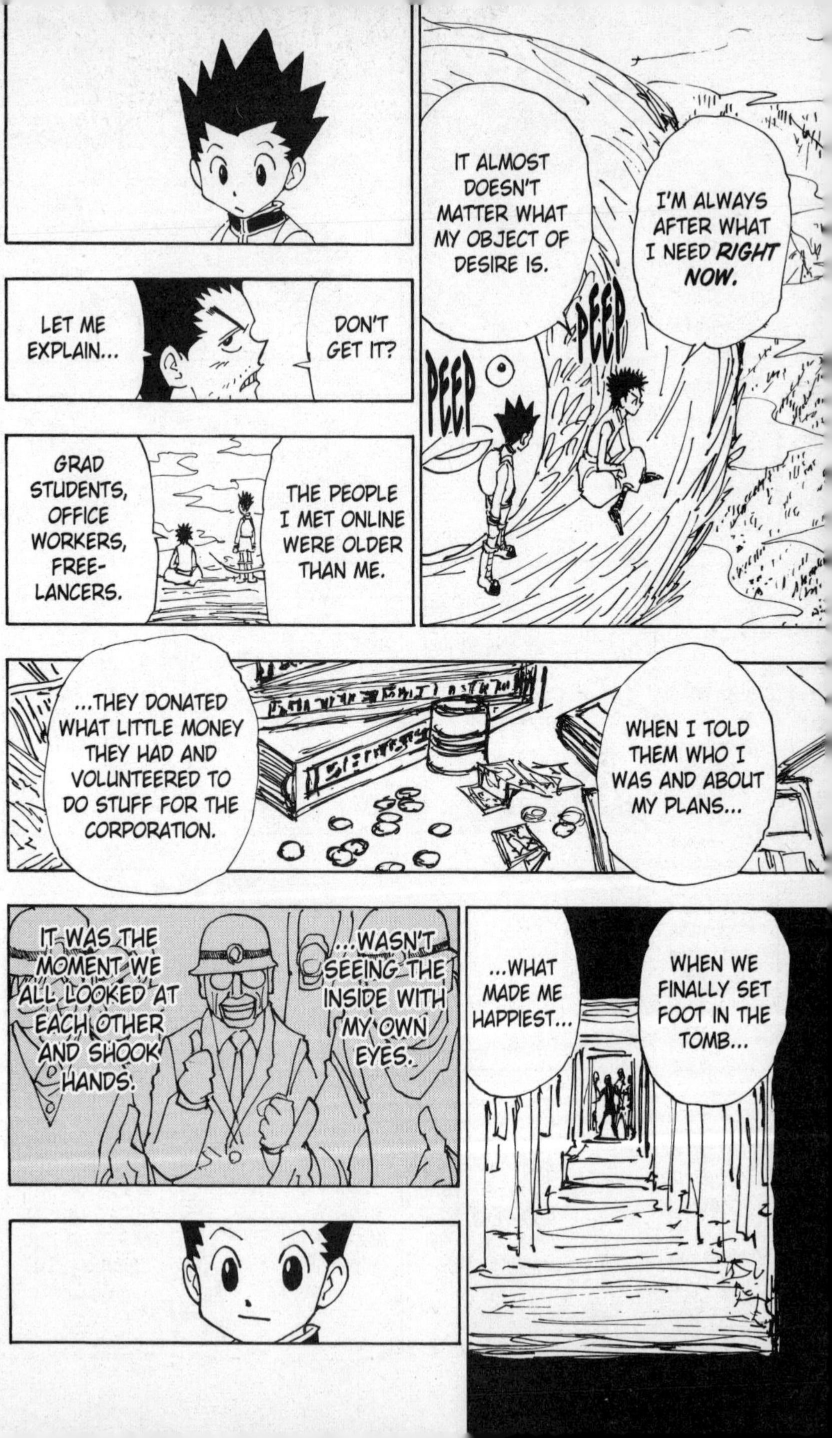
I'M ALWAYS AFTER WHAT I NEED *RIGHT NOW.*
IT ALMOST DOESN'T MATTER WHAT MY OBJECT OF DESIRE IS.
PEEP
PEEP
DON'T GET IT?
LET ME EXPLAIN...
THE PEOPLE I MET ONLINE WERE OLDER THAN ME.
GRAD STUDENTS, OFFICE WORKERS, FREE-LANCERS.
WHEN I TOLD THEM WHO I WAS AND ABOUT MY PLANS...
...THEY DONATED WHAT LITTLE MONEY THEY HAD AND VOLUNTEERED TO DO STUFF FOR THE CORPORATION.
WHEN WE FINALLY SET FOOT IN THE TOMB...
...WHAT MADE ME HAPPIEST...
...WASN'T SEEING THE INSIDE WITH MY OWN EYES.
IT WAS THE MOMENT WE ALL LOOKED AT EACH OTHER AND SHOOK HANDS.

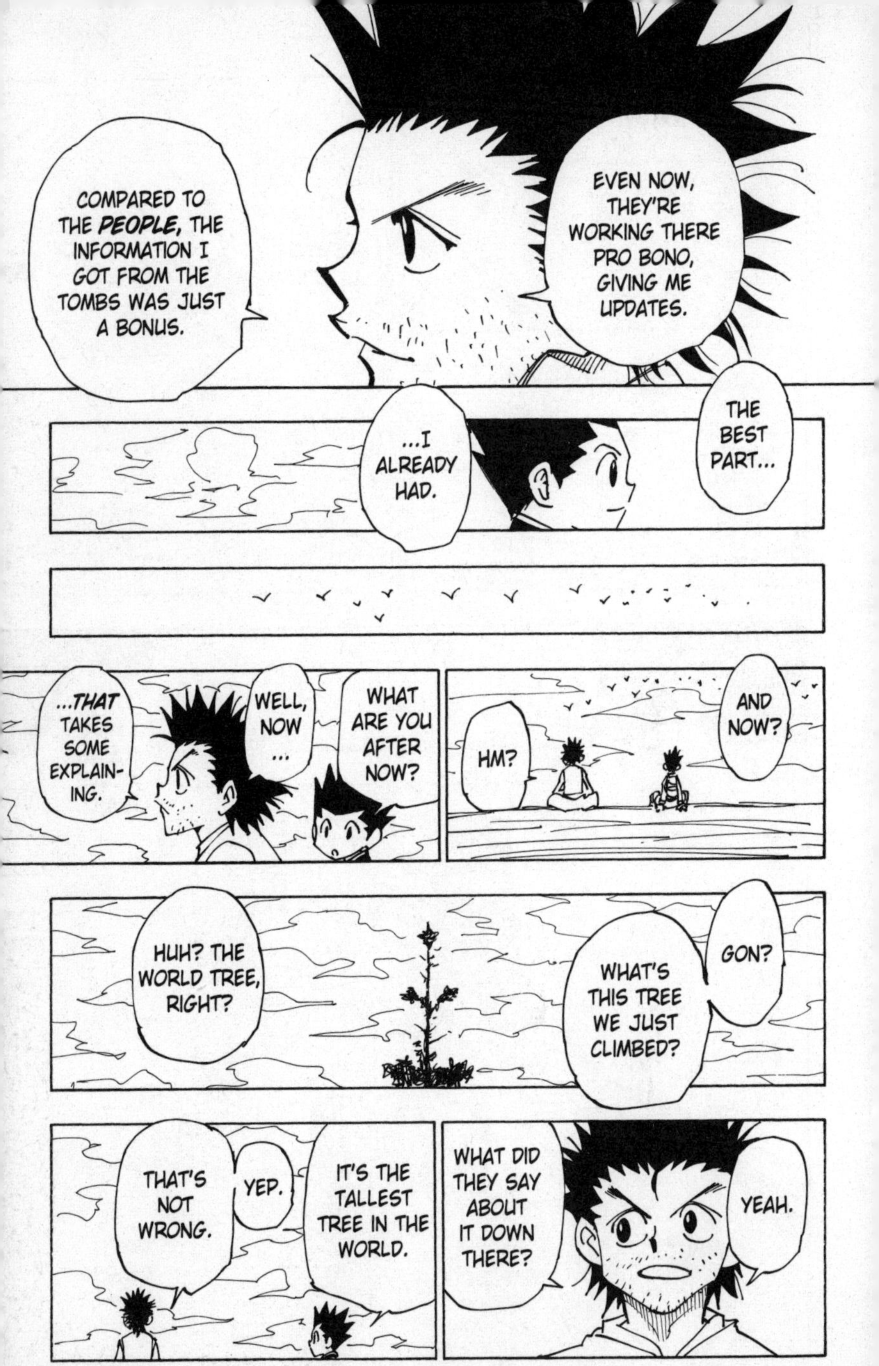
EVEN NOW, THEY'RE WORKING THERE PRO BONO, GIVING ME UPDATES.
COMPARED TO THE *PEOPLE*, THE INFORMATION I GOT FROM THE TOMBS WAS JUST A BONUS.
THE BEST PART...
...I ALREADY HAD.
AND NOW?
HM?
WHAT ARE YOU AFTER NOW?
WELL, NOW ...
...*THAT* TAKES SOME EXPLAINING.
GON?
WHAT'S THIS TREE WE JUST CLIMBED?
HUH? THE WORLD TREE, RIGHT?
YEAH.
WHAT DID THEY SAY ABOUT IT DOWN THERE?
IT'S THE TALLEST TREE IN THE WORLD.
YEP.
THAT'S NOT WRONG.

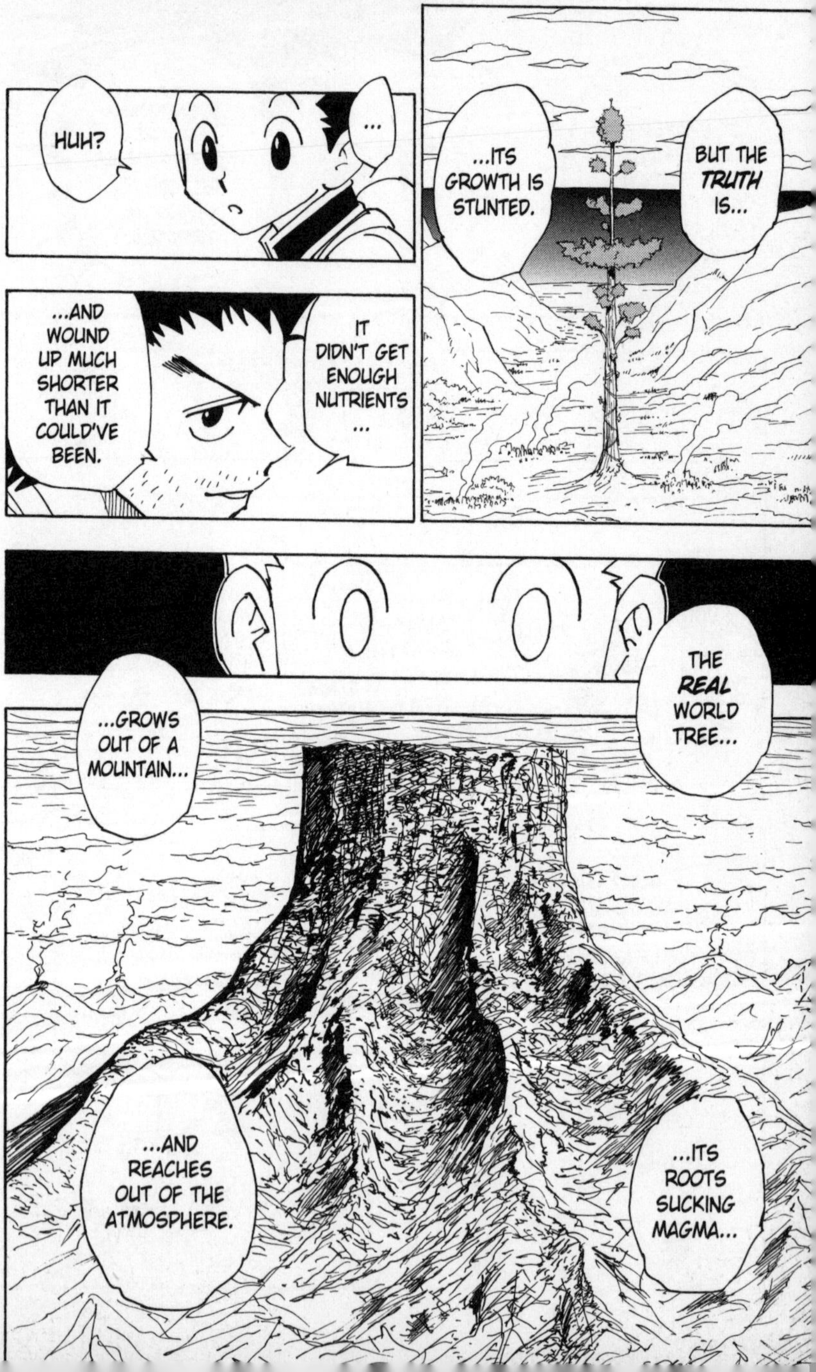
BUT THE TRUTH IS...
...ITS GROWTH IS STUNTED.
...
HUH?
IT DIDN'T GET ENOUGH NUTRIENTS ...
...AND WOUND UP MUCH SHORTER THAN IT COULD'VE BEEN.
THE REAL WORLD TREE...
...GROWS OUT OF A MOUNTAIN...
...ITS ROOTS SUCKING MAGMA...
...AND REACHES OUT OF THE ATMOSPHERE.

IT'S *OUTSIDE*...
...OF THIS WORLD.
THIS WORLD ...?
THE MAP YOU KNOW.
THE ANTS YOU GUYS FOUGHT WERE FROM OUTSIDE TOO.
THE GAME WAS OVER ...
THAT'S SOMETHING THEY DON'T TEACH YOU IN SCHOOL.
THERE...
ZERO HAND.
ADULTS WITH COMMON SENSE...
...TRY NOT TO OPEN PANDORA'S BOX.

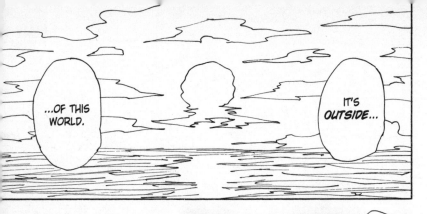

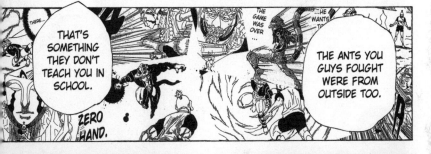

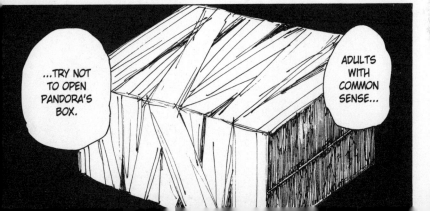

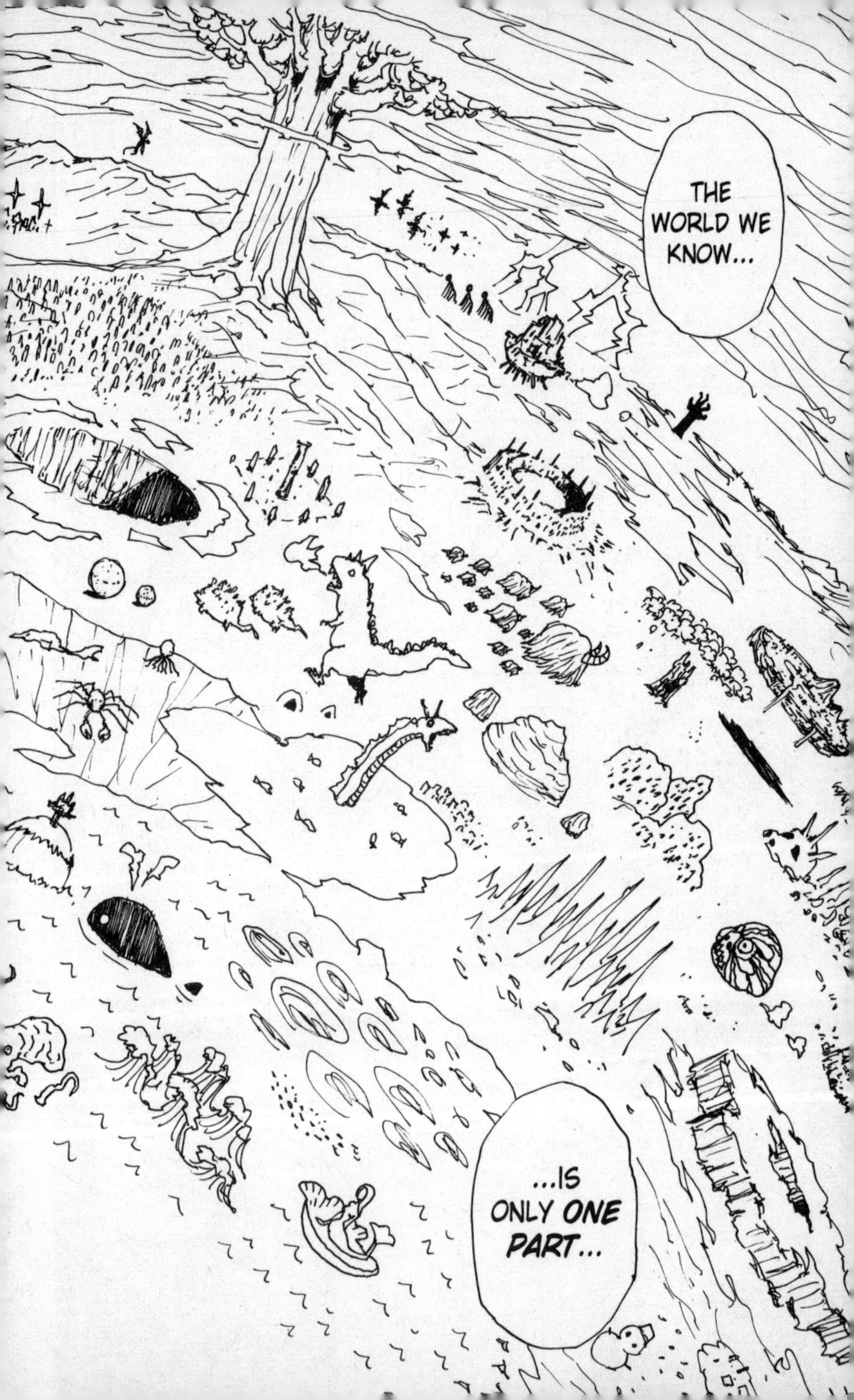
THE WORLD WE KNOW...
...IS ONLY ONE PART...

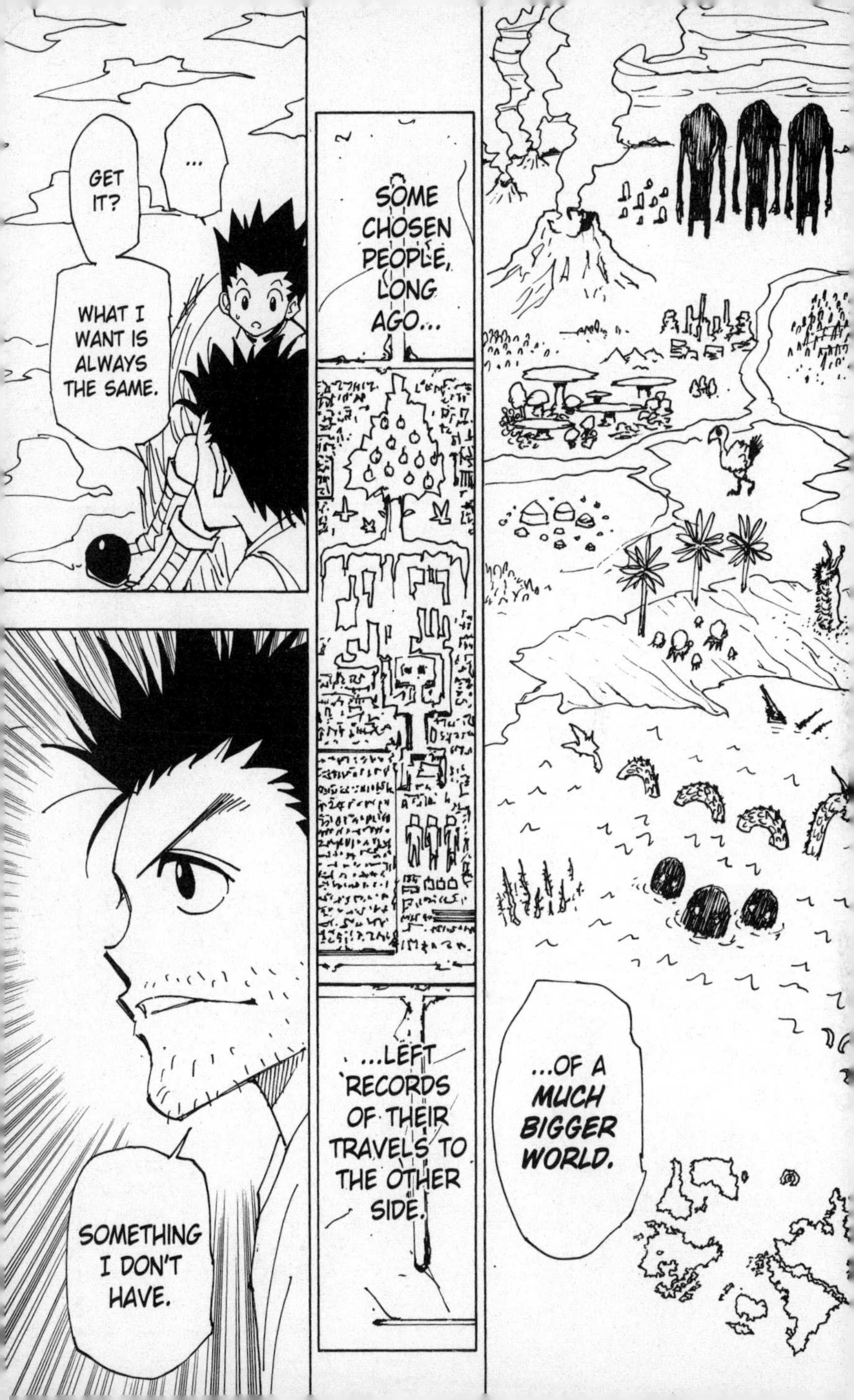

GET IT?
...
WHAT I WANT IS ALWAYS THE SAME.
SOMETHING I DON'T HAVE.
SOME CHOSEN PEOPLE, LONG AGO...
...LEFT RECORDS OF THEIR TRAVELS TO THE OTHER SIDE.
...OF A *MUCH BIGGER WORLD.*

PROMO TWO

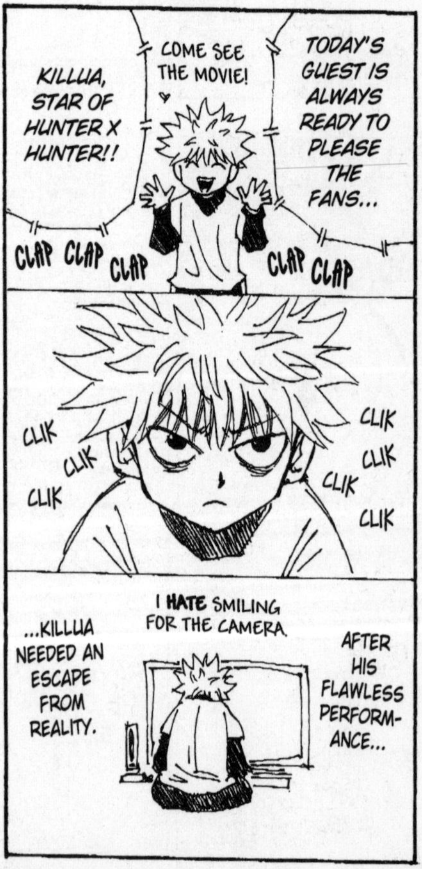
TODAY'S GUEST IS ALWAYS READY TO PLEASE THE FANS...
COME SEE THE MOVIE! ♥
KILLUA, STAR OF HUNTER X HUNTER!!
CLAP CLAP
CLAP CLAP CLAP
CLIK CLIK CLIK CLIK
CLIK CLIK CLIK
AFTER HIS FLAWLESS PERFORMANCE...
I **HATE** SMILING FOR THE CAMERA.
...KILLUA NEEDED AN ESCAPE FROM REALITY.

HUNTER×HUNTER the Movie:
PHANTOM ROUGE
PROMO COMIC STRIP

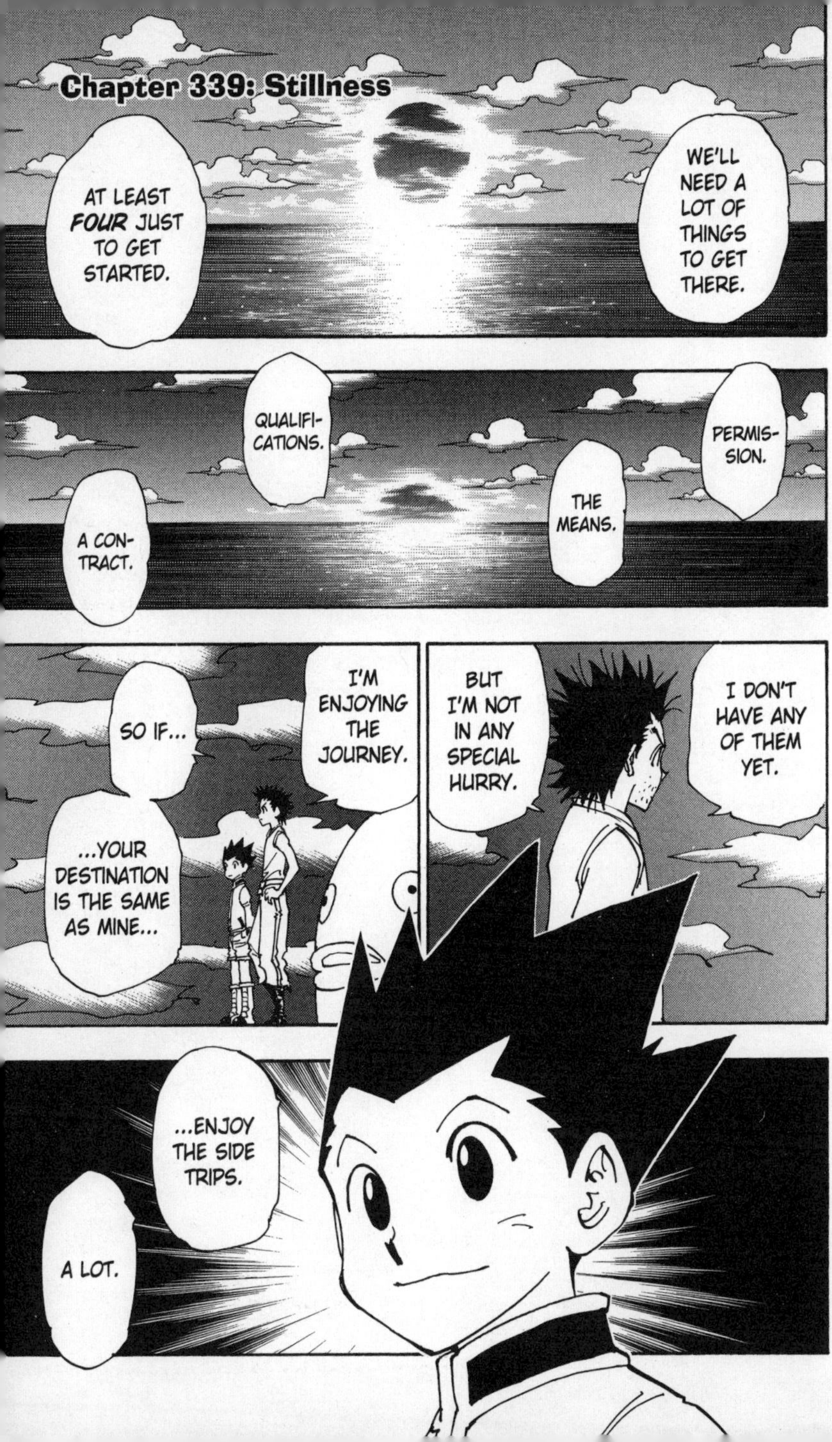
Chapter 339: Stillness
WE'LL NEED A LOT OF THINGS TO GET THERE.
AT LEAST FOUR JUST TO GET STARTED.
PERMISSION.
THE MEANS.
QUALIFICATIONS.
A CONTRACT.
I DON'T HAVE ANY OF THEM YET.
BUT I'M NOT IN ANY SPECIAL HURRY.
I'M ENJOYING THE JOURNEY.
SO IF...
...YOUR DESTINATION IS THE SAME AS MINE...
...ENJOY THE SIDE TRIPS.
A LOT.

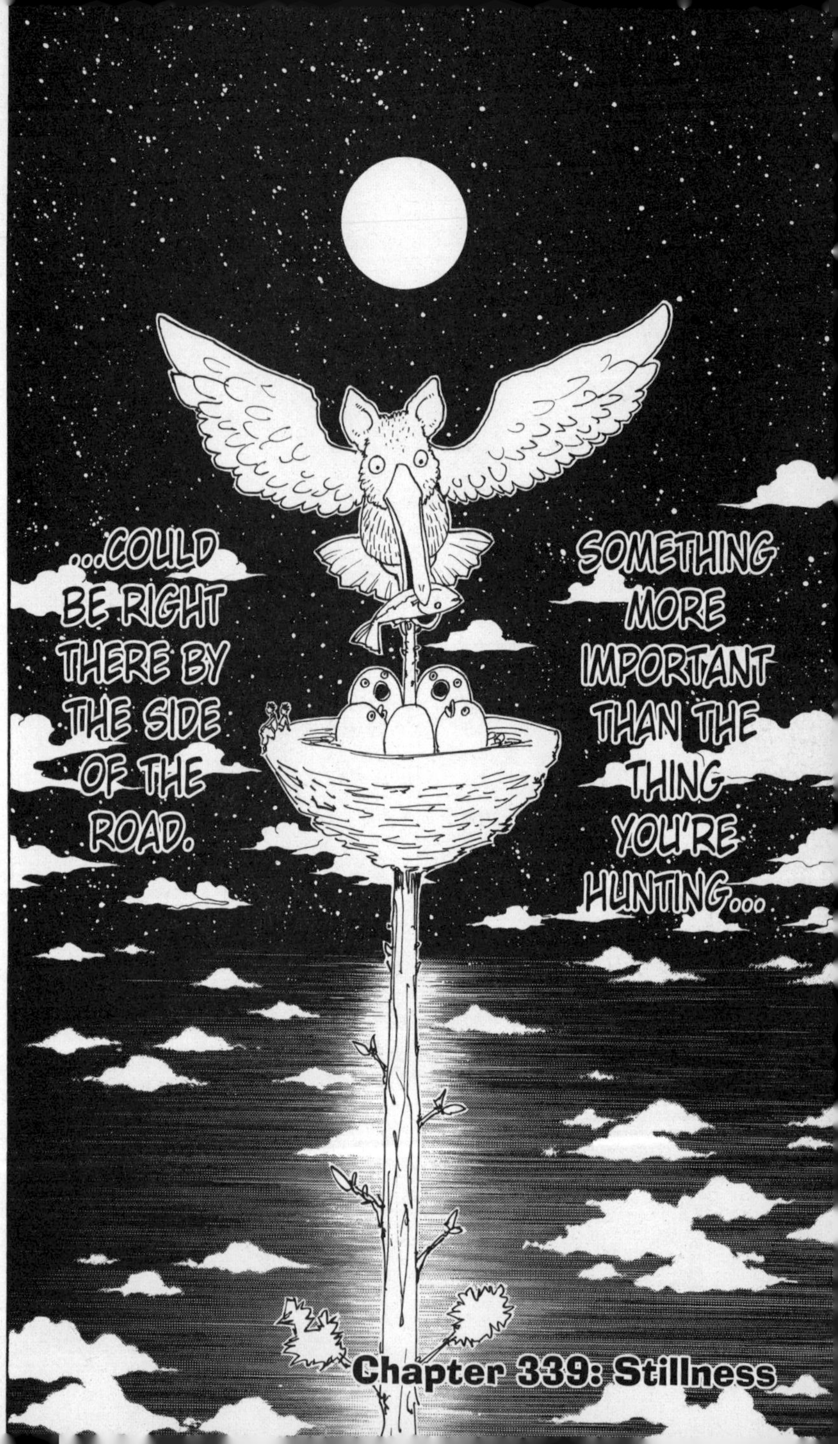
SOMETHING MORE IMPORTANT THAN THE THING YOU'RE HUNTING...
...COULD BE RIGHT THERE BY THE SIDE OF THE ROAD.

Chapter 339: Stillness

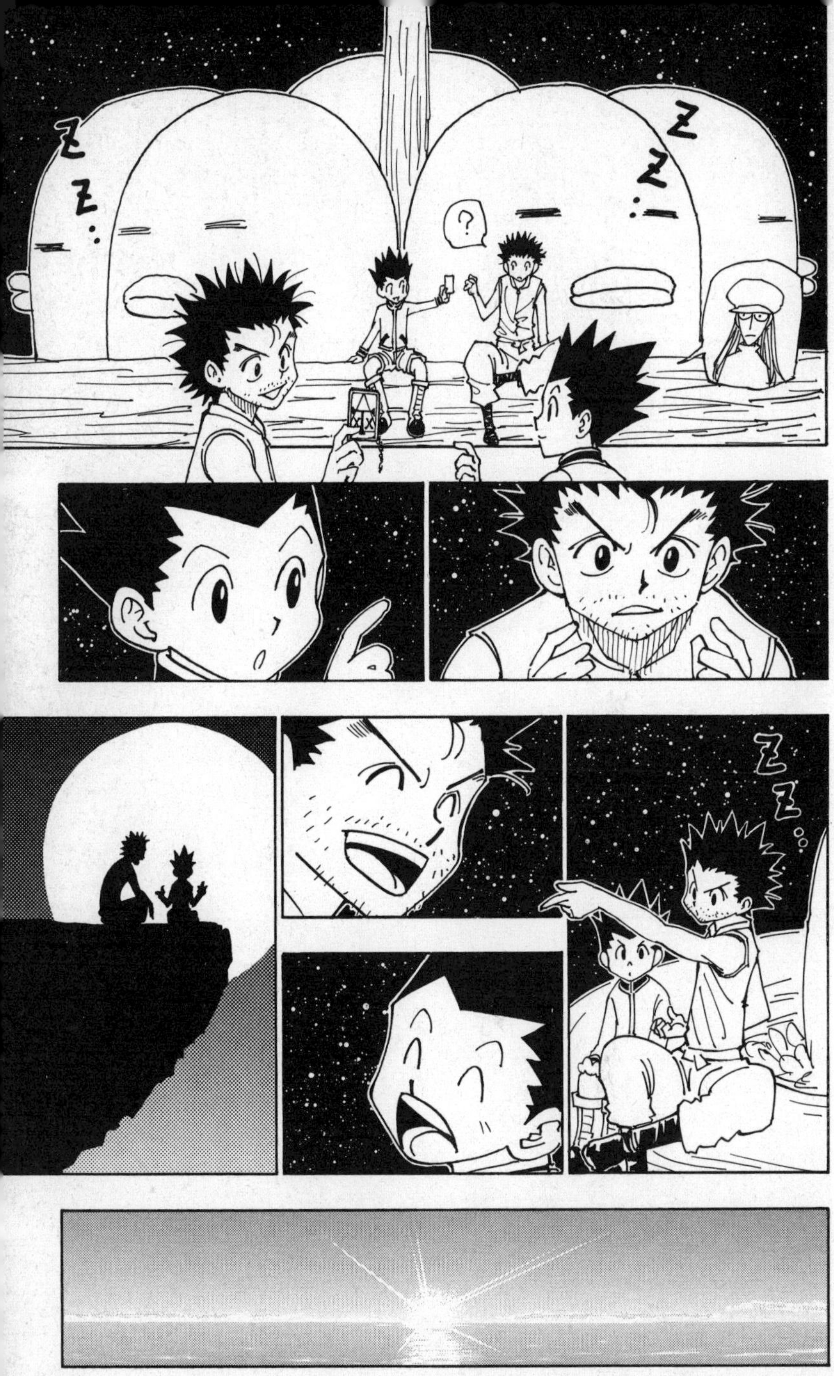
Z Z Z
?
Z Z
Z Z

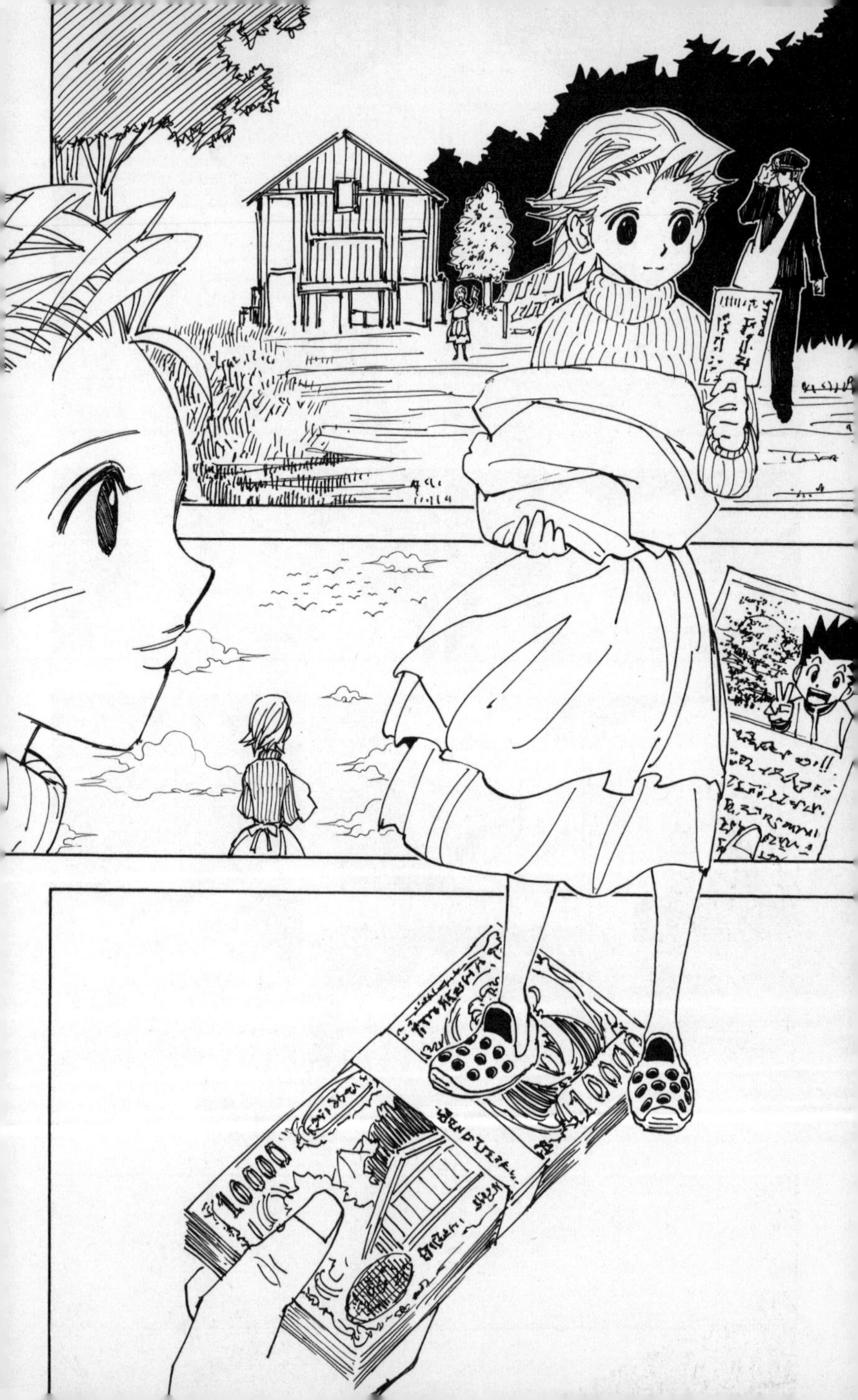

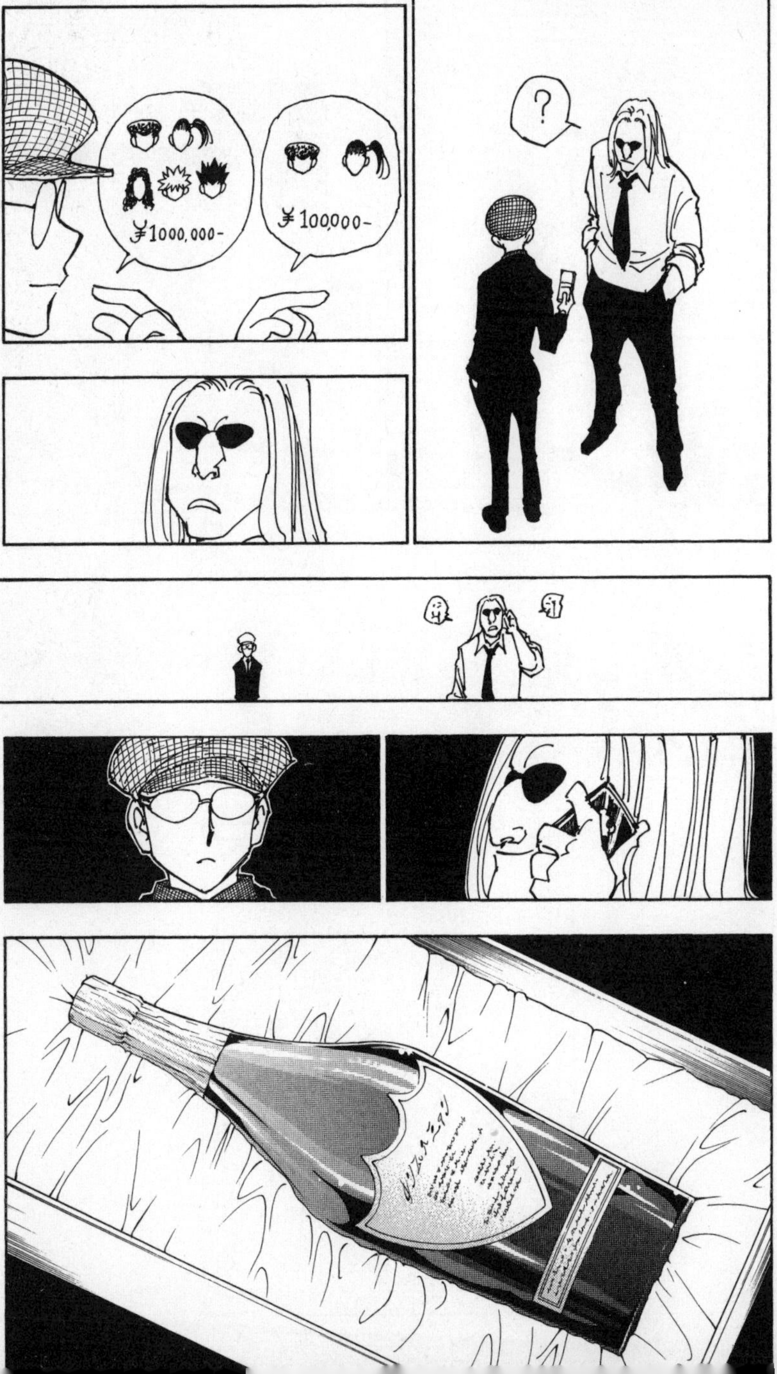
?
¥100,000-
¥1000,000-

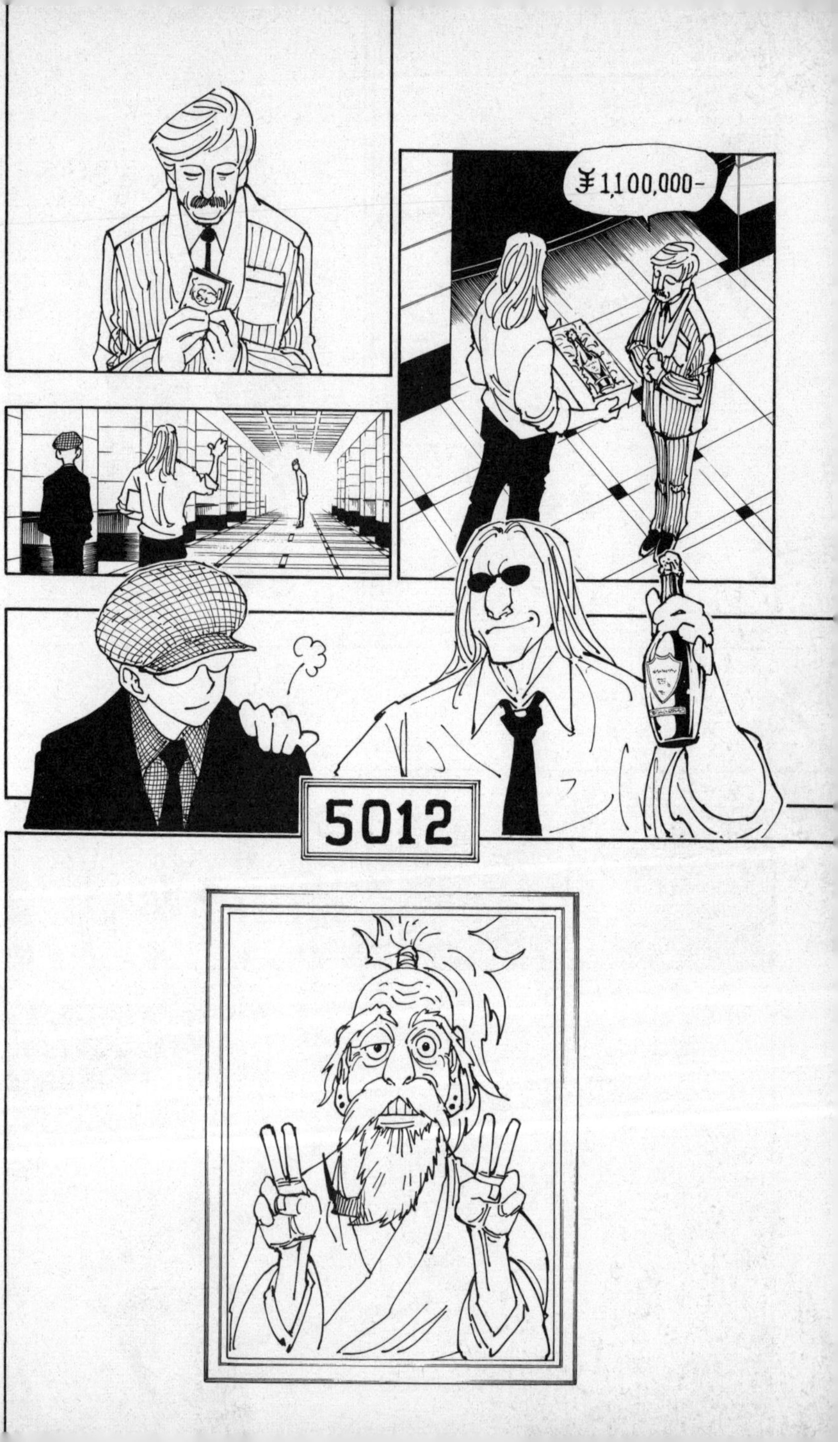

¥1,100,000-
5012

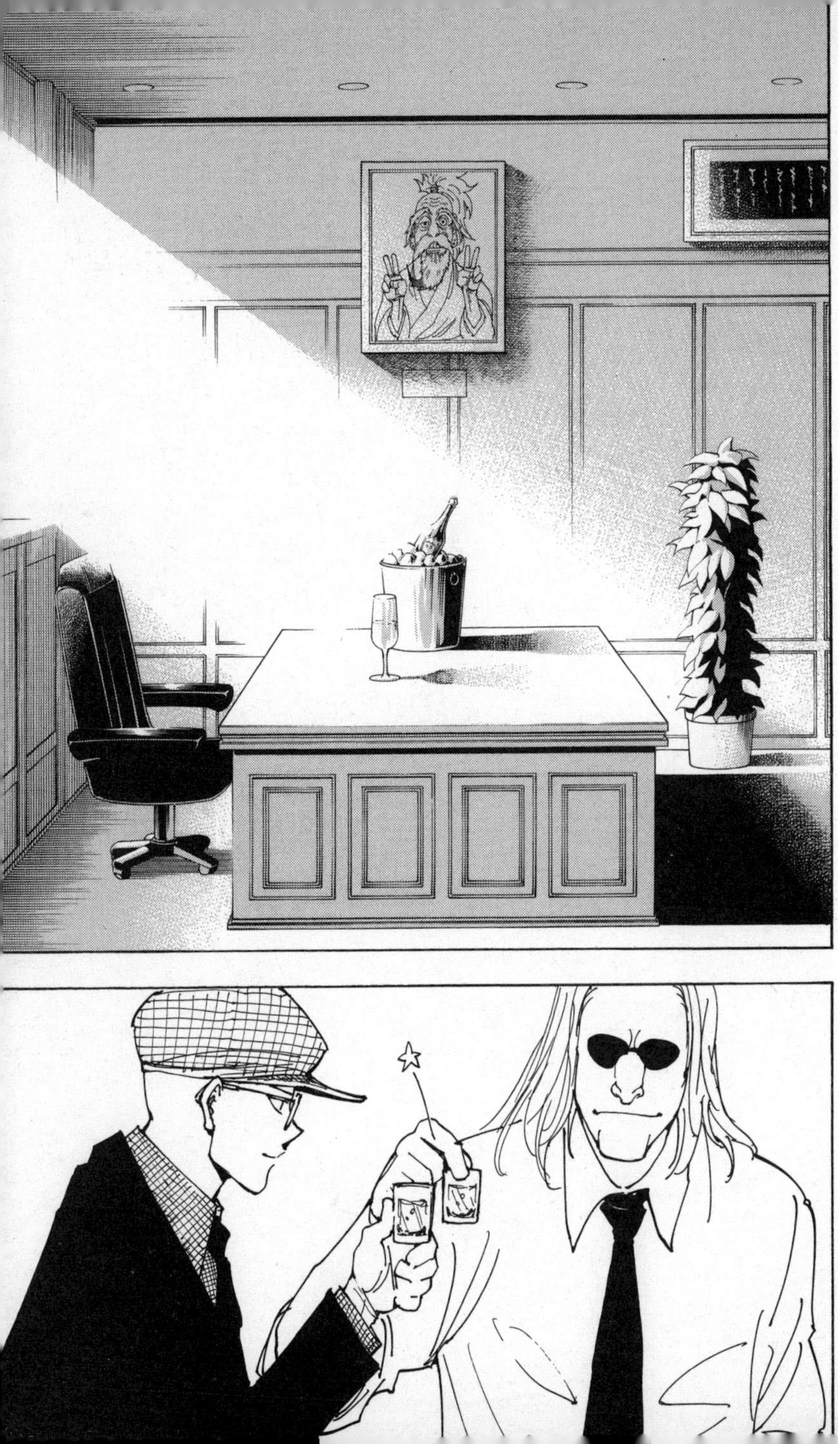

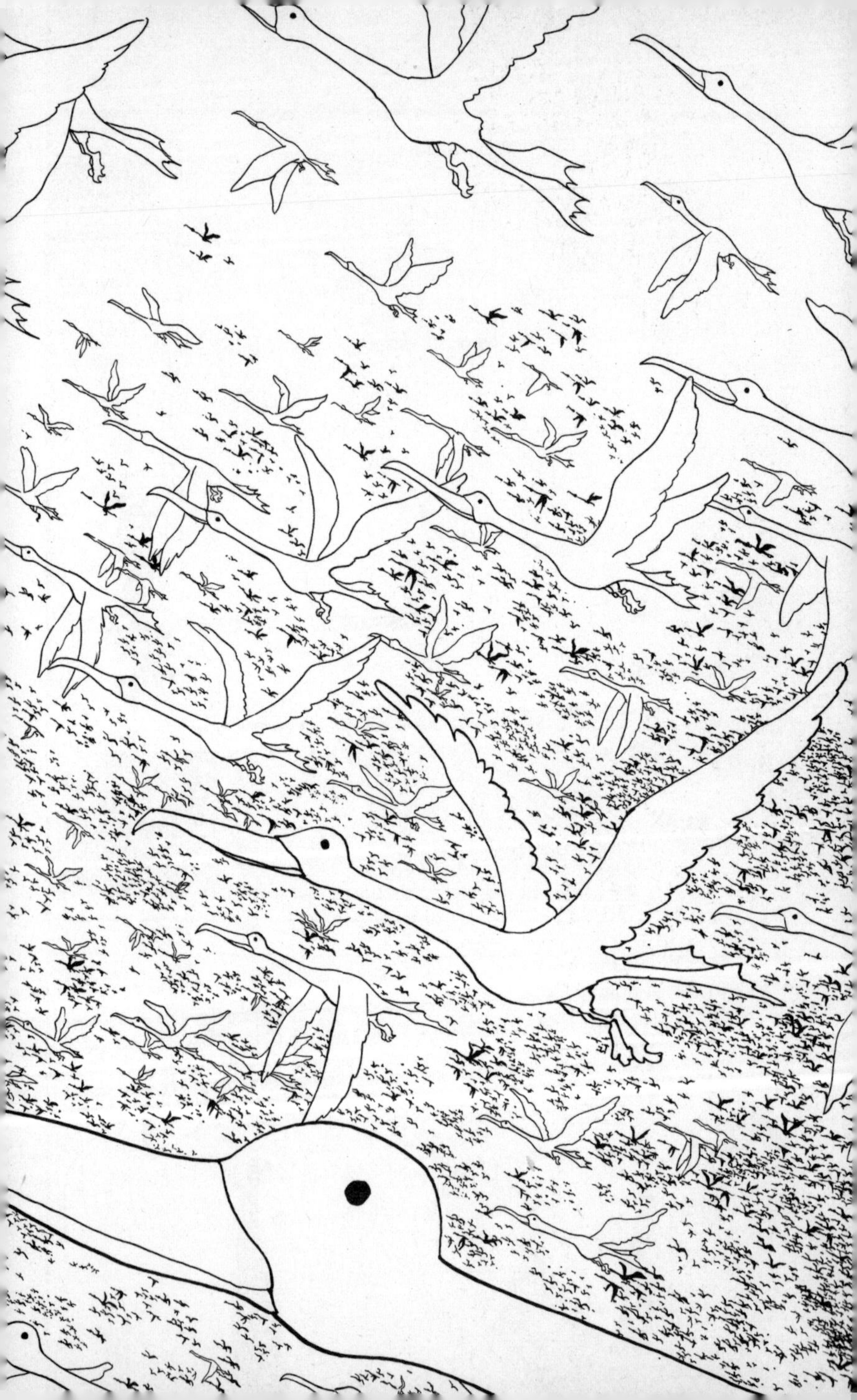

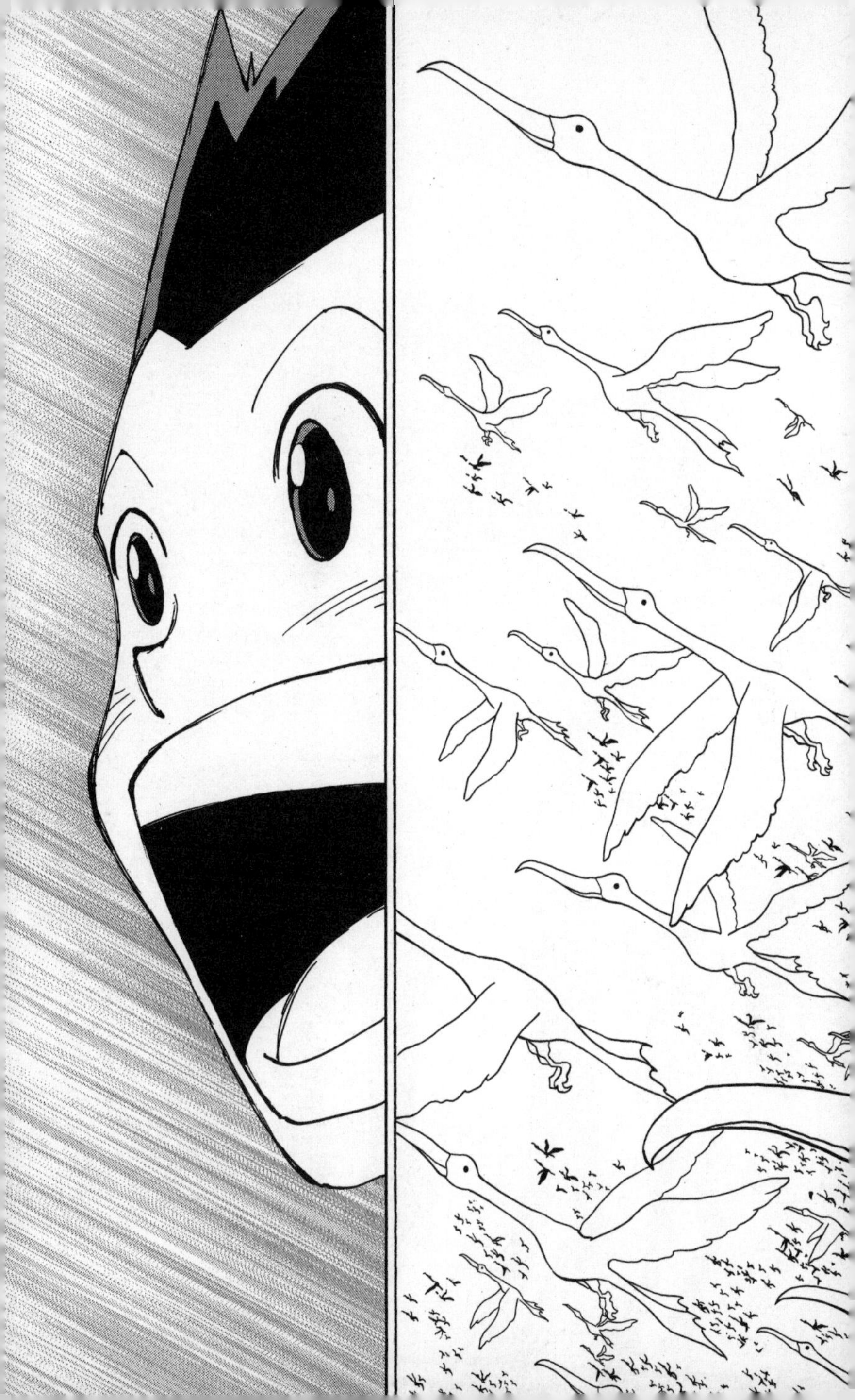

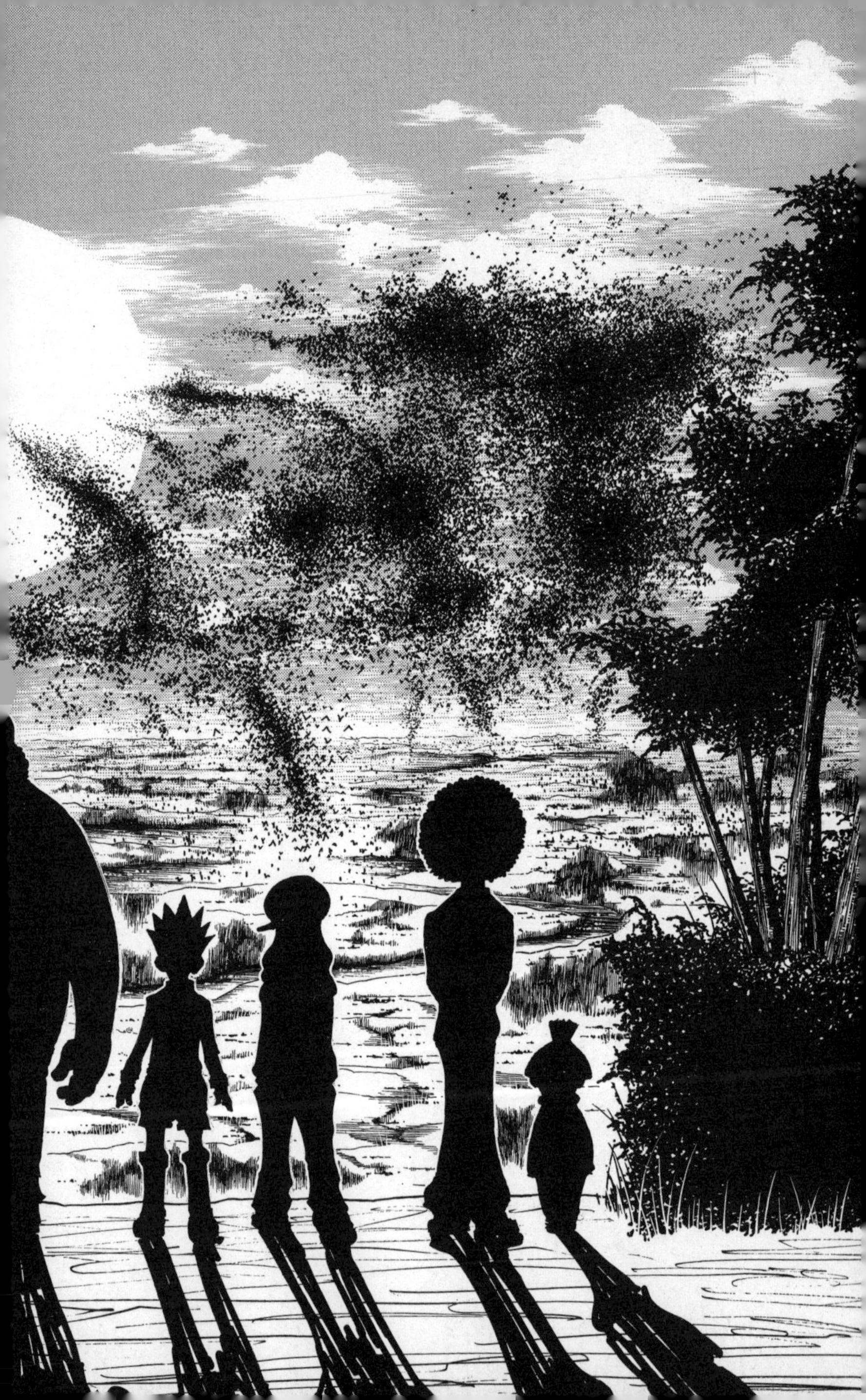

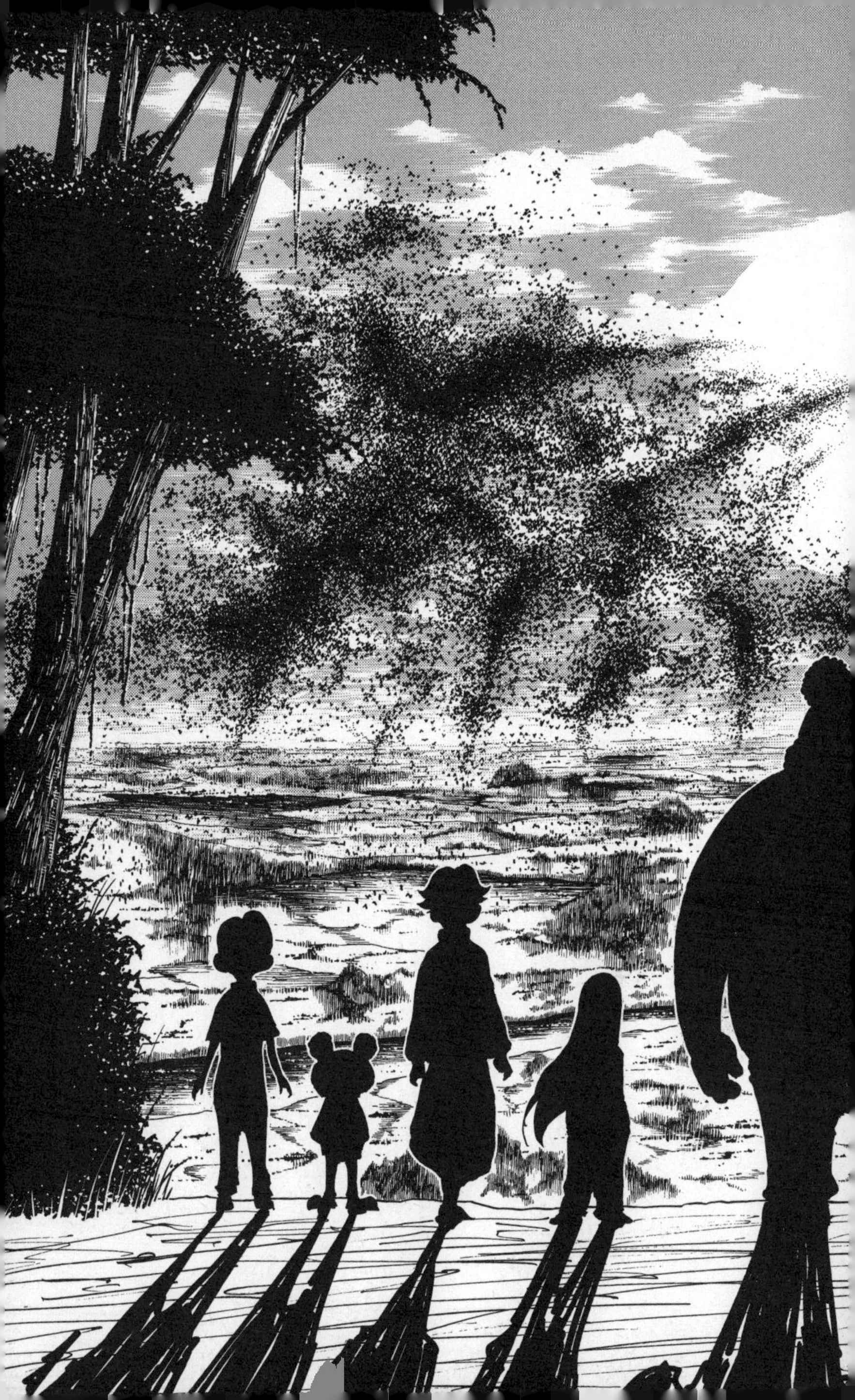

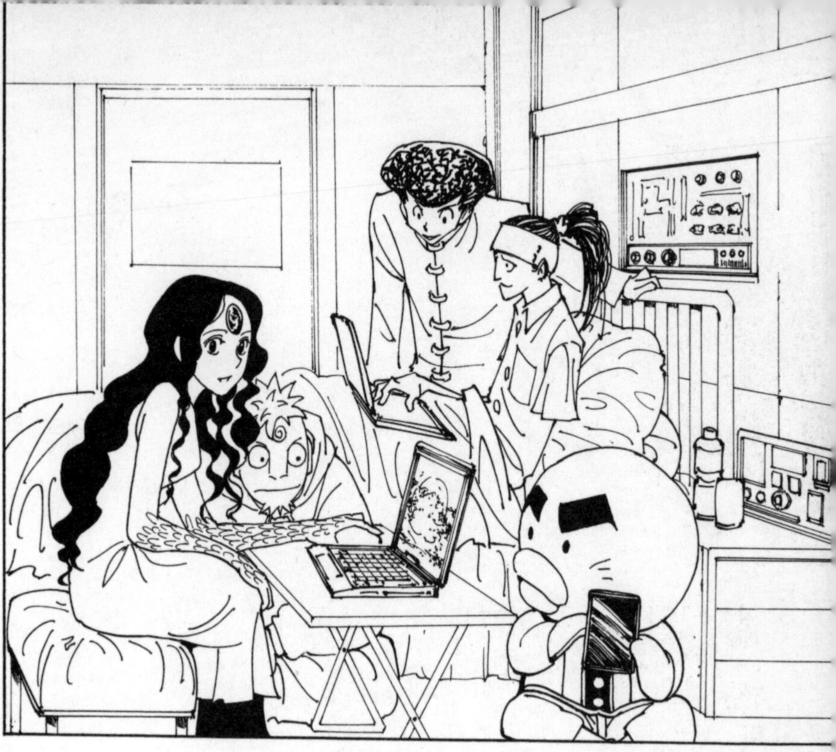

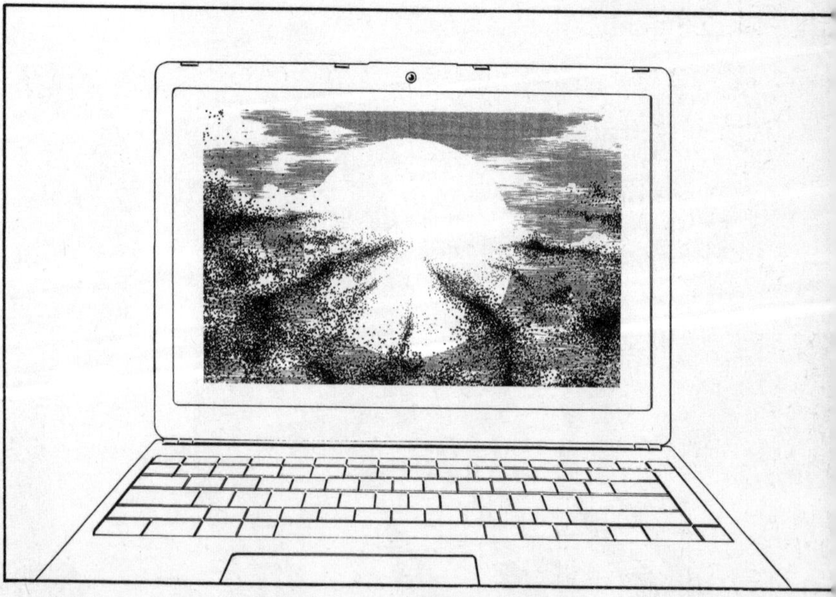

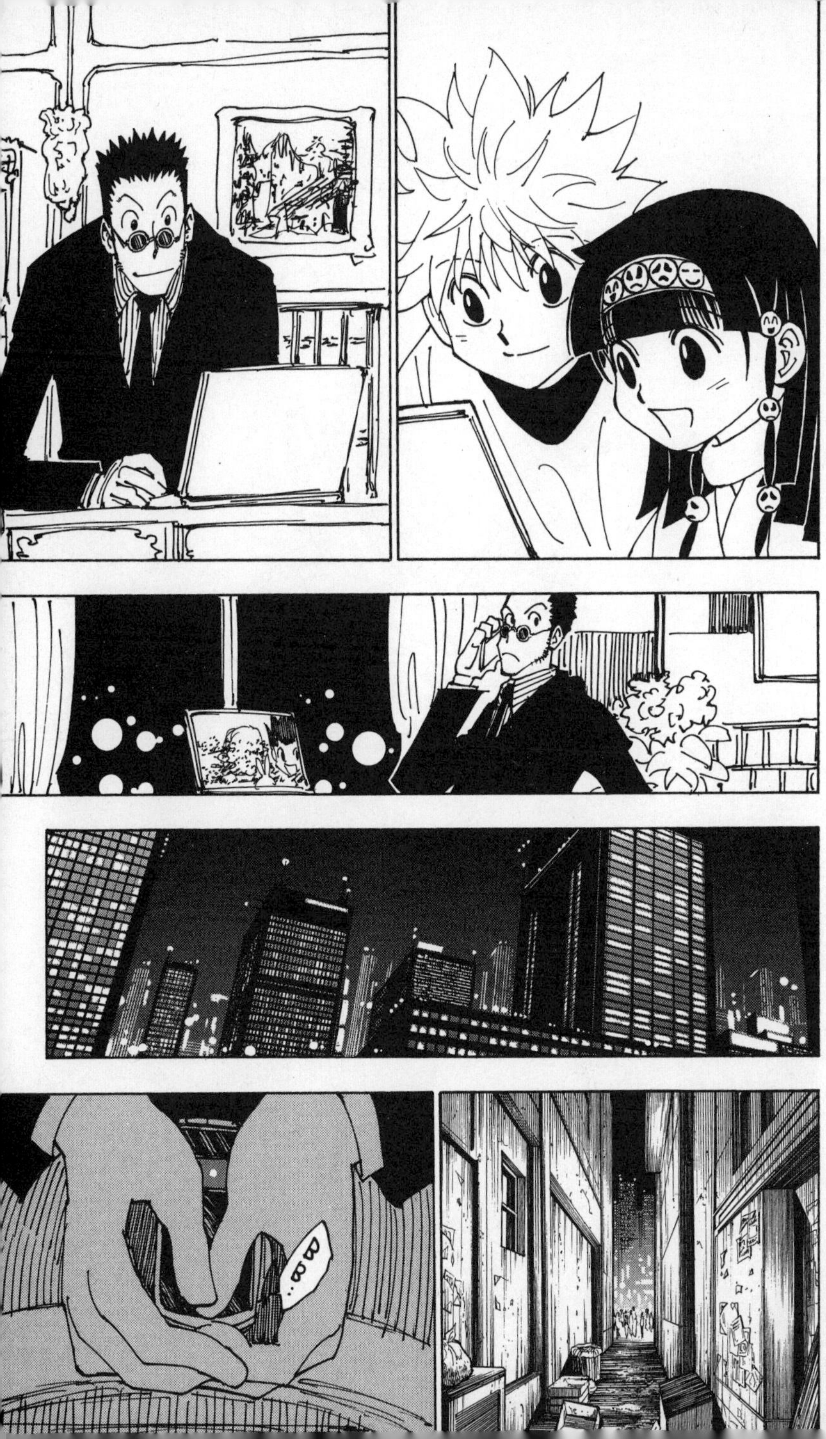
BB..

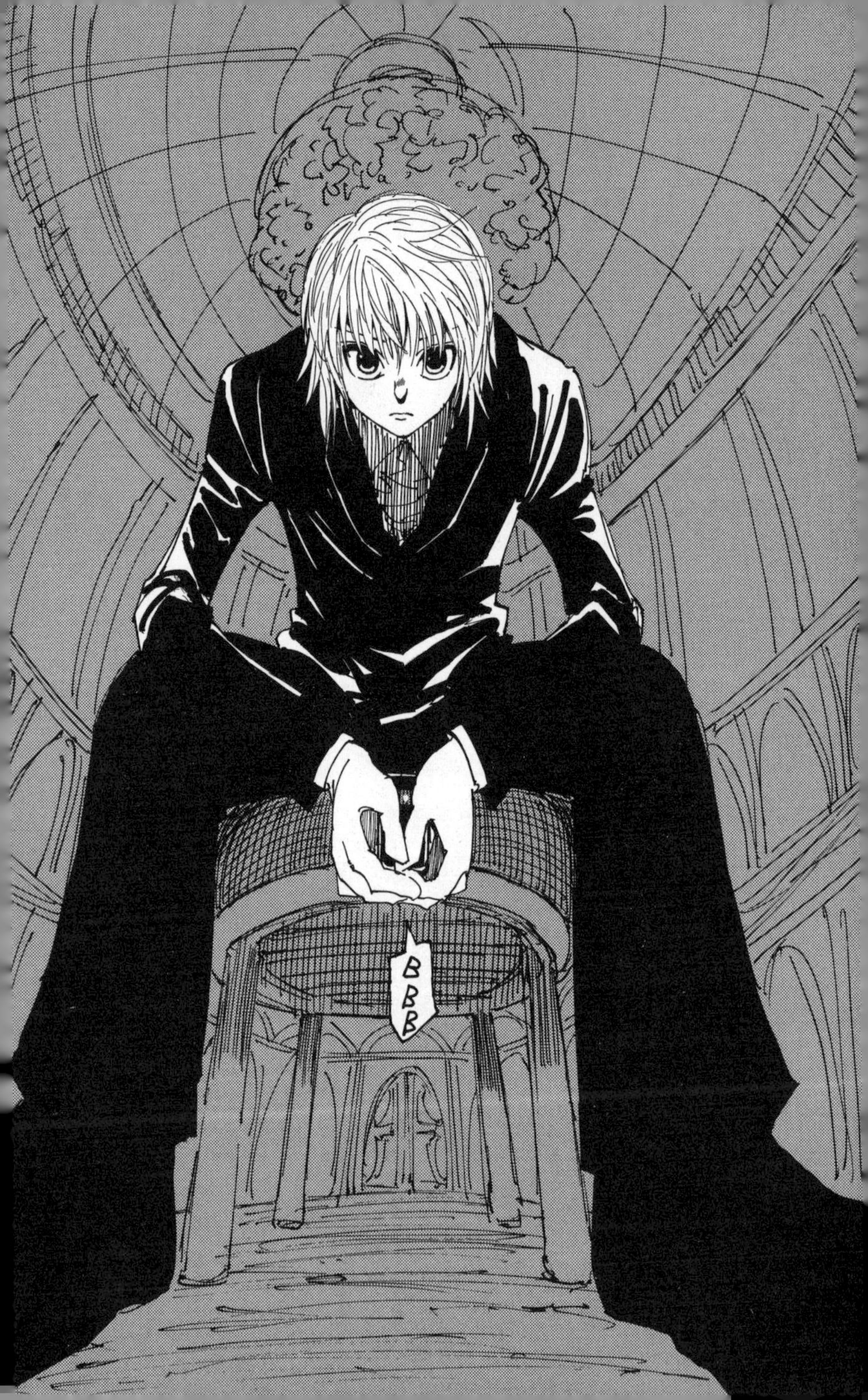
BBB

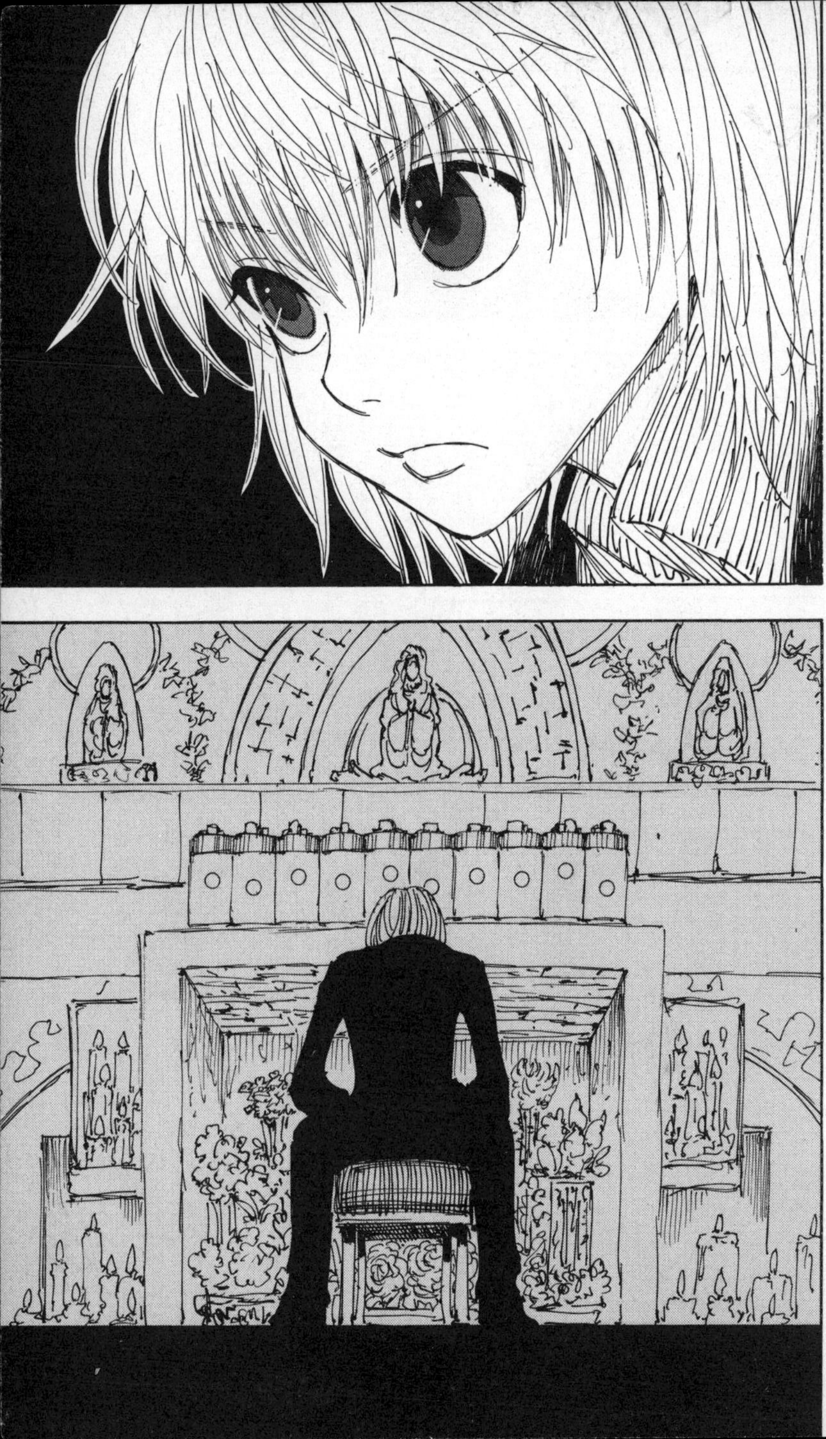

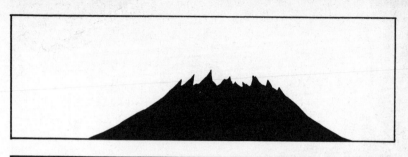

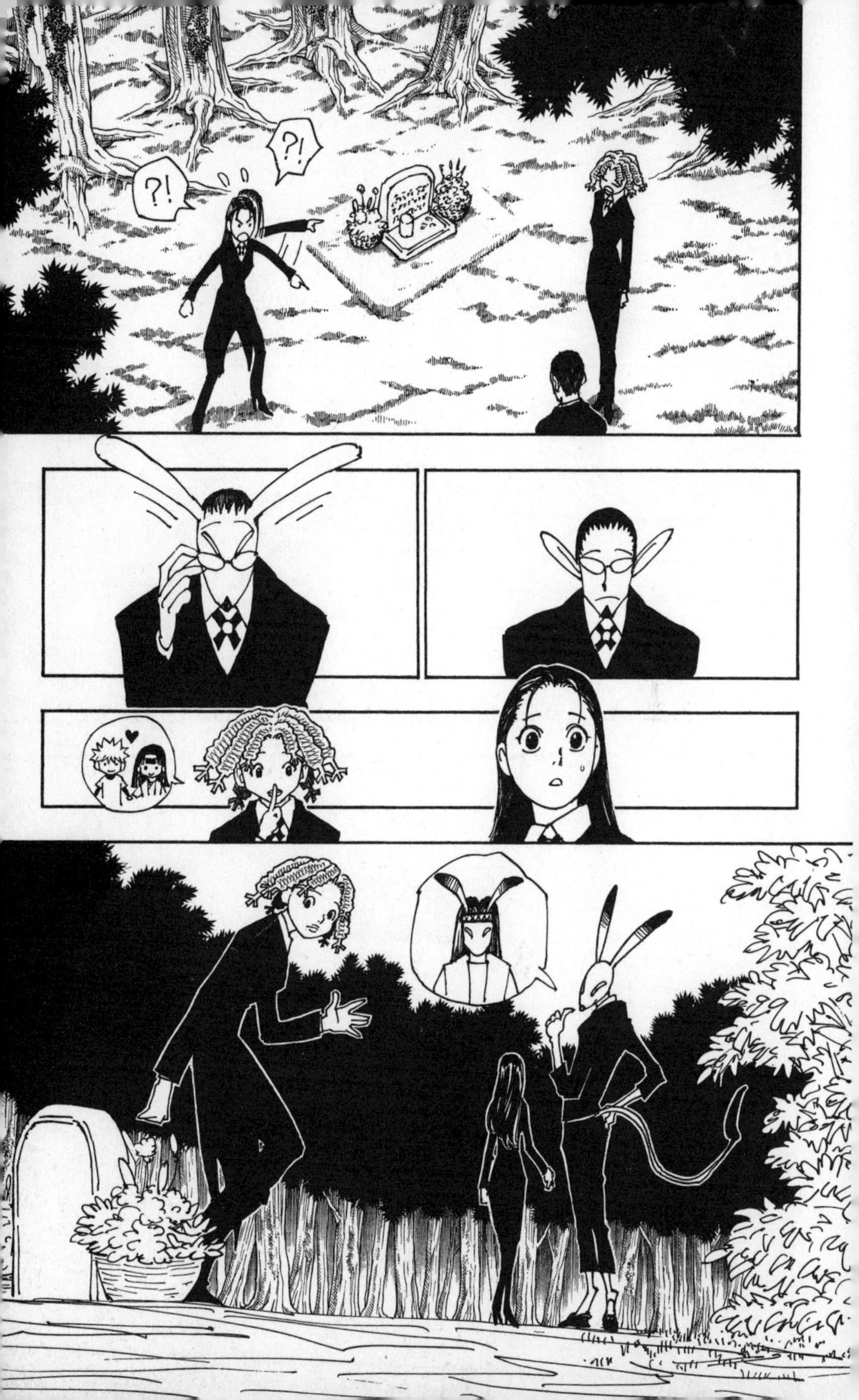
?!
?!

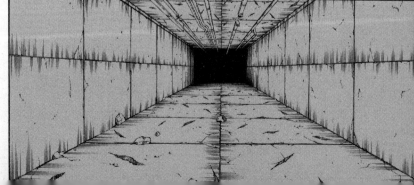

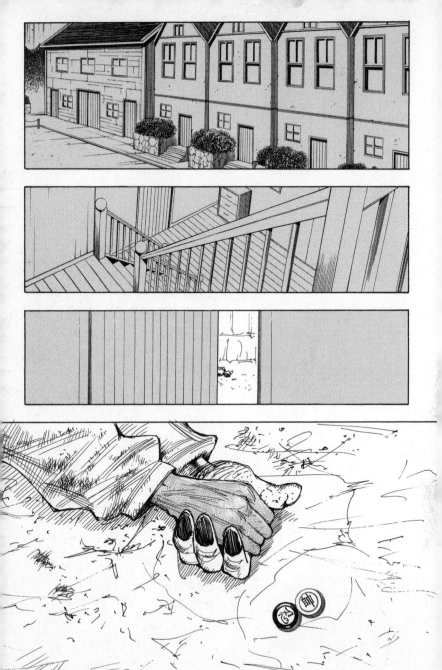

HUNTER×HUNTER
the Movie:
PHANTOM ROUGE
PROMO COMIC STRIP

NAME THAT TUNE

YOU DON'T MIND IF I WIN? I'M ONLY HERE FOR PR.
I'M NOT CLEVER OR MATURE ENOUGH TO TILT THE BALANCE IN YOUR FAVOR !!
DING!!!
"TAMAHIME-SAMA"!!
WRONG!
KURAPIKA DOESN'T KNOW ANY POP CULTURE TRIVIA.
WHAT WAS IT?
"FASHION MONSTER."

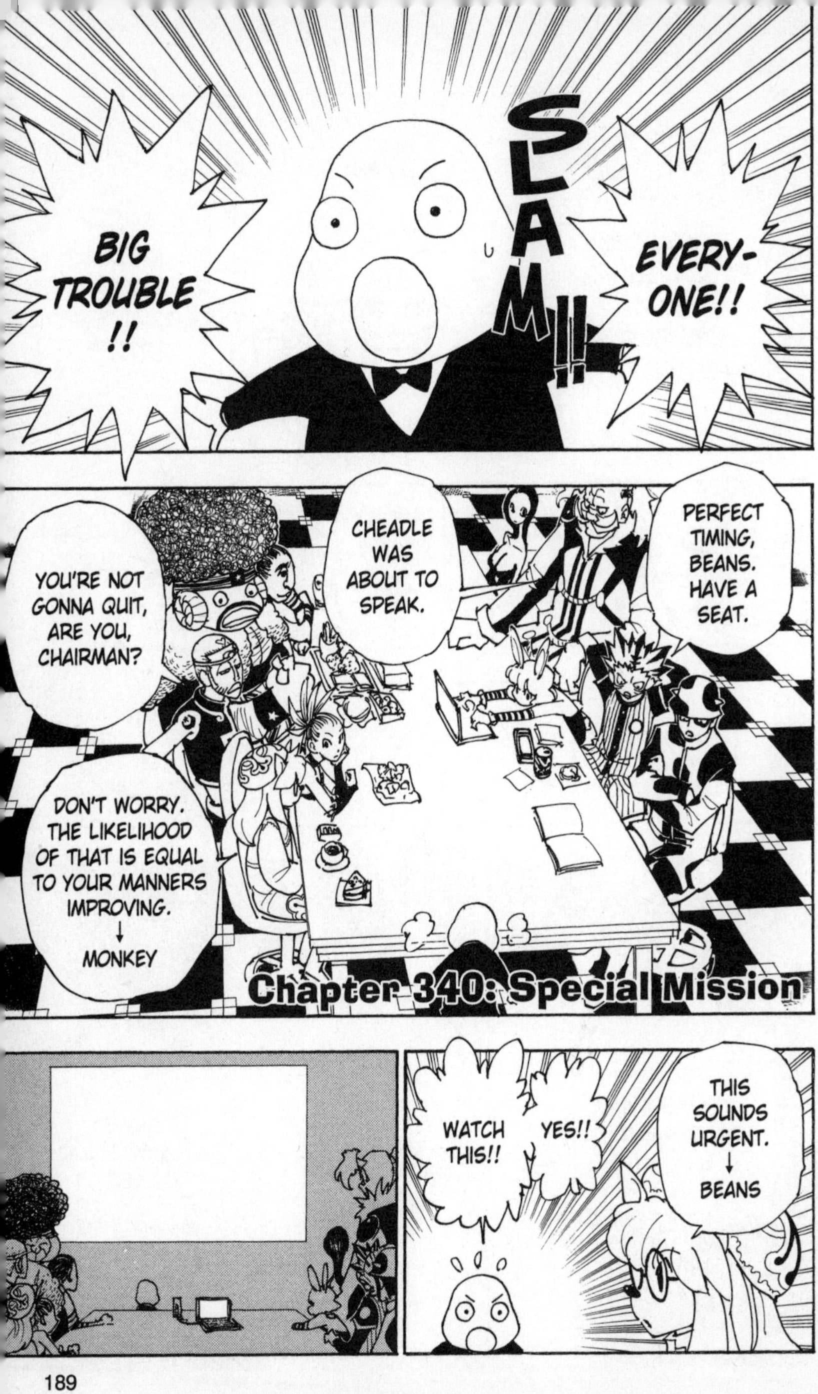
EVERY-ONE!!
SLAM!!
BIG TROUBLE!!
PERFECT TIMING, BEANS. HAVE A SEAT.
CHEADLE WAS ABOUT TO SPEAK.
YOU'RE NOT GONNA QUIT, ARE YOU, CHAIRMAN?
DON'T WORRY. THE LIKELIHOOD OF THAT IS EQUAL TO YOUR MANNERS IMPROVING. ↓ MONKEY
Chapter 340: Special Mission
THIS SOUNDS URGENT. ↓ BEANS
YES!!
WATCH THIS!!

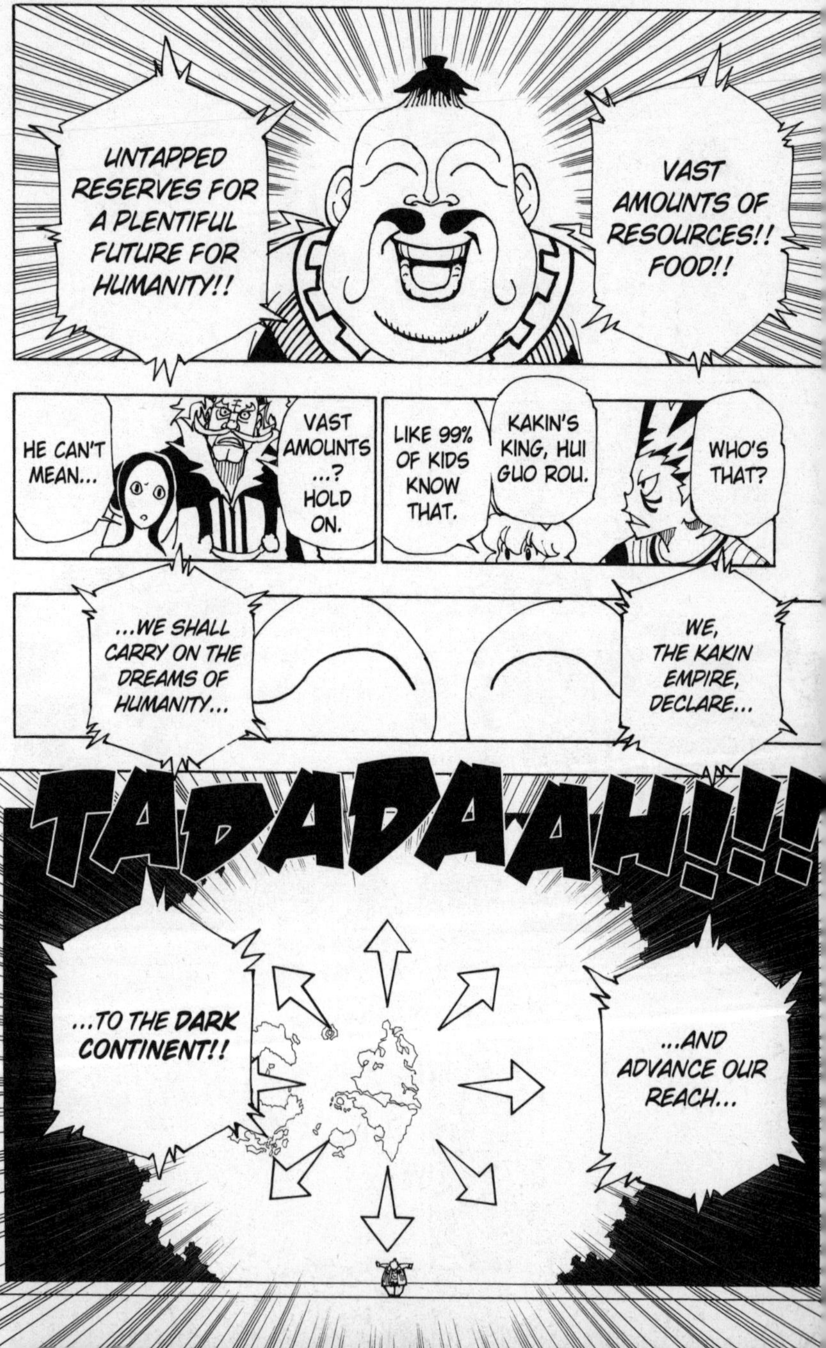
VAST AMOUNTS OF RESOURCES!! FOOD!!
UNTAPPED RESERVES FOR A PLENTIFUL FUTURE FOR HUMANITY!!
WHO'S THAT?
KAKIN'S KING, HUI GUO ROU.
LIKE 99% OF KIDS KNOW THAT.
VAST AMOUNTS ...? HOLD ON.
HE CAN'T MEAN...
WE, THE KAKIN EMPIRE, DECLARE...
...WE SHALL CARRY ON THE DREAMS OF HUMANITY...
TADADA-AH!!!
...AND ADVANCE OUR REACH...
...TO THE DARK CONTINENT!!

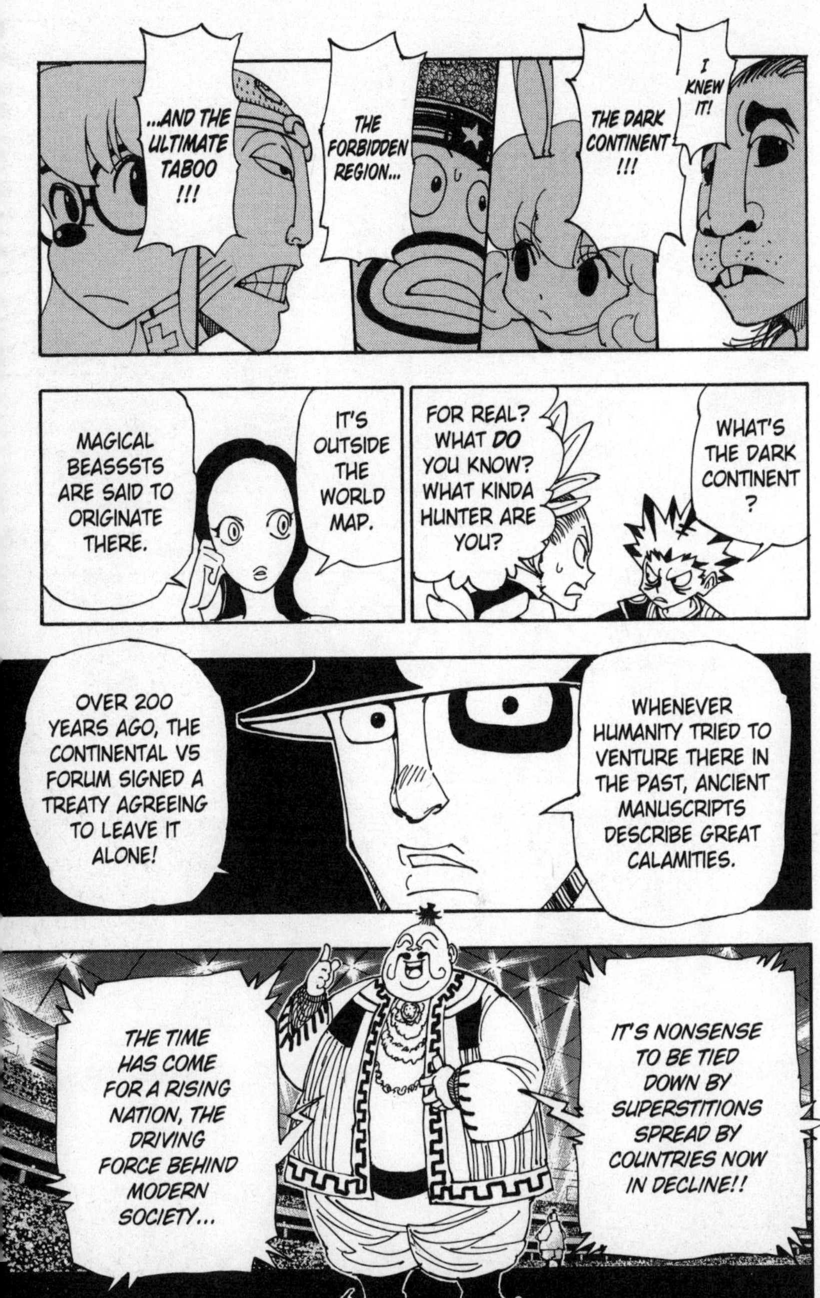
I KNEW IT!
THE DARK CONTINENT!!!
THE FORBIDDEN REGION...
...AND THE ULTIMATE TABOO!!!
WHAT'S THE DARK CONTINENT?
FOR REAL? WHAT DO YOU KNOW? WHAT KINDA HUNTER ARE YOU?
IT'S OUTSIDE THE WORLD MAP.
MAGICAL BEASSSTS ARE SAID TO ORIGINATE THERE.
WHENEVER HUMANITY TRIED TO VENTURE THERE IN THE PAST, ANCIENT MANUSCRIPTS DESCRIBE GREAT CALAMITIES.
OVER 200 YEARS AGO, THE CONTINENTAL V5 FORUM SIGNED A TREATY AGREEING TO LEAVE IT ALONE!
IT'S NONSENSE TO BE TIED DOWN BY SUPERSTITIONS SPREAD BY COUNTRIES NOW IN DECLINE!!
THE TIME HAS COME FOR A RISING NATION, THE DRIVING FORCE BEHIND MODERN SOCIETY...

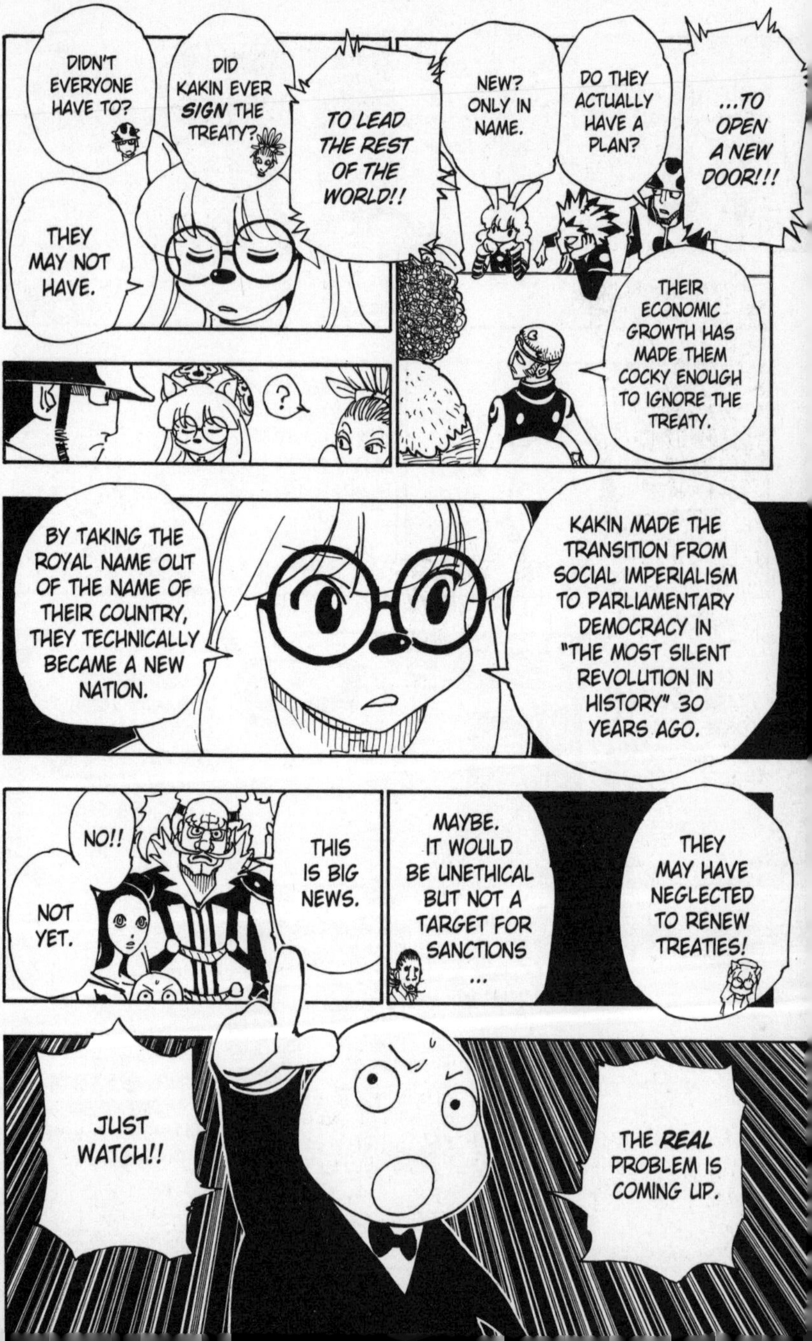

...TO OPEN A NEW DOOR!!!
DO THEY ACTUALLY HAVE A PLAN?
NEW? ONLY IN NAME.
TO LEAD THE REST OF THE WORLD!!
DID KAKIN EVER *SIGN* THE TREATY?
DIDN'T EVERYONE HAVE TO?
THEY MAY NOT HAVE.
THEIR ECONOMIC GROWTH HAS MADE THEM COCKY ENOUGH TO IGNORE THE TREATY.
?
KAKIN MADE THE TRANSITION FROM SOCIAL IMPERIALISM TO PARLIAMENTARY DEMOCRACY IN "THE MOST SILENT REVOLUTION IN HISTORY" 30 YEARS AGO.
BY TAKING THE ROYAL NAME OUT OF THE NAME OF THEIR COUNTRY, THEY TECHNICALLY BECAME A NEW NATION.
THEY MAY HAVE NEGLECTED TO RENEW TREATIES!
MAYBE. IT WOULD BE UNETHICAL BUT NOT A TARGET FOR SANCTIONS ...
THIS IS BIG NEWS.
NO!!
NOT YET.
THE *REAL* PROBLEM IS COMING UP.
JUST WATCH!!

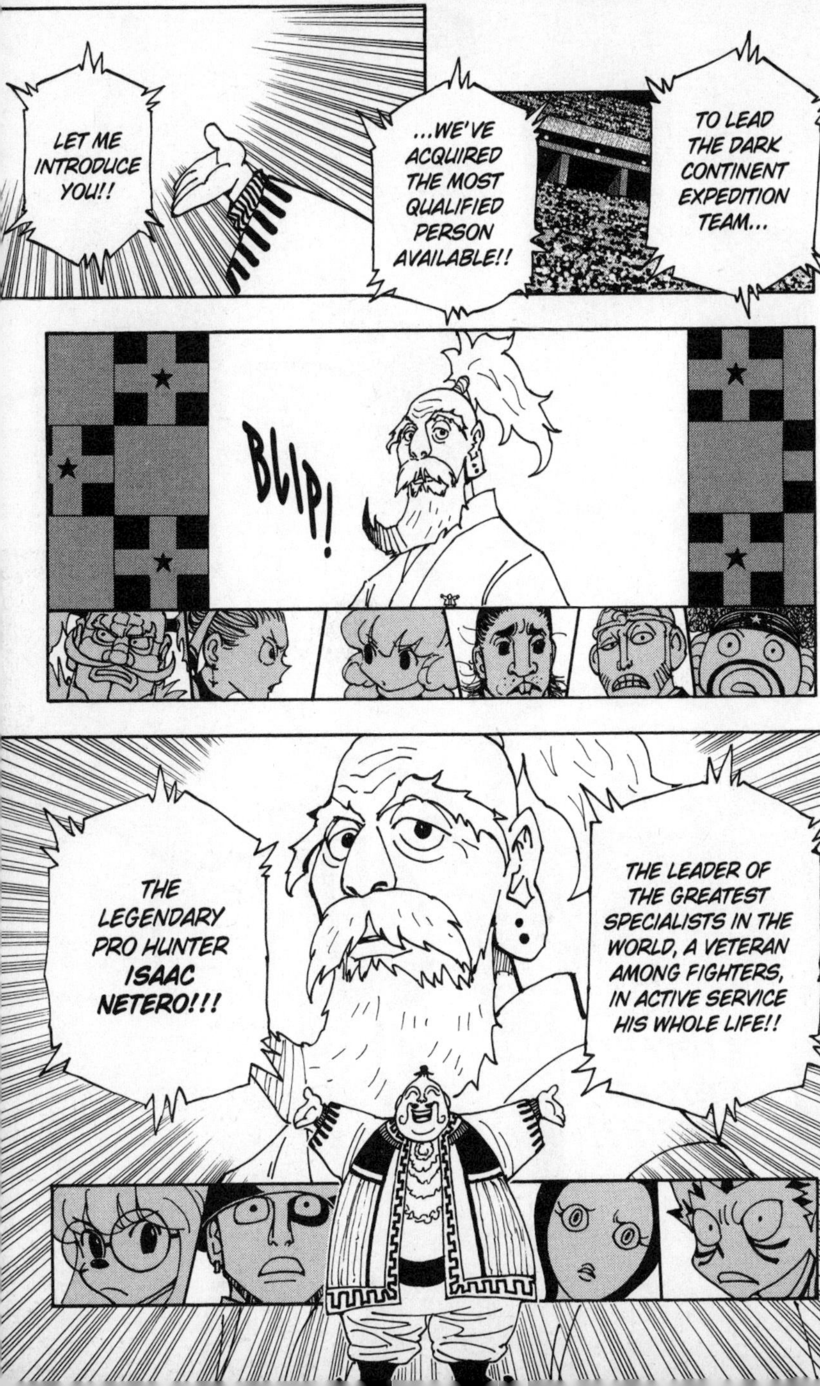
TO LEAD THE DARK CONTINENT EXPEDITION TEAM...
...WE'VE ACQUIRED THE MOST QUALIFIED PERSON AVAILABLE!!
LET ME INTRODUCE YOU!!
BLIP!
THE LEADER OF THE GREATEST SPECIALISTS IN THE WORLD, A VETERAN AMONG FIGHTERS, IN ACTIVE SERVICE HIS WHOLE LIFE!!
THE LEGENDARY PRO HUNTER ISAAC NETERO!!!

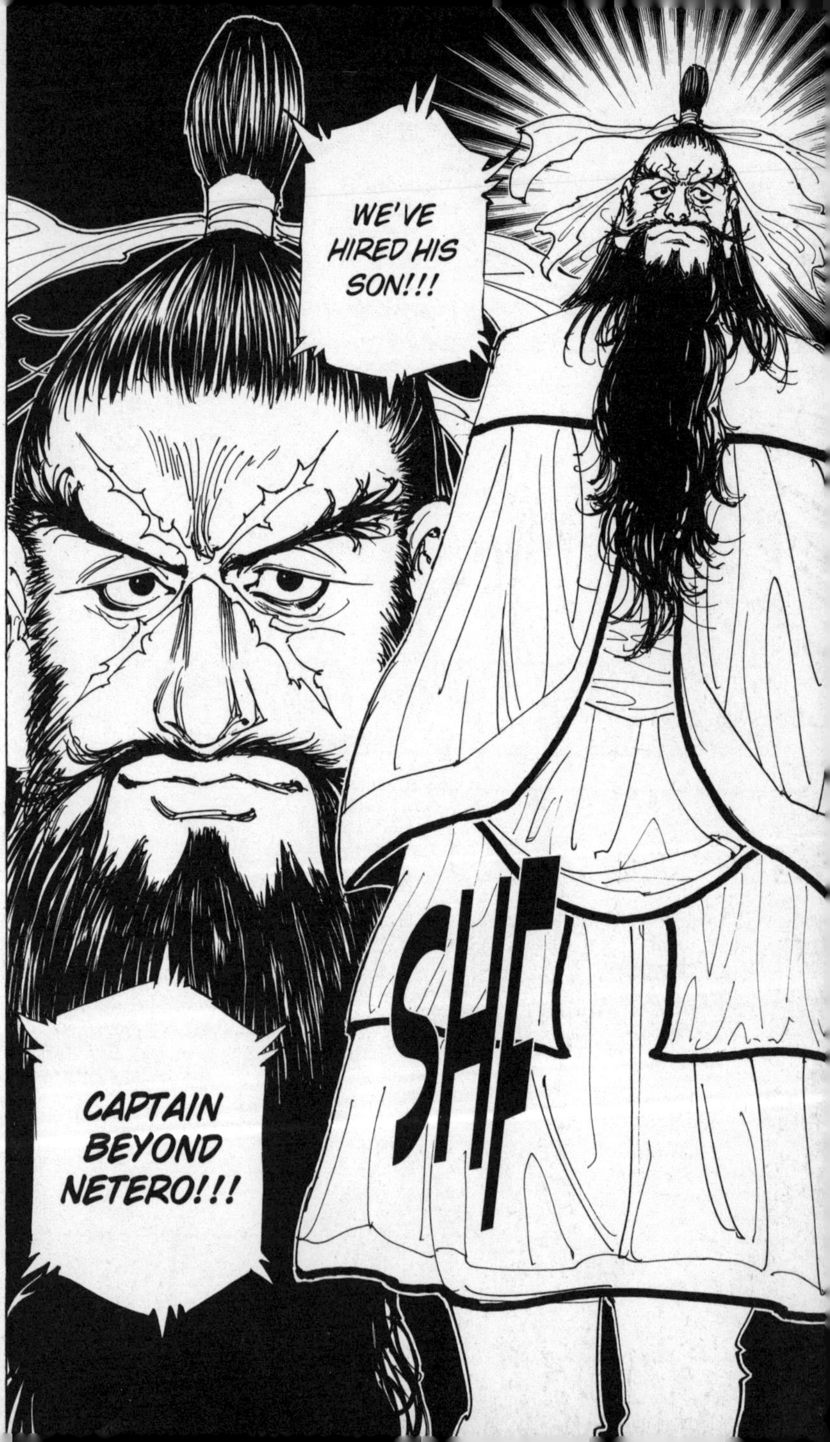
WE'VE HIRED HIS SON!!!
SHF
CAPTAIN BEYOND NETERO!!!

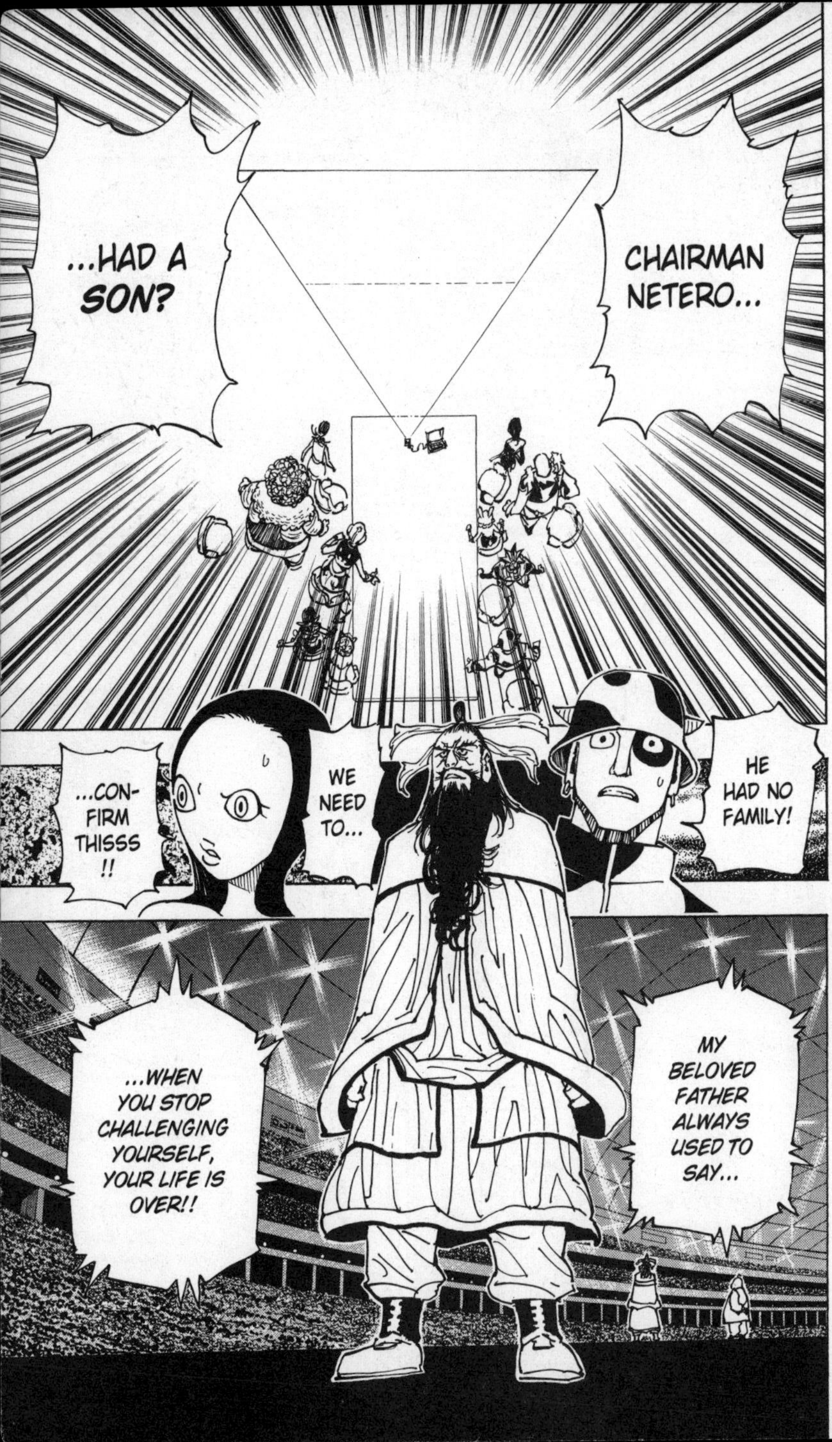
CHAIRMAN NETERO...
...HAD A SON?
HE HAD NO FAMILY!
WE NEED TO...
...CON-FIRM THISSS!!
MY BELOVED FATHER ALWAYS USED TO SAY...
...WHEN YOU STOP CHALLENGING YOURSELF, YOUR LIFE IS OVER!!

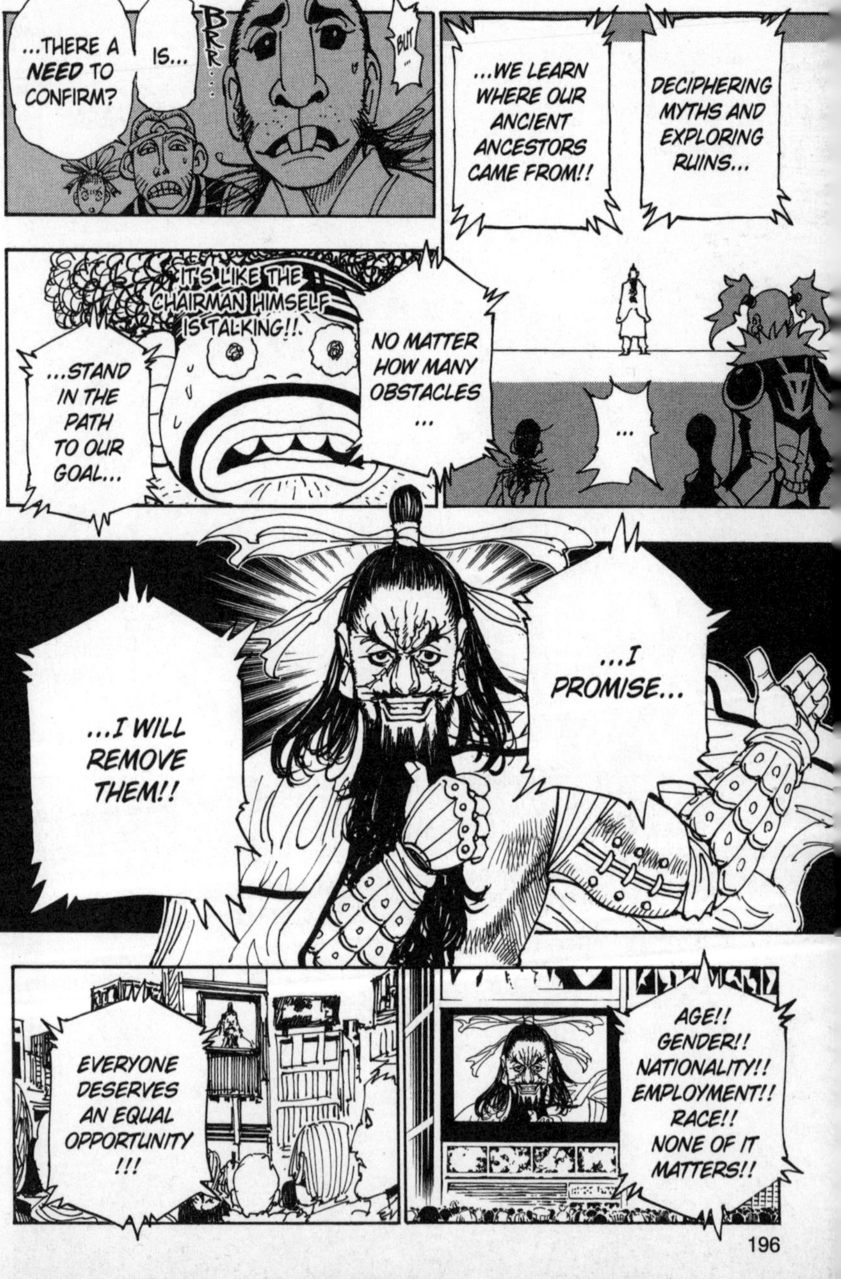
DECIPHERING MYTHS AND EXPLORING RUINS...
...WE LEARN WHERE OUR ANCIENT ANCESTORS CAME FROM!!
...
BUT ...
BRR...
IS...
...THERE A NEED TO CONFIRM?
IT'S LIKE THE CHAIRMAN HIMSELF IS TALKING!!
NO MATTER HOW MANY OBSTACLES ...
...STAND IN THE PATH TO OUR GOAL...
...I PROMISE...
...I WILL REMOVE THEM!!
AGE!! GENDER!! NATIONALITY!! EMPLOYMENT!! RACE!! NONE OF IT MATTERS!!
EVERYONE DESERVES AN EQUAL OPPORTUNITY !!!

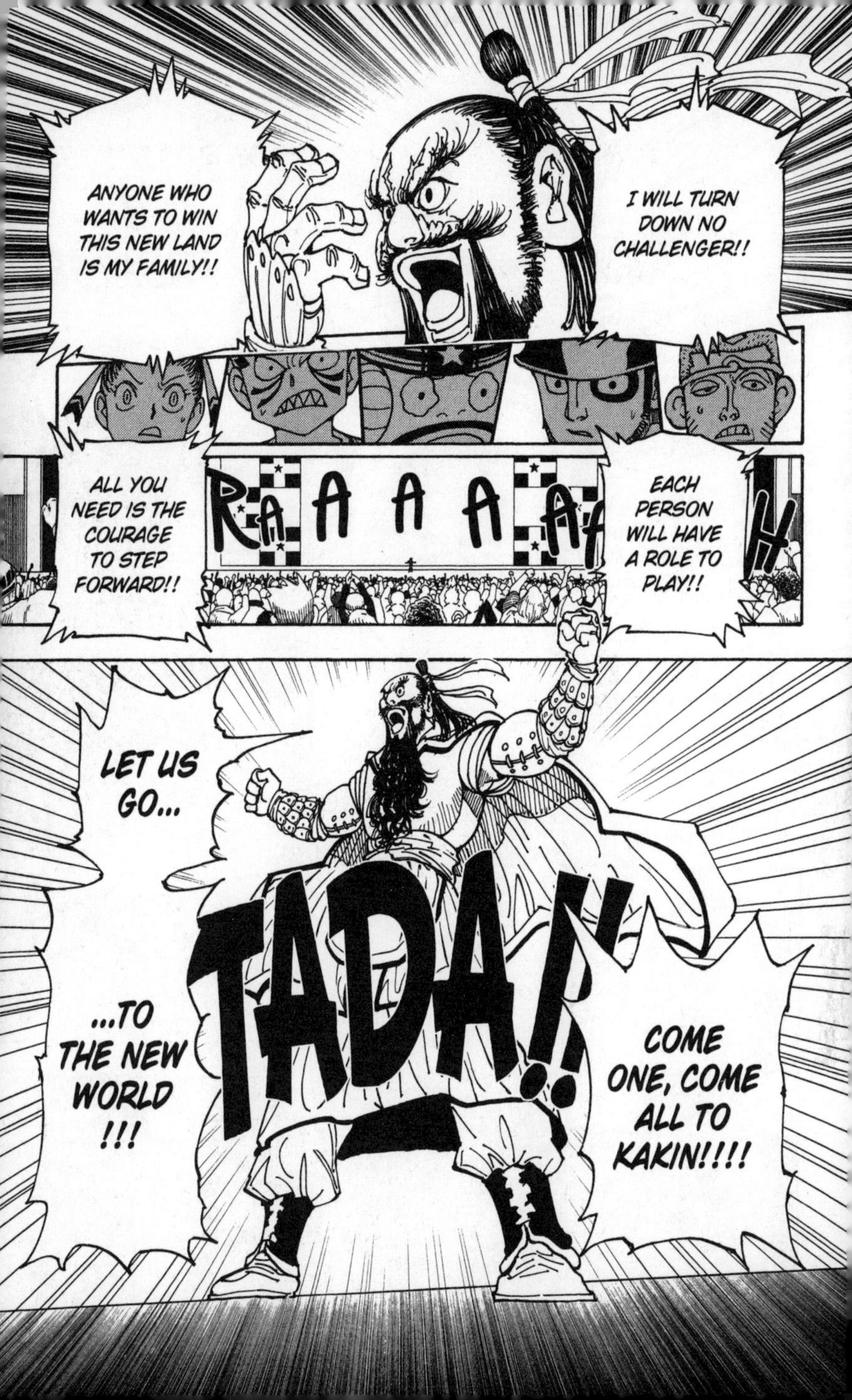
I WILL TURN DOWN NO CHALLENGER!!
ANYONE WHO WANTS TO WIN THIS NEW LAND IS MY FAMILY!!
EACH PERSON WILL HAVE A ROLE TO PLAY!!
RAAAAAH
ALL YOU NEED IS THE COURAGE TO STEP FORWARD!!
LET US GO...
...TO THE NEW WORLD!!!
TADA!!
COME ONE, COME ALL TO KAKIN!!!!

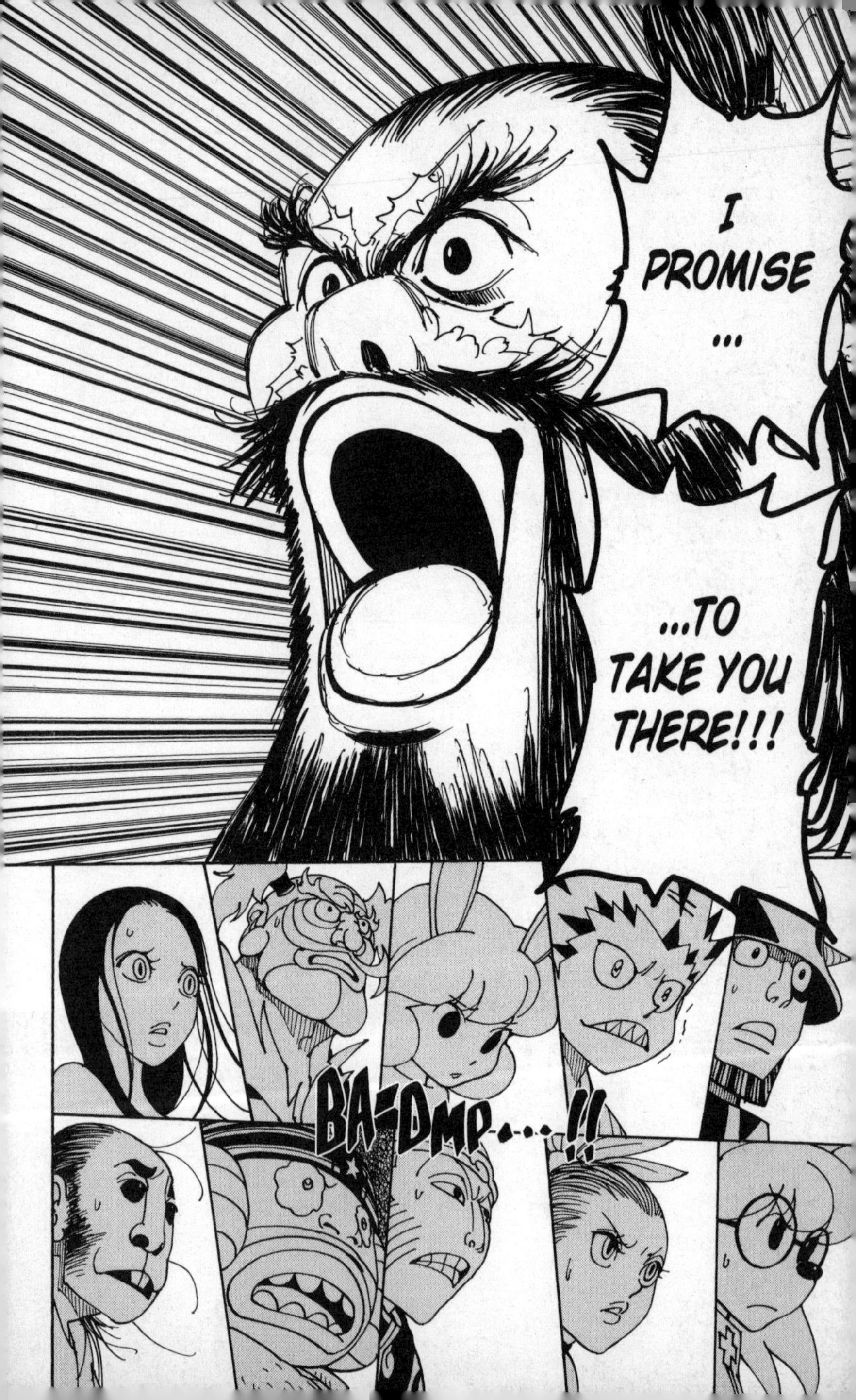
I PROMISE ...
...TO TAKE YOU THERE!!!
BA-DMP....!!

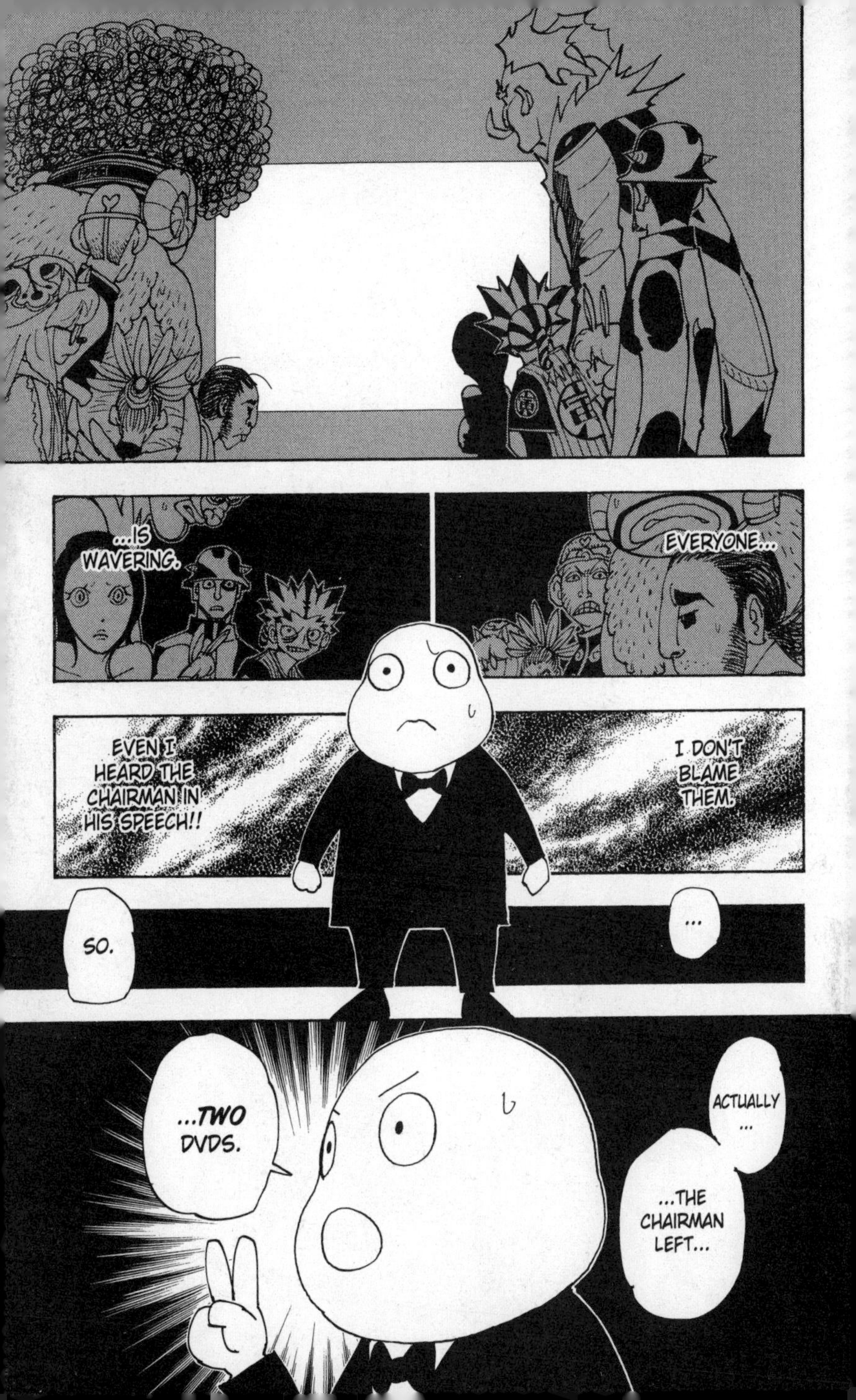
EVERYONE...
...IS WAVERING.
I DON'T BLAME THEM.
EVEN I HEARD THE CHAIRMAN IN HIS SPEECH!!
...
SO.
ACTUALLY ...
...THE CHAIRMAN LEFT...
...TWO DVDS.

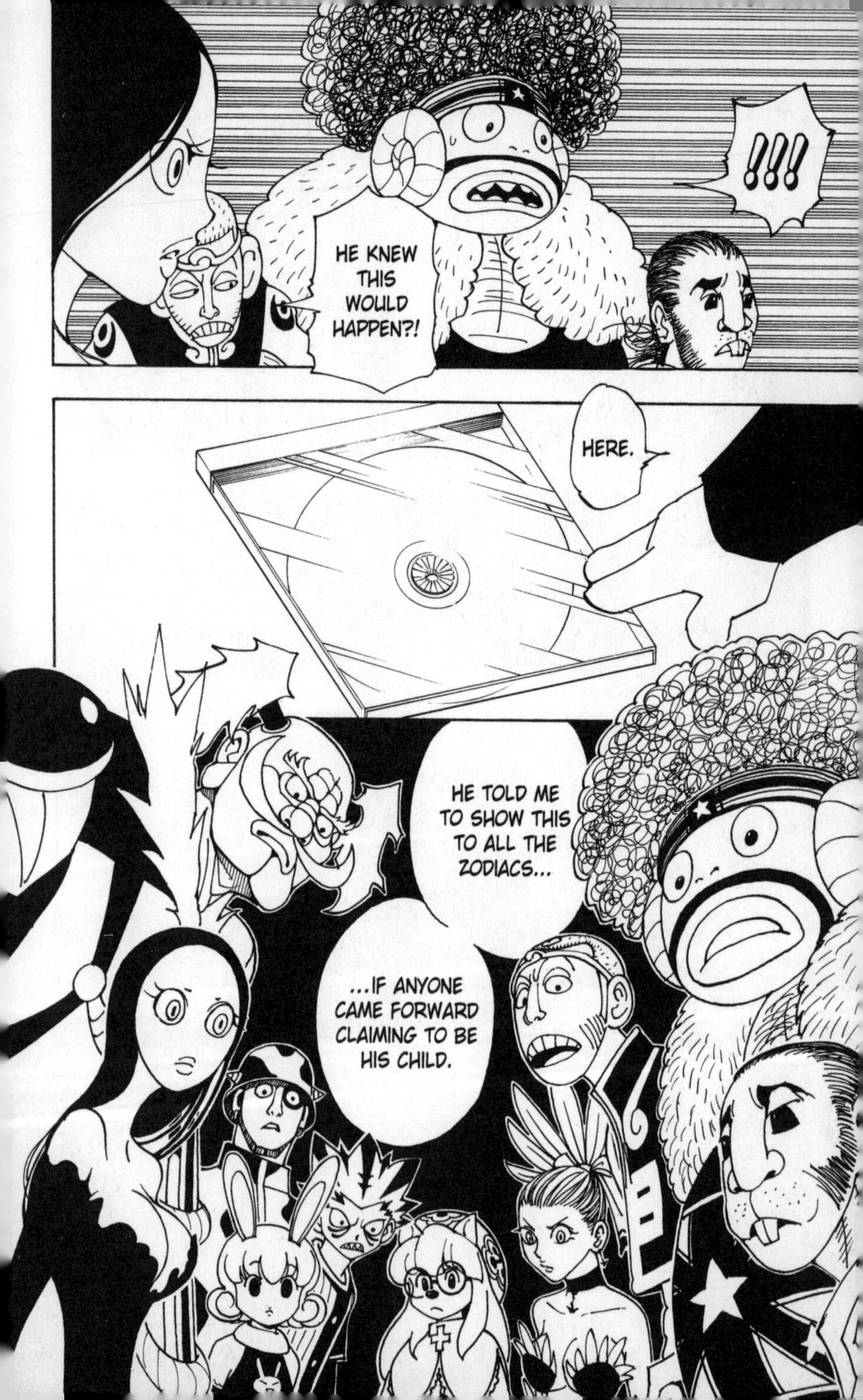
!!!
HE KNEW THIS WOULD HAPPEN?!
HERE.
HE TOLD ME TO SHOW THIS TO ALL THE ZODIACS...
...IF ANYONE CAME FORWARD CLAIMING TO BE HIS CHILD.

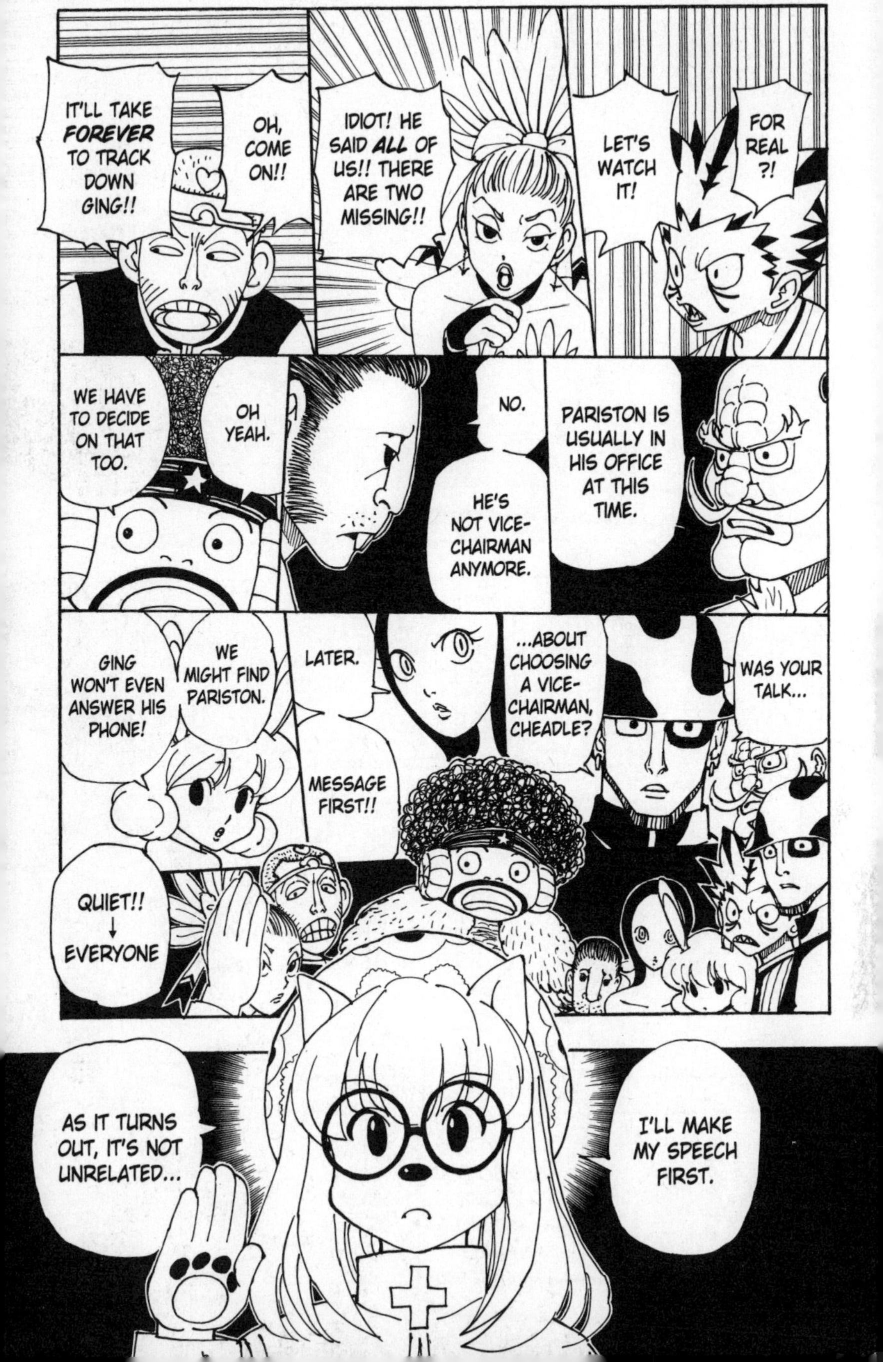
FOR REAL?!
LET'S WATCH IT!
IDIOT! HE SAID **ALL** OF US!! THERE ARE TWO MISSING!!
OH, COME ON!!
IT'LL TAKE **FOREVER** TO TRACK DOWN GING!!
PARISTON IS USUALLY IN HIS OFFICE AT THIS TIME.
NO.
HE'S NOT VICE-CHAIRMAN ANYMORE.
OH YEAH.
WE HAVE TO DECIDE ON THAT TOO.
WAS YOUR TALK...
...ABOUT CHOOSING A VICE-CHAIRMAN, CHEADLE?
LATER.
MESSAGE FIRST!!
WE MIGHT FIND PARISTON.
GING WON'T EVEN ANSWER HIS PHONE!
QUIET!! ↓ EVERYONE
I'LL MAKE MY SPEECH FIRST.
AS IT TURNS OUT, IT'S NOT UNRELATED...

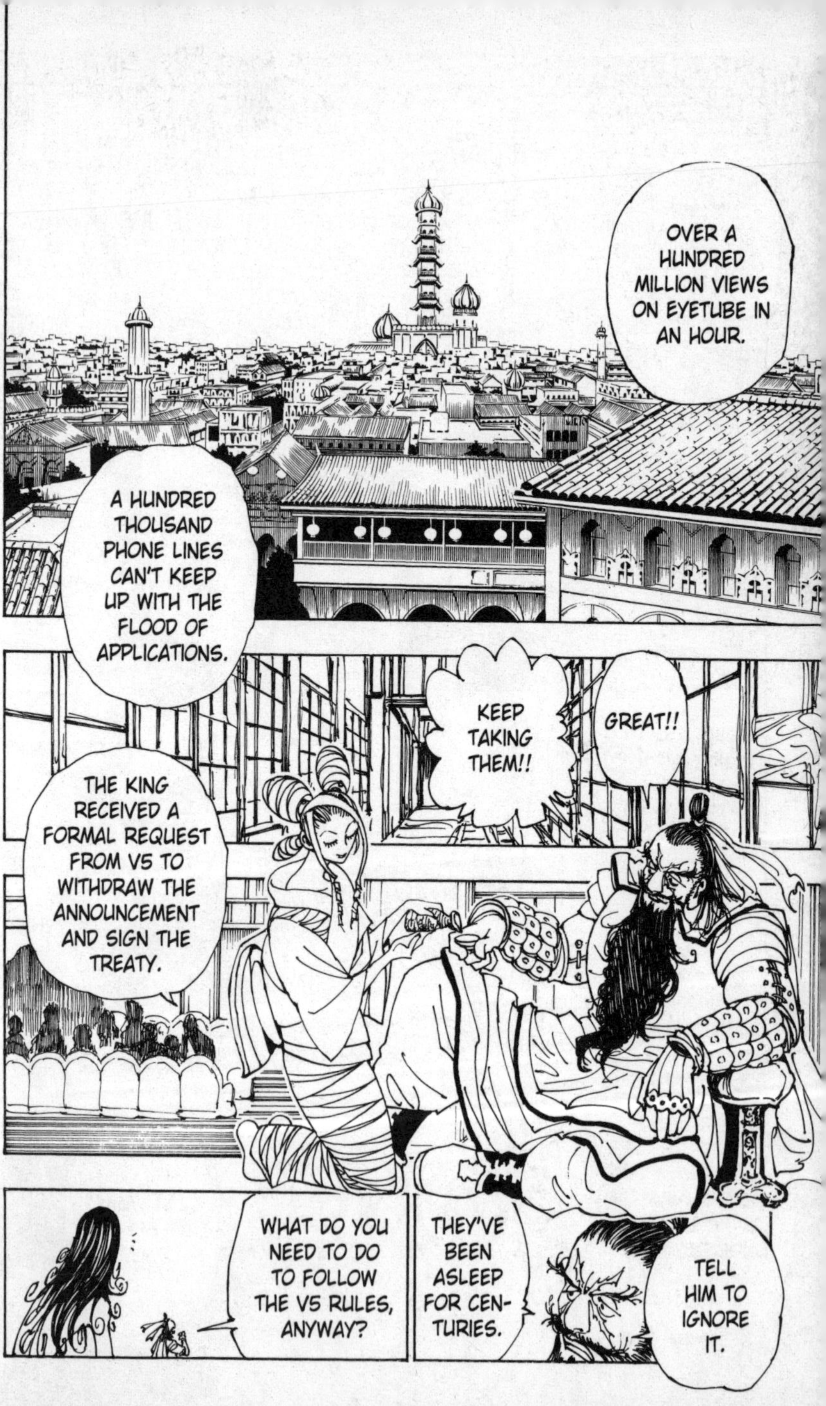
OVER A HUNDRED MILLION VIEWS ON EYETUBE IN AN HOUR.
A HUNDRED THOUSAND PHONE LINES CAN'T KEEP UP WITH THE FLOOD OF APPLICATIONS.
GREAT!!
KEEP TAKING THEM!!
THE KING RECEIVED A FORMAL REQUEST FROM V5 TO WITHDRAW THE ANNOUNCEMENT AND SIGN THE TREATY.
TELL HIM TO IGNORE IT.
THEY'VE BEEN ASLEEP FOR CEN-TURIES.
WHAT DO YOU NEED TO DO TO FOLLOW THE V5 RULES, ANYWAY?

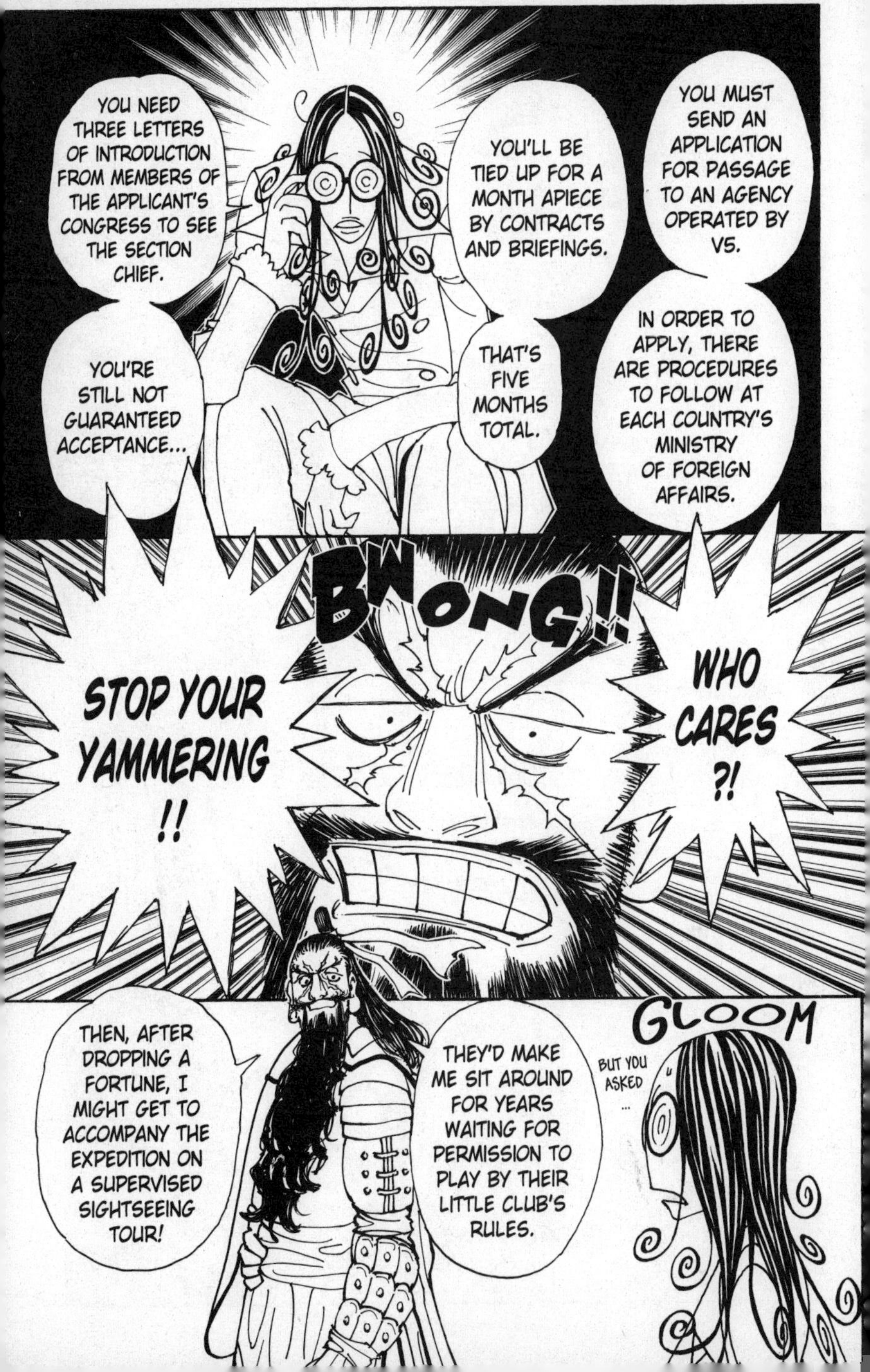
YOU MUST SEND AN APPLICATION FOR PASSAGE TO AN AGENCY OPERATED BY V5.
IN ORDER TO APPLY, THERE ARE PROCEDURES TO FOLLOW AT EACH COUNTRY'S MINISTRY OF FOREIGN AFFAIRS.
YOU NEED THREE LETTERS OF INTRODUCTION FROM MEMBERS OF THE APPLICANT'S CONGRESS TO SEE THE SECTION CHIEF.
YOU'LL BE TIED UP FOR A MONTH APIECE BY CONTRACTS AND BRIEFINGS.
THAT'S FIVE MONTHS TOTAL.
YOU'RE STILL NOT GUARANTEED ACCEPTANCE...
BWONG!!
WHO CARES ?!
STOP YOUR YAMMERING !!
THEY'D MAKE ME SIT AROUND FOR YEARS WAITING FOR PERMISSION TO PLAY BY THEIR LITTLE CLUB'S RULES.
THEN, AFTER DROPPING A FORTUNE, I MIGHT GET TO ACCOMPANY THE EXPEDITION ON A SUPERVISED SIGHTSEEING TOUR!
GLOOM
BUT YOU ASKED ...

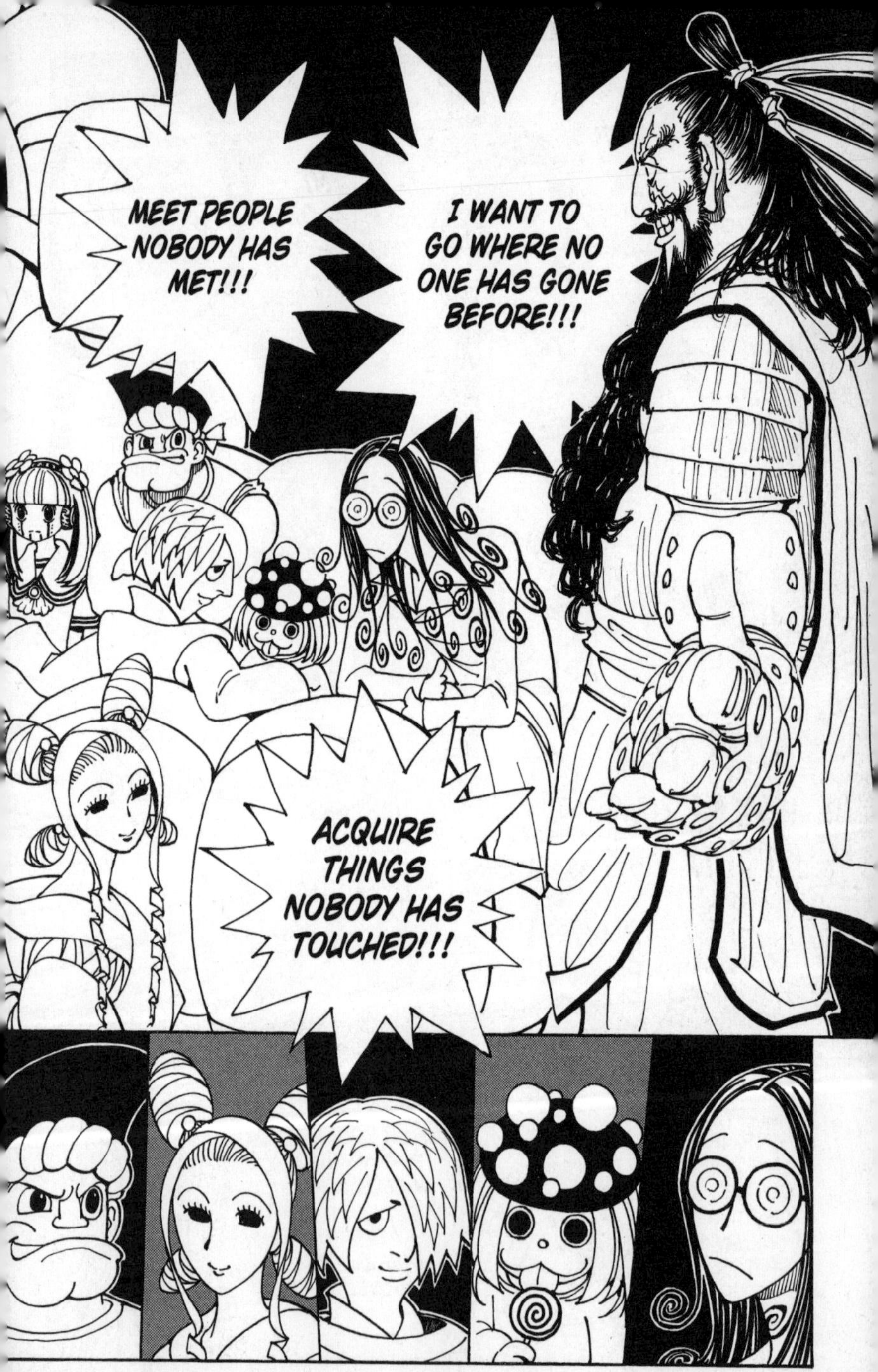
I WANT TO GO WHERE NO ONE HAS GONE BEFORE!!!
MEET PEOPLE NOBODY HAS MET!!!
ACQUIRE THINGS NOBODY HAS TOUCHED!!!

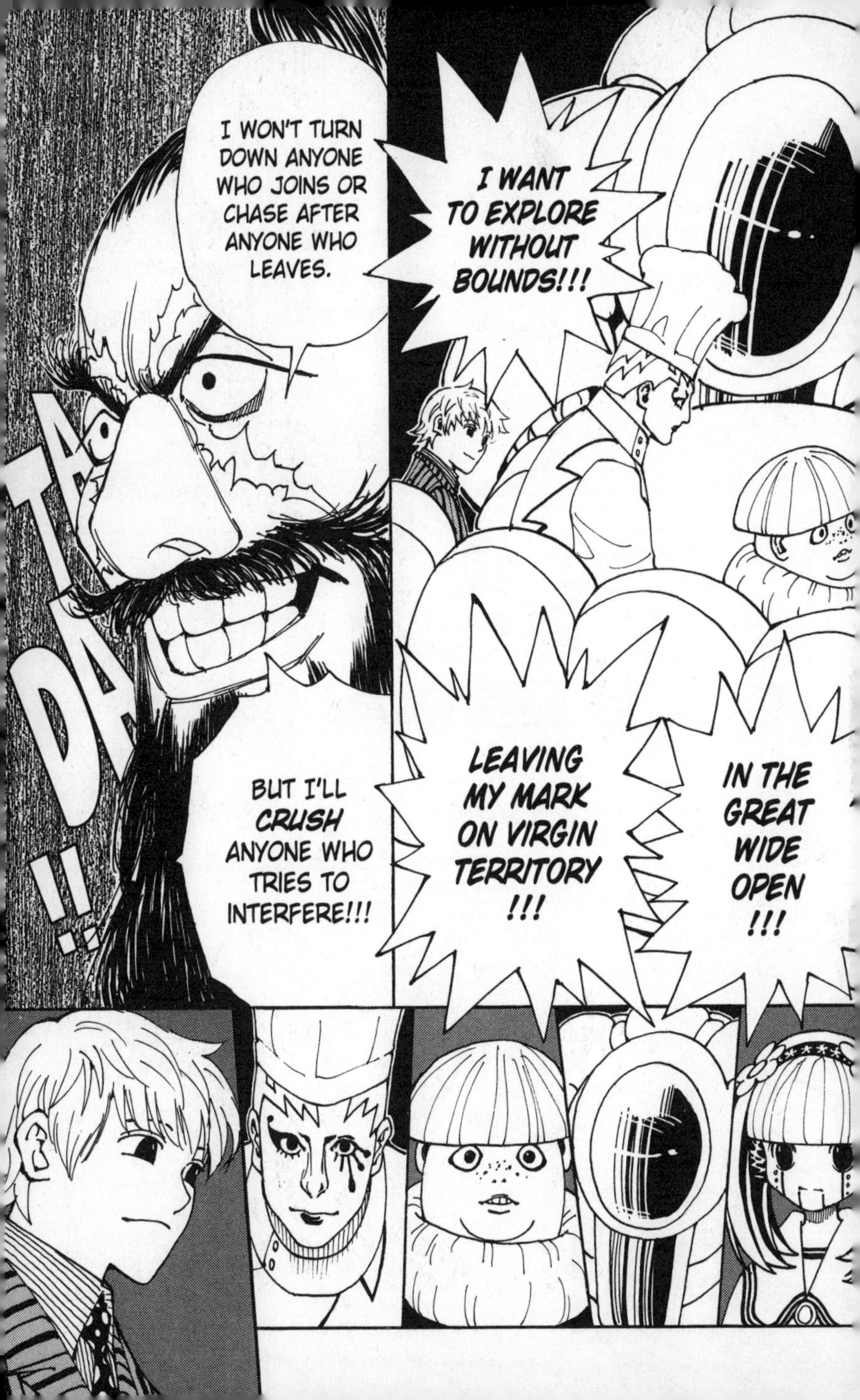
I WANT TO EXPLORE WITHOUT BOUNDS!!!
IN THE GREAT WIDE OPEN!!!
LEAVING MY MARK ON VIRGIN TERRITORY!!!
I WON'T TURN DOWN ANYONE WHO JOINS OR CHASE AFTER ANYONE WHO LEAVES.
TADA!!
BUT I'LL *CRUSH* ANYONE WHO TRIES TO INTERFERE!!!

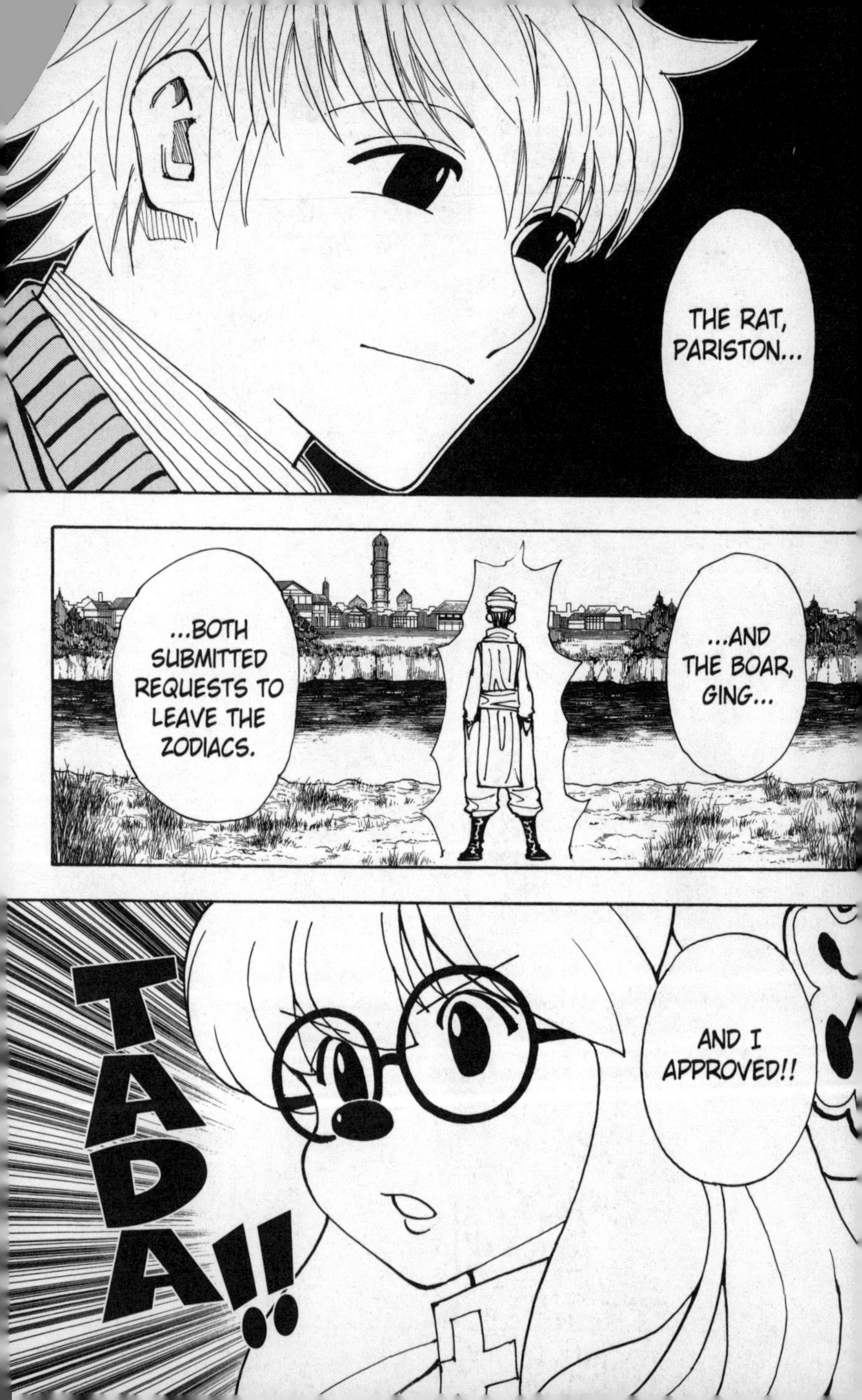

THE RAT, PARISTON...
...AND THE BOAR, GING...
...BOTH SUBMITTED REQUESTS TO LEAVE THE ZODIACS.
AND I APPROVED!!
TADA!!

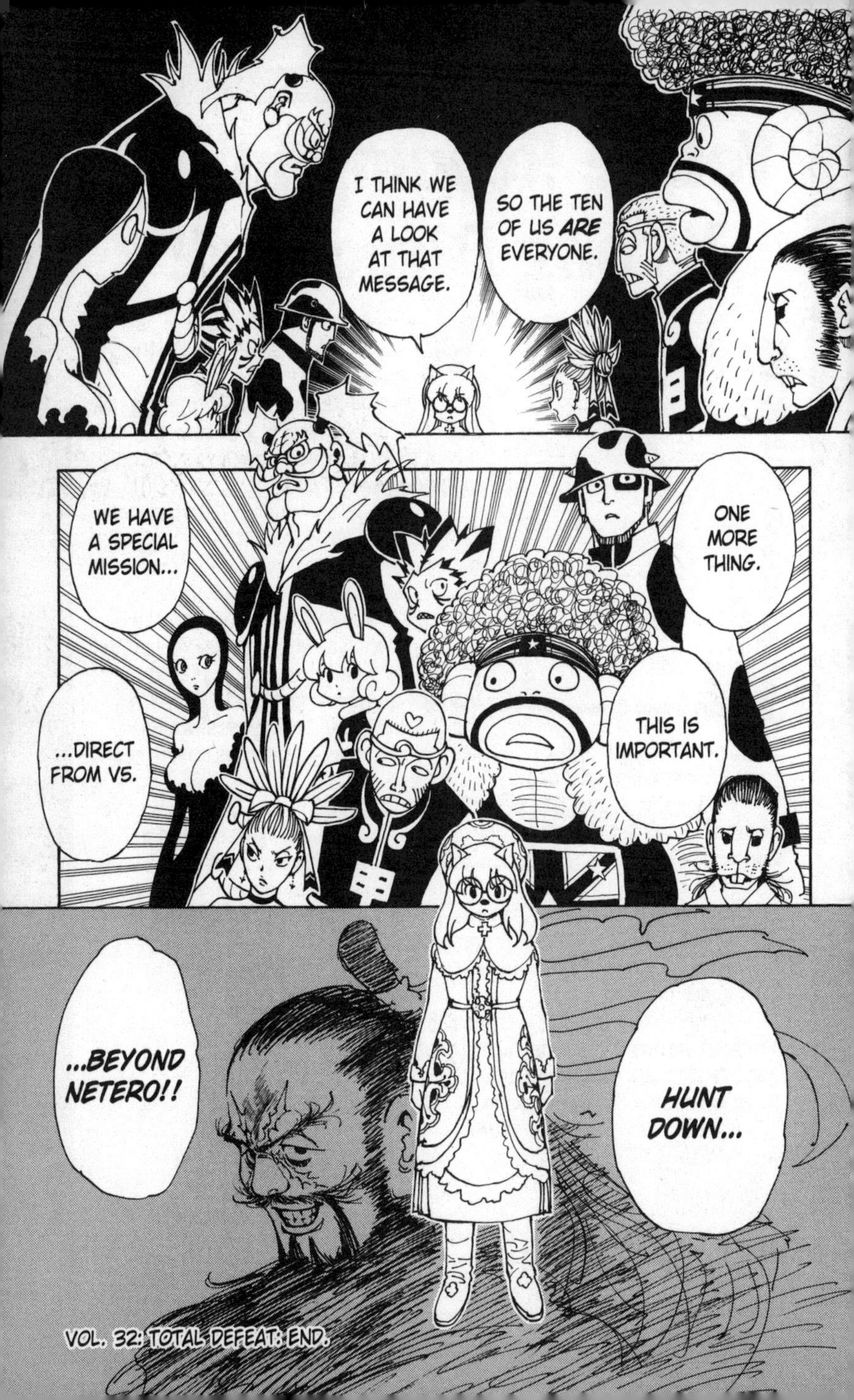
SO THE TEN OF US *ARE* EVERYONE.
I THINK WE CAN HAVE A LOOK AT THAT MESSAGE.
ONE MORE THING.
THIS IS IMPORTANT.
WE HAVE A SPECIAL MISSION...
...DIRECT FROM V5.
HUNT DOWN...
...BEYOND NETERO!!
VOL. 32: TOTAL DEFEAT: END.

You're Reading in the Wrong Direction!!

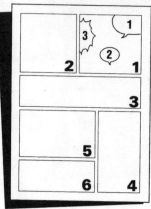

Whoops! Guess what? You're starting at the wrong end of the comic!

…It's true! In keeping with the original Japanese format, **Hunter x Hunter** is meant to be read from right to left, starting in the upper-right corner.

Unlike English, which is read from left to right, Japanese is read from right to left, meaning that action, sound effects and word-balloon order are completely reversed… something which can make readers unfamiliar with Japanese feel pretty backwards themselves. For this reason, manga or Japanese comics published in the U.S. in English have sometimes been published "flopped" – that is, printed in exact reverse order, as though seen from the other side of a mirror.

By flopping pages, U.S. publishers can avoid confusing readers, but the compromise is not without its downside. For one thing, a character in a flopped manga series who once wore in the original Japanese version a T-shirt emblazoned with "M A Y" (as in "the merry month of") now wears one which reads "Y A M"! Additionally, many manga creators in Japan are themselves unhappy with the process, as some feel the mirror-imaging of their art skews their original intentions.

We are proud to bring you Yoshihiro Togashi's **Hunter x Hunter** in the original unflopped format. For now, though, turn to the other side of the book and let the adventure begin…!

—Editor